**INDUSTRIAL SOCIOLOGY:**
An Introduction

# INDUSTRIAL SOCIOLOGY:
## An Introduction

Maria  Hirszowicz

*With a guide to
the literature by*
Peter Cook

Martin  Robertson · Oxford

First published in 1981 by Martin Robertson & Company Ltd.,
108 Cowley Road, Oxford OX4 1JF.

**British Library Cataloguing in Publication Data**

Hirszowicz, Maria
   Industrial sociology: an introduction.
   1. Industrial sociology
   I. Title
   306'.3     HD6955

ISBN 0-85520-425-7
ISBN 0-85520-426-5 Pbk

Typeset in 10/11 and 9/10pt IBM Press Roman by
System 4 Associates Limited, Buckinghamshire.
Printed and bound in Great Britain by Book Plan Limited, Worcester.

# Contents

| | | |
|---|---|---|
| | *Preface* | vii |
| 1 | Industry and Society | 1 |
| 2 | Man and Technology | 27 |
| 3 | Small Groups in Industry | 50 |
| 4 | Motivations to Work | 71 |
| 5 | Sociology of Supervision: The Foreman | 98 |
| 6 | Managerialism | 125 |
| 7 | The Changing Image of the Working Class | 141 |
| 8 | Sociology of Trade Unionism | 172 |
| 9 | Industrial Conflict | 201 |
| 10 | Industrial Democracy | 229 |
| | *Guide to the Literature* by Peter Cook | 251 |
| | *Bibliography* | 270 |
| | *Name Index* | 292 |
| | *Subject Index* | 300 |

# Preface

Over the last decade industrial sociolology has dealt with the most sensitive and important problems of social life. This increasingly complex field of study has been covered by many theories and research findings that have gradually built up an impressive body of knowledge.

The purpose of this book is to draw together some of the most significant achievements in industrial sociology. The task is, however, not an easy one, since one has to strike a balance between selecting 'classic' studies of lasting importance and spelling out implications of new research contributions. In a textbook that has to satisfy the requirements of a concise introduction, one inevitably has to choose from many topics and from the authors covering each topic. It was decided to include, in the first place, those topics that have been relatively well explored by social scientists and give the reader an insight into the complexity of the problems faced in industrial life. Special attention is also paid to lines of study that reveal new aspects of social processes in industry and challenge the conventional wisdom of the established lines of thought.

Of course, the need to integrate many different perspectives and approaches in a comprehensive whole poses enormous difficulties and I am only too aware of the many deficiencies of this endeavour. Industrial sociology has been strongly affected by the polarization of theoretical positions and research methods, which results in many divergent views on the substance of industrial societies (such as, scientific management, human relations school, organizational sociology, disputes between Marxists, neo-Marxists and their critics — for background reading on these various schools of thought, see Blackburn, 1972; Rose, 1975; Silverman, 1970; Sofer, 1972). In my opinion there is no one best theory to deal with sociological problems, no universal methodology for their successful exploration. I try to demonstrate that progress in industrial sociology consists in a transition from the all-embracing assumptions favoured by many social scientists in the past to a more cautious but open-minded approach that critically integrates historical, comparative and descriptive studies into meaningful generalizations. In other words, the emphasis in this book is on the importance of

vii

empirical studies for the understanding of industrial life and on the interactions between empirical findings and theoretical generalizations. The history of the discipline itself is for this purpose of major importance: the reader interested in this aspect of industrial sociology is referred to many books dealing with this subject.

Special attention is paid to the discrepancies between old concepts and new facts of industrial society. I aim to substantiate the view that industrial structures and industrial relations develop through open-ended processes of social actions and interactions characterized by both continuity and change and that in industry, as in all other spheres of social life, we face many options that depend as much on human decisions as on any inevitable fate. These decisions become part of the forces operating in the social environment and the 'logic' of these decisions, including interests, passions and biases, is in itself part of the field of social study. Seen from this perspective, industry appears to be a peculiar mixture of the highest rationality incorporated in technological development and social endeavours in which individual and collective purposes conflict and contradict each other and pose a constant challenge to the cooperation on which industrial activities must be based.

The book was written with special reference to Great Britain and the reader is particularly referred to the English authors whose contributions to industrial sociology seemed to me most impressive. I hope, however, that some of the issues presented in this study might be relevant for other industrial countries, including Eastern Europe where interest in sociological studies carried out by Western scholars is enormous.

The book attempts to set out the background of theory and research findings with which students need to be familiar in order to undertake more advanced courses. For readers who want to embark on more specialized studies in industrial sociology, Peter Cook has prepared a guide to the literature.

My thanks are due to Peter Cook, not only for this guide but also for all his friendly and critical help in editing my typescript, compiling important statistical information and making innumerable suggestions and amendments. I should also like to express my gratitude to Dr Howard Spier, who as the first reader of the study helped me enormously with his critical remarks and linguistic alterations, which eliminated much of the sociological jargon from the text. Among the many people who assisted in the preparation of this book, I should especially single out Ms Liz Paton who was a terrific editor and revised my typescript in a most imaginative and meticulous way. A special note of gratitude is due to Dr Richard W. Brown for his valuable suggestions, which allowed me to carry out important alterations to the content and structure of this book. I would like finally to thank Professor Stanislaw

Andreski, with whom I have had the privilege to work for many years in Reading and whose stimulating and unorthodox views have greatly influenced my way of thinking.

*Maria Hirszowicz*
*May 1981*

# CHAPTER 1

# Industry and Society

The concepts of industrialism and industrial society have become part of everyday vocabulary; they reflect the new stage of social organization in which human life is dominated by industrial production. Ecological change and new environments, occupational structure, urbanization, work and leisure, consumption and cultural interests — all are related directly or indirectly to industrial development.

Yet the nature of the relationship between industry and society is by no means clear. If the general impact of industry on society is obvious enough, opinions vary on the *extent* of its influence and the *manner* in which it operates. Technological determinism, evolutionism, historical materialism, the economic interpretation of history and functionalism — all offer differing explanations of what happened in the past and what may be expected in the future. Even if we ignore 'grand theory' and simply describe what happens in society during the development of an industrial economy, we cannot avoid 'macro' interpretations of the nature of the industrial system. And since industry is but a part of society, and at each stage industrial activities are directly affected by the social order within which they take place, theories of industrial society are unavoidably linked with industrial sociology at both its macro and micro level.

## CONCEPTUAL FRAMEWORK

Industrialism is usually defined as a new type of social organization dominated by the factory system of production. An equivalent term is industrial society', in which, according to Aron, large-scale industry is the most characteristic form of production (Aron, 1967, p. 73). The concept of industrialization has a more dynamic connotation; it is understood as the 'transformation of society through development of modern industry and technology, accompanied by far-reaching political and social changes' (*Encyclopaedia Britannica*). A wider meaning of this concept is that:

Industrialisation refers to the actual course of transition from the preceding agricultural or commercial society towards the industrial

1

society...[and involves] a central dynamic force at work....By industrialisation we have meant the totality of relations involving workers, employers and society as they develop to make use of the new machines, processes and services that modern technology has made possible. [Kerr *et al.*, 1973, pp. 41 and 279]

A preoccupation with industry and industrial development is by no means new. Social thought in the nineteenth century became concerned with the impact of industry on human life. It is, however, twentieth-century theory that has popularized the concept of *industrial society* as opposed to the more specific distinctions between various forms of social and political organization (capitalism, communism and socialism, developed and developing countries, Western democracies and totalitarian states, etc.). The most important studies to have popularized the ideas of industrialization and industrialism are those by Aron (1967), Dahrendorf (1972) and Kerr *et al.* (1973). The latter opens with the following characteristic statement:

The world is entering a new age — the age of total industrialisation. Some countries are far along the road; many more are just beginning the journey. But everywhere, at a faster or slower pace, the peoples of the world are on the march towards industrialism. [Kerr *et al.*, 1973, p. 29]

Although one is inclined to think that modern developed societies are determined by machines and industrial production, some scholars argue that machines are by no means the only spectacular feature of technology in developed societies. For Ellul, the two most relevant features of modern technology are its *rationality* and its *artificiality*. Machines are in this respect no more than a part of the contemporary artificial and rational environment:

In technique, whatever its aspect or the domain in which it is applied, a rational process is present which tends to bring mechanics to bear on all that is spontaneous or irrational. This rationality, best exemplified in systematization, division of labour, creation of standards, production norms, and the like, involves two distinct phases: first, the use of 'discourse', in every operation; this excludes spontaneity and personal creativity. Second there is the reduction of method to its logical dimension alone. Every intervention of technique is, in effect, a reduction of facts, forces, phenomena, means, and instruments to the schema of logic.

The second obvious characteristic of the technical phenomenon is artificiality. Technique is opposed to nature. Art, artifice, artificial: technique as art is the creation of an artificial system....The world that is being created by the accumulation of technical means is an artificial world and hence radically different from the natural world.[Ellul, 1965, pp. 78–9]

Ellul prefers the concept of technological society to that of industrial society. A similar view is held by other writers; some go so far as to use the term 'post-industrial society' to describe the present stage of development of the Western world. There is a general agreement underlying the concept of industrialism (and post-industrialism) that technological development has changed the whole fabric of society in the contemporary world. Thus many periodizations of modern history use stages of technological development to mark the major steps in the evolution of our civilization.

Faunce distinguishes three stages of social history relating to the development of machine technology: (1) the application of inanimate sources of power to the production process; (2) modernizing the machinery of material handling, and (3) mechanizing quality control and decision-making (Faunce, 1968, pp. 44–8).

Slichter divides the history of the United States into three periods according to the stage of economic development: (1) the earliest period up to 1880–1900, when preconditions for the industrial order were created by a progressive rise in the capital-output ratio, that is, by a steady growth of accumulated capital as compared with income; (2) the years 1900–1929, when a tremendous increase in the use of energy took place through the application of electrical and internal combustion – the consequent increases in productivity led to increasing income as compared with accumulation; and, (3) the third period, marked by a technological revolution in managerial practices and by industrial research, which contribute more to industrial growth than the application of more capital or more powerful energy sources (Slichter, 1966, pp. 52–86).

Miller distinguishes four periods of technological progress: *modern craft* from 1400, based on the application of hand-directed tools and the use of wood, iron and bronze, and characterized by a highly skilled labour force; the *machine age*, which began in 1785 and was distinguished by the application of steam, the use of machinery, steel and copper as the main raw materials and a growing army of semi-skilled labourers; the *power age* after 1870, with its automatic machinery, a mixture of skilled and semi-skilled labour and the use of alloyed steel, light alloys and aluminium; and the *atomic age*, which began around 1953 and brought with it atomic energy, automated factories, a wealth of new materials including plastic and new metals, and growing demand for a highly trained labour force (in Allen, *et al.*, 1951).

## SOCIAL CORRELATES OF INDUSTRIAL DEVELOPMENT

All societies that have established an industrial factory-based mode of production display common features that go beyond the productive sphere of social life and seem to justify the concept of a new *industrial civilization* as opposed to pre-industrial systems. Despite the different definitions of industrial society, there is a common view that it represents a new stage of human history in which the entire social order has been completely transformed according to needs of industrial development. The scope of this transformation is so wide that some observers speak of a new era of human experience rather than of a historically unique type of society in a specific period of social history.

Large-scale production, the use of inanimate sources of energy, technical division of labour, high rate of economic growth expressed in increased real income per capita, radical transformation of the environment, dominance of theoretical and applied knowledge, and overall rationalization of organizations in which people carry out their everyday activities, are but a part of the new social experience. The nature of this experience is in itself subject to many different interpretations. For some, this experience is primarily linked with business civilization:

Industrialism is a configuration of technology, economy and business values, one of the most widely spread culture systems in human history. No modern institution has escaped the influence of the economic organization of society: the school, the church, the home, the recreational institutions are built upon human values arising from the material framework of modern civilization. Industrial society refers to more than machines and markets — it refers to men and institutions locked in a network of relationships dominated by industrial ideas and business values. [Wilkie, 1961, p. 221]

Other observers are inclined to believe that the social framework and the ethos of industrialization vary according to the type of industrial elites that promote and carry out the process of technological change. The common ground for all these views is the trends and features associated with economic development and industrial growth.

The growth of industrial output throughout the world is the most spectacular social phenomenon of the last 100 years (see Table 1.1). Recent decades have brought a further acceleration of economic growth, a trend illustrated by the index of world industrial production for the period 1960–1975 (see Table 1.2). These world figures conceal, of course, the spectacular rate of growth of advanced industrial countries as compared to Third World countries.

The increasing importance of industry for the national economy is reflected in changes in the *structure* of the national product in all highly industrialized countries. Thus, for instance, in the United States, agriculture's share in private production income declined from 39.5 per cent in 1799 to 12.7 per cent in 1929, while the share of industrial

TABLE 1.1
INDEX OF WORLD INDUSTRIAL OUTPUT, 1860–1958 (1953=100)

| | |
|---|---|
| 1860 | 4 |
| 1880 | 8 |
| 1900 | 16 |
| 1913 | 28 |
| 1920 | 26 |
| 1938 | 51 |
| 1953 | 100 |
| 1958 | 133 |

*Source*: Patel (1970) p. 59

TABLE 1.2
INDEX OF WORLD INDUSTRIAL PRODUCTION, 1960–1977
(1970=100)

| | |
|---|---|
| 1960 | 52 |
| 1963 | 63 |
| 1968 | 89 |
| 1969 | 96 |
| 1970 | 100 |
| 1971 | 104 |
| 1972 | 112 |
| 1973 | 122 |
| 1974 | 127 |
| 1975 | 124 |
| 1976 | 135 |
| 1977 | 142 |

*Source*: *Monthly Bulletin of Statistics*, December 1976, page x; and *Statistical Yearbook* New York, United Nations, 1975 and 1978.

production increased from 12.8 per cent to 36.2 per cent (Woytinsky and Woytinsky, 1953, p. 431). Patel notes that there are also striking similarities among advanced countries as far as the structure of industrial production is concerned:

In the early phase of industrialisation — stretching from a few decades to half a century in the United Kingdom, France, Germany, the United States, Italy, Japan and the USSR — the producer goods sector grew one and a half to more than two times as fast as the consumer goods sector....Once industrialisation had reached a fairly high level and the proportion of consumer goods had fallen to around one third, the differences in the rates of growth of both these sectors narrowed down significantly, with the producer goods sector expanding only a little faster than the consumer goods sector. This general pattern of industrial growth — producer goods expanding nearly twice as fast as consumer goods in the early phase of industrialisation and the gap between the rates of growth for the two sectors narrowing down later on — appears to have been a characteristic feature of economic development in all the major industrial countries. [Patel, 1970, pp. 64—5]

The concept of industrial society implies a close interconnection between productive forces and other aspects of social life. On the basis of comparative studies, several indicators have been found to be highly correlated with the Gross National Product (GNP) in the world economy. Among the items for which the correlation is particularly high (Pearsonian coefficient ± 0.75 and higher) are: volume of domestic mail per capita, female life expectancy, the percentage of the labour force employed in agriculture, radios per million inhabitants, non-agricultural employment as a percentage of the population, government employees as a percentage of the population of working age, the percentage of GNP originating in agriculture, inhabitants per doctor, newspaper circulation per million inhabitants, primary and secondary school pupils as a percentage of population aged 15—64, percentage of the population of working age, inhabitants per hospital bed, wage and salary earners as a percentage of the working population, the crude birth rate, the infant mortality rate, television sets per million, the percentage of the population in localities of over 20,000 (Patel, 1970, pp. 64—5). These indicators are related to production and consumption patterns, occupational structure, urbanization, the level of education and health service provision. Some of these traits are the direct components of industrial growth; others are the effects of increased affluence.

Industrial development goes hand in hand with rapid urbanization (see Table 1.3). Both industrialization and urbanization generate a whole complex of structural changes in all parts of society. These changes are complementary to each other and therefore are subject to never-ending adjustment.

To understand the complexity of the changes taking place in industrial societies we can refer to the concept of *infrastructure*, which allows us to analyse institutions complementary to both technological and ecological change. The infrastructure designates the basic amenities and institutions necessary for the normal functioning of the productive parts of the economy through the supply of basic services to those sectors. It has two sub-divisions:

(1) the *economic* infrastructure, which includes institutions that supply services in transport and communications, power, irrigation (i.e. ports, railways, motorways, power stations); and

(2) the *social* infrastructure, which includes institutions and

establishments that supply services concerned with health, safety, law and education.

TABLE 1.3
GEOGRAPHICAL DISTRIBUTION OF THE POPULATION IN
ENGLAND AND WALES, 1801–1971 (000s)

| Year | Urban | Rural |
|------|-------|-------|
| 1801 | 1,506 | 7,386 |
| 1851 | 8,991 | 8,937 |
| 1901 | 25,058 | 7,469 |
| 1951 | 35,336 | 8,423 |
| 1968 | 38,325 | 10,268 |
| 1971 | 38,151 | 10,598 |

Source: *Annual Abstract of Statistics* London, HMSO, 1975, p. 24.

The marked development of infrastructure has become a dominant trait of modern society. It goes without saying that this means unavoidable transformations in the nature of individual and social needs and the ways of satisfying them. Some hold that personality traits too are affected by the new industrial order. For instance, Inkeles (1960) has given the following list of characteristics:

a readiness for new experiences and an acceptance of innovation;
an inclination to form opinions about problems that go beyond the immediate environment and that acknowledge the diversity of attitudes and opinions about these problems;
an orientation towards the present and the future rather than towards the past;
an orientation towards planning and organization;
efficacy — i.e. an attitude based on the belief that man can control his environment;
calculability — i.e. confidence that the world in which we live is essentially predictable and dependable;
an awareness of, and respect for, the dignity of others;
faith in science and technology;
a belief in distributive justice — i.e. in the distribution of rewards based on contribution and not on arbitrariness or the possessions of the person concerned.

Whichever characteristics are regarded as the most relevant, there is probably agreement that: (a) there is a *close interrelation of all spheres of social activity* imposed by the interdependence of modern economies; and (b) there is *a fast pace of change regulated by the tremendous speed of technological progress.*

The necessity for constant and massive adjustments and readjustments combined with the rapidity of changes make predictions and projections more important than ever before. Since technology seems to play the major part in these processes of transformation of the present world, the following questions identified by Kerr and his associates (Kerr *et al.*, 1973, pp. 29–39) seem to be particularly relevant for an understanding of the future:

Which features of the economy and the larger society does technology fully control?
Which features are merely influenced?
Which features are relatively independent of technology?

## CONVERGENCE THESIS

The impact of industrialism on social life explains the fascination with technological determinism in the social sciences. The technological explanations denounced several decades ago as vulgar materialism have recently been resurrected as dogma by scholars of varying methodological and philosophical backgrounds.

For many observers, the principal differences between nations stem from their varying stages of economic development. It may be expected, the argument runs, that once the disparities have disappeared, a common pattern of cultural and political life will emerge as the inevitable result of the standardizing and all-embracing industrialization of the modern world. The argument has become popular enough to be termed the 'convergence theory'. In its milder form the convergence theory assumes *some* basic similarities among all industrial societies, and seeks to single out those factors where the similarities are most strongly pronounced. In a stricter version, however, adherents assume that all industrial societies are essentially alike in their basic features.

Feldman and Moore suggest that convergence is limited to 'core' elements of the industrial system; they regard all industrial systems as having the following attributes (1962, p. 146):

a factory system of production;
a stratification system based on the division of labour and a hierarchy of skills;
extensive commercialization of goods and services and their transfer through the market.
educational systems capable of filling the various niches in the occupation and stratification system.

It is pointed out that a common basic technology produces similar effects primarily in those areas of social life that are closest to technology, while other aspects of social life that are not related to technology might be relatively unaffected:

Social arrangements will be most uniform from one society to another when they are most closely tied to technology: they can be more diverse the further removed they are from technology. The areas closest to technology will be most conformist; those farthest from the requirements of its service the most free. [Feldman and Moore, 1962]

Goldthorpe presents the 'stricter' version of convergence theory as follows:

...it is notable that in spite of possibly different origins, current American interpretations of the development of industrial societies often reveal marked similarities. Basically, it may be said, they tend to be alike in stressing the standardizing effects upon social structures of the exigencies of modern technology and of an advanced economy. These factors which make for uniformity in industrial societies are seen as largely overriding other factors which may make for possible diversity, such as different national cultures or different political systems.
Thus, the overall pattern of development which is suggested is one in which, once countries enter into the advanced stages of industrialization, they tend to become increasingly comparable in their major institutional arrangements and in their social systems generally. In brief, a *convergent* pattern of development is hypothesized. [Goldthorpe, 1964, p. 97]

In this form the basic idea of the convergence theory is that of *internal structural consistency*:

The logic of the convergence thesis seems to be that other parts of the social structure are conceived of as having to change in order to meet the requirements of the industrial system of production and distribution. [Kerr *et al.*, 1973, p. 18]

Along similar lines, the concept of *systemness* that is often applied emphasizes the increased complexity and growing interdependence of all forms of social life. A growing systemness means that in the course of development and advancing differentiation, the elements of industrial society become more interdependent than previously. This in turn accounts for an irreversible transition of society towards increased complexity. The concept has been elaborated in detail by Smelser:

For purposes of analyzing the relationships between economic growth and the social structure, it is possible to isolate the effects of several interrelated technical, economic, and ecological processes that frequently accompany development. These may be listed as follows:

(1) In the realm of technology, the change *from* simple and traditional techniques *toward* the application of scientific knowledge.

(2) In agriculture, the evolution *from* subsistence farming *towards* commercial production of agricultural goods. This means specialization in cash crops, purchase of non-agricultural products in the market, and often agricultural wage-labour.

(3) In industry, the transition *from* the use of human and animal power *towards* industrialization proper, or 'men aggregated at power-driven machines, working for monetary return with the products of the manufacturing process entering into a market based on a network of exchange relations'.

(4) In ecological arrangements, the movement *from* the farm and village *toward* urban centres.

These several processes often, but not necessarily, occur simultaneously. [Smelser, 1968, p. 126]

Chodak (1973, p. 55) defines the concept of systemness as follows:

the multiplication of the channels and volume of societal exchanges;
the differentiation of new, specialized roles, institutionalized organizations and autonomous systems, and their increasing interdependence;
the proliferation of systems and systemic interconnections within systems;
the development of worldwide structures.

Emphasis on the standardizing effects of industrial development has become the core of convergence theory. The assumption that with industrial technology and an industrial economy, social structures and social institutions are characterized by a large degree of structural consistency is fundamental to all predictions of the future of the modern world, both in its communist and non-communist parts. Inkeles and Bauer point out that Soviet Russia is in many aspects surprisingly similar to capitalist states, and contend that the similarities seem to increase in spite of the differences in political systems (Inkeles and Bauer, 1959, pp. 377–98).

A more comprehensive theory of convergence has been given by Rostow (1971), who does not limit himself to industrialization but deals with modern history as a whole in order to explain the transition from traditional to economically advanced society. This transition he explains in terms of five successive stages of growth:

(1) *Transitional society* – characterized by the so-called productivity ceiling due to technological limitations. In such societies about 75 per cent of the work force must be occupied in agrarian activities in order to survive. The surplus is used for various forms of non-productive

consumption, be it maintaining harems, constructing monuments or retaining servants. Political systems in such societies tend to be authoritarian and hierarchical, vertical mobility is limited and the world perspective is fatalistic.

(2) A society in which *the preconditions for economic 'take-off'* manifest themselves. This is the case in modern centralized states (late seventeenth and early eighteenth century in Europe) where the surpluses accumulated by the tax system allow for public expenditure in such fields as education, defence, transportation and public security but, above all, for the expansion of international and external markets.

(3) *The 'take-off'* itself — at this stage economic growth becomes a self-sustaining and self-reinforcing process. This happens because new industries develop and the profits are saved and reinvested allowing for further increases of industrial activity and stimulating at the same time the demand of urban employees. Industry also expands into the agricultural sector and covers more and more aspects of social life.

(4) *Societies driving towards maturity* — i.e. developing in full their productive capacities, technological and entrepreneurial skills and the institutions necessary for further development.

(5) The stage of *mass consumption* — societies in which productivity is so high that mass consumption of durable goods becomes a reality. At this stage the number of workers supplying services increases, welfare expenditure grows, more and more collective needs are satisfied.

Rostow emphasizes that the manner in which a given society proceeds from one stage to another depends on many factors. For example, the take-off period in France or England was completely different from the take-off stage in the Soviet Union, where the state was the main driving force of economic development.

The most pronounced view on convergence is given by Kerr *et al.*:

We set forth in *Industrialism and Industrial Man* the view that industrial systems, regardless of the cultural background out of which they emerge and the path they originally follow, tend to become more alike over an extended period of time; that systems, whether under middle-class or communist or dynastic leadership, move towards 'pluralistic industrialism' where the state, the enterprise or association, and the individual all share a substantial degree of power and influence over productive activities. [Kerr *et al.*, 1973, p. 296]

They do not deny that in the modern world there are also dissimilarities and variations in the social order. These they believe, however, are relics of the past, due to the persistence of social practices that, once adopted, tend to acquire a life of their own. Countries that embark on industrialization differ in many respects. They have different cultures, social structures, institutions and elites that carry out programmes of modernization. Middle classes, dynastic elites, colonial rulers, revolutionary intellectuals and nationalist leaders operate in different ways and apply their strategies in different circumstances. The varying trajectories of development (that is, the diversity and disparity of different societies) are explained by the variety of social and cultural forms in which development takes place, by the character of leading industries, by the date of the start of change, by demographic characteristics, etc.

However, in spite of variations in the pattern of industrialization, industrial systems tend to become increasingly similar over an extended period of time. First, there is the growing distance between the industrialized stage of development and the pre-existing non-industrial stage in which heterogeneity prevailed, elites were highly differentiated and ideologies contributed to the diversity of human societies. While the pre-industrial order is fading away, 'the elites tend to wear grey flannel suits', the ideological controversies become more barren, and the cultural patterns of different societies intermingle. Secondly, technology becomes a unifying force since 'at one moment of time there may be several best economic combinations or social arrangements, but only one best technology' (Kerr *et al.*, 1973, p. 266). Technology itself imposes requirements on such social factors as skills and the training of workers involved in industrial processes, determines the occupational structure, which is the major component of modern social stratification, and makes workers more or less dependent on their work place and more or less mobile. Thirdly, progress is expressed in the disappearance of the plurality of economies — that is, the industrial, artisan and agricultural economies. In the same way, a rising living standard and increasing leisure create opportunities to read, travel and compare, while the new life style encourages people to live in the metropolitan centres, which are now the natural habitat of man. Fourthly, since all industrial societies must educate their members so as to enable them to conceive instruction, follow directions and keep records, education becomes a leading industry and greatly contributes to industrial development. There is also the omnipresent state, which becomes an important instrument for running the economic, social and administrative affairs of modern societies. Finally, the 'managerial revolution' has become a universal phenomenon, since the productive enterprise becomes, both in the private and public sectors, a large-scale organization directed by professionals.

As a result of these trends there emerges a 'pluralistic industrialism'. As it has been explained:

The term is used to refer to an industrial society which is governed neither by one all-powerful elite (the monistic model) nor by the impersonal interaction of innumerable small groups with relatively equal and fractionalised power (the atomistic model in economic theory). The complexity of the fully developed industrial society requires, in the name of efficiency and initiative, a degree of decentralisation of control, particularly in the consumer goods and service trade industries; but it also requires a large measure of central control by the state and conduct of many operations by large-scale organisations.

It will be an organisation society, but it need not be peopled by 'organisation men' whose total lives are ruled by their occupational roles.

Industrialism is so complex and subject to such contrary internal pressures that it never can assume a single uniform unchanging structure. but it *can* vary around a general central theme, and that theme is pluralism. [Kerr *et al.*, 1973, pp. 270, 276 and 271]

The pluralistic industrial society is thus a society in which the state controls conflicting forces and interests and, at the same time, ensures an increase in democratic control by different groups over the economy and the activities of the state itself. Four models of pluralistic industrialism were distinguished by the authors in a postscript:

(1) state socialism (sovereignty of the state over the enterprise);
(2) social capitalism of the American type (sovereignty of the enterprise);
(3) social capitalism of the English type (influence of organized labour and the consumer over the state and enterprise);
(4) state syndicalism (self-government of workers and consumers).

## VARIATIONS IN THE CONVERGENCE THESIS AND ITS CRITICS

An optimistic forecast of the outcome of the progressive industrialization of the world is by no means a necessary feature of the convergence theory. There are scholars who, while following the same methodological line, assume that the development of industrial order creates in the last resort a basis for totalitarianism: the end of free competition, a growing concern for efficiency, the political apathy of the masses who are dominated by the mass media, the disappearance of enlightened groups able to counteract the growing influence of organizational elites — these are for many the prevailing features of the future order. Many students of Western and Eastern societies are thus by no means certain that the world will follow a democratic path. On the contrary, they assert that democracy and social pluralism are bound to disappear or be eliminated under the impact of technological growth and large-scale organizational structures.

One of the foremost spokesmen of this approach is Mills, who foresaw an increasing alienation of labour among both manual and non-manual workers. In his study of power elites, he predicted the disappearance of 'the public' and the emergence of mass society manipulated by omnipotent elites (Mills, 1974, pp. 140–9, 581–6). Ellul also argues that technology allows the state to become totalitarian:

We have noted that this occurs as a result of the accumulation of techniques in the hands of the state. Techniques are mutually engendered and hence interconnected, forming a system that tightly encloses all our activities. When the state takes hold of a single thread of this network of techniques, little by little it draws to itself all the matter and the method, whether or not it consciously wills to do so.

   Even when the state is resolutely liberal and democratic, it cannot do otherwise than become totalitarian. It becomes so either directly or, as in the United States, through intermediate persons. But, despite differences, all such systems come ultimately to the same result. [Ellul, 1965, p. 284]

It has been some time since the convergence theory was first proposed, but its appeal has not diminished among scholars concerned mainly with technological change and its impact on the modern world. However, many other writers voice caution in accepting the assertions of convergence theory and point to the various factors that reduce the validity of such predictions. There is a growing awareness that the convergence theory developed as a reaction to a simplified view of the differences between communist and Western societies. Insofar as communist states are concerned, there was the so-called totalitarian model of the 1940s and 1950s. Friedrich and Fainsod were the most outspoken champions of this approach, which emphasized the totalitarian nature of the communist state and contrasted it with the institutions and values of Western democracies (Friedrich and Brzezinski, 1956; Fainsod, 1953). With the liberalization and modernization of the Soviet political system after Stalin's death, the totalitarian model was subjected to much criticism. One major objection was its tendency to over-generalize features of Soviet society that were but a passing stage of economic and social development. Since, in the meantime, Soviet Russia has attained the level of a highly industrialized state, one is inclined to adopt the view that Stalinism was a peculiar and historically conditioned form of Soviet economic development, and one of the many strategies adopted by industrializing elites – very much in line with the Russian tradition of oriental despotism. Moreover, advanced forms of liberalization in other communist countries, especially Poland and, in the early sixties, Czechoslovakia, draw the attention of scholars to the impact of national and cultural differences on the trajectory of the process of industrialization. In these circumstances, the concept of industrial society became a kind of common denominator for developed societies with different economic and political structures. The convergence thesis acknowledged the many similarities that seemed to emerge from the confusion of social, political and economic factors in East and West in the first half of the twentieth century.

Seen from a historical perspective, the convergence thesis may be considered an expression of the optimism of the 1960s, when the world appeared to be heading safely towards economic growth, the liberalization of political systems, national revival and inter-state cooperation. This optimistic picture of the world is apparent in the concluding chapter of *Industrialism and Industrial Man*:

The age of ideology fades.... The age of Utopias is past.... An age of realism has taken its place.... The conflict of ideologies is blunted and fades between societies... consensus develops wherever industrialisation is successful... the cultural patterns of the world intermingle and merge .... The rising standard of living and increasing leisure create the capacity to read and travel and compare.... Progress brings the great metropolitan centre and the city as the natural habitat of man.... Out of education may also come a new call for freedom: [Kerr *et al.*, 1973, pp. 164–8]

In the late 1960s and 1970s new phenomena arose that made the easy and optimistic predictions of the convergence theory less plausible than before. Firstly, there was a new pattern of 'socialism' in the developing countries, the distinctive features of which differ markedly from the communist experience. The 'socialist' industrialization in Third World countries challenges many of the values of advanced industrial societies and there are few signs of significant changes in this respect in the foreseeable future. The revolutionary turmoil in Iran is another example of new trends contrasting with the values and aspirations of the Western World. A shift towards religious fundamentalism and theocratic government may be an alternative pattern of development and reveals the appeal of spiritual movements that run counter to the very ethos of industrial civilization. Thirdly, there are the more recent developments in Soviet Russia and in the communist bloc in general. After a brief period of liberalization, the USSR under Brezhnev adopted a neo-Stalinist position that contrasted with the Krushchev era. Pressure on other communist countries increased. The invasion of Czechoslovakia in 1968 revealed the underlying resistance to 'socialism with a human face' in the Soviet bloc. Fourthly, a feeling of insecurity has developed in the West, where economic recession accompanying extremist political unrest has undermined the previous self-confidence, especially of the 1950s. The concept of the industrial society as synonymous with an affluent society governed by democratic institutions and based on a general consensus no longer seems as obvious as it did two decades ago.

The technological determinism of the convergence theory is thus challenged from many different perspectives. For many, the concept of industrial society is too wide to convey any direct meaning unless it is broken down into sub-systems that differ in their cultural traits and forms of social organization. It should also be noted that growing discontent with the negative aspects of technological progress in the West has also given rise to serious doubts about the wisdom of un- restrained industrial growth, and has stimulated the search for alternative programmes that would deny the dominance of technology over human lives.

Advocates of the convergence theory contend that the divergencies of societies are less significant than their converging trajectories. Their critics, however, emphasize that, at least for the time being, the diver- gencies are important and serious enough to merit investigation for their own sake. They also point out that the predictive value of the convergence theory is based on the assumption that the present trends will continue, which is by no means certain since the short- and middle- range development might basically change the existing social order on which the long-term macro forecast is being based. Furthermore, critics of the convergence theory draw attention to the influence of the inter- vening variables on social systems. They point to the forms of economic organization that generate many different trends in modern society; the differences between the market economy and the command economy seem to be serious enough to merit separate treatment. Differences between socio-political and cultural systems are also widely acknow- ledged as generating varying trends in social development.

From what has been said, it follows that we can distinguish between *stages* of industrialization and *modes* of industrialization (Giddens, 1974, p. 63). In other words, societies can be compared in terms either of their greater or lesser industrial advancement or of the social forms within which this advancement takes place. The differences between various types of economic organization relate to the latter, as do the social and political forms associated with them.

## POST-INDUSTRIAL SOCIETY

At present much attention is paid not only to the general features of industrialism but to its transformation into something that some sociologists are inclined to refer to as post-industrial society. Daniel Bell (1970) ascribes the following characteristics to the new post- industrial order:

Ours is no longer primarily a manufacturing economy — the service sector accounts for more than half of total employment and more than half of the gross national product.

There has been a shift from property or political criteria to knowledge. What is evident everywhere is a society-wide uprising against bureaucracy and a desire for participation so that 'people ought to be able to effect the decisions that control their lives'.

And Touraine declares:

A new type of society is now being formed. These new societies can be labelled post-industrial to stress how different they are from the industrial societies that preceded them, although — in both capitalist and socialist nations — they retain some characteristics of these earlier societies. They may also be called technocratic because of the power that dominates them. Or one can call them programmed societies to define them according to the nature of their production methods and economic organization. [Touraine, 1971, p. 3]

Heilbroner (1977) points out that there are three different meanings that are usually attached to the concept of post-industrialism:

(1) A post-industrial society will be one in which a preponderance of economic activity is located in the 'tertiary' (or service) sector of the economy (p. 49).
(2) A post-industrial society will depend for its growth on 'qualitative' rather than 'quantitative' factors (p. 52).
(3) A post-industrial society can also be regarded as a 'post-capitalist' society — that is, as a system in which the traditional problems of capitalism will give way to a new set of problems related to the altered organizational structure of a post-industrial world (p. 56).

Whether these and other characteristics mean that the most important traits of modern industrial societies will disappear is another matter. Heilbroner argues that we in fact face both change and continuity and points out that continuity manifests itself in the relatively constant number of blue-collar workers (the increase in the proportion of white-collar employees is mainly offset by the drastic reduction in the number of people employed in agriculture). In spite of his argument about the decline of business civilization, he also expresses doubt as to whether structural characteristics and social problems related in industrial capitalism would wither away in the future.

The cardinal notion of post-industrialism is that industry is no longer in the foreground, even though it continues to play a crucial role. One of the most important aspects of the 'post-industrial society' emphasized by observers is the new social structure characterized not only by a shift from agriculture to industry, but also, and to a growing extent, by a shift from the production of goods to the supply of services and by the growth of administrative functions. The growth of industry is no longer marked by increasing numbers of manual labourers; technological development and high productivity are linked to a decreasing proportion of blue-collar workers in the economies of the highly developed countries. Modern societies are not only, or even primarily, societies of industrial workers: they are at least as much societies of clerks, or of those who supply services. 'The typical nineteenth-century view was that society would become an immense factory; today we should be more likely to visualise it as an immense bureaucracy' (Aron, 1967, p. 117). The shift of the working population towards tertiary industries is supported by Berg's analysis of the United States' labour force (see Table 1.4).

TABLE 1.4
PROFILE OF THE AMERICAN LABOUR FORCE, 1900–1980

|  | 1900 % | 1930 % | 1950 % | 1960 % | 1970 % | 1980 % |
|---|---|---|---|---|---|---|
| *White-collar*: |  |  |  |  |  |  |
| Professional and technical | 4 | 7 | 9 | 11 | 14 | 16 |
| Managers and proprietors | 6 | 7 | 8 | 11 | 11 | 10 |
| Clerical | 3 | 9 | 12 | 15 | 17 | 18 |
| Sales | 5 | 6 | 7 | 6 | 6 | 6 |
| Total | 18 | 29 | 36 | 43 | 48 | 50 |
| *Blue-collar*: |  |  |  |  |  |  |
| Skilled workers | 10 | 13 | 14 | 13 | 13 | 13 |
| Semi-skilled workers | 13 | 16 | 20 | 18 | 18 | 16 |
| Unskilled workers | 13 | 11 | 7 | 6 | 4 | 4 |
| Total | 36 | 40 | 41 | 37 | 35 | 33 |
| *Service workers* | 9 | 10 | 11 | 12 | 12 | 14 |
| *Farm workers* | 38 | 21 | 11 | 8 | 4 | 3 |
| No. of workers (millions) | 29 | 49 | 62 | 67 | 79 | 95 |

*Source*: Berg (1979) p. 61.

The distinctive aspect of services is that they require the exercise of symbolic rather than physical capacities. The possession of knowledge is more important than the possession of physical force and skills. Continuous innovation is the most important aspect of the development of knowledge. Innovation is not, however, confined to technology, but extends to all spheres of social life, which are increasingly subject to centralized social planning. It follows that knowledge becomes the most important productive force. It allows for self-sustained growth, in contrast to the previous pattern of development. The growing importance of knowledge means, in turn, that the leading institutions of social life are no longer factories and industrial firms but bureaucracies and research institutes, where real progress is made and transmitted to the rest of society.

Political authority also evolves: industrial and finance capitalists lose their privileged position vis-à-vis the technocrats, who become the leading elite of technological societies as planners and decision-makers. It follows that the source of social conflict shifts from property relationships to power: more and more depends on the decision-makers and all groups in society are vitally concerned to have their interests taken into consideration when long-term plans are drawn up and implemented.

One can conclude that, according to these views, industrialism is a social system geared towards the production of goods, while post-industrialism is a system aiming at the scientific creation and implementation of the most effective technologies.

Important structural characteristics of advanced societies are also reflected in the various terms used by social scientists for the emerging social order. These include: the employee society (Drucker, 1963); the organisational society (Presthus, 1979); the consumer society (Jones, 1965); the mass society (Giner, 1976); the new acquisitive society (Zweig, 1976); the administered society (Gross, 1964). Many of these descriptions can be applied to both communist and Western countries that have reached a certain stage of economic development.

## DILEMMAS OF ECONOMIC GROWTH

Whether or not one agrees with the concept of post-industrialism, there is no doubt that attempts to identify new traits in advanced industrial societies are fully justified in the light of the experience of the last few decades. Whether this experience confirms the optimistic predictions of the early theories of post-industrialism is, however, another matter.

It should be noted that most analysts of advanced, post-industrial societies have paid little attention to the problems posed by unrestrained economic development. Even less consideration has been given to the idea of possible limits to such unrestrained growth. Technological development raised expectations throughout the nineteenth and twentieth centuries. Most people have tended to take economic growth for granted, their concerns were the shortcomings of the social organizations within which this growth took place. Many went as far as to explain the negative aspects of social organization by inadequate technological development.

But there was a rapid change of mood in the late 1960s. In 1971, Forrester presented the main ideas underlying the new approach. He argued that the world economy has certain basic characteristics:

It is too complex to be understood by common sense and intuitive thinking.

The goals of different sub-systems of this complex whole are often contradictory. Thus what may be regarded as a success for one sub-system may be damaging to the totality. Equally, the effects for the system as a whole may be detrimental to some of its sub-systems.

Short-term and long-term solutions frequently conflict; short-term decisions may be detrimental in the long run, while long-term decisions are often unpopular and even unacceptable for society at a given moment.

The world economy is ruled by its own laws and does not respond to political slogans and *ad hoc* measures. It can be regulated only by its laws, in the same way as nature can be conquered only by accepting and using the laws of nature.

A principal conclusion of Forrester's study is that because the globe – the natural environment of man – is limited, the growth of our economy must come to an end. This argument is summarized in the introduction:

Exponential growth cannot continue forever. Our greatest immediate challenge is how we guide the transition from growth to equilibrium. There are many possible mechanisms of growth suppression...Unless we come to understand and to choose, the social system by its internal processes will choose for us. [Forrester, 1971, p. 8]

Forrester's approach was developed in studies by the Club of Rome, whose first report was published as the famous *Limits to Growth* (Meadows *et al.*, 1972). The Club of Rome, a group of prominent intellectuals from ten countries, initiated research into what they called 'the predicament of mankind'. Following Forrester's approach, they shifted their interest from the present to the future – in contrast to many other studies, which seek to understand connections between the present and the past. Following the technocratic assumption that man should look forward in order to make decisions and choose the best course of action, they are concerned with the problems the world will face if the present trend of economic development continues. Their findings may be summarized as follows:

(1) Unrestrained growth implies unlimited resources; yet in the course

of this growth the resources are rapidly exhausted, including raw materials, energy sources and arable areas.

(2) Unlimited growth is linked with the demographic explosion. This means that the pressure on limited resources is on the increase, as each underdeveloped country attempts to catch up and solve its own problems.

(3) Unlimited growth increases pollution on a scale unknown before, releases wastes and may cause a catastrophic contamination of the environment.

### Natural limits to industrial growth

The Club of Rome's report was severely criticised. Much of the criticism proved justified, and was acknowledged even by members of the Club in a later edition of their report. Nevertheless, some of the major conclusions reached by Forrester and the Club of Rome are accepted today as evident truth, or at least as genuine problems to be tackled. Many studies have provided new evidence of the various negative aspects of unrestrained growth.

It should be noted that, as a result of these arguments, the relationship between economic growth and the level of affluence has also been questioned. It has been argued that, despite a further increase in industrial output, living standards may fall. This is owing to greater costs of raw materials, greater numbers of people to be supported by those in work, and greater expenditure of effort and funds for the removal of waste and for fighting pollution. Novick refers to the demand-induced shortage of energy and in general to 'demand-induced scarcity'. He argues that each stage of industrial growth puts further pressure on irreplaceable global resources and is itself an additional obstacle to unrestrained growth (Novick, 1976).

### Economic limits to growth

In October 1973 Western economies faced a major economic oil crisis. Unemployment in the EEC countries rose from an average of two millions in 1960–1970 to six millions. Inflation increased from an average of 3.3 per cent in 1957–1973 to 13 per cent in 1974 and 8 per cent in 1978. The rate of annual growth, which oscillated around 5 per cent in 1960–1970, dropped to 2 per cent in 1974–1978. The dollar was rapidly devalued and petro-dollars from the Arab countries further destabilized the world economy.

There is no doubt that in the new circumstances the developed industrial countries coped with these difficulties much better than the less-developed parts of the world, where the effects of stagflation are particularly severe. Among the industrialized nations, the Common Market countries have proved quite successful — at present they control about 40 per cent of world markets. France and Germany, where living standards in 1950 were only one-third of that of America, reached three-quarters of the American level in subsequent years. Similarly in Great Britain, in spite of problems posed by stagflation, there has been a considerable improvement in living standards in the past decade.

Despite all these achievements most governments are faced in the long run with the dilemma of applying deflationary policies (that is, to curb inflation by drastically restraining economic activity). As Shanks comments:

...what is clear is that, somewhere around the middle to late 1960s, something started to go badly wrong. The mould began to break. The 'fine-tuners' lost control of the machine. And ten years later, we are scrambling about in the ruins trying to recreate a world order which we only imperfectly understand. [Shanks, 1978, p. 18]

### Social limits to economic growth

A new approach to the limits of growth has recently been provided by Hirsch (1977). He rejects the ecological argument but points to new problems posed by increasing consumption and rising expectations in modern society. According to Hirsch, the dominant ideology of recent decades has been the satisfaction of increasing human needs by means of economic growth. This is in contrast with the trend of previous centuries, when the satisfaction of human wants was primarily based on the redistribution of existing goods. This ever-growing consumption cannot, however, continue indefinitely, for the simple reason that human needs shift from material products to the so-called positional goods — that is, values accessible to individuals but that cannot be awarded to everybody. Leisure, land, unspoiled rural or suburban environment, leadership and education are positional goods: the more people want them, the less chance they have of satisfying their desires. Every soldier carries a field-marshal's baton, Hirsch argues, but all soldiers cannot become field-marshals. This simple truth means that, in spite of our affluence, a stage is reached when our expectations must give way to disappointment. The few can only win at the expense of the many — that is, the old problem of the redistribution of a limited stock of values returns at a higher level of economic development. Social limits to growth aggravate the distributional struggle. Conflicts do not disappear: on the contrary, they assume new forms and an increasing intensity, since pressure on positional goods increases their scarcity.

How are these trends likely to affect the two main systems of communism and capitalism? Very few studies deal with the future of communism in the context of limits to growth, but there is a profusion of publications on the prospects for the capitalist world.

One of the most penetrating analyses of the capitalist economy is that by Heilbroner (1977), who discusses the decline of what he calls the 'business civilization'. By distinguishing between the universal, the specific and the unique traits of this civilization, Heilbroner develops his analysis on many levels using different time perspectives. Heilbroner follows both Marx and Schumpeter in anticipating the decline of the capitalist order. Unlike Kerr and his associates, he pays far more attention to the economic, political and cultural forces that weaken the powers of resistance of the capitalist order than to technological factors alone.

As far as the immediate future of capitalism is concerned, Heilbroner points to the increased tendency towards state intervention and central planning as the only way of keeping capitalism alive. He believes that capitalism, as a system of privileges enjoyed by those who either own substantial property or occupy leading positions in the business world, can be maintained only as long as the system can solve its own contradictions. These consist of the tendency of capitalism to develop generalized and local disorders that require governmental intervention, and to accelerate negative environmental changes, that is, depletion of resources and pollution.

As far as the medium-term future of the 'business civilization' is concerned, Heilbroner dismisses the apocalyptic theory of a proletarian revolution. But at the same time he notes that growing affluence does not guarantee social harmony: on the contrary, it is often associated with the undermining of the values upon which the capitalist order rests. Among the novel attributes of post-industrialism that Heilbroner regards as being the result of these trends, the following seem to him most important: (a) the lessening of the margin of safety in Western societies owing to the shift of society's activities in the direction of services in which strikes are much more damaging; (b) the development of the need for a secure and stable environment and the resulting feelings of entitlement to basic provisions from the state: here prolonged education and affluence seem to be the underlying causes of these attitudes; and (c) a growing tendency to exert active control over social forces through the exercise of political will. Affluence becomes in itself a factor that generates social disorder. Inflation is the result not only of such factors as the shortage of raw materials or defective monetary policies, but of the new rights and expectations of a labour force capable of enforcing demands that exceed the increase of the national income. When it comes to carrying out unpleasant tasks and jobs, affluence also means reduced incentives. A contest for power between the owners of capital and the scientific−technical elite also creates problems, as does the uninhibited and unrestrained development of scientific research.

Adjustments to cope with these new problems imply the use of political machinery that functions as an at least partly autonomous force, able to modify some pressures in the system and to impose certain restraints on the forces that operate within it. Much depends in these circumstances on the ability of different societies to make use of their existing economic, political and social institutions. If many of the problems are thus common to countries like the Soviet Union, USA, Sweden or Great Britain, the methods of dealing with them and the possibility of a successful outcome will vary from one country and one system to another.

The same uncertainty applies, according to Heilbroner, to the long-term perspective. Neither in the West nor in the East can the present rate of growth be maintained for ever, since it will lead to the depletion of resources and the destruction of the environment within the lifetime of only a generation. Yet this very prospect causes new tensions and antagonisms — a struggle for the redistribution of wealth between classes and nations. Heilbroner asserts that in the long term the rights of property will inevitably be assailed or ignored. This will result in a greater role for the central authorities in the allocation and redistribution of resources. He is also convinced that the cultural resources of the 'business civilization' are on the wane because of the commercialization of life and a disregard for the value of work. The only method of legitimizing the 'business civilization' is by growth; once growth is brought to a halt, all arguments for private property lose their appeal.

As we see, Heilbroner goes far beyond technological determinism in his analysis of future prospects. His analysis brings him to a position contrary to that of 'industrial pluralism' put forward by Kerr *et al.*; rather he expects the development of 'statist' structures and 'statist religion' characterized by 'the elevation of the collective and communal destiny of man to the forefront of public consciousness, and the absolute subordination of private interests to public requirements' (Heilbroner, 1977, p. 95).

Ignoring the shortcomings of long-term prophecies, the important methodological point from Heilbroner's theory is the necessity to look at both present and future economic life in terms of the interplay of economic forces, political institutions and cultural changes that go far beyond the requirements of developing and changing technologies. The concept of a post-industrial society seen from this perspective depends much more on the combination of all these factors than on a one-sided emphasis on productive processes, which seemed to dominate the last decades of modern industrial society.

## CONCLUDING REMARKS

A comparison of economic problems in both Western and communist countries helps us to understand the interrelationship between industry and society. The functions carried out by workers, managers and a growing army of white-collar employees in industrial enterprises are very much alike in both communist and capitalist countries as are the technological and human skills. Technology, equipment, occupational groups and basic organizational principles are, however, only part of the story. We cannot disregard the objectives of industrial activities, the norms and rules adopted in industry, the environment in which enterprises operate and the conflicts and contradictions people face while pursuing their aims. Enterprises cannot be analysed as isolated social systems; they respond to the totality of the economic, social and political pressures to which they are exposed, and fulfil their social functions according to the changing laws and rules of the social field in which they operate. Workers in the United States and in Soviet Russia may have much in common in terms of working in similar industries, having the same occupational training and even displaying identical personality features, yet they will react differently according to whether they work within the command economy or are exposed to market forces, whether they deal with authoritarian or democratic rules of conduct, and whether they depend upon autonomous institutions like the trade unions and occupational associations or are subject to the monolithic and arbitrary regulations of the party-state.

The differences are particularly striking when we analyse group conflicts at the macro level, and when we compare the institutional settings that determine the collective activities of workers in West and East. In fact it is hardly possible to speak about the united action of employees under communist rule when workers are deprived of the possibility of organizing and acting independently to promote their interests. Hence the difference between the two systems in the nature of industrial conflict, in the role of trade unionism, in the forms of industrial action and in the meaning of industrial democracy. The differences are not limited to communism and capitalism alone. They can also be found if we compare various societies within the communist camp (to mention only China and Russia or Yugoslavia and Bulgaria) or the variety of industrial societies in the non-communist world.

All this does not mean that we should reduce social research of industrialism to area studies in which the particularities of different systems are explored and duly reported. Convergence and divergence, continuity and change, similarities and differences are not poles apart but appear to be intrinsic features of the industrial world. It follows that generalizations are important if made with caution and with necessary qualification, taking account of the social, economic, political and cultural frameworks within which industry operates.

It is in the realm of ideas that the problems posed by rapid change and the high complexity of technological development are particularly grave. The pace of change makes it very difficult to adjust concepts and beliefs to the new circumstances. However, when dealing with social aspects of industry, 'artificiality' of the industrial system does not allow us to dismiss the old ideas, and formulate fresh rules of conduct. From this point of view, industrial sociology poses as many problems as it solves, since it too is subject to the fallacies and difficulties of a changing and conflict-ridden environment. Industrial sociologists are by the very nature of their discipline torn between conflicting values of social justice, between the need for the preservation of the productive means of their society and demands of different groups directly involved in, or affected by, production processes. At the same time, the complexity of social facts accounts for the abundance of explanations and approaches that, while on the surface contradicting each other, in fact reflect only the diversity and variation in industrial life.

The grasp of the changing reality is determined to a great extent by concepts and theories based on past and often obsolete experience. The nineteenth-century masters dominate our thinking, the ideologies that were genuinely progressive a few decades ago exercise an irresistible attraction in spite of new circumstances that contradict them, and the magic of absolute and infallible solutions lures many industrial sociologists into the false feeling of professional certainty. It is enough, however, to follow the development of the discipline in more detail to see the relative nature of all theorizing, and to understand that real progress cannot be achieved by using a master key supplied by any of the big names of the past.

The European perspective on industrial life dominated by the intellectual outlooks of Marx, Durkheim and Weber, and the American development of industrial studies via scientific management, the human relations school and organizational theory, give us the necessary background to pursue the study of industry. As we shall see, many of the contributions stemming from these lines of thought have preserved their relevance and importance; others have faded away, giving place to alternative and more advanced explanations.

# CHAPTER 2

# Man and Technology

## TECHNOLOGY AND THE DIVISION OF LABOUR

The impact of technology on human life can be analysed in terms of what people produce and how they produce it. The antecedents of work behaviour can be found in all species; for example, higher mammals spend much time on gathering food, providing shelter, caring for their young and protecting their territory. Man is distinguished by the fact that he produces tools with which to work: the entire evolution of mankind can be described as the process of developing and channelling the means of production.

As far as individual producers are concerned, technology determines the rhythm and content of their working day. In primitive societies, hunting and gathering were the main types of productive activity. The rhythm of daily activity was dictated by natural factors, and the dynamic interaction with nature shaped human life. Cooperation was spontaneous and determined by common interests, the division of labour was rudimentary and the distinction between functions carried out by different members of human groups depended largely on sex and age. Developments in agriculture led to basic changes in working activities. New forms of division of labour and cooperation emerged. The rise of ancient civilization marked the turning point in the history of human work. A division between agricultural and non-agricultural activities coincided with the development of urban centres, where specialized crafts and trades were grouped. The distinction between manual and non-manual tasks became more and more pronounced, and non-agricultural manual labour came to be subdivided into many different skills based on different techniques. While small-scale production was based on direct cooperation within the workshop, indirect bonds between producers were maintained throughout the market. Motivation for productive activities changed accordingly: some were producing mainly to satisfy their own needs, others were producing commodities for the market, and yet others were subject to direct compulsion and reduced to the status of slaves toiling to satisfy the needs of their masters.

In modern civilizations, non-agricultural forms of production were originally based on artisanship. Individuals were designated by their trade: carpenters, saddlers, barbers, smiths, cobblers, haberdashers, grave-diggers, tailors, dressmakers — all were artisans differentiated both by the nature of the products they supplied and by the skills they possessed. They passed their techniques and trade secrets from one generation to the next. The social forms in which artisans were organized were known in Western Europe as guilds, which existed from medieval times to the eighteenth century to carry out different functions on behalf of their members. The guilds supervised the education of apprentices and journeymen, regulated the membership and controlled the prices of the products so as to secure a decent income for their members. They also used common funds to cover expenses for funerals and acted as pressure groups and representative bodies vis-à-vis local councils and sovereign authorities. The work of artisans was highly specialized and trade secrets were jealously guarded. (See Schneider, 1957, pp. 31–6.)

Work based on craftmanship has certain characteristics that distinguish it from the manual labour of the modern factory. Craftmanship was the result of a long period of apprenticeship; it implied full control by the artisan over the work process; it was characterized by a variety of tasks and complex operations; it presumed the full responsibility of the producer for the final product. It is true that artisans' work contained many tedious and repetitive elements, which were usually carried out by the apprentices. The apprentices hoped, however, that in due time they would acquire the intermediate status of journeymen and carry out more complicated tasks, and would one day become the masters themselves.

During the manufacturing period, which extended in England from the middle of the sixteenth century to the final third of the eighteenth century, a further evolution of technology took place. Manufacturing could generally be described as great numbers of workers working together at the same time and in one place in order to produce the same sort of commodity by using their manual skills under common supervision. In *Capital*, Marx described the two-fold origin of manufacture. Some manufactures arose by assembling workers belonging to various crafts to manufacture a complete product — for example, a carriage. This involved tailors, locksmiths, upholsterers, glaziers, painters and many other craftsmen. But once the craftsmen became exclusively occupied in such highly specialized activities as making carriages, they lost the ability to produce the whole range of products. These were heterogeneous manufacturing units. Other manufacturing was created by the employment of a number of workers who all performed the same kind of work, such as making paper or needles. At first they worked in the traditional manner, but gradually the work was redistributed so that the workers performed disconnected, isolated operations. The fragmentation of the process of production allowed for increased specialization by the workers in relatively simple manual operations. This was serial manufacturing.

In the first case we have the combination and merging of what was previously independent; in such manufactures craftsmen are co-operating while stripped of their independence. In the second case there is a division of what was once united: a former craftsman's skills are fragmented and divided among a set of workers, each of whom carries out part of what constituted his previous task. In both cases, however, the handicraft remained the basis of production. (Marx, 1979, pp. 455–67.)

The eighteenth-century industrial revolution began with the replacement of the craftsman's tools by mechanical implements. The spinning machine invented by John Wyatt was most characteristic of this development. The basic change consisted of the emancipation of tools from the limitations of human organs: 'The Jenny...even at the very beginning, spun with twelve to eighteen spindles, and the stocking-loom knits with many thousand needles at once' (Marx, 1979, p. 495). Once the workman handling a single tool was superseded by a mechanism operating with a number of similar tools, it was only a matter of time before the motive power was improved by replacing human muscles or other primitive sources of energy by more effective ones. The invention of the steam engine by Watt in 1784 was a major step in this direction. From this moment technological progress has been marked by the development of machines separated from the constraints of human strength and less dependent upon manual skills.

While in handicraft workmen made use of tools, in the factory the machine makes use of man; he becomes a mere appendage of the machine. The decisive stage was reached when machines could be produced by machines. The factory system could spread, bringing a degree of mechanization previously unknown.

An organized system of machines to which motion is communicated by the transmitting mechanism from an automatic centre is the most developed form of production by machinery. Here we have, in place of the isolated machine, a mechanical monster whose body fills whole factories, and whose demonic power, at first hidden by the slow and measured motions of its gigantic members, finally bursts forth in the fast and feverish whirl of its countless working organs. [Marx, 1979, p. 545]

The division of labour remains, but changes its character.

In so far as the division of labour re-appears in the factory, it takes the form primarily of a distribution of workers among the specialized machines, and of quantities of workers, who do not however form organized groups, among the various departments of the factory, in each of which they work at a number of similar machines placed together; only simple co-operation therefore takes place between them. The organized group peculiar to manufacture is replaced by the connection between the head worker and his few assistants.... Thus although, from a technical point of view, the old system of division of labour is thrown overboard by machinery, it hangs on in the factory as a tradition handed down from manufacture...the lifelong speciality of handling the same tool now becomes the lifelong speciality of serving the same machine. [Marx, 1979, pp. 545–7]

The equipment of  factories used nowadays has changed much since Marx wrote *Capital*; however, many of his observations remain valid so long as man's domination by machines remains essentially the same. In many modern industries workers were, and still are, functioning as mere appendages to machines, and the whole progress of technology in recent decades has not liberated them from this dependence:

[Man] supplements without loss whatever human faculties the machine lacks, whatever imperfection hampers the machine in the satisfaction of its needs. If it lacks eyes, he sees for it; he walks for it, if it is without legs; and he pulls, drags, lifts, if it needs arms. All these things are done by the factory worker at the pace set by the machine and under its direction and command. [Marot, 1918; quoted by Friedmann, 1955, p. 178]

The emergence of manufacturing heralded a new work pattern in which the skills of the producer became less and less relevant to the final product. This development has continued in modern factories where producers are no longer regarded as people endowed with special skills but are named according to the establishment in which they work. Steel workers, textile workers, miners, glass workers, are all names describing employees in different industries, irrespective of their functions and skills. All of them are designated as factory workers, industrial workers or simply workers; all these general categories reflect the changing status of the manual labour force. Several decades later, Schneider, an American sociologist, commented:

...the tool is merely the extension of the man's hand; the hammer obeys the impulses of the worker, operates by the energy supplied by the worker, responds to his thoughts, habits, skills...the worker in modern industry is exactly the opposite relation to the machine; it is the machine which determines the worker's actions, the energies he will expend, the skills he can employ...power is supplied from a distant source, the speed of the process is controlled automatically, needed skills are reduced to elementary movements. [Schneider, 1957, p. 152]

It is clear from these observations that the nature of workers' tasks is moulded by technological development; the division of labour between machines and aggregates of machines is the decisive factor in shaping human work, structuring social relationships and affecting the whole rhythm of individual life. In some industries, such as steel, technological processes require 24-hour attendance so that shift-work is essential. In some plants, machines require the cooperation of closely knit teams of workers; in others they act as atomized individuals. Every technological change degrades certain skills while elevating the holders of other skills to the ranks of a labour aristocracy. Some technologies compel workers to live in remote communities, while other industries disperse workers in large urban agglomerations. Lorry drivers, navvies, assembly-line workers, printers, miners, watchmakers, gasmen and railwaymen are highly differentiated occupational groups though all are described as 'manual workers'; the occupational composition of the working class is shaped and reshaped at every stage of technological development.

The usual distinction between unit production, mass production and process production corresponds roughly to the principal differentiations in industrial *work* in manufacturing industries, as well as to the principal differentiations in industrial life. At the same time, it marks the historical sequence in productive methods from old craft industries, through large-scale production with its preponderance of semi-skilled labour, to the modern automated industries where differences between manual workers and non-manual technicians are less pronounced (see Meissner, 1969).

Present-day industry offers...three kinds of machines which also mark three stages of automation, with a number of intermediate forms. First, the dependent machines where feeding, control, and regulation constantly depend on the hand of man: these are the machines widely disemminated in the workshops by the first industrial revolution and restrained to the extent that the latter has been prolonged and survives. In the second place, the semi-automatic machines....Finally, born of the perfecting of the first two, automatic machines (independent) in which the worker is eliminated in the role of operator. Other functions appear, such as supervision, control, and especially regulation... Muscular work is here insignificant or non-existent.

The most disagreeable work seems, therefore, to be that in which automation is so to speak, stopped in its tracks, for possibly very different reasons: technical difficulties of automatization, neglect or ignorance of their interest by hidebound industrialists, low wages of unskilled workers in a given region or industry, etc. [Friedmann, 1955, pp. 177–9]

## MASS PRODUCTION

Comparing methods of production used at the earlier stages of indus- trialization, we notice that the main development is the semi-automation of many aspects of work processes. Early machines were completely dependent on man: the workers controlled them, regulated their move- ments, adjusted them to new tasks and used their skills to improve the quality of the end product. The introduction of more sophisticated machinery meant that workers became an extension of the machine itself, carrying out the simplest of fragmented operations. Once the needs of machines are reduced to the simple and repetitive operations carried out by mass production workers, the road to full automation is open so that the human being can be eliminated from the process of production altogether. Whether this happens or not depends on the costs involved. So far, automation is confined to selected indus- tries while the semi-automated, man–machine systems based on sup- plementary, repetitive operations of the workers have become the predominant feature of many industries (Brown, 1977b).

The automobile industry was the first in which mass production methods were fully utilized. Ford is rightly regarded as a pioneer of the new technology. In 1914, mass production technology appeared for the first time at Ford's Highland Park plant where three principles were observed:

(1)  the planned and continuous progression of the car through the shop;
(2)  the delivery of the work to the mechanic instead of the reverse;
(3)  the fragmentation of tasks into their constituent parts, each component of the partitioned operation being allocated to a worker or group of workers.

Behind all these changes was an immense effort on the part of planning departments to set up the most effective scheme of work processes. Intellectual effort and skills lay with the engineers who designed the productive processes and subdivided the functions. The worker was left to perform the relatively simple tasks according to schedule. As Nevins and Hill state, the plant itself became kinetic:

A kinetic plant: – moving, moving, moving; every segment – presses, furnaces, welders, stamps, drills, paint-baths, lathes – in use every minute; not an ounce of metal or a degree of heat avoidably wasted; and the economy in time and labor matching the economy in materials. [Nevins and Hill, 1957, p. 7]

The advantages of mass production are obvious. There is no need to spend money on training skilled workers; simplified operations can be performed after only a few days of training. Such methods shortened the time needed to produce motor cars and provided the market with surprisingly cheap products. The interchangeability of easily available parts greatly simplified repairs and maintenance, and the rapid increase in the demand for low-priced cars enormously increased the profits of the motor car producers and enabled them to pay good wages to the workers whose productivity rose because of the new technology. The automobile industry was for many decades the leading example of technological advancement. At the same time, it revealed the seamy side of mass production technology, well-described in books by Walker and Guest (1952), Chinoy (1955), and Touraine's study of Renault (1955), which have become classics of industrial sociology.

But the abundance of literature on the motor industry creates a certain imbalance; many generalizations about mass production are based almost exclusively on studies of automobile workers and do not take into consideration the differences between various industries in terms of production technology. The assembly line has become a sort of symbol of modern industrial work, even if the actual number of workers thus employed is rather limited. There is also a tendency to underestimate the monotony and repetitiveness of pre-industrial forms of production:

Many tasks in agriculture such as sowing, harvesting by the sickle or the scythe, winnowing with a flail were (and still are, in many European peasant communities in which old techniques persist) repetitive and monotonous labor. Spinning with a wheel or a spindle, weaving on the old handloom and basket-making offer other examples. We are used to contrasting the work of artisans with mechanized labor; but were not the journeymen and the apprentices assisting the masters often given tasks of slight interest? [Friedmann, 1955, p. 131]

There are, however, substantial differences between the traditional pattern of repetitive work and the requirements imposed on workers in the machine age. Firstly, what was regarded in many pre-industrial trades as a transitory period of apprenticeship has become in modern industry the dominant pattern of work throughout the whole of a man's life. Secondly, the physiological and psychological effects of repetitiveness cannot really be compensated for as long as the worker's performance is controlled by machines and reinforced by the payments system. Thirdly, there is a difference in the meaning of repetitive jobs for the mass producer as compared with those performed by peasants or independent craftsmen — the work is performed for the employer's benefit and under his control. Fourthly, there is a radical change in the industrial environment: working with large numbers of workers in huge workshops dominated by machines creates tensions. Finally, there is a discrepancy between the kind of work performed by semi-skilled workers and the values of the outside world, where lack of skill, of initiative, of independence and of responsibility are usually regarded as being of low status.

## RESPONSES OF WORKERS TO MASS PRODUCTION

From the beginning, mass production methods posed at least as many problems as they solved. It is true that many negative aspects of human toil could be eliminated: 'hard' labour disappeared; the use of human force was reduced to a minimum; hygiene and safety at work were improved. At the same time, it was noted at a very early stage that simplified, repetitive jobs caused a new phenomenon of industrial fatigue, the result not so much of physical effort as of the tedium of daily work. In England, the first studies on industrial fatigue were made during the First World War by the Industrial Fatigue Research Board (1924–1934). Since then many studies have appeared covering different aspects of the subject.

Social psychologists who study workers' responses to job characteristics refer to the theory of stimulation to explain the adverse effect of monotony on human beings. Deprived of sensory variety, individuals develop negative reactions (including boredom and fatigue), reduce their work performance, and attempt to abandon the place in which the adverse experience occurs (at the work-place this leads to absenteeism and high labour turnover).

Many authors emphasize that the degree of boredom in industrial enterprises is closely related to the degree of mechanization of work. One is less likely to become bored if either attention is entirely concentrated on what one is doing, or the tasks can be performed automatically so that one's mind may be directed elsewhere. Boredom is most acute in semi-automatic processes, when neither of these conditions applies — that is, when the task is too absorbing to allow for day-dreaming and too simple to attract the worker's interest.

Boredom has been defined by psychologists and sociologists in various ways. According to Mayo: 'Monotony, like fatigue, is a word which is used to denote any sort of induced imbalance in the worker such that he cannot continue work, or can continue only at a lower level of activity' (1933, p. 54). For social psychologists, boredom is an entirely subjective phenomenon, a state of kind. Fatigue, on the other hand, whether it is based on excessive physical activity or whether it is caused by the sensation of boredom (subjective fatigue), is always accompanied by physical effects such as sleepiness or lethargy (Friedmann, 1955, p. 143).

If we define boredom in terms of the worker's response to his environment and to the type of work he performs, we have to distinguish three questions:

(1) Which objective factors are likely to cause boredom at work?
(2) Are these factors determined by the nature of the tasks only, or are they caused or reinforced by other elements of the worker's situation?
(3) To what extent do personality characteristics affect the worker's response, i.e., which subjective factors influence the susceptibility to boredom at work?

Many scholars argue that the level of intelligence is primarily responsible for boredom: intelligent workers find it more difficult to adapt themselves to repetitive jobs than workers with mediocre intelligence. Friedmann, who notes that many managers and technicians support this view, quotes the following opinion:

Indeed automatization has now reached a point where individual capacities of workmen count for so little that large employers of labor find less keen minds cheaper than keen minds in many berths, because the less keen mind presents fewer labor complications to the boss, is more easily satisfied, feels labor strain less and is less trouble all round.

And he comments:

The testimony which I have personally accumulated in the course of my inquiries is in agreement. Confronted with a new, repetitive, subdivided task, the most intelligent and developed minds are less capable of resistance than their fellows; their output decreases, and they try to change assignments. [Friedmann, 1955, p. 140]

Viteles (1955, p. 542) distinguishes three types of personality that he relates to job attitudes:

people who wish to be completely absorbed in any task they are doing (totality type) and are consequently more sensitive than anyone else to boredom caused by monotony;
people capable of splitting their attention, who are consequently able to endure monotonous jobs;
people capable of creating an active mental life apart from the work they are doing, who are thus relatively indifferent to their environment.

The diversity of elements that contribute to the varying responses of workers to repetitive jobs has been convincingly shown by Wyatt, Fraser and Stock. They demonstrate that, under monotonous working conditions, output and workers' attitudes to their tasks depend upon:

the value attached by workers to repetitive tasks:

some tasks just as monotonous as the others arouse a far higher interest of the workers and achieve a far higher output because the workers find their activities somehow important: the unwrapping of candy poorly wrapped by the machine was considered in the factory as useless and consequently as monotonous while the preparation of boxes which were destined for trade was positively valued... [Industrial Fatigue Research Board, 1934] ;

the continuity of work: many workers resent short and unexpected
  interruptions that prevent them from day-dreaming;
the complexity and variety of tasks, which, though repetitive, could
  absorb the worker physically and mentally.

Similar conclusions can be drawn from Lawler's analysis of the factors affecting employee-satisfaction. He argues that it depends basically on three general job characteristics:

1. *The job must allow a worker to feel personally responsible for a meaningful portion of his work* [autonomy dimension] ...
2. *The job must involve doing something that is intrinsically meaningful or otherwise experienced as worthwhile to the individual...*
3. *The job must provide feedback about what is accomplished*... Such feedback must come from doing the task itself... [it] may come from some other person. [Lawler, 1973, pp. 158–160]

Lawler points out (p. 161) that in view of these three dimensions, those with well-developed higher needs will react differently to dull and meaningless jobs from those with low expectations of intrinsic outcomes.

Other experimental studies support these generalizations, even if firm conclusions relating to increased variety cannot be made. Wyatt, Fraser and Stock believe greater productivity results from more varied work, but other research does not confirm this (Industrial Fatigue Research Board, 1928). According to Turner and Lawrence (1965, p. 36), motor variety and optional social interaction at work are negatively related to absenteeism. Bonjean and Vance (1968), who tested a random sample of 332 salaried workers, discovered that the lower the 'self-realization' the more likely were: day-dreaming; aggressive feelings towards supervisors; aggressive feelings towards co-workers; restricted output; errors at work; the postponing of difficult tasks and decisions; a preoccupation with material rewards; thinking about other jobs; lack of interest in work; and lack of specialization at work.

In studies of people's complaints about their work, repetitiveness and standardization of tasks do not seem to be the major cause of dissatisfaction. According to Conant and Kilbridge (1965): assembly-line workers complain mostly about being tied to the job, which prevents them leaving the place of work except during breaks; fatigue is very often the result of having to remain for hours in one position and repeating the same movements (swollen legs, aching backs, pain in the neck, are very common complaints); the pacing of work seems to be one of the most unpleasant aspects of assembly-line work. In all these respects the difference between conveyor-belt work and repetitive jobs at individual machines was significant for those workers asked to assess their work. While working at individual machines, workers have more influence on structuring their working day, can pace their work and have more control over their movements. In an investigation of an American mid-western manufacturing company, sixty-one workers with previous experience of assembly-line work were interviewed. Their assessments of the differences between assembly-line and bench work are shown in Tables 2.1 and 2.2.

TABLE 2.1
FEATURES LIKED AT BENCH WORK

|  | *No. of workers:* |
|---|---|
| Freedom from being tied to the job | 55 |
| Quality assignability | 53 |
| Individual incentive opportunity | 53 |
| Ability to contribute to quality | 52 |
| Opportunity to make a complete assembly | 50 |
| Ability to set own pace | 48 |
| Greater amount of variety at work | 47 |
| Learning time | 38 |

*Source*: Conant and Kilbridge (1965)

TABLE 2.2
FEATURES DISLIKED AT ASSEMBLY LINE

|  | *No. of workers:* |
|---|---|
| Inability to control quality | 57 |
| The group incentive scheme | 43 |
| The attachment to line | 42 |
| Pacing of time | 37 |

*Source*: Conant and Kilbridge (1965)

This research was carried out in a firm that had originated a job enrichment programme by abandoning the assembly line and going over to bench work with every worker regulating his own speed and being individually responsible for the operations performed. The workers appeared to favour the new methods and no social differences were discovered between those who approved of the new methods and those who preferred the old ones. Some elements of assembly-line work were favoured by the majority: 32 workers expressed satisfaction with the small number of work elements in their previous jobs; 44 liked the short training time; and 45 approved of the assembly -line social relations pattern.

It has been noted in other studies that workers are relatively satisfied with repetitive tasks in industries where wages exceed the average. Research into the attitudes and job satisfaction of workers in the motor industry in England demonstrates the following principle:

Most previous writers, we would suggest, have tended to over-simplify the problems of workers' response to the stresses and constraints of assembly-line technology (and have tended to assume greater uniformity in this respect than proves to be the case) because they have left out of account one important *variable*; that is, the orientations which men *bring* to their employment and which *mediate between* the objective features of the work situation and workers' actual experience of, and reaction to, this situation. [Goldthorpe, 1966]

Other writers point out that human reactions to tedious fragmented jobs are determined by personality factors, habits and learning processes as well as by other components of work processes, including remuneration, social pressures and 'the climate' of the enterprise concerned. One should also mention individual expectations and aspirations, cultural background, and many situational factors that influence not only direct reactions but also the pace of eventual adjustment to work conditions. This is shown diagrammatically in Figure 2.1.

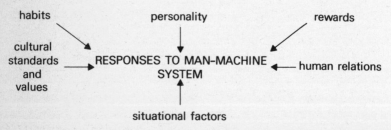

FIGURE 2.1 *Factors affecting responses to man–machine system*

The question of the adaptation of industrial workers to industrial conditions seems open to conjecture. The tentative generalizations based on empirical findings are best summarized in what has been called the 'tolerance theory' of workers' adaptation. This explains ways in which 'people can achieve toleration of what is to them, and may appear to others as, an unsatisfying or impoverished work situation' (Biddle and Hutton, 1976, p. 833). Biddle and Hutton analyse job satisfaction not in terms of motives, needs and attitudes but in terms of 'the living space' — the psychological territory that serves to protect the individual's inner world and sense of worth. They summarize many scattered findings and interpret them in the light of a connection with their own empirical studies of workers employed in technologically different sections of a large engineering company.

Biddle and Hutton point out that in situations where the congruence between the required and the permitted living space was low (that is, when the workers were faced by a dissonance between their needs and a situation that they could not change) they tended to suppress their negative feelings and even to deny their existence. Adaptation manifested itself in three different ways:

(1) Workers developed some form of individual toleration: where wages were high enough they resorted to economic instrumentalism; where wages were not satisfactory they seemed to find compensation in some sort of positive self-image shared by other workers as well.
(2) Workers could adjust by shifting their attention to group relationships and by developing meaningful and rewarding bonds with the members of the group.
(3) Finally, workers could react by withdrawing totally from the system through absenteeism and high labour turnover.

## THEORIES OF THE ALIENATED WORKER

The transformation of the worker into a mere appendage of the machine and the degradation of human labour brought about by the fragmentation, standardization and simplification of tasks, find their reflection in theories of the 'alienated worker'. The concept first appeared in the early nineteenth century in Germany, where the Young Hegelians denounced the plight of industrial labourers. Later, the same idea could be found in the writings of the young Marx. Marx combined the Hegelian notion of alienation, its materialistic interpretation as elaborated by Ludvig Feuerbach, and the criticism of industrial civilization levelled by the Left Hegelians. Marx's concept of alienation at work was an integral part of his materialist and dialectic philosophy. He pointed out that the division of labour not only accounted for increased human productivity, but also resulted in man's growing dependence upon the blind forces loosed by technological and economic change. The Marxist approach to alienation contains two major points. The first relates to the growing discrepancy between human nature and the world of technology, which imposes unbearable strains on the worker. Technology *per se* is to blame in this case:

What constitutes the alienation of labour? First, that work is *external* to the worker, that it is not part of his nature; and that, consequently, he does not fulfil himself in his work but denies himself, has a feeling of misery rather than well-being, does not develop freely his mental and physical energies but is physically exhausted and mentally debased. The worker, therefore, feels himself at home only during his leisure time, whereas at work he feels homeless. His work is not voluntary but imposed, *forced labour*. It is not satisfaction of a need, but only a *means* for satisfying other needs. Its alien character is clearly shown by the fact that as soon as there is no physical or other compulsion it is avoided like the plague....

We arrive at the result that man (the worker) feels himself to be freely active only in his animal functions — eating, drinking and procreating, or at most also in his dwelling and in personal adornment — while in his human functions he is reduced to an animal. The animal becomes human and the human becomes animal! [Marx, 1971, pp. 127–8]

The second aspect of alienation was, however, related by Marx to the 'wicked' nature of capitalism, which Marx regarded as the major cause of the workers' plight. The economy, market pressures, ruthless competition, exploitation — these transformed man into a mere agent of the social forces, which were beyond rational control. This broader view sees the 'real' cause of man's alienation as being rooted in the *type of ownership* of productive capacity (privately owned factories, etc.).

Despite the vehement condemnation of modern technology, Marx was convinced that the machine was here to stay. The solution was, in the first place, to abolish social organization based on the exploitation of workers:

Just as the savage must wrestle with Nature to satisfy his wants...so must civilised man, and he must do so in all forms of society and under all possible modes of production...Freedom in this field can only consist in socialised man, the associated producers, rationally regulating their interchange with Nature, bringing it under their common control ...But it nonetheless still remains a realm of necessity...The realm of freedom can only flourish with the realm of necessity as its basis. [Marx, 1969, p. 260]

Concern with the negative aspects of technological progress seems to have been growing in the last decades. There has been increasing discussion of the adverse effects of modern technology on both the life of the worker and the environment generally. The plight of the working man who is exposed to the requirements of machinery has been illustrated by many empirical studies. The concept of alienation has become popular among sociologists as a catchword of this new trend, and the references to Marx are an indispensable appendage to discussions on industrialism and industrial man. However, in contrast to Marx, most modern sociologists who discuss alienation confine themselves to denouncing the direct ill-effects of modern technology and are much less concerned with broader analyses of economy and society and man—machine relationships. The idea of alienation has become a combination of the heritage of anti-industrialism, the Durkheimian perspective of anomie (see chapter 9), modern criticism of bureaucratic structures, and the Freudian and neo-Freudian denunciation of external social constraints.

In most empirical studies of alienation, attention is concentrated on the direct relationship between worker and machine or, more generally, between worker and technological requirements. The advance of industrialism seems to generate among social scientists a growing uneasiness with the seamier side of the division of labour associated with technological progress. Rising workers' expectations have also stimulated a much more critical approach to the dehumanizing aspects of industrial work; working conditions have become a matter of concern for trade unions, management, large-scale corporations, politicians and governments. This changing perspective on factory work explains the growing popularity of the concept of alienation, and has stimulated empirical studies of the man—machine relationship.

Blauner discusses alienation in terms of powerlessness, meaninglessness, isolation and self-estrangement (Blauner, 1973, pp. 15–34). He compared four industries – printing, textiles, motor cars and chemicals – and found that the changing level of alienation in work could be presented as an inverted U-curve. In traditional craft-style industry, work processes retain their stimuli and social meaning, while mass production methods tend to deprive the workers of their former autonomy and to increase their feeling of alienation. The most advanced system of technology linked with automated production tends, however, to restore the meaning of work and to create new conditions in which workers can regain their social and individual identity. Using his typology of work situations and comparing many research findings in the above four different industries, Blauner was able to make generalizations that can be projected into the future. To the extent to which automation will become the dominant form of production, one can optimistically expect a positive change on the content of work through a decrease in the alienating effects of technology. (Blauner, 1973, pp. 182–3.)

One could argue that Blauner's concept of alienation at work is limited by its technological determinism – that is, it is an explanation of social events based primarily on technological factors. It is also undoubtedly true that the analysis is enterprise-centred, in that he was more concerned with the fragmentation of man's work experience than with the fragmentation of his social, collective existence. While discussing the general tendency of modern industry to use people as objects of labour power, Blauner specified the conditions under which this trend occurred; thus the link is with the mass production manufacturing industries, and there is no need therefore to refer to other variables that might account for the dehumanization of work, for example, the type of *ownership* of production.

Alienation-based theories have their critics. Form, an eminent American sociologist, stated in a study of motor-car production that:

Intellectuals hate machines. While they acknowledge that machines lighten the burden of labor, they see machines unnaturally intruding upon work life...Robbing workers of their skills, machines have isolated workers from one another, their families, and communities. Most important, machines have so estranged workers from themselves that they can only hate their work. [Form, 1973a]

Form argues that, in contrast to this image, most industrial workers declare themselves satisfied with their jobs. His research corroborated these attitudes. He selected four motor-car factories in four countries (USA, Italy, Argentina and India), each representing a different stage of industrialization. Form's findings (and many similar findings) suggest that job characteristics in the motor industry affect workers' satisfaction only marginally, a point I shall discuss in more detail in later chapters.

Does this mean that job monotony can be dismissed as irrelevant from the point of view of the workers? Advocates of the alienation view of the modern worker argue that job satisfaction is a complex phenomenon that must be studied within a wider context – that job characteristics must be related to what we regard as the requirements or standards of a fully developed human personality. Mental health, psychological well-being, personality development – all these factors are beyond doubt affected by the fragmentation of labour and can therefore be assessed on their own merits, even if workers do accept the negative aspects of their occupations and adjust to them accordingly.

## DEALING WITH THE DISRUPTIVE EFFECTS
## OF THE DIVISION OF LABOUR IN INDUSTRY

The negative effects of technology are not only experienced by the workers but, insofar as they cause dissatisfaction, frustration and discomfort, they have direct and indirect repercussions on productivity rates. If we omit the problem of industrial unrest (which will be discussed in more detail in chapter 9), we are still left with high labour turnover, absenteeism and general apathy on the part of workers employed in repetitive jobs. These are all phenomena that affect production negatively, and cannot therefore be disregarded by industrial management.

Under conditions of full employment unskilled and semi-skilled workers are much less interested in retaining their jobs than skilled workers. Indeed, they do not mind changing jobs as often as possible in order to enjoy such benefits as a short break from the monotony of factory life while looking for another job. Absenteeism plays a similar role: the worker affected by monotony finds an easy escape from the rhythm of work and does not much care if he loses a day's wages, especially in those industries where shortage of labour prevents management from taking punitive measures. The enormous cost of absenteeism and high labour turnover, as well as other side-effects of workers' dissatisfaction, are the reason for attempts to deal with boredom and frustration on the shop floor.

In the USA the problem of over-specialization became clear during the Second World War. The need to increase production to bolster the war effort could not at that time be met by assembly work because of the specialist nature of much of the technology. On the other hand, the unavailability of male labour made it necessary to employ women and clerical workers who were much less adjusted to the strains and tensions of factory life. For these reasons, many engineers began to challenge traditional ideas of organizing mass production, and studied alternative ways of attaining high labour productivity.

Later, an enlightened approach to work initiated by the human relations school encouraged many other managers to undertake similar attempts. The post-war decades of relatively high employment exacerbated the problem: absenteeism and high labour turnover were particularly inconvenient in highly competitive industries using expensive equipment. It is not surprising therefore that the claim that repetitive and stressful jobs had adverse effects on the labour force was acknowledged by many companies, which are now ready to conduct experiments in dealing with productivity problems through improved working conditions.

As Sheppard and Herrick put it, the requirements underlying most of the job improvement programmes are relatively simple:

(1)  Change as a regular part of the job.
(2)  Job easily identified with end-product.
(3)  Opportunity to act and decide.
(4)  Opportunity to interact with other people.
(5)  Ingenuity and initiative opportunities.
(6)  Freedom of movement.
(7)  Opportunity to learn something new.
(8)  Mental and physical demands well balanced.
(9)  Attractive physical environment. [Sheppard and Herrick, 1972, p. 175]

Taking into consideration what has been said previously about variations in workers' responses to the industrial environment, additional methods of dealing with boredom and monotony could include:

(1)  the selection of workers best suited to the type of job;
(2)  improvement of the working environment;
(3)  redesigning jobs.

(1) The most traditional approach is careful recruitment and selection of workers so as to avoid allocating workers to tasks for which they are ill-suited. The growing practice among personnel departments of using refined tests is nowadays widespread in larger enterprises. The higher the cost of industrial training, the more important are the selection tests, particularly in jobs with a high labour turnover. Vocational guidance is also widely used so as to give the young worker a preliminary understanding of his job.

(2) On the shop floor many managers attempt to alleviate the workers' discomfort by introducing more frequent breaks, allowing them to listen to music, arranging tea and lunch breaks in well-equipped canteens and paying attention to hygiene and the aesthetic environment. In spite of all the efforts in this direction, technological requirements and economic factors often necessitate physical inconveniences that are difficult to deal with. For example, too much noise can blot out a radio broadcast. Moreover, such attempts to deal with working conditions often meet with obstacles. There may be problems with radio broadcasts if many workers are crowded in one place and have differing standards of entertainment. Breaks during which workers may be encouraged to take physical exercise are by no means enthusiastically accepted by all. Excessive heat and lack of space can easily spoil the most attractively painted workshop, and longer breaks for lunch may be resented by workers who would prefer a shorter working day. These obstacles are well known to all managers who deal with organizational improvements, though they are not always acknowledged by academic minds. In many cases, industry tries to find a way out simply by reducing the working week to four days instead of experimenting with

costly and often ineffective changes in working conditions. There are few detailed studies of the constraints imposed by economic factors in efforts to alleviate the strains of repetitive jobs; one can, however, point to a trend within big corporations to be more generous when allocating money for such purposes.

(3) As for the content of jobs, it is important that repetitive jobs that are resented by workers and cause excessive tension should where possible be redesigned. In contrast to previous efforts to fragment and simplify labour, the attempt should be to enrich the operations performed by workers by making them more complicated and varied. One can distinguish between *horizontal job enlargement*, which consists of varying the tasks an employee carries out, and *vertical job enlargement*, which allows the employee to make more decisions about his work. Guest (1957) indicated the following elements of job enlargement:

increased number of job tasks;
increased variety of job tasks;
self-determination of pacing;
responsibility for work quality;
discretion for working methods;
completion of work units.

Friedmann (1961) describes in detail American and British experiments in job enlargement and summarizes the American experiments as follows:

From the examples given it can be seen that job enlargement does not consist in any sense of a return to craft methods. It does not hand over to one workman the complete construction of a complex machine, like an aeroplane engine or a television receiver. We are dealing with a reaction against the excesses of the division of labour, not with a reactionary attitude. It is a question of taking into account a group of facts, some purely technical and others of a psychological and social kind, which have come under the notice of those who organise, direct, staff and observe mass-production processes, and in consequence of restoring to the content of the job, as it is experienced from day to day and month to month by factory worker and office employee, the importance denied to it, or at least ignored by Scientific Management. [Friedmann, 1961, p. 53]

Apart from widely publicized experiments in job enlargement (Volvo in Sweden have made significant progress in this respect), there are intermediate methods, which usually consist of job rotation so that the workers perform different tasks. Reports indicate that such methods result in greater satisfaction, less absenteeism, reduced labour turnover and a feeling that there is social significance to the tasks performed. In some cases, there have been marked increases in productivity.

It has, however, been noted that job enlargement or job rotation has resulted in some cases in negative responses by workers. Firstly, workers are often reluctant to accept changes that may result in a temporary reduction in their income as they acquire the skills needed for their new tasks. Secondly, the mechanization of tasks means that job redesigning is linked to the application of new machinery, and this is regarded by some workers as unnecessarily expensive or potentially threatening. Thirdly, some workers resist change even if it means reducing boredom at work, while others do not resent repetitive jobs at all. For example, female workers who have demanding household duties often prefer quiet, simplified tasks performed with little effort to the more challenging and complicated duties that require a longer training period and greater involvement. Finally, many workers without industrial training find it easier to adjust to repetitive, fragmented jobs that do not require a prolonged period of training or, in case of immigrant workers, a full command of the language of the host country.

## SOCIAL PROBLEMS POSED BY TECHNOLOGICAL DEVELOPMENT

In spite of many measures intended to alleviate the hardships of mass production technology, the problem is far from being solved. Those industries where labour has been fragmented and tasks simplified to extreme limits are best suited for the replacement of human movement by machines. Yet, full automation is a question for the future, even if some experts predict a rapid expansion in the next few decades. The pace of automation depends on many factors: the threat of mass unemployment is one reason why many governments and considerable sections of the labour force resist rapid technological change.

It seems that the more advanced the country the more pronounced are the negative effects of mass production on the average worker because of the growing discrepancy between his work status and the surrounding cultural standards and expectations.

In the first place, one should take into consideration the rapid increase in education in all advanced and developing countries. The prolongation of compulsory education and general interest in the completion of formal education means that more and more workers enter industry with a good academic record. In the United States the proportion of the adult labour force with one or more years of college rose from 19 per cent in 1960 to 30 per cent in 1978. On the other hand, the proportion of total employment represented by managerial, administrative, technical and professional positions went up only from

20 per cent in 1960 to 26 per cent in 1977 (Rothwell and Zegveld, 1979, p. 59). Research indicates that those with higher educational standards often react unfavourably to dull, repetitive jobs, and, more important, have higher career expectations. This results in more frustration and bitterness as such aspirations are not met in mass production industries.

A detailed analysis of this problem was recently made by Berg in a multi-plant Mississippi textile manufacturing company (Berg, 1973). He found that educational achievement is inversely related to work performance. He pointed out that the same pattern was observed in a comparable study of 762 workers in a Southern hosiery manufacturing plant: productivity and labour turnover were shown to be related to such factors as age and family stability, but did not improve among the better-educated workers. Moreover, among night-shift workers there was an inverse relationship between education and performance measured in terms of productivity and labour turnover (Berg, 1973, p. 96).

Another consideration is that, in the past, as long as the mass production labour force was recruited from unskilled workers and their children, access to high-level technologies and better wages was an obvious advance. The same applied to immigrants from the less industrialized countries and migrants from rural areas. At the moment, however, there is a degree of downward mobility among the lower middle class, which means that many young people whose fathers had white-collar or highly skilled manual jobs enter industry as semi-skilled workers. Unlike skilled workers who, after a period of apprenticeship are moved to more responsible and better-paid positions, or who change their industry or enterprise if they are dissatisfied with their jobs or wages, semi-skilled workers do not and usually cannot expect a change for the better within the industrial system. Even if they are paid relatively well, they know that their present earnings are the best they can hope for — ageing impairs their chances of better-paid jobs and their limited skills bar them from promotion or self-employment. Frustration in unskilled and semi-skilled work has been well described by Chinoy (1955). He found that of forty-seven unskilled automobile workers interviewed, only *four planned or aimed* to get the next best paid job in their section (pp. 47–50).

It is characteristic that in most studies mass production workers do not want their children to have similar jobs but want them to become professionals. To remain on the shop floor means failure, not only for those from a white-collar background but also for children from working-class families, an attitude that might make them more sensitive to the negative aspects of mass production.

A new social philosophy of the affluent society presupposes increasing comfort and the improvement of all aspects of life, including working conditions. It is precisely in countries with the highest standards of living that pressure for redesigning jobs is the strongest. One could also speculate that those more likely to respond negatively to the strains of mass production are young workers. But it is difficult to say whether the underlying causes of their dissatisfaction are primarily the prevailing cultural and social climate or higher expectations characteristic of the younger generation (see Berg, 1973, Ch. VII).

One of the major dilemmas of modern industry is that mass production methods result from an attempt to increase workers' productivity and lower production costs, but that, at the present stage of industrial development, the opposite is frequently the case. Highly competitive industries such as the motor industry are increasingly vulnerable to disruptions caused by absenteeism, high labour turnover and official and unofficial strikes; this is because the very nature of mass production presumes a high degree of coordination and discipline among work units. Those workers who remain in the least challenging industries and fulfil the least popular tasks naturally expect to be compensated by higher wages, and display a spirit of materialism that makes it increasingly difficult to meet their demands. High material aspirations, the characteristic trait of affluent workers employed in repetitive jobs, have become an important economic factor, for they challenge the established patterns of pay differentials and cause many pay disputes to be initiated by skilled workers who feel their relative earnings to be eroded by the semi-skilled mass production workers.

A new problem posed by technological development is the transition to automation. This implies considerable transformation in the composition of the labour force, and causes, at least in the short run, unemployment among workers whose skills become obsolete (Shils, 1963). In all countries where the change to automated industry is taking place there is a considerable growth of unemployment among the unskilled and semi-skilled.

This problem can be particularly acute among school leavers who do not have formal educational qualifications. In view of the growing numbers of unemployed in many Western countries, it would seem sensible to devise special measures for combating the structural unemployment connected with technological change.

In those industrial countries that are fairly competitive, unemployment is kept lower because of compensating factors – extra spending on health, social welfare, education, public works and investment in new industry. But in countries like Britain, in which the ability to compete is low, there are strong pressures for cuts in public expenditure; this makes employment prospects even worse. The mismatching of skills and vacancies is another vital part of the problem, so that high unemployment can coincide with unfilled posts and the use of foreign labour;

but, again, the lack of state provision for adequate retraining makes the problem even more acute. In recessionary times, industrial investment shifts even more markedly into cost-saving automation instead of extending the capacity of prevailing technology. This throws more people out of work without a compensating increase in employment under the new technology. (No wonder technological change is often resisted by the workers; see Rothwell and Zegveld, 1979.) Paradoxically, growing unemployment alters the whole attitude of the labour force to dull, unchallenging jobs — the prospect of being out of work appearing much worse than the strains and tensions of repetitive tasks.

In a way, Marx's theory of alienation, in which emphasis is laid not only on the direct impact of technology but on the social factors associated with technological change, has been shown to be correct, as opposed to those who believed that mechanization would be the solution to the work force's problems.

The man—machine relationship has, as we can see, far-reaching social consequences: each stage of technological development gives rise to new problems not only in the factories but in society as a whole.

# CHAPTER 3

# Small Groups in Industry

In traditional societies work was based on collective effort. Hunting, fishing, farming and trading are examples of cooperation within relatively small units. Some of these units were multi-purpose groups; others consisted of people who separated when their tasks were completed. Even so, these groupings were different from the groupings we find today as a part of large-scale enterprises.

## CONCEPTUAL DIFFICULTIES

Working groups differ from other groups — friends, families, etc., — in that they are brought together in order to collaborate over work, and the pattern of relationships in the group is primarily determined by the task to be done. [Argyle, 1972, p. 104]

Some scholars assume that every large-scale organization is composed of working groups that resemble cells in living organisms (Barnard, 1956). Yet the concept of group is ambiguous if applied without qualification to configurations of employees described as organizational units. One wonders whether a hundred or more workers employed in the same factory workshop should be described as a group at all. Similarly, doubts always arise when we refer to 'groups' in general without taking into account the complexity and intensity of interactions and social bonds that keep people together. The concept of group presents no problems, however, when we refer to a handful of individuals who remain in close contact and who share a sense of identity. An unsupervised group of miners working for years together, a gang of building workers, a crew on a fishing boat or a team of electricians moving from one building site to another are undoubtedly groups in this sense. Ambiguity arises only when we refer to groups when we mean departments, sections or simply organizational work units based on formal divisions regardless of the 'density' of interactions between the members of such units and of the group consciousness. Some writers therefore think it necessary to distinguish between *teams* ('groups of people who cooperate to carry out a joint task') and *technological groups* ('groups of people working in a place, at a speed and in a way determined by the technology, but where there is little interaction between them') (Argyle, 1972, p. 110).

Furthermore, students of organizations often make a distinction between *formal* and *informal* groups. In this context, informal groups are people united by social bonds that have been developed within wider organizational boundaries, or that cut across formal divisions. Others distinguish *networks of social relationships* or *a network of social interactions* within organizations (Merton, 1970). Accordingly, a group may be defined as a number of people with a high density of interaction relationships *within* a broad framework of interpersonal contacts and interpersonal bonds.

If we say that individuals A, B, C, D, E... form a group, this will mean that at least the following circumstances hold. Within a given period of time, A interacts more often with B, C, D, E... than he does with M, N, L, O, P,... whom we choose to consider outsiders or members of other groups. B also interacts more often with A, C, D, E,... than he does with outsiders, and so on for the other members of the group. It is possible just by counting interactions to map out a group quantitatively distinct from others. [Homans, 1968, p. 84]

However, frequent interactions are not necessarily associated with 'we-feelings'; similarly, people who regard themselves as members of the same group. i.e. use the 'we' and 'them' reference, do not have to interact very often provided they feel united by genuine bonds, a point that must be borne in mind when we analyse social relationships at work. Zweig asked a number of workers who their mates were and with how many they worked. Even when they worked in the same departments, his respondents answered in many different ways (Zweig, 1961). To explain this phenomenon he indicated the various groupings to which workers belonged:

strictly bureaucratic groupings devised by management and usually supervised by a foreman;

semi-formal groupings, i.e. consisting of men working under one informal leader in close proximity or united in a team working on a collective bonus;

trade union groups operating at the level of a plant or department;

informal groupings such as tea or dinner groupings, faction groups, regional groups, age groups and so on.

Actually a worker entering a modern factory becomes a focus of a whole web of group relations, not of a single group....The behaviour of the industrial worker can never be satisfactorily described in terms of any one of these groupings above. There is no one single group which can claim to be in full control of his behaviour and attitudes. [Zweig, 1961, pp. 81—2]

A similar point was emphasized by Sayles:

We have found that it is inappropriate to speak of the informal group. Rather we suggest that it is more useful to investigate the relationship among friendship cliques, work teams and pressure or interest groups. Not only is there obviously substantial overlapping in group member-ship, but the internal structure of any one of them is shaped by the membership it includes, as well as by the membership it excludes. [Sayles, 1958, p. 160]

Finally, there are situations in which people working together avoid any commitment to closely knit groups. Sykes (1969a,b) reports in his study on navvies that people working in the same gangs had little to do with each other in their leisure hours, while people sleeping in the same huts did not work together and avoided going out together in the evenings. The small aggregations of men going out for a meal or sitting in a bar were only of a temporary nature. At the same time, mutual help was widespread, strangers were quickly absorbed and the atmosphere was friendly even if the composition of various groups was constantly changing.

## SOURCES OF SOCIOLOGICAL INTEREST
## IN SOCIAL RELATIONS AT WORK

Interest in interpersonal bonds at work is relatively new, but is based on two long-standing and different schools of thought:

(1) *alienation* theory: Marx was one of the first to raise the problem of the atomization and isolation of industrial workers in the new technological environment (Blauner, 1973, pp. 1—6).
(2) the theory of *social anomie*: Durkheim advanced the concept of industrial development as the cause of social disintegration, resulting in the withering away of moral and cultural values and the weakening of social control (Durkheim, 1964).

It should be noted that early empirical studies of small groups in industry were not inspired by either of these traditions but were originated for purely pragmatic reasons. The famous Hawthorne in-vestigations arose out of an attempt by engineers and psychologists to investigate the impact of environmental factors on workers' productivity. Only when the results of the experiments failed to show any correlation between such factors as lighting or rest breaks and productivity were alternative explanations connected to social relationships sought (Roethlisberger and Dickson, 1964). A set of elaborate experiments was carried out and the only constant element in all of them was the existence of closely knit small groups:

Workers left on their own and acting as an experimental group became increasingly friendly towards each other; they were willing to help one another at work and extended their contacts outside the factory.

Being selected as members of the experimental group and enjoying associated privileges made the workers feel superior to their fellow workers and increased their 'we-feeling'.

They enjoyed a considerable freedom in choosing their methods of work and were comparatively free from close supervision.

Relations between the workers and management greatly improved as the former came to appreciate the attention paid to them by the supervisors, who, in turn, were eager to cooperate with the experimental group.

The conventional wisdom of the scientific management approach was then challenged. While Taylor (1911) tended to regard the worker as an 'economic animal', an isolated individual and passive cog in the organizational process, the Hawthorne findings fundamentally changed this perspective (Friedmann, 1955, pp. 37–65). Workers were seen as independent and active personalities, capable of creating a social world of their own and of responding to various stimuli stemming from the social structure suitably adjusted to their interests and psychological needs. The factors that proved of primary importance to the workers' performance were:

*Informal ties between the workers on the shop floor*: belonging to a group meant that workers not only had everyday contact with their workmates, but also enjoyed mutual help; friendships too were cultivated beyond the factory gates and new social bonds developed.

*Informal structure*: group relationships permitted some individuals to emerge as leaders and influence others; autonomous hierarchies were created that affected interactions beyond the purely formal and functional patterns imposed by the administrative organization of work processes.

*Informal control exercised by the group*: belonging to a group meant much more than social contacts and friendly help. The workers were subject to social pressures that proved no less effective in controlling individual work behaviour than the norms and standards imposed by management. The group created or adopted norms of behaviour best suited to their interests; if individual workers attempted to disregard these norms they were exposed to various sanctions and pressures.

Acceptance or rejection by the group was a major concern and few would risk offending their colleagues and friends by their behaviour.

The researchers were, however, reluctant to make any broader generalizations on the basis of their studies. Instead they concentrated on a very detailed presentation of the methods, experiments and findings. But among the few more general ideas put forward by Dickson and Roethlisberger we may refer to the concept of *social organization* and the distinction between *formal* and *informal* organization. By social organization they meant the actual pattern of interaction between the employees, supervisors and managers. Formal organization was regarded as a network of those patterns of interactions prescribed by the rules and regulations of the company. Informal organization designated personal relationships between the members of the organization arising out of their spontaneous interactions, and not necessarily prescribed by the formal rules.

The Hawthorne investigation marked the beginning of what became known as the human relations school. The essence of this new line of thought was the belief that the major evils of industrial life could be eradicated by restructuring the organization of industrial enterprises in order to meet workers' social and psychological requirements. Lack of discipline, disobedience, strikes, high labour turnover, absenteeism — all were regarded as symptoms of poor human relations in industry. Once the importance of human aspects of work and especially of social relations was recognized, one could expect a general improvement in work practices.

One of the most prominent exponents of this school of thought was Mayo, an American anthropologist and sociologist who published several books in which the empirical findings of the Hawthorne studies were used. Mayo to some extent followed Durkheim's arguments on the disruptive effects of the division of labour, social anomie and the atomization of industrial society. He wrote of the seamy side of progress, emphasizing that sociologists should not neglect the negative side-effects of social development. Mayo noted that in the simpler social systems of the pre-industrial world, individuals lived in closely knit local communities and were strictly controlled by the groups to which they belonged. Well-developed family ties, community and kinship bonds, the observation of social codes and well-established patterns of economic activity contributed to the socialization of individuals and reinforced their integration within society (Mayo, 1962). He believed that the new industrial order had brought about a decline in the authority of social codes, diminished the capability of individuals to cooperate effectively with one another, reduced the impact of primary groups on their members, and contributed to the maladjustment of manual workers to their social and occupational roles. He drew a distinction between what he called *established* societies, i.e. traditional communities, and *adaptive* societies generated by the industrial order. In his view, the latter were characterized by a growing discrepancy between the development of technical skills and the complete abandonment of social skills:

...the social structure of civilisation has been shaken by scientific, engineering, and industrial development. This radical change — the passage from an established to an adaptive social order — has brought into being a host of new and unanticipated problems for management and for the individual worker. [Mayo, 1962, p. 66]

For Mayo, the new civilization had brought about anarchy by replacing well-knit social groups with 'a disorganised rabble of individuals competing for scarce goods'. The disorganization caused by industrialism, the disruption of traditional bonds and the growing isolation of individuals found expression on the shop floor, where high labour turnover, frustration and disagreement with supervisors were a direct reflection of this social anomie.

The management problem appears at its acutest in the work of the supervisor. No longer does the supervisor work with a team of persons that he has known for many years or perhaps a lifetime; he is leader of a group of individuals that forms and disappears almost as he watches it...But for the individual worker the problem is really much more serious. He has suffered a profound loss of security and certainty in his actual living and in the background of his thinking. For all of us the feeling of security and certainty derives always from assured membership of a group. If this is lost, no monetary gain, no job guarantee, can be sufficient compensation. Where groups change ceaselessly as jobs and mechanical processes change, the individual inevitably experiences a sense of void, of emptiness, where his fathers knew the joy of comradeship and security. And in such situations, his anxieties — many, no doubt, irrational or illfounded — increase and he becomes more difficult both to fellow workers and to supervisor. [Mayo, 1962, p. 67]

The normative content of Mayo's arguments is generally approved. The real difficulties begin with the question whether the need for closer social bonds at work can be successfully met, in view of the factors that restrain social contact in productive work or reduce them to a superficial level (Brown, 1977a). In other words, the issue of how to overcome social isolation at work remains open: those who attempt to deal with it must consider empirical studies that reveal variations in the cohesiveness of industrial work groups; they also need to understand the limitations on social relationships in work situations.

## TECHNOLOGICAL VARIABLES
## AND SOCIAL RELATIONSHIPS

Modern technology is usually regarded as the principal cause of the depersonalization of work relationships in industrial enterprises. The interpretation of this trend varies, however, as do the predictions of future trends in this respect. Marx was one of the first to emphasize that the division of labour based on modern technology leads not only to the fragmentation of functions performed by individual workers, but also to the social isolation of the workers who are tied to repetitive and standardized tasks; complementarity and cooperation between workers is replaced by complementarity and cooperation between machines (Marx, 1979, p. 508).

One of the most important contemporary studies highlighting this tendency was carried out by Walker and Guest (1952). They investigated the impact of the assembly line on social relations at work and identified factors leading to social isolation at work. They found that the nature of interpersonal relations between workers on the shop floor was basically determined by the functional interdependence of the work performed. Workers tied to their jobs on the assembly line had no opportunity of making contact with their workmates and were limited to casual talk with their nearest neighbours. Even these contacts were severely restricted by the pace of work and noise. Short breaks provided the only opportunities for developing any form of social life, but the contacts that developed during these breaks were highly superficial compared with the bonds arising between team workers. Thus, the physical and functional isolation due to the conditions of assembly-line work led to the social isolation of the workers concerned.

Touraine distinguishes three phases of industrial development with corresponding forms of cooperation among workers (1962, pp. 426–37; 1966, pp. 45–51):

(1) the old system of work, characterized by skilled work or craftmanship: at that stage workers strongly identify themselves with their trades and develop a kind of solidarity, relying at the same time on their own skills and individual techniques;

(2) mass production or semi-automation, where workers can no longer intervene in the productive process: they are segmentalized and reintegrated in a formal and artificial way that affords little room for personal relationships;

(3) the era of full automation when the workers' tasks are no longer determined by the nature of the products they produce or the machines they operate but by the organizational schemes under which they superintend, record and control productive processes.

Under these conditions a new type of work team and group solidarity may develop.

A convincing elaboration of the 'stage theory' may be found in Blauner's work (Blauner, 1973). Here he compares four industries (printing, textiles, motor car and chemical) that represent technological progress from craft and early mechanization, through to mass production and automation. Blauner demonstrated that mass production, far more than any other system, reduced cohesion and inhibited shopfloor social contacts in the motor industry. In the textile industry, social cohesion seemed restricted by the division of work since most jobs were designed on an individual basis. In the small towns, however, where workers belonged to the same local groups, community and kinship ties extended to the factory and supported traditional patterns of shopfloor social contact. The nature of the tasks performed did not inhibit these contacts: workers could converse freely, they did not feel the pressure of time while working, and, not being tied to their jobs, they had many opportunities of socializing not only during official breaks but also outside them. In the larger textile factories, where management disapproved of too much socializing on the job and where pressure of work seemed greater, opportunities for social contacts were fewer. The dispersion of responsibilities contributed to the disruption of social life since the organization of work made it impossible for workers to identify with any work team. Even under these unfavourable conditions, the strength of community ties positively affected social relations on the shop floor. Family and church, the dominant institutions in the small towns, contributed to the workers knowing each other outside their work. Often whole families were employed in one factory so that relatives and neighbours maintained their traditional patterns on the shop floor.

The interpersonal relations of the printing workers were of a different nature. Their freedom from job pressure, relative ease of movement during the working day and lack of close shopfloor supervision made it possible for them to communicate with one another during the working day. As many printing workers worked night shifts, their social contacts were even more developed since the isolated group remained in a 'world of their own'. Many printing workers operated in teams and this brought them still closer together. The highly skilled printing occupation enjoys great prestige and provides relative security. These factors contribute to the strengthening of the feeling of social identity among printing workers. Their leisure is also organized on the basis of voluntary associations: they have their lodges, technical and social clubs, sports teams and fraternal orders. Thus they meet in their occupational community, share many interests and hardly separate work from leisure. They are inclined to talk shop outside the factory, develop close friendships on the job and, in spite of relatively high mobility, maintain social ties arising out of work relations. The off-the-job occupational activities tend to strengthen friendships despite the disintegrating effects of urban life.

The other group discussed by Blauner was the chemical workers, whose interpersonal relationships were characterized by the existence of clearly defined, independent work teams, collective responsibility, freedom from constant or close supervision, and personal commitment to their job. Blauner notes that 'A number of workers mentioned their surprise at the readiness with which more experienced employees taught them their jobs and helped them with their problems' (Blauner, 1973, p. 146). He points out that in one chemical plant the workers ranked 'friends at work' as one of the most important influences on their employment situation — more important than interesting work, job security or pay.

Blauner's pioneering inter-industry comparisons can be related to a number of other studies in which different occupational groups are investigated and social relationships shown to be determined by the nature of the work performed. Trist and Bamforth's study (1951) illustrates the rapid transformation of social relationships as a result of changed methods of coal mining. Several studies on British manual workers highlight the specific patterns of social relationships that occur and provide invaluable insights into the impact of technology on social relations at work. In contrast to many technology-oriented theories, they present the problem in a wider perspective of industrial relations and community life (Brown *et al.*, 1972; Brown and Brannen, 1970; Hollowell, 1968; Dennis *et al.*, 1956; Scott *et al.*, 1963; Sykes, 1969a, b; and Wilson, 1972).

## THE FUNCTIONS OF INFORMAL
## RELATIONSHIPS AT WORK

Cooperation among workers is not confined to the implementation of their tasks, but exists in many other aspects of factory life. An account of the logic of spontaneous informal cooperation has been presented by Etzioni (1961; 1964, pp. 58—67). He discusses the relationships between: organizational goals, the kind of power applied towards lower members, the kind of involvement on the part of these members, the social and normative bonds arising out of the compliance structure, and the types of approved leadership. Etzioni subdivided the types of organizational control into coercive power (based on the use of physical means), utilitarian power (which applies material rewards) and normative power (based on symbolic interaction). These distinctions allow us to distinguish three basic types of organization: those that use coercive power (prisons, concentration camps); those in which control is carried out through remunerative means; and those based on sharing common norms and values (religious and political associations, etc.). While emphasizing that most organizations apply more than one type of organizational power towards their members, Etzioni points out that one type of power prevails in most cases.

The main finding of Etzioni's comparative study is that organiza-tions that differ in the type of control they use will also differ in aspects of organizational structure. This is illustrated in Figure 3.1.

| Types of organization: | coercive (e.g. prisons) | utilitarian (e.g. enterprises) | normative (e.g. political parties) |
|---|---|---|---|
| Types of goals: | imposed | instrumental | moral |
| Power applied: | physical | remunerative | symbolic |
| Type of involvement: | alienative | calculative | commitment |
| Relationship between formal and informal structures: | informal vs formal | partial dualism | fusion |

FIGURE 3.1. *Social correlates of organizational control*

These structural differences seem most pronounced when we study small group relationships. The main point of Etzioni's analysis is that not only the attitudes of the members towards the organizational goals, but also their mutual relationships, are affected by the degree of conflict (or congruence) between their interests and the organizational demands. Prisons and other coercive organizations are characterized by permanent conflict between the authorities and the inmates, which affects the whole structure of group life among the prisoners. The common interests of prisoners in resisting official regulations, the need for collective effort to supply otherwise unobtainable goods, the common fight against 'stool pigeons' and cooperation in avoiding punishments, shape the nature of the prison community and give rise to informal norms and standards that differ completely from those imposed by the authorities.

Organizations based on personal involvement, such as political parties or religious associations, are at the other end of the scale since there are not many points at which divergence between official targets and individual goals arises. Approved informal leaders can easily be incorporated into the official structure and norms and standards emanating from the rank and file can be integrated into the formal code, which in any case is based upon membership consensus.

Social relations in industrial enterprises can be located between these two extremes. Industry operates in such a way that much congruence between the individual interests of workers and official targets can be maintained. Remuneration, that is, wages and other benefits, operates as an inducement and accounts for the attitude described as 'calculative involvement'. On the other hand, contradictions between formal and informal aspects of shopfloor relationships cannot be fully eliminated, and a certain degree of incongruence between managerial goals and workers interests remains. Thus the instrumental activities of workers may go beyond what is approved of by management, and unofficial norms may reflect and reinforce this discrepancy by supporting unorthodox work behaviour.

One of the basic problems in most factories is the output level as related to wages and productivity norms. It is not surprising that workers are interested in regulating work in the most convenient way. In the course of their social interaction, information is exchanged about ways of maintaining desired levels of wages so as to beat the system of what is often regarded as excessive demands on the part of management. Solidarity against supervisors and time-and-motion studies is approved of and, if necessary, enforced through common action aimed at opposing decisions that appear to be to the workers' detriment.

These group phenomena develop spontaneously, but informal cooperation may be purely instrumental without leading to more personal ties. Although one should expect that the more developed the functional bonds of the type described above, and the more often the workers experience the need for informal cooperation, the greater will be their readiness to identify with groups well suited to their aims, to articulate the 'informal' rules and to adopt a code of behaviour that is enforceable through collective pressure. The emergence of informal groups seems to correspond with a work situation in which the contradictions between management and the workers are strong enough to create spontaneous solidarity and to generate genuine cooperation in defending common interests. This is most typical of non-unionized enterprises (or of enterprises in which the unions are remote from the shop floor) in which defence of common interests cannot be expressed through formal workers' representation.

The analysis of complex organizations supports the claim that social bonds depend upon organizational factors, including the intensity of industrial conflict, that are built into the worker–management relationship. The integrative function of small groups operates in contrasting ways: the group's commitments may be compatible with targets set by management, or they may consist of helping workers in opposing those targets and resisting managerial pressures by means of solidarity and well-coordinated action. Drucker expresses the view that restrictions of output under restrictive union rules and 'feather-bedding' are 'only the part of the iceberg that is above water. Much more important are the invisible, unwritten, informal restrictions decreed by the custom and common law of every plant' (Drucker, 1960, p. 83).

Not surprisingly, as a result of such practices, managerial attitudes towards reinforcing social bonds among workers differ considerably: the more tense the atmosphere in the work-place and the greater the conflict between workers and management, the greater is the likelihood of hostility towards all forms of workers' unity and the more pronounced are attempts to atomize and isolate the workers irrespective of the recommendations by human relations specialists.

## GROUP DYNAMICS

So far, I have discussed small groups in close relationship to the industrial setting in which they operate. One should, however, bear in mind that social relationships do not exclusively depend on the environment but also have dynamics of their own. Once people are brought together and interact with each other, new processes are generated. These processes can be studied both in natural surroundings and under laboratory-type conditions — the major issue is that of general regularities that occur in many different social groupings.

Group dynamics is defined as

that division of social psychology which investigates the formation and change in the structure and functions of the psychological grouping of people into self-directing wholes. The formation and change of the group do not take place automatically and inevitably but are a consequence of the efforts of its members to solve their problems and satisfy their needs. A dynamic group is thus in a continuous process of restructuring, adjusting, and readjusting members to one another for the purpose of reducing the tensions, eliminating the conflicts, and solving the problems which its members have in common. [Bonner, 1959, pp. 5–6]

Homans' well-known scheme assumes that there is mutual dependence between what he called the *external* and the *internal* systems of the group phenomenon. This is shown in Figure 3.2. As far as work groups are concerned, mutual interaction is primarily determined by the links between the division of labour and the type of communication. By the division of labour Homans means that the tasks performed by a group of workers are divided into a series of separate activities, such as wiring, soldering, checking, etc., each being performed by an individual or sub-group of individuals. Interaction arising out of those activities consists primarily of communication:

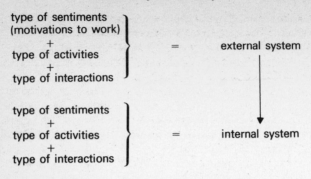

FIGURE 3.2    *Scheme of group dynamics*

'we can without danger call interaction communication provided we remember that communication is not necessarily verbal' (Homans, 1968, p. 101). The operations performed can be carried out: (1) without any communication between the workers involved, who would thus only communicate with their supervisors; (2) by small teams carrying out routine functions and communicating in a very limited way; (3) by a team cooperating without any pre-established programme, which would mean constant communication between all members of the team on decisions regarding the allocation of tasks, attempts mutually to adapt the operations to be performed, checking the progress of collective activities, etc. In each of these cases the scheme of interactions will be different, ranging from pyramidal to multi-dimensional contacts.

Configurations of this type are not confined to small groupings, but occur in all circumstances where people cooperate. Communication may be verbal, but in many work situations it is standardized and translated into elaborate signs and symbols transmitted without words: a signalman shows a red light to indicate that a line is blocked, a computerized device points to the danger of infringing the parameters of safety, a siren announces danger, etc. In many cases, verbal and non-formalized communication is combined with non-verbal and mechanical messages and interactions.

This external system consists of activities and interactions not only aiming at the performance of everyday tasks, but also directed towards the implementation of organizational duties, the satisfaction of economic needs, or the elimination of undesirable effects associated with working conditions or supervisory practices, etc. It is on the basis of the external system that personal relationships between people develop. The totality of those relationships is what Homans called the internal system. As he stated:

When a number of persons have come together to form a group, their behaviour never holds to its first pattern. Social life is never wholly utilitarian: it elaborates itself, complicates itself, beyond the demands of the original situation. The elaboration brings changes in the motives of individuals.

If the interactions between the members of a group are frequent in the external system, sentiments of liking will grow up between them, and these sentiments will lead in turn to further interactions, over and above the interactions of the external system. [Homans, 1968, pp. 109 and 112]

This 'internal system' has become the subject of many detailed experimental studies in social psychology. Argyle (1972) points out that the merit of Homans' analysis is the distinction he makes between behaviour that is primarily work-oriented (that is, related to the handling of external tasks) and behaviour that is primarily sociable (that is, related to coming to terms with other human beings). What Homans defined as an internal system is synonymous with a set of social bonds between the members of the group. Argyle lists the following ways of maintaining and reinforcing personal contacts between people: sociable chat, gossip, discussion of current affairs, jokes and games, telling funny stories, discussion of personal problems and non-verbal communication, including communicating interpersonal attitudes (smiling, frowning, etc.), communication of emotions, and signalling preferences and attitudes (Argyle, 1972, pp. 111–14).

According to Argyle, the formation of groups is subject to certain regularities that are connected with the stages of development of social bonds among people. These stages include: forming, storming, norming, performing, and (if the existence of the group is coming to an end, dissolving. The first stage is characterized by anxiety and dependence; the second by conflicts, polarization and exploration; the third by the development of cohesion, mutual support and the formation of norms (Argyle, 1972, p. 116).

The important distinction made by social psychologists is between membership groups and reference groups, which affect the attitudes and behaviour of individuals by normative or comparative influence respectively (Kelly, 1952). In some cases merely belonging to a work group does not necessarily mean accepting its norms and standards. The dynamics of identification with a group is a topic needing further exploration. As long as this identification does not take place, many mechanisms I have so far discussed do not operate.

Studies in group dynamics cover a variety of factors affecting group formation; of these, competition and cooperation seem most relevant in shaping social relationships. The former causes disruption and the dissociation of inter-human norms; the latter accounts for mutual interdependence and stronger group commitment. Group commitment is really social *cohesiveness*, which could be defined as the total field of forces that act on members to remain in the group and that resist disruptive influence. Cohesiveness, in turn, can be linked with the concept of *integration*, described by Stogdill (1959, p. 213) as 'the ability to maintain structure and functions under stress'.

The major problem of group dynamics is the *mechanisms* that determine greater or lesser identification with the small group and higher or lower levels of group cohesiveness. Summarizing the numerous studies and findings in this field, Argyle enumerates the following integrative factors: physical proximity, homogeneity, the degree of mutual cooperation, the incentive system, the benefits of belonging to a group, external threat, size of the group and intensity of social interactions (Argyle, 1972, pp. 117–20). Each of these factors operates in work situations, which allows us to apply findings in social psychology to the exploration of group dynamics in the industrial setting.

An example of the importance of general studies for the understanding of social relationships at work is the research carried out by Festinger and his colleagues (Festinger *et al.*, 1963). It is pointed out that the process of making friends implies, as a necessary condition, contacts between people. So we can refer to *passive* contacts (contacts that simply happen) and *active* contacts (contacts deliberately brought about). They argue that, because social norms prevent active contacts with total strangers, 'the passive kind of contact is probably, in most instances, the more important factor in determining whom one meets...and with whom one makes friends (Festinger *et al.*, 1963, p. 154).

Work situations are one of the most typical ways in which people make passive contact. Whether more meaningful relationships develop out of these contacts depends on many factors, of which homogeneity seems to be one. Rice (1958) gives the following principles derived from his study:

(1) Group stability is more easily maintained when the range of skills required of group members is such that they can all comprehend all the skills and, without having, or wanting to have them, can aspire to their acquisition.

(2) The fewer the differences in prestige and status within a group, the more likely is the internal structure of a group to be stable and the more likely are its members to accept internal leadership.

The variety of the factors that affect face-to-face relationships undermines the naive belief that all that is needed on the shop floor is the expert and skilful manipulation of group influences so as to channel social forces in a direction favourable to the aims of management. Research into conflict situations casts new light on what was originally seen only as a lack of developed inter-human relationships and indicates that the communication system does not appear to be the main factor in shaping social bonds. Sherif's experiments in the development of inter-group conflict are the best example of this point (Rohrer and Sherif, 1951). In a series of summer camps, teenage boys were assigned to two groups. These were at first separated, but were subsequently made to interact in competitive games with the object of bringing about conflict situations. Sherif found the following pattern of group dynamics:

When individuals try to attain an end by cooperating with each other they become a group, develop specific norms and form a social hierarchy.

When two groups seek to realize incompatible ends, so that one group cannot attain its target unless the other group fails to attain its target, mutual hostility develops while in-group feelings rise accordingly.

The reconciliation of aims does not reduce mutual hostility. It is only when the hostile groups must attempt, in cooperation, to solve common problems (such as repairing a lorry needed for an excursion) that there is a considerable relaxation of animosity (Rohrer and Sherif, 1951, pp. 388–426).

As far as the formation of norms and ideas under group influence is concerned, the extent to which collective pressure results in a change of attitudes is indirectly suggested in an experiment reported by Cohen (1964). Studying the behaviour of people induced by small rewards to express ideas contrary to their known convictions, psychologists discovered that, after a time, a change of attitudes occurred. Cohen explains this phenomenon in terms of dissonance dynamics:

If a person is led to express outwardly an attitude which is discrepant from his actual private attitude, a state of dissonance results. Since the behavior is fixed, dissonance in such a setting can be reduced by changing one's attitude so that it becomes consistent with the behavior one has engaged in publicly. There is no dissonance remaining because private attitude and public expression are now consistent with each other. [Cohen, 1964, pp. 82–3]

All these studies in group dynamics, and many others that have not been mentioned here, open new avenues in studying social relations at work. They reveal the complexity of the group phenomenon, identify the factors that affect various dimensions of group behaviour, and help to specify these factors in a work situation.

## THE IMPORTANCE OF GROUP AFFILIATION
## FOR WORKERS

The group-oriented approach, with its emphasis on social contacts at
work, regards group affiliations as a very important factor in enriching
and developing the worker's personality and in integrating the individual into the established order. Two assumptions are taken for
granted:

(1) that work constitutes one of the central life interests of industrial
workers — thus social relations developed on the shop floor have
exceptional significance for them;
(2) that for this reason small face-to-face groups are the most effective
means of social control over individuals who belong to the groups.

Both these assumptions have, however, been criticized by many
scholars. In his study of the central life interests of industrial workers,
Dubin (1956) opposed the view that 'work has to be considered a
central life interest for adults in most societies' and that 'informal
human relationships at work are important to the individual industrial
man'. He described an investigation carried out in 1952–53 in three
American plants. He showed that only 24 per cent of his sample could
be regarded as job-oriented; only 9 per cent of workers reported that
important social contacts and personal relationships had developed at
work; the remainder referred to their interactions *outside* the enterprise
as being important and meaningful. The explanation of these findings is
to be sought, according to Dubin, in the inevitable *segmentation* of
modern social life:

This segmented character is revealed in the round of daily activities
where one kind of activity succeeds another in the succession of days
and particularly the weekdays when leisure time actively replaces
remunerative work; in the physical separation of such significant locales
as place of residence and place of work; and in the numerous autonomous organisations that serve special, and sometimes very esoteric
interests in our lives. [Dubin, 1956]

Dubin asserts that, for the individual, participation in some sectors or
segments of social experience is less important than in other sectors
where social experience is of value to him. Since work is far from being
the most significant experience for the worker, he will find inter-human
contacts outside work far more challenging and rewarding. Orzack
(1959) compared the central life interests of professional nurses with
those of the workers studied by Dubin. He found that 79 per cent of
professional nurses were work-oriented, as compared with 24 per cent
of industrial workers.

Dubin's views have been corroborated by a major British study where it was found that the social contacts of workers in the automobile industry were extremely limited (Goldthorpe *et al.*, 1969). Very few closely-knit groups were found: about 76 per cent of skilled workers and 66 per cent of the less skilled said they would not object to being moved to another job away from the man with whom they had so far been working; 60 per cent of workers in the first category and over 80 per cent in the second stated that they had not one single close friend among their work-mates with whom they would like to meet for recreational activities.

...given that among the affluent workers we studied economic considerations have predominantly determined their choice of job, or at any rate are now the main factor binding them to their present employment, it is not surprising that, in general, they show no great concern over maintaining stable relationships with any particular set of work-mates. So far as work goes, emotionally significant experiences and 'significant others' tend neither to be looked for nor, thus, to be greatly missed in their absence. [Goldthorpe *et al.*, 1969, p. 53]

For these workers, 'those of their kin who were reasonably available represented a major source of friends and companions'. Neighbours also seemed to be of some importance in contrast to work-mates. In this respect, affluent manual workers seem different from white-collar workers, who draw much more heavily on friends made at work. The authors note:

Consistently with the findings of other research, the white collar employees we studied appeared not to define their work in an almost exclusively instrumental way. For these men, certain work associates at least were likely to be 'significant others', and thus the nature of their relationships with these persons was a feature of some importance within the work situation as they viewed it – a source of support or gratification; or if relationships went wrong, of resentment and distress. For our manual workers, on the other hand, and notably for the semi-skilled men, expectations from work were clearly more restricted. The work-place was where they came to earn their living, to sell their labour for the best return they could get; and while shop-floor cameraderie and an unobtrusive foreman might in some degree make their jobs less taxing, highly meaningful and rewarding social relationships in work seem rarely to have been anticipated or sought. [Goldthorpe *et al.*, 1969, pp. 66–7]

From what has been said, one could draw the general conclusion that the importance of social relationships at work varies according to how meaningful the job is. Blauner's comparative study (1973) substantiates this in that the least degree of social involvement occurs under those conditions in which the alienation of workers is most pronounced. But, in the light of his findings and many others, alternative interpretations of the 'meaning of work' are also possible. First, one could argue that, if workers find other fields more stimulating and meaningful than factory life, it may be because they have been deprived of the opportunity to develop genuine social interactions on the shop floor. Secondly, a lack of concern for intimate relationships at work does not necessarily mean that people do not appreciate the opportunity. The textile factories in small localities discussed in Blauner's study are the best example of the continuation of social bonds developed outside and cultivated at the work-place. Thirdly, under certain conditions, workers accept isolation and depersonalization on the shop floor providing they are compensated for by other advantages related to the job, and by opportunities of a more active social life off the job. One can further expect that, in those occupations requiring a high degree of mobility, more intimate contacts may even be avoided as interfering with the necessity of changing one's work-mates (Sykes, 1969 a,b).

There also remains the question of the degree of segmentation of social life in different social and ecological settings: large cities seem to pose a different problem in this respect than smaller communities. The atomization of social structure in urban areas, the lack of facilities for developing work contacts into meaningful relationships beyond the factory gates, the anonymity of everyday life in high blocks of flats and on housing estates, and the dispersion of employees into different areas, increase the importance of family and kinship as opposed to limited and short-lived work relationships.

The importance of local community bonds and their impact on social relationships at work has been highlighted by many sociologists. Gouldner speaks of friendly and egalitarian contacts between supervisors and workers in a small factory in a rural community. He quotes one mechanic who explained that

the bosses associate with the men. They will drink with them at the saloon or restaurant, and there is a fine sentiment. That's something you don't see in other plants. Each of the departments has a bowling team. The Company buys bowling shirts for the men, and the bosses bowl right along with the men. They are sociable that way. They hunt and fish together. [Gouldner, 1964, p. 39]

Gouldner comments that these relationships developed because the factory employees grew up together and had known each other for many years. Many workers as well as managers owned small farms and thus came to know each other and had mutual friends. Personal relationships were forged by the character of the rural community in which everybody knew everybody else and where contacts out of work were more frequent and more intimate than in big cities.

Referring to small-scale surveys covering social behaviour in work and non-work situations, Argyle notes that in work groups

there is much more talk about the task in hand, as opposed to general chat; more concealment of personal problems, of irritation with the others, financial situation and ambitions, more concern with what the others think of one, and more concern with personal appearance; a greater need for reciprocity from others before helping them a second time. [Argyle, 1972, p. 114]

All these findings indirectly show that social relations at work are meaningful and important for the members of work groups.

Studies of occupational communities have shown that segmentation is not a universal phenomenon. In many trades it does not occur, irrespective of ecological circumstances. There is a wide spectrum of occupational communities and patterns of sociability are rather associated with the style of life and reflect the differences between the traditional working-class culture and the more recent culture of the 'new' working class (Salaman, 1974). In the first case, work relationships depend not only on the circumstances in which people work together, but also on the traditions and ways of life they regard as natural and proper.

Cross-cultural comparisons reveal significant differences in the degree of integration of workers with their working community. Dore (1973, p. 214), for instance, notes that in his sample of Japanese workers 83 per cent belonged to some sport or social club or hobby group organized exclusively for members of the firm or the union. Only 14 per cent belonged to any outside social, political or religious organization. In his sample of British engineering workers, 56 per cent belonged to some social group organized by the enterprise and 34 per cent to other outside organizations. In other words, their links with the work-place and work-mates at leisure time were much weaker. On the other hand, Dore points out (p. 212) that in both the British and Japanese factories two models of behaviour clash with each other: one is home-oriented and requires leisure time to be spent with wife and family; the other requires leisure time to be spent on escapades with work-mates – pursuits that reinforce the social bonds with work mates.

Finally, it should be noted that the degree to which social relations develop can be underestimated by researchers who are unfamiliar with an industrial setting. Donald Roy, whose studies supply us with first-hand evidence of factory life based on participant observation, noted that he was unable for some time to grasp the nature of social relationships among operators engaged in highly repetitive, monotonous tasks. He thought the workers had little in common and it was only after some time that he realized that his first impression was superficial: 'The interaction was there in constant flow. It captured attention and held interest to make the long day pass' (Roy, 1960).

Many of the findings I have discussed are easier to interpret if we bear in mind that the differences between groups and networks of social relationships are often only a matter of degree. A lack of well-structured groups with clear boundaries does not necessarily mean that employees are not involved in meaningful social interaction. Daily contact with work-mates, supervisors and shop stewards, meetings with a few friends, casual relationships with people working in close proximity, participation in occasional social events — all these belong to what sociologists call the social system of a factory, even if the nature of the work performed prevents the formation of small, cohesive face-to-face groups.

CHAPTER 4

# Motivations to Work

The many theories on the topic of motivations to work and the enormous number of books about it reflect the preoccupation of industrial
sociologists with the question of making workers more cooperative
and more productive, and also concern with their psychological well-
being.

There are undoubtedly many theoretical reasons why one should
find motivational issues challenging and interesting. Weber's concept
of value-orientated action, Durkheim's notion of social control, studies
in socialization, modern theories of decision-making – all emphasize
the complexity of the processes that underlie individual actions. Is
it sufficient to define motives very generally as the 'hypothesized
causes of observable behaviour'? When we wish to understand why
someone does something we normally concentrate on *rational
aspects* of individual behaviour, that is, the *purposes* of the given
activities as compared with impulsive, emotional actions. However,
delving into motivations takes us further still, for we attempt to discover the ultimate 'causes' that underlie the choice of the given
objective. In other words, we are looking for the needs and desires
behind the purpose of a specific action. And, finally, the explanation
*why* people want this or that is not confined to revealing individual
motives. Social psychologists and sociologists are usually interested
in the social causes that make people desire some things more than
others, or display certain attitudes, or conform to certain norms or
pursue certain values.

Campbell lists seventy-six meanings used by psychologists to describe social motives and related phenomena. This variety reflects not
so much conceptual confusion as the multitude of factors to which
reference is made when motivations are studied (Campbell, 1968,
pp. 100–1). We are dealing with issues related to human nature and
human needs; the mechanisms of choosing between alternative courses
of action; the impact of culture; institutional and organizational constraints – all these can hardly be covered by a *single theory* of human
motivation (Lawler, 1973).

71

Nowadays it is recognised increasingly that human action must be seen from various perspectives if its many facets are to be understood. There is no one sovereign explanation, no single ruling motive, no dominant psychological process which can adequately characterise the doings of men. Appreciation of human complexity has led many psychologists to realise that the theoretical approaches...only partially overlap; each focuses on somewhat different aspects of human interaction. Many of their apparent conflicts reflect fixation by some theorist on the outdated and grandiose notion that there can be one general theory which will embrace all social psychological phenomena. This notion is no more than a prejudice. Physics, it should be remembered, has a muddle of theories. There is need in social psychology for a variety of conceptual frames and theories to embrace the richness of human behaviour. This is not to say that any formulation, no matter how vague, will do: it must serve a role in carrying inquiry forward. [Deutsch and Krauss, 1965, p. 215]

It is not surprising that in view of the variety of approaches there is fragmentation of the study of motivation, but this chapter is an attempt to define motives as broadly as possible and thus leave room for many different approaches and perspectives.

## MOTIVATIONS TO WORK AND SOCIAL STRUCTURE

Why do people work? The answer will vary depending on the circumstances in which people use their muscles and brains in productive processes. The satisfaction of direct needs, coercion, remuneration, identification with the tasks performed — these are the main driving forces of physical and mental activities. In different societies and in different types of organizations, some driving forces clearly predominate: the toil of slaves in mines, the study of scholars immersed in their work, the activities of businessmen, the labour of factory workers, the daily efforts of housewives — all these reflect the various social conditions under which people work and the differences in motivational patterns associated with these conditions.

Etzioni (1961) distinguishes 'coercive' organizations, which are based upon the application of physical sanctions; 'utilitarian' organizations, which exercise remunerative power based on control over material resources and rewards; and 'normative' organizations, which rely on the allocation and manipulation of symbolic rewards. He points to the close relationship between the functions and goals of the given organization and the type of power applied to secure the compliance of its lower members (see chapter 3). Galbraith enlarges this scheme by referring to compulsion, pecuniary compensation, identification and adaptation as four variations in attitudes and motivations in social systems based on various *types* of production. His argument is that compulsion as a motivator has a long association with land, while money rewards are closely connected with capital (Galbraith, 1969, p. 146).

The question of how people are motivated to work is, thus, directly related to the nature of social and organizational structures within which men pursue their productive activities. Although most social scientists would certainly agree that different methods for motivating the labour force are usually intermixed, they do not fail to notice that it is the social organization of work and the power structure that largely determine the motives and their effectiveness in a given society.

Discussion of motivational patterns associated with industrial society can be found in studies on the position of the labour force in the twentieth century that set up models of the 'committed worker' (Moore, 1965, pp. 37—44). It is generally claimed that industrialism is associated with the evolution of calculative and instrumental attitudes to work, and that the exceptional role of pecuniary motivations in industrial society is economically, socially and culturally conditioned and reinforced by the spirit and ideology of acquisitiveness. This tendency towards individual acquisition is often contrasted with the values prevailing in pre-industrial societies in which individuals are expected to share their possessions with kinsmen and neighbours. For Rostow, societies are nowadays structurally committed to a highly consumerist way of life (Rostow, 1971, p. 81). Kornhauser argues that a central belief of our societies is that people want more than they already have, and that their efforts to advance their interests are generally desirable (Kornhauser *et al.*, 1954, pp. 79—80). Yankelovich (1974, p. 22) identifies the following elements inherent in the work ethos of modern industrial culture:

The 'good provider' theme: the breadwinner, i.e. the man who provides for his family, is the 'real' man.
The independence theme: to make a living by working means to 'stand on one's feet', i.e. to avoid dependence on others.
The success theme: 'hard work always pays off'.
The self-respect theme: hard work of any type has dignity whether it be manual or non-manual.

Many sociologists believe that pecuniary interests determine the attitudes to work of manual workers, and indicate that most other needs can be satisfied outside of work in leisure time. Dubin, in his pioneering study of the major outside interests of modern workers (1956), advances the concept of the segmentation of social life where workers divide their interests between different segments of social life and regard their work-place primarily in terms of making a living.

But other sociologists point out that the logic of industrial life adds new dimensions to the meaning of work — that the activity itself is valued (Friedman and Havighurst, 1954). Morse and Weiss (1955) posed the question: 'If by some chance you inherited enough money to live comfortably without working, do you think you would work anyway or not?' Eighty per cent replied that they would keep working. A typical listing of reasons why people work beyond retirement age contains the following:

the importance of exercising minds and muscles;
the maintenance of high morale by achieving results that absorb people and give them emotional satisfaction;
the self-esteem that results from status identification with the occupation performed;
continuation of the companionship of work colleagues (Clark, 1966, p. 121).

When we ask why some of these needs cannot be satisfied outside the work-place, the limitations imposed by the character of modern life come to mind. Indeed, numerous sociological studies indicate the following: social atomization of the urban population; overcrowded households that restrict the development of independent manual hobbies; poor sport and recreation facilities; weakening of family ties; rigid division of time into work and leisure; emptiness of modern culture as far as the development of active creative interests is concerned. There are also other factors that account for people's psychological dependence on work and the extra-economic aspects of life associated with it.

In some occupations and jobs, the 'work-is-life' principle is reinforced by the restrictions of the individual's work tasks or by the organizational requirements to which they are constantly exposed. Scientists absorbed in their research, executives whose life is centred on the firm, people who work long hours in shifts or are isolated at work from external influences, are bound to rely on their work communities much more than average. Galbraith predicted that identification and adaptation would increase with the development of the technostructure, especially at the heart of entrepreneurial corporations where the individuals' goals and the interests of the enterprise merge into an indistinguishable whole (Galbraith, 1969, p. 159). Some scholars expect the same to occur among industrial workers provided the establishment of industrial democracy allows them to be integrated with the enterprise. Alternatively, others argue that the shortening of the working week will sever employees' links with their firms and shift their interests towards outside activities.

CHANGING PERSPECTIVES ON WORKERS' NEEDS

It is certainly insufficient to say that in modern society most people have to work in order to be paid for their efforts. A statement of this kind helps us to understand the nature of the social order, but not the needs and desires that motivate people to enter employment and fulfil their everyday tasks.

As far as industrial workers are concerned, the concept of workers' needs varies in different schools of thought, depending upon the assumptions and values that are taken for granted. The scientific management approach is primarily concerned with the economic needs of workers, that is, it implies a model of economic man. The human relations approach is characterized by the shift of interest towards the model of social man. Psychological studies based on the theory of alienation focus attention on the need for self-actualization, and organizational theory tends to be concerned with the complex and dynamic character of human needs.

The model of *economic man* assumes that workers are exclusively, or almost exclusively, motivated by financial rewards. Schein (1970, p. 56) presents the general line of thought as follows:

man is primarily motivated by economic incentives and will do whatever affords him the greatest economic gain;
since economic incentives are controlled by the organization, man is
essentially a passive agent to be manipulated, motivated and controlled by the organization;
man's feelings are essentially irrational and must be prevented from
interfering with his rational calculation of self-interest;
organizations can and must be designed in such a way as to neutralize
and control man's feelings and therefore his unpredictability.

The assumptions of the model of *social man* have been thoroughly investigated by the human relations school, which substantiated them through studies showing the importance of small groups in industry and their impact on individual workers. Mayo (see chapter 3) pointed out that the disregard for social needs of the workers to belong and to be appreciated resulted in apathy, carelessness and low productivity, the management being perceived as 'the enemy' against whom the workers ganged up. Once the 'rabble hypothesis' was discarded, as happened in the Hawthorne experiment, cooperation among the workers developed, they gave themselves wholeheartedly to work and their productivity dramatically improved.

A model of *creative and self-actualizing man* developed in the course of discussion on alienation in industry. It became a significant element in organizational requirements and individual needs are empha-sized. The concept of the self-actualizing man has been discussed most thoroughly by Argyris, who postulates a basic incongruity between the needs of a mature personality and the requirements of formal organizations (Argyris, 1964, p. 64). It is assumed that human beings in our culture had to develop from: a state of passivity as infants to a state of increased activity as adults; a state of dependence as infants to a state of relative independence as adults; the capability of behaving in only a few ways as infants to the capability of behaving in many different ways; erratic, casual, shallow, quickly abandoned interests to more profound interests; a short time perspective to a much longer time perspective; the occupation of a subordinate position in family and society to the aspiration to occupy an equal and/or supra-ordinate position relative to their peers; and a lack of awareness of self to an awareness of and control over self. What bureaucratized, formal systems in fact achieve is the reduction of men to the infant position, thus depriving them of the attributes of adult life. This either gives rise to feelings of frustration, conflict and failure, or to constant conflict between the individual and the organization.

All these models differ in what they consider to be the *most* important needs affecting workers' responses to managerial goals. An attempt to combine various types of needs into one dynamic model has been made by Maslow, who distinguishes five kinds of needs that he regards as basic and common to all human beings: physiological, safety, love, esteem and self-actualization (Maslow, 1976, pp. 117–35). He regards these as forming a hierarchy so that at every stage it is only by satisfying the preceding needs that people become preoccupied with the higher needs.

It is quite true that man lives by bread alone — when there is no bread. But what happens to man's desires when there is plenty of bread and when his belly is chronically filled? At once other (and 'higher') needs *emerge* and these, rather than physiological hungers, dominate the organism. And when these in turn are satisfied, again new (and still 'higher') needs emerge and so on. This is what we mean by saying that the basic human needs are organised into a hierarchy of relative prepotency. [Maslow, 1976, pp. 120–1]

Maslow did not deny that the hierarchy of needs varied in many cases because of individual preferences, situational constraints or cultural factors; he only argued that the order of needs he presented was predominant.

Physiological needs in Maslow's view come first simply because of their importance for human survival; as long as these are not satisfied, people are usually unable to think about anything else.

The importance of safety needs is seen most clearly in the compulsive—obsessive neuroses of people when seeking all means possible to stabilize the world around them. There are other aspects of safety needs, such as the need for an environment free from threats. Among those enumerated by Maslow, one can mention: a preference for some kind of undisrupted routine or rhythm; a preference for an organized, predictable world; a common preference for familiar rather than unfamiliar things, for the known rather than the unknown.

Their physiological and safety needs satisfied, people tend, according to Maslow, to seek love and affection, friendship and intimate family ties — urges very different from the sex drive, which, for Maslow, belongs to physiological needs.

Now the person will feel keenly, as never before, the absence of friends, or a sweetheart, or a wife, or children. He will hunger for affectionate relations with people in general, namely, for a place in his own group, and he will strive with great intensity to achieve this goal. [p. 124]

The need for self-esteem comes next, provided that life experiences have not discouraged people from pursuing their aspirations. Reputation, prestige and appreciation are all highly valued and, their other needs satisfied, people seem unremitting in their efforts to attain them. Esteem needs are divided by Maslow into two categories: in the first is a desire for strength, achievement, adequacy, mastery, competence and independence; in the second, a desire for reputation, prestige, status, recognition, importance and appreciation.

The highest need, according to Maslow, is for self-actualization, self-fulfilment and the self-expression of potential ability. Some individuals aim at intellectual achievement, others at artistic or athletic achievement, whilst many find it most rewarding to fulfil to perfection the social roles assigned to them.

The term refers to man's desire for self-fulfilment, namely, to the tendency for him to become actualized in what he is *potentially*. This tendency might be phrased as the desire to become more and more what one is, to become everything that one is capable of becoming. [p. 126]

Maslow's principal idea is that men are never satisfied, since every step taken towards implementing their desires leads to new 'needs'. His approach has been enthusiastically welcomed by industrial sociologists, who see in it the answer to the apparently insoluble contradiction between the different models of man.

## CONTRACTUAL OBLIGATIONS AND
## INDUCEMENT–CONTRIBUTION THEORY

Many students of organizational behaviour believe that whatever the merits of theories of human needs may be, they have, in fact, little bearing on the way people work. Modern organizations do not in reality rely on men's desires and drives and can to some extent disregard them. This is because workers are under a contractual obligation to perform their tasks in the way prescribed by the organizations that employ them. Udy traces contractual work back to traditional societies where it played a subordinate role as an alternative to familiar reciprocity, and he stresses the importance of the institution of contractual work in 'a new occupational system grounded in industrial technology' (Udy, 1970, p. 95).

Contracts, whether they are employer-related, job-related or occupation-related, specify the duties of the employee to be performed in return for certain benefits. By taking up employment a person is said to be agreeing that his behaviour is to be regulated by another's will and decisions. A contract implies, in other words, an equilibrium between contributions and inducements: the employee will remain in employment and carry out his work as long as he received satisfactory rewards. Similarly, the firm will accept his services as long as his contribution seems satisfactory compared with the cost of keeping the contract in force. The employee's identification with the goals of the firm is conditional and instrumental, and lasts only as long as the contract remains in force. During that time he is prepared to do what he is told, to observe the standards of performance imposed on him and to substitute organizational values and preferences for his own. He behaves like an actor hired to play a role designed for him. Barnard stresses that

the most ineffective services in a continuing effort are in one sense those of volunteers, or of semi-volunteers; for example, half-pay workers. What appears to be inexpensive is in fact very expensive, because non-material incentives – such as prestige, toleration of too great personal interest in the work with its accompanying fads and 'pet' projects, the yielding to exaggerated conceptions of individual importance – are causes of internal friction and many other undesirable consequences. [Barnard, 1956, p. 221]

Barnard points out that, in contrast to individual behaviour, organizational behaviour may be analysed without reference to psychological motives, needs or feelings.

Every effort that is a constituent of organisation, that is, every coordinated cooperative effort, may involve two acts of decision. The first is the decision of the person affected as to whether or not he will contribute this effort as a matter of personal choice. It is a detail of the process of repeated personal decisions that determine whether or not the individual will be or will continue to be a contributor to the organisation...The second type of decisions has no direct or specific relation to personal results, but views the effort concerning which decision is to be made non-personally from the view-point of its organisation effect and of its relation to organisation purpose. This second act of decision is often made in a direct sense by individuals, but it is impersonal and organisational in its intent and effect. [Barnard, 1956, pp. 187–8]

The most important element in contract theory, as far as motivations are concerned, is its ability to explain the mechanisms by which commitment to organizational goals can be secured. An individual's loyalty, responsibility, submission to superior orders, initiative and inventiveness cannot be secured other than through selection, promotion, demotion and dismissal. These must be based on anticipation of the ability and willingness of the employee to respond to organizational requirements and to do his best to follow his contractual obligations. It has been noted, however, that an employee is often prone to limit his contribution to the 'satisfactory' level without attempting to maximize it. Moreover, everyday control of what is regarded as an adequate performance is often very difficult. In these circumstances a distinction must be made between motivations *to* work and motivations *at* work, a distinction that places serious limitations on contract theory (March and Simon, 1958). Clearly, in many cases the motives to work are insufficient to cause the employee to observe the contract and fulfil his tasks as expected. In most situations the employee is faced with a number of alternatives regarding the extent and form of submission to contractual obligations. The question of how to motivate people *at* work remains valid even if they operate within contractual relationships.

## OUTCOME-ORIENTED BEHAVIOUR AND EXPECTANCY THEORY

The main weakness of the inducement—contribution theory is its failure to predict variations in the behaviour of employees subject to the same organizational stimuli. These variations cannot be understood unless we take into consideration (a) the many different *objectives* (outcomes) for which people are striving in concrete work situations; (b) the *circumstances* in which they pursue and carry out their plans; and (c) the way they *perceive* the end-to-means relationship. We are dealing, in other words, with innumerable decisions in which general needs and organizational stimuli belong to a broad framework within which many volitional, cognitive and situational factors affect employees' decision-making.

As far as objectives are concerned, many industrial psychologists argue that we should shift the emphasis from basic human needs towards the factual *outcomes* for which people are striving. These outcomes can be interpreted in terms of their ability to satisfy, directly or indirectly, one or many needs. 'Some outcomes are sought as ends in themselves...while others are sought because they lead to other outcomes...' (Lawler, 1973, p. 51). In the first case the outcome directly satisfies a person's needs, in other cases they lead to an outcome or a set of outcomes that satisfy a particular need or a set of needs.

Money is the best example of an objective regarded as highly desirable by most people, yet it seldom appears to be an end in itself. Opsahl and Dunnette (1966) distinguish five theories that explain the role of money as an incentive. In these theories, money is:

(1) A generalized conditioned reinforcer on account of its association with primary reinforcers (need-satisfiers).
(2) A conditioned incentive. A new, learned drive for money is established because money is continually associated with primary incentives.
(3) An anxiety reducer.
(4) A 'hygiene' factor, i.e. lack of it causes dissatisfaction, while it contributes little to satisfaction when present.
(5) A universal instrument used to obtain desired outcomes.

The desirability of the outcome is, however, but one of the factors that affect human decisions at work. 'Expectancy theory' applies to explanations covering the other factors mentioned by Lawler. In the first place, motivation is influenced by the expectancy that effort or action on the part of the person will lead to the intended performance, which can be labelled as E–P (effort–performance) expectancy. Expectancy also applies to the relationship between performance (P) and outcome (O), i.e. the expectation that the given performance may lead to a given outcome. Motivation does seem to be greatest when E–P is high for successful performance and low for unsuccessful performance and when P–O is high for positive outcomes and low for negative ones.

In the case of productivity...people will be motivated to be highly productive if they feel they can be highly productive and if they see a number of positive outcomes associated with being a high producer. [Lawler, 1973, p. 52]

Many studies support the expectancy theory. Stedery and Kay reported the performance of those who perceived a goal set up for them as challenging and those who saw it as impossible. In the first case, the number of sub-standard items produced decreased by 28 per cent; in the second, it increased by 35 per cent (1971, p. 298). Distinctions between conditions of certainty, uncertainty and risk have also been investigated. Here, most theorists emphasize that models of decision-making have paid insufficient attention to decisions taken against a background of risk and uncertainty.

As we see, the relationships between effort and performance and between performance and outcome are determined by objective factors; however, at the same time, their motivational impact depends on the *subjective perception* of these relationships. The influence of previous experience, the process of socialization and the amount of information available play an important part in shaping these perceptions. Purposive behaviour is comprehensively analysed in terms of needs, expectations, views of the path—goal relationship and the level of freedom in the environment.

## CULTURE, SOCIALISATION, AND ATTITUDES TO WORK

Models of purposeful, outcome-oriented behaviour tend to disregard the impact of socialization on attitudes to work. These attitudes can be traced to different socialization processes that predetermine human behaviour.

The impact of culture is sometimes presented as a set of programmes imposed on man and that shape his reactions to the external world. The choice between acceptable and unacceptable alternatives, the norms of behaviour followed, the orders of preference and the perception of work — all depend to a great extent on upbringing, social background, experience of life and the influence of primary groups through which the individual learns social behaviour. The differences between workers coming from rural areas and those from urban centres, the occupational subcultures, the peculiar traits of local communities, the differences in workers' behaviour according to ethnic background, are all issues that have been discussed by sociologists concerned with cross-cultural comparisons.

In recent years a considerable number of studies have concentrated on the 'subculture of poverty', and its impact on workers whose lives have been shaped by it. The view that poverty creates a subculture of its own was put forward by Lewis in 1959 (Lewis, 1959, 1966). The subculture of poverty was, he noted, characterized by: lack of participation and integration into the institutions of the larger society; lack of any organization beyond the level of a nuclear family; family and sexual practices at variance with the outside culture; and feelings of helplessness, dependence and inferiority (Holman, 1978, pp. 106–7).

By the time slum children are aged six or seven they have usually absorbed the basic values and attitudes of their sub-culture and are not psychologically geared to take full advantage of changing conditions or increased opportunities which may occur in their lifetime. [Lewis, 1966, p. 50]

An important contribution to this subject is a study by Davis (1969). He argues that in similar conditions different cultures impose different responses. The cases he examined can be regarded as determined by the subculture of poverty. The workers he describes behave in ways contrary to middle-class standards, yet there is some logic and rationality in their responses to situations. Their behaviour is determined not merely by different standards resulting from different life experiences, but also by the nature of the problems they face:

The habits of 'shiftlessness', 'irresponsibility', lack of 'ambition', absenteeism and of quitting the job, which management usually regards as a result of the 'innate' perversity of underprivileged white and Negro workers are in fact *normal responses* that the worker has learned from his physical and social environment. These habits constitute a system of behaviour and attitudes which are realistic and rational in that environment in which the individual of the slums has lived and in which he has been trained. [Davis, 1969, p. 150]

Davis points out that managers expect workers to be punctual, responsible and willing to get on in life. They do not, however, take into account that these attitudes need to be learned through formal training, family pressure, job incentives, etc. As far as underprivileged workers are concerned, their socialization includes quite different values and standards. They learn even in childhood to limit their ambitions, to concentrate their efforts on mere subsistence, to accept poor nutrition and medical care and to seek prestige and respect only within their own slum culture, which does not appreciate ambition and education but acknowledges only thrift, shrewdness and the ability to live on the fringe of legal activities. They have poor housing and families to look after, and lack steady or well-paid jobs. Nor are underprivileged workers responsive to middle-class-oriented punishments such as dismissal from work; in contrast to middle-class workers, they can always *expect* family support; casual jobs are not regarded as degrading; and overcrowding in the home is not thought to be a calamity. Even those without families can join a commune, sharing money and possessions.

Having studied several cases of underprivileged workers, Davis concludes that organizational methods cannot change work attitudes, as long as they are at odds with their subculture. He dismisses those who believe increased hardship would compel such workers to change their behaviour patterns. Unemployment, low wages and lack of social facilities do not encourage the underprivileged worker to greater effort but, on the contrary, reinforce preferences and habits opposed to employment requirements:

If he does change his work habits, if he does become ambitious, if he does begin to crave respectability, then industry and society must have the homes and steady jobs and education to offer him in return for his great effort. [p. 163]

Himes, in his study of two Southern communities, points out that the black boys he studied were not subject to the influences that shaped the attitudes of white children in regard to work. They never met skilled adult workers and had never had the opportunity to acquaint themselves with the daily routine of industrial life; thus, one could speak of a 'trained unreadiness for smooth transition from family, school and neighbourhood to the social world and technical role of work' (quoted in Fromkin and Sherwood, 1974, p. 134).

Liebow describes the life of about twenty unemployed street-corner men. He argues that they lack the education and skill required for better-paid jobs and, being unable to support their families, they turn to the company of those who resemble them:

It is the experience of the individual and the group; of their fathers and probably their sons. Convinced of their inadequacies, not only do they not seek out those few better-paying jobs which test their resources, but they actively avoid them, gravitating in a mass to the menial, routine jobs which offer no challenge — and therefore pose no threat — to the already diminished images they have of themselves. [Liebow, 1967, p. 54]

All these studies are characterized by a tendency to explain individual behaviour in terms of the central values of the culture to which the individual belongs. A response to employment is, from this point of view, determined by the whole structure of social life, the patterns of socialization and collective experiences, which provide us with the best clues to the preferences and standardized reactions of an individual exposed to organizational stimuli.

Further observations on workers' motivations have been accumulated through studies of industrialization in underdeveloped countries. It has been found that the classic inducements based on monetary incentives fail to motivate workers brought up in pre-industrial cultures and exposed to various kinds of social pressures. Moore argues that:

A part of the motivational framework for economic development depends upon a growing orientation to an exchange economy, and to exchange stripped of part of its archaic social appurtenances. In many underdeveloped areas of the world, the consumer has a fairly fixed level of demand. In these situations, even if the labourer (or, for that matter, manager or merchant) becomes involved in a monetary system, his demand for money has more or less early limits and is perhaps confined to highly specific products. [Moore, 1965, p. 43]

Moore is particularly concerned with the clash between a relatively stabilized traditional economy and the new demands of the industrialization processes. He claims that under the old system the motivational structure remains stable and is adjusted to the entire social framework; once the transformation occurs, there is a growing incongruity between established attitudes and the new economic and technological requirements. The social control over human needs and social norms imposed by traditional societies is, under new conditions, a serious obstacle to industrial development. The destruction of the old *structures* is no answer to the problem so long as no new *cultural* standards arise to replace the old ones.

Moore rightly points out that modern industry is no longer satisfied with the 'motivated worker'; it expects him to be committed, that is, to identify with the trade or job, and even with his firm. Studies of different subcultures demonstrate that this commitment is the result of a long process of socialization and that, in some circumstances, the relevant attitudes are unlikely to arise.

## STUDIES IN PAYMENT SYSTEMS

An important part of the study of work motivation is devoted to comparisons of different incentive plans, including individual incentives, group incentives, promotion schemes, profit-sharing, etc. By studying the relationship between the type of incentive and the resulting output, one accumulates empirical evidence of worker responses to various rewards and benefits.

The crucial empirical question about pay as a motivator of job performance is not the traditional one of 'Are incentive plans efficient motivators of effective job performance?' but the differential one of 'Under what conditions is pay a significant motivator of effective job performance?' [Opsahl and Dunnette, 1966]

Payment by results is one of the most widely applied and most controversial methods of motivating people at work. It is not surprising that research in this area abounds, although the findings are far from conclusive. Argyle refers to an American survey according to which the introduction of 514 incentive schemes was followed by an average 39 per cent increase in output, a decrease in labour costs of 11.6 per cent and a wage increase of 17.6 per cent. He also quotes findings on six British factories in which incentive schemes were introduced: output rose by 60 per cent as compared with the increase in earnings of 20 per cent (Argyle, 1972, p. 85).

Payment by results has, however, many in-built drawbacks that in many cases outweigh its advantages. The main problem is that of fixing the norms and establishing the payments per unit of output. In theory, time-and-motion studies are supposed to provide a fair assessment of the average time required for a given performance; this was, at least, what Taylor (1911) believed when he introduced his incentive schemes. This is not, however, the way the system works. Firstly, workers try to outwit their time-and-motion study men, so that the assessments are based on observations of workers deliberately working slowly. Secondly, the workers themselves quickly learn that negotiating *new* payments through the unions is more effective in increasing their incomes than 'busting' the rates. This gives rise to endless bargaining over piece rates and may lead to industrial unrest. Thirdly, the introduction of new production methods, which is standard practice in many enterprises, poses serious problems of reassessing the rates in view of the changing relationship between individual effort and the contribution of new technology. In most factories, collective agreements indicate that changing rates should follow substantial technological improvements; however, defining these improvements may cause friction between management and workers.

The practice of restraining output is exercised in capitalist and communist countries alike; the phenomenon has been well described in the literature on the social aspects of payments systems.

*Goldbricking* takes place when workers discover that whatever they do they cannot earn much more than they are guaranteed under basic payments. If, for instance, £4.35 is the guaranteed day's wage and the workers find out that even by using all their effort they are unable to earn much more than, say, £4.90 per day, they may attempt to slow production so as not to exceed the basic minimum, and will often try to work slightly below it. We know that the positive value of incentives depends, among other things, on their being easily attained; workers tend to evaluate 'extra money' in terms of extra effort spent. If they find it more profitable to save their energy and peace of mind by avoiding the opportunity of getting a few shillings, then clearly such an incentive system is not functioning. Even if the ceiling of extra earnings is higher, so that workers are interested in increasing their output, a 'saturation' point is reached when the extra rewards are less and less attractive in comparison with the effort applied. This is a law of diminishing marginal returns: the more the worker produces, the more energy he has to spend on exceeding average output, so that if the basic rates remain the same the cost exceeds at a certain point the rewards to be expected (Roy, 1952). This is recognized by some incentive schemes, which contain a progressive scale of remuneration for increased output. In the same way, overtime is paid at a higher rate if extended over a certain number of hours. There is, however, a threshold of profitability involved; all managers realize sooner or later that there is no effective way of inducing workers to increase output indefinitely.

*Quota restrictions.* In circumstances where workers feel they can raise output relatively easily and considerably increase their earnings by producing more than is guaranteed by the average minimum, they may still use their skill and ingenuity to maintain a sound balance between output level and wage increases, and avoid reaching the highest limit of income based on maximum productivity (Roy, 1952). They obviously have good reasons for doing so, since these attitudes can be found worldwide wherever the piecework system exists. Hickson (1961) listed five causes of the restriction of output:

1. Uncertainty about the continuance of the existing 'effort-bargaining' between the workers and management.
2. Uncertainty about the continuance of employment.
3. Uncertainty about the continuance of existing social relationships.
4. The desire to continue social satisfactions derived from the practice of restriction.
5. Desire for at least a minimal area of external control over one's own behaviour. [Hickson, 1961]

The point is that, in assessing their short-term interests, workers take into account the indirect consequences of satisfying them; they assume that increased productivity will be of no benefit to them over a period of time. It frequently happens that once a certain level of output is reached within the limits of extra earnings and becomes 'the average', the management either cuts the basic rate so as to put an end to excessive income, or changes the productivity norms to increase the output required as a necessary minimum. Alternatively, if the extra production goes beyond what the enterprise needs, some of the workers are made redundant so as to adjust the labour force to the level of output anticipated. Workers are aware of these possibilities and try to counteract them by all means available, even at the cost of limiting their own earnings by producing below the feasible

average of output. Their efforts find expression in group evaluation
of what the fair output should be and in enforcing a quota against
individuals reluctant to recognize the group's long-term interests.

*Saving the reported output.* Even when the basic rates are relatively
well calculated and workers are induced to do extra work, they often
do not claim credit for the extra production achieved on a particular
day or week and leave aside some product (by not reporting it) 'for
a rainy day'. The reason for this is simple: workers are used to frequent
fluctuations in earnings based on piecework and seek to prevent them
by equalizing output. They know they have good days and bad days
depending on their mood, work flow and many other accidental
factors; if they put something aside on a good day, they will have
something in reserve on a bad day. At the same time, they seek to
prevent revision of the productivity norms on the basis of a temporary
peak. Workers may also restrict their output so as to give an impression
to a supervisor of lower productivity. Once they have 'something up
their sleeve', they can converse, relax or whatever, making up for lost
production later.

The disruptive effects of payment by results explain why many
managers prefer daily work payments even if these result in reduced
productivity. Paying the worker for time spent at work has the obvious
advantage of removing the tensions and conflicts involved in determining norms and piecework payments. At the same time, more emphasis
is put on the general motivation of employees, their skills, career
prospects and commitment to their duties. The negative effects of
the system are, however, considerable in many industries. Where tasks
are repetitive, lack of interest and boredom seem to be the immediate
results of abandoning a piecework system. There are strong incentives
to reduce output because of overtime earnings: the less workers produce during the day, the more chance they have of overtime work.
The lack of any direct feedback between performance and rewards
encourages workers to multiply their 'gains' by saving effort at the
expense of their productivity. This tendency cannot be effectively
counteracted by exhortation and other indirect inducements.

In these circumstances many enterprises attempt to combine the
two systems by using more or less complicated schemes of incentives
along with a guaranteed minimum wage. This is assuming that the
average or less-motivated worker will be content with the minimum,
while others will try to exceed the norms and make extra money. As
happens only too often, these methods give rise to all the problems
I have just discussed in reference to the two systems: restriction of
output through fear of the introduction of new norms; calculating the
benefits of overtime as offsetting the extra inducements of increased
production; endless bargaining over payments, etc.

Clearly, no incentive applies satisfactorily to all workers in all circumstances. Individual and social differences between workers make it impossible in practice to devise a successful and perfect method applicable to all of them. One of the few studies corroborating this conclusion was carried out by Dalton (1955), who analysed the earning records of 84 out of 300 production workers in an industrial department. The production ceiling for average workers was 150 per cent and a performance near 100 per cent was regarded as perfectly normal. Dalton compared those who tended to exceed average earnings with those who were constantly below normal production. The first group consisted of nine men who were labelled 'rate busters' by their fellow workers: their output was over 150 per cent. The second group totalled twenty-five men, whom Dalton described as 'restricters': their output was below 100 per cent.

The attitudes of 'rate busters' and 'restricters' were quite different. One 'rate buster' explained: 'I'm here to make money. If any of these damn loafers think they can stop me, let them try it.' On the other hand, the restricters asserted that 'you've got to keep your nose to the wheel....And even if things was fixed so you could make your regular bonus by working like hell — I still wouldn't want it if I had to make somebody sore to get it or have the whole shop down to me' (Dalton, 1955, p. 41).

Dalton was particularly interested in the characteristics of these two contrasting groups. He found the following factors most relevant:

Family background: 'restricters' were mostly sons of unskilled workers from urban conglomerations with experience of youth gangs. The 'rate busters' came either from rural areas or were from lower-middle-class families.

Social participation: the 'restricters' were well integrated into shopfloor life, while the 'rate busters' lived a life of their own both in the factory and outside it, enjoying hobbies such as modelling, photography, collecting, guns, etc.

Spending and saving: the 'rate busters' proved to be acquisitive, while the 'restricters' enjoyed a flourishing social life and spent money on themselves.

Dalton also noticed some differences in political attitudes, ideologies, religion and ethnic background.

The variety of factors involved meant that no reasonable prediction about individual workers was possible, but once some regular patterns were established they could be used as a guideline by managers. As Dalton put it:

The executive does not need to explain the responses of each worker. It is enough for him to be able to predict what most people will do. In this connection it should be emphasised that the theory of motivation at present generally applied in industry promotes full effort from probably less than 10% of the work force. [Dalton, 1955, p. 49]

In view of all these difficulties, some firms attempt to combine individual incentives with group ones, and even with collective incentives based on the idea of profit-sharing. The advantages and disadvantages of such schemes have been widely discussed in the economic and sociological literature (see Lupton, 1972, Part III). There are also managers who believe that a solution to the problem of effective inducements lies in the direction of industrial democracy, in making workers responsible for the firm and allowing them to identify with its success. This belief is officially expressed in communist Yugoslavia where private profits have been eliminated and replaced by collective forms of ownership. Whether practical experience justifies such hopes remains to be seen (see chapter 10).

## JOB SATISFACTION AND PRODUCTIVITY

Studies in job satisfaction have a long history. The belief that a happy worker is likely to be more productive lay at the basis of many research projects sponsored by managers eager to find ways of increasing workers' productivity. Later development brought a marked shift of emphasis: the well-being of the worker — and subsequently his satisfaction — became the leading theme in many sociological investigations (Form and Geschwender, 1962; Mumford, 1970; Handyside and Speak, 1964; Blauner, 1973).

The two main areas of studies related to job satisfaction at work are: explorations in the *causes* of job satisfaction/dissatisfaction; and evaluations of its possible impact on workers' performance.

Opinion polls show a relatively high percentage of workers who declare themselves satisfied at work, although the percentage of dissatisfied workers fluctuates from one year to another. In America in 1973, 77 per cent of workers were satisfied (Strauss, 1974, p. 75) and in Great Britain comparable figures were 82 per cent for men and 88 per cent for women (*Social Trends* 1970, p. 90). However, interpretation of these data is not easy because of the different methods by which satisfaction is measured. The difference between asking people the simple question 'Are you satisfied?' and enquiring about more specific aspects of their jobs is important.

Some opinion polls suggest there has been a considerable erosion of job satisfaction in the USA: according to a Gallup Poll, the percentage of satisfied employees fell from 87 per cent in 1964 to 77 per cent in

1973 (Yankelovich, 1974, p. 34). Other studies suggest there might have been fluctuations. In the USA, the percentage of satisfied workers remained fairly steady between 1948 (76 per cent) and 1958 (78 per cent); it rose to 89–90 per cent in 1966 and fell to 87 per cent in 1971, a trend that hardly indicates any considerable decline in job satisfaction.

An analysis of the impact on job satisfaction of factors such as age, sex, race and education reveals conclusive differences, but these seem to be limited in most cases (with race being a notable exception) to minor fluctuations in the number of the dissatisfied minority. The findings of a 1973 poll in America are shown in Table 4.1.

TABLE 4.1
VARIATIONS IN JOB SATISFACTION, USA, 1973

|  | *Satisfied* | *Dissatisfied* | *No opinion* |
|---|---|---|---|
| Overall | 77 | 11 | 13 |
| Sex |  |  |  |
| men | 78 | 12 | 10 |
| women | 76 | 10 | 14 |
| Colour |  |  |  |
| white | 80 | 10 | 10 |
| non-white | 53 | 22 | 25 |
| Education |  |  |  |
| college | 84 | 10 | 6 |
| high school | 75 | 13 | 12 |
| grade school | 71 | 9 | 20 |
| Occupation |  |  |  |
| professional and business | 85 | 10 | 5 |
| clerical and sales | 81 | 13 | 6 |
| manual workers | 80 | 13 | 9 |
| Age |  |  |  |
| under 30 years | 72 | 20 | 8 |
| 30–49 | 83 | 9 | 8 |
| 50 and over | 74 | 7 | 19 |

*Source*: Yankelovich (1974) p. 75.

As we shall see, interpretation of these findings is no simple matter and many theories and approaches have been put forward to explain the causes of satisfaction at work. Lawler (1973) has identified four main theories: the fulfilment theory, the discrepancy theory, the equity theory and the two-factor theory.

The fulfilment theory assumes that the satisfaction of needs or the achievement of desirable outcomes is essential to make workers happy. Those whose needs are more fulfilled are supposed to be more satisfied: those who earn more should be more satisfied than people with lower incomes; the same applies to other aspects of work, for example, an interesting job, a higher or lower position, job security.

The discrepancy theory introduces an important variable regarding what people think about what they receive: their assessment of the job will depend less on the absolute amount of the benefits they receive from it, than on their *perception* of those benefits measured by the discrepancy between what they receive and (a) what they wish, (b) what they think they should receive, and (c) what they think they can receive in the circumstances.

According to the equity theory, satisfaction is determined by the perceived ratio of what a person regards as his net cost and the return he gets: an over-reward will bring about a feeling of guilt, while an under-reward will give rise of feelings of unfairness.

The two-factor theory takes into account, on the one hand, the factors that cause job satisfaction and, on the other hand, the factors that cause dissatisfaction. The first category — the satisfiers — was identified by Herzberg (1968) as related to higher needs like self-actualization, ambition, etc.; job dissatisfiers were found in such factors as the level of payments, job security, etc. (Lawler, 1973, pp. 61–87).

To this list should be added theories that seek to explain the *dynamics* of job satisfaction. The significant contributions in this field are those of March and Simon (1958), Strauss (1974) and Stagner (1969).

Simon and March analysed the dynamics of aspirations in terms of the theory of decision-making. Simon regards the level of aspirations as being the result of environmental constraints (or environmental opportunities), on the one hand, and of previous learning, on the other hand. According to general rules widely substantiated by social psychology, we normally assume that, in the long run, the level of aspirations of an individual is adapted to the possibilities of satisfying them, and that these possibilities depend partly on external circumstances and partly on the ability of the individual concerned; in simple terms, people want what they think they can get. There is, however, an element of previous learning in the formula; after all, we determine what is within our reach only by our own and other people's experiences. The greater the previous successes, i.e. gratifications from the environment, the higher our expectations, and vice versa.

A similar point has been elaborated by Stagner, who notes that:

Children and adolescents who have had an accumulation of 'success' experiences have higher aspirations than those who have more 'failure' experiences. Thus, children from upper class families, with advantages in home background, intelligence, education, etc., characteristically have higher aspirations than those from poorer homes.

The executive...will set his sights higher and strive for increasingly more income, power and status. The worker, with a low income and probably some failures to look back upon, tends to hold his aspirations down and to strive for only fairly short-run, reasonably attainable goals. [Stagner, 1969, p. 144).

Assuming a given level of aspiration, an individual can be regarded as making his decisions in terms of achieving the goals within the limits of his expectations. He will be looking for satisfactory alternatives, and using his order of preferences when making his final choice regarding the possible outcome of his actions. It may happen, however, that in spite of intensive search, the individual does not find a satisfactory solution to his problems. What then? Since the search cannot last indefinitely, a normal individual tends to reformulate his expectations so that they can be satisfied under the given circumstances. On the other hand, relative ease in reaching some goals usually results in a rise in expectations so that one tends to seek new, more satisfactory alternatives. The dynamics of aspirations is thus affected both by external circumstances and by individual characteristics. An older worker accustomed to high wages and respectable jobs will desperately seek any job as soon as he finds out there are few opportunities available for people over a certain age. Employees satisfied with a moderate income during an economic depression will reject the same level of pay as unsatisfactory during periods of a boom and full employment.

The weakness of Simon's model lies in its disregard of the *variety* of possible responses to dissatisfying work situations. According to his model, dissatisfied workers either quit, or, if they perceive no better alternative, reduce their expectations to reach a new balance of satisfaction with what they can achieve. Strauss challenges the approach to motivations based on the concept of higher needs and offers instead a scheme of variations in responses to unsatisfactory jobs. This is elaborated in Figure 4.1. The scheme reflects the fact that in most cases workers faced with dull, unchallenging jobs do not necessarily quit or modify their expectations but rather adopt an attitude of being neither satisfied nor dissatisfied — they are apathetic. Apathy is a form of adjustment to adverse conditions through concentration on any instrumental benefits that may be received. It explains, according to Strauss, why a worker expresses satisfaction with a job while at the same time frequently saying he would change it if he could. It also explains why a worker prefers work to idleness, even if his job does not

TYPE OF WORK

| | | non-challenging | challenging |
|---|---|---|---|
| | expressive | Dissatisfaction and unstable 3 | Satisfaction 1 |
| EMPLOYEE ORIENTATION | instrumental | Satisfaction 4 | Dissatisfaction and unstable 2 |

FIGURE 4.1 *Types of adjustment to work*

Source: Based on Strauss (1974) p.87.

fulfil many of his possible needs. The dynamics of adjustment and its resulting reflection in job satisfaction are illustrated by Strauss with reference to box 3, where a man seeking the possibility of self-expression at work is faced with a dull, unchallenging job. Adjustment to this situation — unless he quits his job — is two-fold. He will either look for substitutes at work or outside that will leave him satisfied with his situation, or he will gradually adopt an apathetic attitude. In regard to workers in box 2, the dissatisfied ones will be either those who are faced with a situation at work to which they did not have time to adjust, or those unable to adjust at all but who still cannot quit their jobs.

The important distinction between satisfaction *with the job* and satisfaction *at the job* helps us to clarify at least some difficulties in interpreting the ambivalent attitudes of many workers who on the one hand report that they are satisfied and, on the other hand, complain about various aspects of their present jobs. Daniel has stated:

All surveys show that nearly all workers are satisfied with their jobs. They have made the best bargain in terms of their opportunities as they see them and accept it. So it is not surprising that these workers are satisfied with their jobs... This satisfaction is largely associated with sources of attachment to the job, which is a very different thing from the relative opportunities that different jobs provide... In this case, satisfaction with the bargain one has made does not make the cost less painless. [Daniel, 1969]

This distinction needs to be remembered when we come to consider the impact of job satisfaction on workers' performances. One might expect that dissatisfaction with the nature of the contract would lead workers to quit, thus explaining high labour turnover; alternatively, dissatisfaction with different aspects of the job, when linked to a conviction that the contract itself is generally satisfactory, leads us to expect stability in the labour force. And, indeed, some sociologists have observed a 'new industrial feudalism' — a situation in which an employee feels trapped in his job by the many benefits he can achieve (promotion, longer vacations, good pension, substantial wage increases for long service, etc.), and yet may at the same time loathe every minute spent at his work.

If there is a correlation between reported job satisfaction and labour turnover and, to some extent, absenteeism too, then the association between job satisfaction and productivity is less conclusive. Some correlation — usually a weak one — has been reported in many studies, but in other studies this relationship does not appear. A possible interpretation of the findings can be as follows:

Job satisfaction accounts for higher productivity but other factors weaken this relationship.

Job satisfaction is not the cause but the *result* of higher productivity, although it may appear also in circumstances unrelated to high output.

Both job satisfaction and productivity are determined by some third factor — hence their association.

As I have said, the first view dominated the early writings of industrial sociologists; nowadays the inclination is to accept the other two explanations, with the notable exception of Herzberg (1968) whose theory of motivators constitutes an attempt to reintegrate job satisfaction and productivity.

Having reviewed ample evidence on the relationship between job satisfaction and performance, Vroom states that the data lead to 'The inescapable conclusion that the conditions necessary to make membership in a system attractive and satisfying to a person are not identical with those which are necessary to motivate the person to perform effectively within his role' (Vroom 1969, p. 199). Vroom and other social and industrial psychologists believe that the weak correlation between job satisfaction and productivity revealed in most studies does not reflect the impact of satisfaction on productivity, but rather the reverse — high performers being in many cases happier than low ones. As Lawler and Porter state:

If we assume that rewards cause satisfaction and that in some cases performance produces rewards, then it is possible that the relationship found between satisfaction and performance comes about through the action of a third variable — rewards. Briefly stated, good performance may lead to rewards, which in turn lead to satisfaction; this formulation then would say that satisfaction rather than causing performance, as was previously assumed, is caused by it. [Lawler and Porter, 1967]

This is shown diagrammatically in Figure 4.2. In connection with this model of the relationship between performance and job satisfaction, Lawler and Porter state that:

Extrinsic (money) rewards are imperfectly related to performance because no system of rewards gives full justice to individual achievements.

Extrinsic rewards are more likely to be related to good performance because to a great extent they are awarded by the individual to himself.

Both extrinsic and intrinsic rewards are affected by what a person feels he should receive.

In most cases these factors will result in a positive but low association between performance and job satisfaction.

There will, however, be a negative relationship, in that a good performance will be associated with dissatisfaction when rewards are either unrelated or negatively related to performance. In such a situation, the best performers will be the most dissatisfied.

On the other hand, if the good performers are given significantly better rewards there will be a strong positive association between job satisfaction and performance.

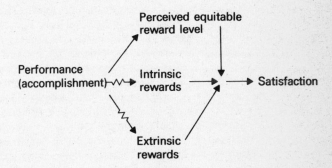

FIGURE 4.2 *Model of the relationship of performance to satisfaction*

*Source:* Lawler and Porter (1967).

However, one should note that some studies have found no relationship between performance and job satisfaction (for example, Leavitt, 1963). The explanation for job satisfaction is to be sought in the cumulative effects of many factors, of which performance is only one. Rewards may be quite considerable, yet an employee may feel that what he and everybody else receives is quite unsatisfactory. Similarly, satisfaction with high earnings (extrinsic reward) may be overshadowed by the fact that the job is so unchallenging that it does not offer any other substantial intrinsic rewards.

One should also take into consideration the fact that the impact of job satisfaction on productivity may in fact be positive, but without being reflected in the often imperfect statistics. The only conclusive evidence would be to demonstrate somehow that under controlled conditions job satisfaction in a factory or within a work group has increased without there being positive effects on productivity. However, such before and after experiments are almost never quoted in the relevant literature.

The relationship between job satisfaction, labour turnover and absenteeism poses fewer problems. As far as labour turnover is concerned, there is ample evidence that dissatisfied employees are more likely to quit their jobs. Whether or not they do so will depend to a great extent on market conditions: the incidence of turnover is directly related to fluctuations of the labour market. As far as absenteeism is concerned, this appears to be affected by both dissatisfaction *with* the job and dissatisfaction *at* the job. In the second case, absenteeism is a response to job drudgery, although the evidence is not conclusive in this respect.

It should be noted that social scientists have, in recent years, tended to abandon the instrumental approach to job satisfaction. Instead of looking for a relationship between job satisfaction and productivity, they are more interested in the *quality* of working life and use the concept of job satisfaction as only one of many indicators of workers' well-being. The change of emphasis is very important: the new approach does not imply that the worker *should* be satisfied, but simply reflects a desire to create a working environment that adds to the value of the working man's life irrespective of his feelings about it. One can conclude that with improved social conditions and rising expectations workers might be even less content with their jobs than formerly. This should not, however, exclude or nullify attempts at making the best of the working environment — an approach that is closely linked with the concept of social justice.

Desirable aspects of jobs that add to the quality of working life have been identified by Emery and Thorsrud (quoted in Rosow, 1974, p. 6) as follows:

The need for a job to be reasonably demanding in terms other than sheer endurance, by providing a minimum of variety (not necessarily novelty).

The need to be able to learn on the job.

The need for a minimal area of decision-making that the individual can call his own.

The need for a minimal degree of social support and recognition in the work-place.

The need for the individual to relate what he does and what he produces to his social life.

The need to feel that the job leads to some sort of desirable future (not necessarily promotion).

The satisfaction of these requirements is seen more and more frequently as leading to a stage at which any erosion of extrinsic rewards makes it necessary to compensate by boosting work-place morale in order to secure not so much the maximum, as satisfactory performance.

# CHAPTER 5

# Sociology of Supervision: The Foreman

Industrial sociologists have produced many studies about the foreman's role in industrial enterprises. This interest reflects the attention paid by management to the human problems of supervision. Rationalization of supervision is based on the assumption that 'organizations are people', and that these people have to be properly directed and supervised. The last and most sensitive link in the chain of command in industry is the shopfloor supervisor: decisions reached in offices and laboratories have to be implemented on an everyday basis by foremen who occupy a position analogous to non-commissioned officers in the army.

## THE CHANGING ROLE OF FOREMEN

In small industrial enterprises in the eighteenth and nineteenth centuries, foremen as they operate today were practically unknown. There were either sub-contractors acting as intermediaries between groups of skilled workers and the entrepreneur, or the master craftsman heading groups of workers. Gradually, with the stabilization and expansion of the labour force, the foreman emerged as the officer and agent of the owner of the factory — combining the functions of a production planner, cost clerk, administrator and personnel officer. He was responsible for the smooth running of the technological processes and for work discipline. Operating as an agent of the employer the foreman enjoyed considerable power and authority at a time when most employers were able to rule with an iron hand. The state of the labour market and the lack of unionization allowed the foreman to dismiss workers who displeased him, to be arbitrary, to pay favourites and generally to abuse his position vis-à-vis people who were working under his supervision.

Some observers note that the authoritarian power of the foreman is still considerable in small non-unionized firms where there is a labour surplus. They also have considerable influence on workers' earnings. In many small companies based on traditional production methods, foremen exercise influence over wage—work bargaining. In the footwear industry, for instance, it has been found that:

the foreman's piecework pricing activity determines shop prices;

the foreman makes decisions about work loads and work allocation — for example, on the amount of hand-cutting performed by press cutters, or the allocation of 'good' and 'bad' priced work among machinists;

he can mitigate the effects on a worker's earnings of factors outside the worker's control, like paying extra for cutting poor material or performing alternative work;

he is an intermediary between workers and more senior management — he can put pressure, for instance, on work study staff in order to get a quick job reassessment (Goodman *et al.*, 1977, p. 171).

In modern medium and large factories the position of foremen is completely different. The scope of their decisions is considerably reduced, their power over employees is almost non-existent, their mediatory functions are less important and their discretion in rule-setting and problem-solving is very limited. All of this is the result of the technological, organizational and institutional changes that have taken place in modern industry:

Separate engineering departments are concerned with problems relating to production technology.

Personnel officers and personnel departments are responsible for recruitment and promotions, and also organize workforce training to the required standards.

Organizational planning regulates and programmes work flow, and devises rules indicating the various courses of action to be adopted in special circumstances like job-switching, remunerating extra effort, etc.

Trade unions discuss shopfloor grievances with management and act as the intermediaries between workers and their higher supervisors.

Under these circumstances, foremen are merely part of the bureaucracy, with very few first-line supervising functions. It does not follow, however, that these few functions are always easy to perform; foremen are given only limited organizational power and usually have to rely on their innate skill and experience in dealing with human problems arising on the shop floor. Unlike army sergeants, they are also less frequently promoted from the rank-and-file; they often gain their position via college education, and often lack the know-how characteristic of the traditional foreman in older industries. The need for training foremen in supervisory skills is thus greater than ever before. In many technical colleges, the curriculum includes only a token element of study in industrial management, although on-the-job training organized by personnel departments often compensates for this.

## FOREMAN – THE MAN IN THE MIDDLE

Sociologists investigating the position and functions of foremen in industry invariably point out that foremen are caught between two different social and organizational structures: on the one hand, they maintain daily contact with rank-and-file employees, whom they supervise; on the other hand, as part of management, they are exposed to the pressures of their own superiors from whom they receive instructions and orders. This position is reflected in expressions applied to foremen such as 'marginal men', 'men in the middle' or 'victims of double talk'.

If an intermediate-level officer is to be a real leader, he has a dual role to play. He must accept the norms and values of superior authority, thus serving as an agent of the impersonal and coercive organisation of which he is part. To the extent that he does this effectively his superiors regard him highly. At the same time, he must win the willing followership of the men under him, so that he wields over them authority that they have themselves given him. He will be rated highly by the men to the extent that he shows 'consideration' for them and to the extent that he mingles freely with them and represents them against the cold machine which is the overall organisation. [Gibb, 1965, pp. 894–5]

This statement reflects the conflicting requirements built into the foreman's role because of his location between the managers who represent the interests of the firm and the workers who do not necessarily identify with the enterprise and seldom obey unquestioningly the orders and rules given to them. The marginal or middle position implies, however, more than that.

In organizational terms, foremen are the lowest part of the authority structure with the boundaries of their prerogatives and functions loosely defined. It is noticeable that the functions of foremen vary in this respect from one enterprise to another.

In terms of group interests, the position of the foreman is also somewhat marginal and often ambiguous. Foremen are supposed to act on behalf of management but their close cooperation with the workers often makes it difficult to maintain a one-sided identification. They understand workers' grievances better than do the distant managers, and they are too close to the realities of shopfloor life to accept arbitrary decisions without reservation. In any case, a one-sided identification with management often proves counter-productive since it alienates the workers. An experienced foreman will be cautious to avoid taking sides and is able to predict with accuracy both shopfloor and trade union responses to events. Foremen tend to behave less like bureaucrats obeying orders to the letter and more like 'politicians' negotiating and looking for workable solutions without committing themselves to the interests of any of the parties involved.

In terms of their cultural background, in many enterprises foremen form a group apart and do not identify themselves socially either with the workers or with higher level management. Dalton (1951), who studied the career patterns of 226 individuals and among them 93 first-line foremen and 61 general foremen, found that the key ethnic and social characteristics helping foremen in their promotion were different from those of the majority of the labour force. Foremen do not automatically merge with higher management either. Their class origin is more lower-middle class than that of higher management, their education inferior, their class identification ambiguous since they do not regard themselves as 'professionals' or 'executives' as most managers do. Very much like army sergeants, many of them do not expect to be promoted to higher management but expect rather to advance if at all, in their technical capacity.

The ambiguity of foremen's status is reflected in their level of unionization. In England a Social Survey on Workshop Industrial Relations gave the following for a sample of 598 foremen from 319 organizations:

32% of total in unions
24% in construction
33% in metal handling
24% in other manufacturing
(Dunkerley, 1975, p. 136).

This clearly indicates the conflicting expectations and pressures built into the foreman's role. The concept 'role' usually refers to the formal and social requirements associated with various positions. As long as social or occupational role is regulated by a set of consistent demands the concept does not pose any problems. The situation becomes more complicated when we deal with either conflicting demands, ambiguous demands or very few demands. The analogy with the actor playing his role according to a scenario written in advance does not make sense in such circumstances, for foremen are supposed to improvise and to find their own way in the face of many different expectations and conflicting demands, of which the following can easily be identified:

the organizational requirements — which are meant to be implemented through effective supervision and control;
managers' demands — not necessarily geared towards improving the performance of supervisors if this implies a substantial limitation of their own authority and is therefore against their own personal interests;
workers' expectations — the foreman's behaviour is very important for

workers, who assume that supervision will be exercised along lines acceptable to them.

the norms adopted by the foremen themselves and the extent to which they act as an occupational group with their own interests.

How do role conflict and role ambiguity affect the foreman? Several studies show that the incidence of ulcers among foremen tends to be disproportionately high, which is a symptom of the stress built into the foreman's job (Warr and Wall, 1978, p. 145). There is also ample evidence of lower job satisfaction among people faced by role conflict and role ambiguity. Whether role conflict and role ambiguity are the *source* of job dissatisfaction among foremen has not been fully tested, but some studies do suggest that this might be the case.

## THE SEARCH FOR THE BEST STYLE OF
## SUPERVISION IN INDUSTRY

Urwick, one of the founders of scientific methods of management, stated that:

The art of organisation consists in determining the correct method to apply at each point and to each aspect of an undertaking, and so to build up a structure in which the method or methods used at each point and the degree to which they are used result in the balance which is most effective for the purpose of the undertaking. [Urwick, 1947, p. 68]

Accordingly, many attempts have been made to determine the most effective supervision in industry. At first, efforts were concentrated on purely organizational issues, such as the distinctions and definitions of the functions performed by supervisors, the range of control, the relationship between the line and staff officers, the boundaries between the prerogatives of lower and middle management, the incentives and sanctions left to the discretion of foremen, etc. Most studies were normative and relied more on direct practical experience and common sense than on empirical research. For example, the distinction between 'headship' and leadership was unknown. It was assumed that the foreman was endowed with authority by the very fact of his being in office.

Opinions on the duties of direct supervisors were far from unanimous. Taylor (1911) argued on behalf of functional supervision. He pointed out that the functions of foremen were too complicated to be performed by a single person; they should be broken up into their component parts so that there would be gang boss, speed boss, repair boss, inspector, shop disciplinarian, scheduling and routing clerk, and cost and timekeeping clerk, etc. Other students of organizations disagreed with Taylor, and emphasized that the scalar line of authority was one of the main principles of scientific management. Fayol stressed that 'A body with two heads is in the social as in the animal sphere a monster and has difficulty in surviving' (quoted in Gross, 1964, vol. I, p. 132). The unity of command and unity of direction were also stressed by Gulick and Urwick, the leading scholars in organizational theory.

An interesting point was raised by Follett (1971), who argued that supervision could be depersonalized by obeying the rules of the situation. Once people are accustomed to the procedure that should be applied to a particular situation, there is no point in giving orders and receiving them.

If those in supervisory positions should depersonalise orders, then there would be no overbearing authority on the one hand, nor on the other that dangerous *laissez-aller* which comes from the fear of exercising authority. Of course we should exercise authority, but always the authority of the situation. [Follet, 1971, p. 155]

The underlying assumption of this argument is that there is no divergence of interests between management and workers, and that all problems can subsequently be solved by analysis: 'Our job is not how to get people to obey orders, but how to devise methods by which we can best *discover* the order integral to a particular situation' (Follet, 1971, p. 155).

The human relations approach, which developed in opposition to classical theory, takes credit for discovering the social and psychological aspects of supervision in industry. The Hawthorne investigators showed the importance of supervisor—worker relationships and substantiated the view that it was only through voluntary consensus by the workers that the foreman could exercise his full authority over them. The foreman was regarded as the crucial link between workers and management. The difference between headship and leadership was re-emphasized and problems of leadership qualities and of leadership style became one of the major research topics in industrial sociology. The Hawthorne findings suggested that the employee-oriented leadership style could raise workers' morale and boost their productivity. The need of employees to talk about their problems could be satisfied by a sympathetic supervisor provided he was aware of the social skills needed in dealing with industrial problems.

The critical arguments about leadership style were given in studies carried out by White and Lippitt (1953, 1960). They attempted to investigate the effects of different leadership styles on group performance and members' attitudes. To start with, two groups of five boys each were subjected to an experiment in which the effects of the authoritarian and the democratic style of leadership were compared. Subsequently, four groups of schoolboys were organized at after-school clubs where they participated in all kinds of handicraft activities. The groups were directed by leaders who were instructed to act in a specific way — either authoritarian, democratic or laissez-faire. Later the leaders were moved to other groups with instructions to apply a new style of leadership so as to exclude the impact of personality factors on the members of the group. The effects of the experiments were spectacular.

The democratic style of leadership proved the most successful all round. Although the performance of the group that was led in an authoritarian way was slightly higher, the total balance of the effect of democratic supervision was definitely more positive: the leader was much more popular than in two other groups where greater dissatisfaction with the leader was manifested; psychological dependence on the leader was at the same time less; there were many more suggestions and group initiating activities; there was a feeling of responsibility and commitment to tasks; the atmosphere among the boys was much friendlier; spontaneous sub-groups were larger, mutual admiration and appreciation were often expressed; there was no victimization or manifest aggression, unlike in the authoritarian groups; individual differences seemed more pronounced.

The groups that were directed by authoritarian leaders were much less reliable and more aggressive; there was a feeling of discontent with the leader and more tension, although dissatisfaction did not show on the surface; there was no incentive to seek recognition among peers, no initiative in the search for necessary information for the accomplishment of a task. The positive element consisted in a high degree of friendliness among the boys; the authors concluded that the spirit of rebellion and aggression seemed to be a cohesive force.

The laissez-faire groups were superior in one respect only: the boys showed much more responsibility in obtaining for themselves the information necessary to carry out their tasks. They showed some initiative when left alone but not in the direction of productivity. Their performance was poor, dissatisfaction with the leader quite common, but the atmosphere was much friendlier than in aggressive groups.

Parallel to the laboratory-style experiments of social psychologists, a number of field studies in industry have been carried out to corroborate the thesis about the relationship between leadership style and the performance of workers. The most intensive investigations in this area were conducted by the University of Michigan where the human relations approach was enthusiastically adopted. The research laid particular emphasis on field studies, surveys and field experiments, which were supposed to supply new data to corroborate the findings of the Lewin School and of Mayo and Roethlisberger's studies (see Sofer, 1972; Rose, 1975, pp. 161—5). The Michigan scholars compared supervisors whose departments attained a high output with those with poor productivity records, and found that the supervisors of high-production groups were those who:

were less supervised by their own supervisors;
put less emphasis on production goals;
made the employees participate in decision-making;
were employee-oriented;
spent more time on supervising people than on production itself;
were able to define their position clearly in relation to the company
   (Kahn and Katz, 1960).

In the field studies, matched work teams were compared with regard to output, job satisfaction and foreman behaviour so as to make sure that in the matched pairs the conditions of work were very similar. Foremen were interviewed and workers were asked to reply to questionnaires on the behaviour of their foremen and on their own job satisfaction. At the same time output ratios were compared. The most important findings were those indicating the positive effects of the foreman's involvement in leadership activities, and of his employees' orientation to productivity. It was also demonstrated that job satisfaction increased when supervision was not too 'close' but rather more general.

Another important contribution to the employee-centred and democratic style of supervision was presented by Coch and French (1948), who studied the response of workers to industrial change. In the factory where they carried out their investigations, technological change and the switching from one product to another were strongly resisted by the workers. The negative attitudes of the employees were expressed in their grievances over the piece rate that accompanied the new methods of production, in high turnover, low efficiency and restriction of output, and in marked hostility and aggression towards the management. The project involved the formation of experimental groups which were allowed to participate in the planning and carrying out of the changes. In each of the experimental groups the scope of participation was different: two groups participated fully in planning the changes, and one group was permitted to participate only through representation. The control group was allowed no participation at all. The groups were matched with respect to previous efficiency, to the amount of change involved in the transfer and to group cohesiveness. The results of the experiment are very interesting:

(1) The control group showed the usual drop in productivity with its accompanying phenomena such as expressions of aggression, restriction of output, high labour turnover, etc.

(2) The experimental group in which participation through represen- tation was applied proved successful as far as the time of relearning was concerned and, in spite of the initial drop in productivity, recovery was speedy and was followed by the development of permissive and cooperative attitudes.

(3) In the two groups with full participation, no drop in production occurred, and later a considerable rise in productivity was recorded.

A second experiment was then carried out: the non-participation group was assigned to new jobs while participation was fully applied. The group showed the same patterns of positive response to change as other groups with total participation techniques; a high level of produc- tivity was reached, no marked aggression occurred; no turnover took place. It could then be rightly argued that the results obtained de- pended on the experimental treatment and not on personality factors in the group. Coch and French conclude their experiment by arguing that:

It is possible for management to modify greatly or to remove com- pletely group resistance to changes in methods of work and the ensuing piece rates. This change can be accomplished by the use of group meetings in which management effectively communicates the need for change and stimulates group participation in planning the changes. [Coch and French, 1948]

The experiment was repeated later on in a Norwegian factory, where nine four-man groups were allocated to producing new products with a new piece rate. The conclusions were very similar (French *et al.*, 1960).

Such studies are used as arguments for a new leadership style based on participative techniques and on the reduction of authoritarian attitudes by supervisors. McGregor (1960), who incorporated these findings into his discussion of the traditional and the new styles of management (theory X and theory Y), argued for a new technique of managerial activities based on the following principles. Management remains responsible for organizing the elements of productive processes. However, people are not by nature either passive or resistant to organi- zational goals unless those attitudes are shaped by previous experience. It is the responsibility of management to develop the human potential for assuming responsibility, cooperating with management and identify- ing with organizational goals. The managers then need to arrange organizational conditions and methods of operation so that people can achieve their personal goals by directing their efforts toward organizational objectives.

A full summary of the human relations approach to methods of supervision has been presented by Likert (1961), who argues for the participative style of management, for lessening the degree of direct supervision and for applying the employee-oriented approach. Likert lists a set of requirements that, as he concluded from case studies, were associated with successful leadership:

> employee-centred attitude;
> enthusiasm and commitment to high performance goals;
> empathy and understanding;
> developing a high degree of group loyalty;
> technical competence.

## THE RETREAT FROM THE
## 'BEST STYLE OF SUPERVISION' APPROACH

In contrast to many spokesmen of the human relations school, Likert (1961) was aware of the many intervening factors that might affect the results of the new supervision techniques. He argued that apart from the attitudes and behaviour of the leaders one should also take into account:

> the relationship between the lower grades of supervisors and their own overseers, who might be unwilling to give up authoritarian, non-participative methods;
> the nature of work tasks;
> the composition of the group and its members' attitudes to organizational goals;
> the social environment in which the organization operates.

The number and scope of these additional factors cast some doubt upon the validity of the experiments in participative, democratic and employee-oriented techniques. Further experience reinforced these doubts, and contributes to a large extent to a growing criticism of the indiscriminate application of the 'new style of management' as advocated by McGregor and Likert.

In spite of enthusiastic support for the new style of management evinced by industrial sociologists and scientifically oriented managers, the practical results were rather disappointing. Social scientists were at first only too ready to believe that the failure of the new methods was primarily due to the ineptitude of the management in making use of them. Subsequent discussions, however, revealed the complexity of factors that accounted for the difficulties found when adopting the new supervisory style. Three main points were shown to be decisive in the effectiveness of supervision:

(1)  the low effectiveness of the supervisors' training courses;
(2)  the minor role played by improvements in leadership style as compared with technological and organization change;
(3)  new experiments that undermined the belief that there was any 'one best method' of supervision and leadership.

Fleishman (1956) reports that it was only immediately after training that positive changes in the behaviour of foremen were observed. After a time they returned to their old ways of dealing with people. He suggests that the attitudes of foremen depend much more on the supervisory style of their own superiors; those foremen whose supervisors are more considerate tend to behave in the same way, regardless of whether or not they have undergone any training in human relations.

Homans (1965) points out that the differences in productivity resulting from contrasting methods of supervision are relatively unimportant since they do not affect more than 15 per cent of total output. At the same time, considerably larger increases can be achieved by technological improvements and advances in materials and planning. Moreover, changing methods of work allow managers to reduce considerably the differences in output of different work groups.

There is also increasing evidence that the same supervisory style gives different results when applied to different work groups. Methods that are appropriate on the assembly line fail to produce positive results in small-batch production; the effective style of supervision with bank employees proves useless when applied to sales teams, etc.

Tannenbaum and Seashore (1964) attempt to explain the shortcomings of these studies by criticizing their approach of regarding problems of supervision in purely individualistic terms, that is, by concentrating on the attitudes of rank-and-file employees while ignoring the total industrial environment within which such teams operate. There is, moreover, evidence for a lack of a positive relationship between supervision, job satisfaction and productivity. It has therefore been assumed that the explanation consists in discovering the rules of effective supervision, but here again the emphasis was on small units while the working of the total system was disregarded. Thus, Tannenbaum and Seashore conclude:

Our present approach thus implies a more holistic conception of organizations. ... in some respects this applies to a sociological as well as a psychological definition of the problem. It has become unmistakably clear that the behaviour of people in organizations cannot effectively be studied from a psychological viewpoint, traditionally defined. [Tannenbaum and Seashore, 1964]

A very similar conclusion has been reached by Cartwright and Zander:

From the beginning it has been assumed that morale, group effectiveness, and leadership are all intimately related to one another. But as more and more research has been completed it has become increasingly clear that the relations among these different aspects of group life are exceedingly complex. As is so often true, the accumulation of facts has revealed that simple formulations are inadequate. The belief that a high level of group effectiveness can be achieved simply by the provision of 'good' leaders, though still prevalent among many people concerned with the management of groups, now appears naive in the light of research findings. [Cartwright and Zander, 1960, p. 487]

And Golembiewski states the following:

Supporters of any all or nothing view have one thing in common: they will often be surprised to find that the research literature does not consistently support any one leadership style. The reason for this lies not in any failing of the research itself, but in the simple fact that there is no 'best' style. Indeed the question which kind of leadership should we use? prevents any useful answer. The question should be, rather, Which kind of leadership, when? [Golembiewski, 1961]

The conclusion from all this is that instead of looking for a general formula for the best method of supervision one should concentrate instead on the method of supervision best suited to the particular circumstances. Indeed, in the course of systematic research, several factors have been found to account for the effects of different styles of leadership:

*Personality factors*. Vroom points out that people who are more dependent and are pronounced authoritarian types themselves, have a preference for authoritarian leadership, while those who are independent in character are more effective when they are allowed to participate in decision-making (Vroom and Mann, 1960).

*Cultural factors*. In groups with well-established authoritarian patterns, authoritarian leaders seem to be much more effective than (other things being equal) in groups where democratic procedures form an established rule; some students of industry even argue that participative leadership may be inherently ineffective when applied to blue-collar workers (Centers and Bugental, 1966).

*The nature and structure of the task*. Where tasks are new and can be performed in many different ways, individual contributions are very important and the democratic style of leadership that encourages these contributions is fairly successful, but when tasks become established and routinized there is more scope for authoritarian and managerial power (Vroom and Mann, 1960). Vroom and Mann found that package handlers in a large company, who lacked independence in their work, were much more concerned with employee-centred supervision than truck-drivers and despatchers who worked in an individual and independent way and who were mostly satisfied with a production-centred and authoritarian approach.

*The attitudes of the members regarding the tasks, the personality of the supervisors, the nature of organizational goals, etc.* Blau and Scott suggest that 'supervisors whose approach is inconsistent with their disposition (i.e. normal mode of conduct)...are apparently less likely to command the loyalty of subordinates' (Blau and Scott, 1963, p. 163). This is the case with supervisors who primarily express loyalty to superiors rather than to their workers.

*The wider social context of supervisor–employee relationships.* Turner (1955) indicates that there is a greater degree of positive feeling between worker and foreman when interaction between them is frequent and includes informal contacts going beyond that necessary for the course of work.

*Situational factors.* There is plenty of evidence that in some circumstances, like, for instance, a crisis situation, people willingly accept authoritarian leadership that they would otherwise resent and oppose. An interesting example of this aspect is to be found in a study by Hamblin (1958), who examined the effects of crisis situations on the acceptability of a leader. He began his experiment with:

the centralisation hypothesis, based on Weber's concept of bureaucracy where influence may be more centralized in crisis than in non-crisis periods;

the replacement hypothesis, according to which every leader will be removed from power if he fails to cope successfully with any serious domestic or international crisis.

The experiment involved the before-and-after observations of twelve three-person groups in a crisis situation, and twelve more three-person groups in a control situation. The crisis was created by changing the rules of the game in which the groups were engaged in such a way that confusion and frustration arose as a result of unexpected and misleading manipulation. For each member of the group, the influence and acceptance ratio was measured by observing and reporting the number of his suggestions in group problem-solving that had been accepted by the group. The high influencers, that is, those whose influence was greatest, had more influence during periods of crisis than during periods of non-crisis. It was found, however, that if the observations were continued for a longer period of time the influence of persons who enjoyed high prestige at the start did not rise but, rather, tended to decrease. In other words, short-term observations seemed to support the centralization hypothesis while long-term observations refute it. The explanation is supplied by the replacement hypothesis. In periods of crisis, old leaders tend to be replaced by new ones when the members of the group find that the former leaders are unable to cope with the crisis situation.

## THE CONTINGENCY THEORY

To answer the question why there is no single best style of leadership, Fiedler's contingency theory (1969) challenges the human relations approach to leadership as being too exclusively oriented towards the leadership style without taking into account the intervening variables. Along with leadership traits, the nature of the task and positional power prove to be most important. Fiedler distinguishes two components of leadership: the *way* in which people achieve their leadership positions; and the *degree of success* they enjoy once they have acquired their status of leader.

In his earlier experiments Fiedler showed that psychologically distant leaders of task groups were more effective than the leaders who tended toward warmer, psychologically closer relations with their subordinates. He concluded that psychological distance seems to facilitate effective role relations with the emphasis on performance of the tasks. People who are personally uninvolved are more inclined to be professionally oriented, to follow the policy imposed by the top management and to see to effective implementation of board decisions. At the same time, the subordinates who feel most secure with their superiors do not pay much attention to their work and are less concerned with the well-being of the enterprise, and this indifference inevitably affects their performance.

At this point we should also ask why psychological distance might be relevant to team performance. The most plausible answer seems to be that we cannot adequately control and discipline people to whom we have strong emotional ties. If a man is emotionally dependent on another, he cannot afford to antagonise him since this might deprive him of the other man's support. Similarly, we can evaluate only those people objectively, and we can control only those, on whose goodwill we do not depend. [Fiedler, 1960, p. 596]

Fiedler's theory was based and tested on a series of field studies. This programme of research, spread over fifteen years, accounts for a whole range of factors that affect the performance of the supervisors. His studies contain two main findings. Firstly, he distinguishes between leaders who will tell people what to do and how to do it and those who are prepared to share their leadership responsibilities with the members of the group by involving them in the planning and execution of the tasks. In order to operationalize this concept of authoritarian and permissive (supportive) leadership he devised two simple tests. In one of them the individuals were required to think of all people with whom they had ever worked and then to describe the one person with whom they had most difficulty in working together — in other words, to depict their *least preferred co-worker* (LPC). In another test they were asked to characterize their most as well as their least preferred co-worker on a number of personality traits. The two tests proved to be highly correlated and could be used interchangeably. The relationship between these tests and authoritarianism—permissiveness was also close. An individual who described his least preferred co-worker in favourable terms (i.e. received a high LPC score) was most likely to be permissive and considerate, while the individual who tended to describe his least preferred co-worker in unfavourable terms (i.e. had a low LPC score) was found to be assertive and managing. The tests permitted leaders' behaviour to be ranged on a scale from permissiveness and passivity at one extreme, to strong control and activity at the other.

Secondly, the groups subject to examination were also studied in terms of their performance, but for methodological reasons the specific traits of the groups that were attributed to the particular tasks they were carrying out were randomized. The research consisted of comparing high and low performance groups in connection with the leadership style; but allowing for intervening factors could have explained why in some of the most effective groups leaders of the authoritarian type prevailed, whilst in others permissive leaders achieved better results. The explanation was found in what Fiedler referred to as the *favourability* of the environment. He realized that in situations that were either very favourable for the leader or very unfavourable, the best effects were achieved by high control and a great degree of activity on the part of the leader, whereas in situations that were moderately favourable for the leader a passive and permissive method of leadership was most effective.

|  | Success of the leader | |
| *Degree of favourability* | *Authoritarian* | *Permissive/supportive* |
| Very high | + | – |
| Medium | – | + |
| Low | + | – |

This simplified presentation does not do justice to the factors that determine, according to Fiedler, a greater or lesser degree of favourability. They depend upon (1) leader—members relations; (2) the structure of tasks, and (3) the organizational power of the leader.

(1) Leader—member relations depend on the attractiveness of the leader to his group members and on whether he is trusted and respected: one can assume that a leader who is personally more attractive wields more influence over the group than someone who is less popular. Personality traits thus play an important part in the behaviour of the leader. Interestingly enough, authoritarian leadership is very effective, both in situations where a leader is very unpopular and where he enjoys trust and respect.

(2) The task structure has been operationalized by Fiedler into four areas:

(i) decision verifiability — the degree to which the correctness of a decision can be objectively proved;
(ii) goal clarity — the task requirements being more or less explicitly stated and more or less known to the group;
(iii) goal path multiplicity — the degree to which there are many or few procedures available for performing the task;
(iv) solution specificity — the number of possible correct solutions.

The model also throws new light on phenomena which were rather difficult to fit into our usual ideas about measurement in social psychology. Why, for example, should groups differ so markedly in their performance on nearly parallel tasks? The model — and our data — show that the situation becomes easier for the leader as the group moves from the novel to already known group-task situations. The leaders who excel under relatively novel and therefore more difficult conditions are not necessarily those who excel under those which are more routine, or better known and therefore more favourable. Likewise, we find that different types of task structure require different types of leader behaviour...in business organisation...the routine operation tends to be well structured and calls for a managing, directive leadership. The situation becomes suddenly unstructured when a crisis occurs. Under these conditions the number of discussions, meetings, and conferences increases sharply so as to give everyone an opportunity to express his views. [Fiedler, 1960, pp. 549—50]

(3) Power is described by Fiedler in terms of the influence inherent in the formal position of the leader regardless of his personal relationships with the members. This power is determined by organizational factors: the right to promote and demote, to suspend, punish and remunerate. Authoritarian leadership proves to give best results in situations where the organizational power of the leader is either very high or very low: in the first case, subordinates accept his style as a self-evident necessity; in the second case, authoritarian style appears to be a means of compensating for a lack of organizational power.

## EXCHANGE THEORY

So far I have discussed factors accounting for more or less effective supervisory performance without much reference to the concept of power and interests. Organizational power appears in Fiedler's contingency theory, but it constitutes only one of the many elements in the supervisor—subordinate relationship.

A different approach is taken by those sociologists who look at supervisors in industry (and supervisors in general) mainly in terms of their organizational positions in the organizational power structure. It should be noted, however, that this power-related approach can be successfully applied to informal relationships between the leader and his followers provided we look at these relationships in terms of *exchange theory*. Gouldner (1960) defined reciprocity as 'the pattern of exchange through which the mutual dependence of people, brought about by the division of labour, is realised. Reciprocity, therefore, is a mutually gratifying pattern of exchanging goods and services'. Homans referred to the same phenomenon in an article under the significant title 'Social behavior as exchange' (1958).

A pioneering study on exchange theory was carried out by Pelz (1952), who started with the traditional assumptions of the human relations school and looked originally for connections between the human relations skill of foremen and workers' satisfaction. His investigations covered about 700 supervisors and 7,000 employees. Forty work groups classified as having high morale were compared with the same number of low morale groups. One would have expected that the supervisors of high morale groups would be rather employee-oriented — at least this was the assumption of the human relations approach — but this was not so. Pelz then drew a new distinction between those supervisors who had some influence with their superiors and those who had not, and divided the groups accordingly. He found that in those groups where the supervisor was influential and at the same time displayed skills in human relations there was much greater satisfaction than in groups where the foreman, although employee-oriented, had no influence whatsoever. By comparing the groups supervised by management-oriented supervisors with the groups directed by employee-oriented foremen, he found that the latter were even less popular if they had no influence with their superiors that they could use in their commitment to the workers.

Pelz's findings leave many unanswered questions, especially if we bear in mind that in some cases foremen, even if they are fairly influential, may be unable to change the negative characteristics of a job and would thus be regarded as being part of an oppressive system. We might also predict that so long as foremen are not given credit for those aspects of work situations that are most appreciated by the worker, and are not blamed for what is disliked, the attitudes of workers toward their foremen may well be neutral.

On the whole, however, it may be concluded that the influence of the foreman is regarded as an important factor by workers. Their skill in dealing with people should not mean that they display psychological empathy with the work force, but that they have a talent for negotiating and concluding deals that are satisfactory both to the workers and to the management. The limited power that the foreman has can be used in exchanging benefits granted by the management for concessions and contributions by the workforce.

In his study of bureaucracy, Blau points out that in the welfare agency he investigated:

The supervisor was to some extent subject to the control of his subordinates, because he depended on their co-operation. To discharge his responsibilities he had to maintain relationships with them that encouraged ready compliance with his requests. [Blau, 1955, pp. 168–9]

Blau notes that newly appointed supervisors were particularly responsive to group pressures because they were interested in establishing a cooperative relationship with their subordinates. Among other things, the supervisor permitted his subordinates to break many minor rules, which in turn enhanced the controlling power of the superiors.

By voluntarily relinquishing some of his prerogatives the supervisor created social obligations. His requests for co-operation when he could issue orders and his promises of future help, his toleration of agents, his references to his identification with them and his considerate manner — all these served to oblige agents to him....In fact the supervisor surrendered some of his immediate power in exchange for greater ultimate power. [Blau, 1955, p. 169]

Blau emphasizes, however, that the power inherent in the position of supervisors creates special dilemmas. He points out that the situation of an informal leader in a group is different from the position of an official supervisor who is placed *a priori* in a dominant status in comparison with his subordinates by having access to resources and institutional mechanisms giving him power over the others regardless of whether he is approved by them or not. It is this position of power that generates new contradictions:

Stable leadership rests on power over others and on their legitimating approval of that power. The dilemma of leadership is that the attainment of power and the attainment of social approval make somewhat incompatible demands on a person. To achieve power over others requires not only furnishing services that make them dependent but also remaining independent of any services they might offer in return. To legitimate a position of power and leadership, however, requires that a leader be concerned with earning the social approval of his followers, which means that he does not maintain a complete indifference to them. [Blau, 1955, p. 203]

A number of other studies illustrate and support the nature of the transaction between the supervisor and his subordinates. An example can be found in a study by Goodman and his associates (1977), in which they analyse the role of the foreman in the footwear industry with respect to workers' earnings. They point out that, because of the uncertain nature of demand, workers' earnings fluctuated and the foreman was able to mitigate this instability by allowing for some 'extras', allocating better jobs, etc. In return, workers were supposed to cooperate beyond the strict obligations of their employment contract. They would be willing, for instance, to be moved temporarily to another job to eliminate a bottleneck. The authors make the important point that these relationships could have ceased if the workers insisted on introducing strict rules regulating the procedures by which work was allocated and earnings established. As long as they abstained from doing so, there was considerable scope for the discretionary power of the foreman.

This last point brings us to the question of how far transactions can take place in situations where the foreman's discretionary power is very limited or non-existent. Gouldner's study (1960), to which I referred above, would suggest that increased bureaucratization contributes to the limitation of supervisory power: a foreman may not be *allowed* to apply 'indulgency patterns', and when he makes use of his formal powers the workers know their rights and are able to use them against the decisions of the supervisors.

A situation in which workers are in a position to 'do favours' for supervisors who can only reciprocate by a tolerant attitude towards breaking the rules has been described by Bensman and Gerver (1963) in their study of crime and punishment in a factory: here the foreman had to tolerate the use of taps that were officially forbidden while at the same time keeping an eye on the offenders so as to prevent more serious breaches of discipline. He had to operate, as the authors point out, at the boundaries of formal and informal in the organization — a situation known to those who are familiar with work activity in the communist countries where officially illegal but nevertheless tolerated practices are common.

In the light of these studies, the picture of the relationships between subordinates and supervisors has been seriously modified. On the basis of empirical observations it is clear that, even within the area of formal supervisory rights to give orders and the formal obligation of subordinates to obey, a wide range of options exists. The novelty of this approach consists in looking at leadership in terms of transactions between the leader and his followers or between the supervisor and the supervised. These transactions are based on power relationships, on the one hand, and on exchange processes on the other.

In terms of exchange theory we can explain many of the empirical findings I have discussed earlier. It seems that in situations where the nature of tasks imposes an authoritarian style of supervision, the workers may be willing to accept it if the tasks they perform are important enough for them, so that they sacrifice their immediate interests for a better work performance by being submissive and obedient. It is only when the tasks are not seen as relevant for their interests that they are inclined to trade their cooperation for minor or major concessions from their supervisors. The transactions between the foreman and the workers based on deliberate concessions on the part of the foreman do not necessarily generate the kind of psychological dependence and submission that occur when the leadership is charismatic. What really matters is a sense of social obligation on the part of the workers towards their superior, so that the foreman/worker relationship is not limited to a series of separate deals but creates social bonds and permanent commitments making the foreman's demands acceptable for other than pragmatic reasons.

In any relationship based on exchange the interests of the two parties are to some degree opposed: the supervisor is always interested in increasing the scope of his discretionary power so as to be able to trade it with his employees; the workers, on the other hand, are interested in increasing their own discretionary power while approving any limitation of the resources at the disposal of the foreman, who then becomes more dependent upon his workers and more willing to accept their terms. In many cases, the resulting conflicts lead the workers and supervisors to depersonalize the power of the managerial staff by imposing general rules and regulations defining in very precise terms the duties and rights of workers and the sanctions for breaking them. The foremen may find this development convenient because they can then give up personal strategies and concentrate on the tasks. To the workers, on the other hand, bureaucratic rules give a feeling of independence from their immediate supervisors, who are prevented from granting favours and hence are deprived of some of their personal power over their subordinates. This trend is regarded by many of those studying industrial relations as being one manifestation of the growth of bureaucracy in industry.

## AUTHORITY OF POSITION AND
## AUTHORITY OF LEADERSHIP

Since Barnard (1956) made the important distinction between authority of position and authority of leadership, more and more attention is being paid to the impact of the power and authority structure on supervisory roles.

One overriding impression conveyed by surveying the literature of the 1960s, in contrast with the preceding two decades, is the re-direction of interest in leadership toward processes such as power and authority relationships. [Hollander and Julian, 1971, p. 515]

Etzioni (1964), who analyses the informal patterns in different types of organizations, makes an important distinction between what he calls officers, formal leaders and informal leaders. Officers are those who are in power and exclusively depend upon it in their relations with their subordinates, without any need for personal influence. Informal leaders were those who are deprived of any organizational power and whose position is determined only by the consensus of their followers. Formal leaders are correspondingly those who combine organizational authority with personal influence.

| Coercive organizations | Utilitarian organizations | Normative organizations |
|---|---|---|
| Officers vs Informal leaders — expressive — instrumental | Officers + Expressive informal leaders | Formal leaders |

*Source*: Based on Etzioni (1964) p. 91.

FIGURE 5.1 *Authority structures in different organizations*

Etzioni argues that in different types of organization different combinations of the authority structure take place, the typical configurations being shown in Figure 5.1. (According to Parsons every collectivity must fulfil two instrumental needs of input and allocation of resources and two expressive needs of social and normative integration; hence the concepts of instrumental and expressive leaders — see Etzioni, 1964, p. 91.) Etzioni argues that dual systems of supervision and leadership are mainly the result of the disparity between organizational *goals* and the *interests* of the lower members. In prisons and other coercive organizations, the officers have little to offer so far as the basic goals of the inmates are concerned. The prisoners pursue their interests despite and against formal prison regulations, which makes both the expressive and instrumental informal leadership very important. In normative organizations, a reverse situation arises. Once informal leaders prove influential and able to command support among the rank and file, they can quite easily be absorbed into the formal authority structure, either by being elected or by being co-opted by the governing body. Industrial enterprises are neither fully coercive nor can they rely upon moral commitment. The employees cooperate with management on an instrumental basis, trying to maximize their benefits within the boundaries of a contractual work relationship. As Etzioni states:

Control in utilitarian organizations is more evenly divided among organizational officials, formal leaders, and informal leaders of the employees. Moreoever, the main concern of these organizations is with the instrumental control of matters such as production and efficiency, and not with control of relations and norms established by the workers, so long as these do not adversely affect the instrumental activities. The particular leadership pattern that evolves depends largely on the relative degree of alienation or commitment of the employees. In industries where the workers are extremely alienated, their informal leaders, whether 'old hands' or union stewards, tend to control most of the expressive activities and a number of instrumental ones. In such factories the foreman and higher-ranking supervisors, even if they wish to participate, are excluded from worker social relations, and the workers set the norms which determine what is considered a proper day's work. ... In factories where the workers are less alienated, and in white collar organizations, the formal leadership exerts considerably more control, especially over instrumental activities. [Etzioni, 1964, pp. 66–7]

Etzioni's analysis brings home the obvious truth that different power and authority structures result in different forms of organizational compliance, and subsequently in differing relationships between supervisors and subordinates. According to this analysis a foreman is part of the authority system, recognized by the employees and accepted as entitled to give orders within his sphere of duties. Very much as in the classical approach, the position of the foreman can be taken for granted on the basis of contractual obligations that give the employee wages and other remunerations in exchange for his cooperation and willing obedience.

In contrast to the traditional school of management, however, this analysis assumes that this calculative approach has its limits: a 'generalized' consensus applies only to a certain area of 'tolerance' within which the employee is prepared to put up with his supervisor's wishes. Neither the boundaries of this area of tolerance nor the consensus to obey are established once and for all, but will change according to the circumstances. In an alienating situation the employees will regard their supervisor more like the enemy than a legitimate leader. Similarly the state of the external labour market and individual possibilities of finding another job can affect the endurance with which an employee is prepared to follow his foreman's wishes. And, finally the work-place consensus is subject to negotiation; trade unions play a major part in the determination of limits upon the managements' right to make decisions concerning different aspects of workers' jobs.

Supervisors who are aware of *their* rights, on the one hand, and of the level of tolerance of the *workers* on the other hand, will operate in such a way as to make balanced decisions. Once they trespass the accepted boundaries, open conflicts arise that may in some cases lead to the establishment of new boundaries but that may also endanger and weaken the position of the supervisor.

## SUBSTANCE VERSUS STYLE

In most of the studies to which I have so far referred, supervision is investigated and interpreted in terms of leadership functions, that is, from the point of view of the psychological influence exercised by the supervisor over his subordinates. The emphasis is on the leadership *style*, the progress of research being marked by the disclosure of various factors that lead to the promotion of one or other more effective leadership style.

It should be noted, however, that supervision implies more than *motivating* people in their performance. Organizational functions, coordination of dispersed efforts into a working whole, prevention of disturbances that may affect the work flow, diffusing conflicts by coping with the situations that generate them — all this belongs to what has rightly been called the *substance* of supervision as opposed to the supervisory style (Gellerman, 1976).

The substance of supervision depends to a great extent on the nature of tasks. An important analysis of the relationship between technology and supervisory activity has been given by Goldthorpe (1959). He describes the changing functions of supervision in the mining industry by comparing the pre-mechanization or 'hand-got' system in the nineteenth and in the early twentieth centuries, the partially mechanized or 'conventional' production, and the fully mechanized system of coal mining. Each technological stage had its own form of supervision.

An assembly line is another example of a semi-automated system in which the conveyor imposes the pace of work, directs the sequence of using materials and tools and determines the output, without much intervention from the foreman. At the same time, as Blau and Scott point out, new responsibilities for supervisors arise. Because of increased absenteeism and labour turnover they have to train new workers, obtain replacements, provide tools and watch closely the supply of materials; they also have to ensure the proper quality of products (Blau and Scott, 1963, pp. 177–8). The pioneering work of Walker and Guest (1952) enables us to grasp the complexity of tasks carried out by the foreman, which include: the distribution of activities in different fields like quality, walk progress, personnel administration, etc.; the types of activity performed by foremen (talking, walking, watching, manipulating, etc.); and the foreman's topic of conversation with other people including workers, other foremen and superiors. All these factors may reflect to some extent individual personality traits and individual preferences and techniques of work, but they do appear to be strongly determined by technological and organizational requirements. Similarly,, the time spent by foremen in conversation with their employees will depend in part on the number of employees under them. The span of control in various industries varies.

There is also evidence that organizational setting affects the substance of supervisory performance in terms of the time and effort required from the supervisors for different tasks. A pioneering study by Guest (1964) gives a detailed account of what the foremen on the shop floor really do. The average amount of time spent by them on different tasks is shown in Table 5.1. The foremen's contacts with other people were very wide as they dealt not only with workers but also with other foremen and superiors, so that of the time spent keeping in touch with other people the foreman's subordinates kept him busy 6.4 per cent of the time – the contacts being usually very brief, often interrupted and in many cases limited to one or two workers to the exclusion of the rest. A general picture of the foreman's activities is shown in Table 5.2. The conclusion drawn is that:

...the profile of time distribution is only a partial reflection of a man's ability, experience and training, Equally important are the unpredictable operational factors, the things a foreman must face, minute by minute, which dictate how he allocates his time. Even the 'best' foreman, when faced with absenteeism, mechanical problems, new operators, schedule changes or material shortages, had to devote large segments of his time to this particular problem on a given day and at the expense of other important supervisory duties. The best selection and training techniques can hardly be expected to pay off, if the conditions of the job make it impossible for a foreman to discharge at all times the full scope of his responsibilities. [Guest, 1964, p. 178]

TABLE 5.1
AVERAGE TIME SPENT BY FOREMEN ON DIFFERENT TASKS

| Topic | % of time |
|---|---|
| Quality | 18.2 |
| Work progress | 13.2 |
| Personnel administration | 11.2 |
| Personal relations and other non-job-related topics | 10.2 |
| Foreman's performance of an operation | 8.1 |
| Tools, jigs, fixtures | 8.1 |
| Materials | 8.0 |
| Employee job performance | 7.6 |
| Production schedule | 5.2 |
| Grievances | 2.0 |
| Injury, illness | 1.2 |
| Housekeeping | 0.5 |
| Work standards | 0.4 |
| Safety | 0.2 |
| Meeting | 0.1 |
| Miscellaneous | 2.4 |
| Topic unknown | 2.4 |

*Source*: Guest (1964) p. 176.

TABLE 5.2
GENERAL PICTURE OF THE FOREMAN'S ACTIVITIES

| % of time | Activity |
|---|---|
| 46.6 | Talks |
| 20.9 | Looks |
| 9.6 | Manipulates |
| 6.9 | Walks |
| 16.0 | Carries, reads, telephones, writes, stands, signals, listens, shows and sits |

*Source*: Guest (1964) p. 177.

Technology and the way work is organized determine the substance of supervision not only in terms of actual tasks and the timetable of the foreman, but also through the number of people he has to supervise. One of the most striking characteristics of mass production is the great span of control — often extending to more than fifty people. In an English sample studied by Woodward (1965, p. 69), the relationship between technology and numbers under a foreman's control was:

| Unit operations: | 10—60 | median 23 |
|---|---|---|
| Mass production: | 11—90 | median 49 |
| Process operations: | 10—40 | median 13 |

In an American survey, however, these striking differences did not appear, which indicates that the relationship between technology and the span of control varies (Zwerman, 1970, p. 69).

In conclusion, it can be said that in earlier studies little distinction was made between personality traits of supervisors and the institutional features of their position. In other words, the emphasis was laid on the way the foreman — as an actor — interprets and plays his role. Not much attention was paid to the requirements or components of his role *imposed upon him* by the nature of the tasks he had to accomplish and the circumstances in which he operated. These studies mark only the beginning of sociological research into supervision. In contrast to the impressive research in leadership carried out by social psychologists, the sociological approach is relatively undeveloped. However, it is only by combining psychological explanations and small-group research with wider studies of organizational and social factors that we can get a better understanding of the role of supervisors in industry.

The new perspective on supervision in industry does not deny the possibility of improving the supervisory style, but at the same time it helps us to understand that improvements will depend to a large extent on a range of factors affecting the supervisor—subordinate relationship. These include:

the *organisational structure* within which supervisory tasks are carried out;

the *nature of the tasks* performed by the supervisor and the relative weight of the possible communications with the work force in his daily schedule;

the *scope of discretionary power* of the supervisor, and the possibility of fair transactions between him and his subordinates;

the *extent* to which the situation is favourable or unfavourable for the supervisor, including his *acceptance* by the subordinates, the nature of the tasks and the organizational control he can exercise.

This multitude of factors means that in many cases adjustments to the supervisory role may be less effective than organizational changes, the impact of which may be more important than the given style of leadership. Reducing alienating work pressures, redefining supervisors' duties, reorganizing the work flow, increasing or decreasing the supervisors' discretionary control, changing the structure of tasks or even changing the composition of the working group, can all result in raising the effective performance of supervisors.

A new approach consists not so much in supplying foremen with some ready-made formula of how they should operate, but rather in allowing them to understand the situations they are dealing with and the possible responses and reactions of the people they have to supervise, so that they can formulate their own diagnoses of the problems they face. It is up to them to use those means at their disposal that they find best suited both to the circumstances and to their own abilities in handling them. It is important to remember that industrial sociology *does not supply ready-made formulae*; but it *helps us to understand* the organizational constraints, the impact of the composition and morale of the group on the leader's performance, the likely effects of various styles of supervision and the transactions that can take place on the shop floor. As far as higher management is concerned, it plays an important part in granting to supervisors the means of organizational control through defining their roles by sanctions, regulations and the exertion of social pressures upon them.

# CHAPTER 6

# Managerialism

## THE DEVELOPMENT OF CORPORATE MANAGEMENT

The growing interest in the sociology of industrial management is clearly connected with the increasing size and importance of modern corporations. Both Adam Smith and Karl Marx, who dealt with the capitalist economy at a relatively early stage of its history, noticed the development of corporate management based on the division of ownership and control. As Marx wrote:

...Transformation of the actually functioning capitalist into a mere manager, administrator of other people's capital, and of the owner of capital into a mere owner, a mere money-capitalist. Even if the dividends which they receive include the interest and the profit of enterprise, i.e. the total profit (for the salary of the manager is, or should be, simply the wage of a specific type of skilled labour, whose price is regulated in the labour market like that of any other labour), this total profit is henceforth received only in the form of interest, i.e. as mere compensation for owning capital that now is entirely divorced from the function in the actual process of reproduction, just as this function in the person of the manager is divorced from owner-ship of capital. ... It is private production without the control of private property. [Marx, 1962, pp. 427 and 429]

An account of the changing nature of business administration in the modern economy was given by Weber (1947, 1968) in his analysis of bureaucracy, which, in his view, incorporates the spirit of rationality. A firmly established hierarchy, governed by rules and regulations, the importance of written documents, training of managers, full-time employment of administrators, formal examinations as pre-conditions of entry into employment and promotion based on seniority — these are for Weber the characteristic features of bureaucratic organizations. Weber contrasted bureaucratic management with administration carried out by laymen on a part-time basis. He emphasized that the bureau-cratic order brought about an unprecedented increase in precision, speed, continuity, know-how, reduction of friction and reliability.

Further studies have explored the issues raised by Marx and Weber.

Some writers have concentrated on the issue of capitalism in which managers have replaced capitalists, while others study the organizational structures of the new monopolies and oligopolies. In 1919, Rathenau wrote of the large German corporation:

No one is a permanent owner. The composition of the thousandfold complex which functions as lord of the undertaking is in a state of flux...This condition of things signifies that ownership has been depersonalized...The depersonalization of ownership simultaneously implies the objectification of the thing owned. The claims to ownership are subdivided in such a fashion, and are so mobile, that the enterprise assumes an independent life, as if it belonged to no one; it takes an objective existence, such as in earlier days was embodied only in state and church, in a municipal corporation, in the life of a guild or a religious order...The depersonalization of ownership, the objectification of enterprise, the detachment of property from the possessor, leads to a point where the enterprise becomes transformed into an institution which resembles the state in character. [Quoted in Berle & Means, 1968, p. 309]

Berle and Means' theory of corporate management (1932) was an important contribution to the study of business administration. In their book they analysed the development of joint stock corporations, drawing attention to the fact that the growth in the number of shareholders, with the consequent fragmentation of shareholders as a group, increased the influence of company managers. Separation of ownership and control leads to the concentration of power in the hands of the business administrators, whom the authors labelled 'the new princes'. This new economic structure is no longer individualistic and based on private property; most enterprises operate as collectivities, even if the process of collectivization is not carried out by the state. Management-controlled corporations are the dominant feature of the new system, as opposed to the owner-controlled firms that dominated the industrial scene in the nineteenth century.

Further development of large-scale corporations fully corroborates Berle and Means' theory. In an American study, Larner reported that 84 per cent of the 200 largest non-financial organizations, and 70 per cent of the next 300, are controlled by managers rather than by owners (see Berg, 1979, p. 145). Similar trends have been observed in Western Europe, and even in Great Britain, which was regarded by many as a stronghold of small firms, large-scale organizations ruled by managers dominate economic life. The nature of this transformation is subject to many interpretations. While some declare that the separation of ownership and control heralds an era of post-capitalist society (Dahrendorf), and brings to power a new managerial class (Burnham), others tend to emphasize that managerial control is carried out according to the rules and characteristics of capitalist market economy and does not in fact erode the power of private capital in society (see Nichols, 1969).

## POWER IN LARGE CORPORATIONS

The power structure in large-scale corporations is normally discussed in terms of three different nuclei of power: the stockholders (either individuals or corporate); the boards of directors, which act as the elected representatives of the stockholders; and the managers, who are elected by the board of directors and function within limits approved by the board.

In theory, the shareholders retain ultimate power over the board of directors and indirectly over the management. However, an important distinction must be made between small shareholders, who own the bulk of the shares and whose impact on company affairs is illusory, and the large shareholders, who exercise considerable influence even if they control only a minority of total shares (in this group, fiduciary institutions play a major part).

The limited role played by the rank-and-file shareholders is the inevitable outcome of several factors, among which the following are most important:

the huge number of small shareholders;

the institution of proxy-voting;

the lack of experience of ordinary people of business matters and inadequate information on what is really going on inside the corporation;

the diffusion of share ownership by individuals between many firms and institutions, which makes it very difficult for the share owner to follow the development of each of the companies whose shares he possesses.

On the other hand, the influence of the large shareholders has increased (because of the same factors) out of proportion to the number of shares they control. Banks, insurance companies and pension funds that hold stocks have both business expertise and access to inside information, and can take full advantage of concentrated voting power as opposed to the disparate voting of small investors. It should also be noted that in many companies there is a division between voting and non-voting shares, with the non-voting shareholders being effectively disenfranchised, whilst the voting shareholders are often members of the family that originally owned, but now controls, the enterprise.

Penrose has demonstrated that, on a purely mathematical basis, the more indifferent is the electorate, the smaller need be the minority determined to enforce its will by block voting.

If a committee or electorate consists of two sections, a 'resolute' bloc and an 'indifferent' random voting group, a small resolute group of people, who always vote together can exercise a surprisingly powerful control over the whole committee. Thus, three resolute votes can control a committee of twenty-three to the same extent that one vote can control a committee of three. Furthermore, a bloc of twenty-three could control, again to the same extent, an electorate of over 1,000.... These blocs have about a 75% chance of carrying the decision in their respective electorates, but, by increasing the size of the resolute bloc, any specific degree of control can be obtained. Blocs three times as great as those mentioned would carry the decisions they desired in nearly 96% of the situations encountered. [Penrose, 1946, p. 54]

The marginal role played by stockholders is best reflected in the composition of corporate capital expenditure. Between 1946 and 1953, out of 150 billion dollars spent in the USA for this purpose, 64 per cent came from internal sources, that is, funds that had been accumulated but not distributed as dividends; a further 18 per cent was raised by current borrowing, while only 12 per cent was raised by the issue of bonds and notes, and of this only one-third was supplied by the issue of stock (Berle, 1954, pp. 37–9). It is argued that this availability of capital protects the corporation from outside interference and that it is when there are no retained earnings to be used that management autonomy is threatened and the stockholders can exercise their power (Galbraith, 1971, pp. 77–85).

Management is also protected from outside interference through the complexity of its financial and technological decisions, by the importance of long-term planning, and by the secrecy surrounding many aspects of industrial and marketing activity. Galbraith refers to a 'corporate liturgy' that is used to lull the board of directors, and even more so the stockholders, into a feeling of power, whereas they are, in reality, manipulated into accepting decisions made on their behalf. The annual meeting of the large American corporation is, he argues, the most elaborate exercise in popular illusion.

## MANAGERIAL CAPITALISM

The separation of ownership and control raises the important issue of the goals of the business enterprise. It can easily be assumed that once family ownership is replaced by corporate ownership the profit motive no longer plays the same role; some observers even go so far as to argue that it disappears altogether. Others claim that we have a situation of 'capitalism without capitalists', that is, a system in which the market economy enforces profitability upon management despite any other objectives they may have.

An indicative study of the impact of the separation of ownership and control on business performance is that by Monsen, Chin and Cooley (1968). They assume that 'the interest of owner controlled firms is more coincident with that of owners' profit maximisation... than is the interest of management controlled firms'. They show that in the years 1952—1963 the thirty-six owner-controlled firms in their sample had a ratio of net income to net worth (return on owners' equity) in the average range of 12.8 per cent, while in the thirty-six management-controlled firms in the same industries, the corresponding ratio was only 7.3 per cent. They summarized their analysis as follows:

This ratio measures the effects of management's efforts to provide a return on the owners' investment...Since among owner controlled firms the ratio of net income to net worth achieved a level 75% higher than among management controlled firms, it appears that the presence of a powerful owner group does produce an appreciable increase of management attention to owner interests. [Monsen, Chin and Cooley, 1968]

The conviction that profit motives give way to other organizational objectives is reinforced by the argument that large-scale corporations can secure high profits by exploiting a monopolistic position in the market, an argument that can apply to both nationalized industries and large private corporations (Carre, 1964).

Numerous studies in decision-making point to the existence of non-profit motives in the strategies of corporate management that are not necessarily compatible with profit maximization: objectives like empire building, control of the market, responsibility to consumers, long-term security and innovative experiments (Stewart, 1979, pp. 80—90). Gordon (1961) asserts that in large corporations delegation of authority means that the professional needs of employees, pressures from non-managerial groups and purely scholarly interests may influence decision-making processes. Gordon points out that, while attempting to secure profits expected by the shareholders, managers are also concerned with other factors, such as their own security, the impact of their decisions on their authority, the firm's growth and the needs of employees. There is also a decrease in the willingness to take risks: security can come before profits. Salaried managers are more interested in long-term growth, and this would appear to be what the larger companies offer. One would think that it is just this type of policy that is most attractive to most institutional and private investors. It is also possible that the managements of larger companies are more, rather than less, sensitive to the stock market and clearly, from their point of view, there is good reason for seeking compromise. There is still little inter-firm mobility at the highest levels and top executives cannot afford to be tainted by failure.

These findings do not remain unchallenged. Larner (1970) points out, for instance, that profits still appear to be the key variable determining the level of executive remuneration in large corporations. He does not deny that managers do not participate directly in firms' profits, but claims that executives' remuneration varies according to their diligence in pursuing the interests of the shareholders as expressed in profits and high dividends. Similarly, Katona argues that managers identify themselves so completely with their companies that maximization of company profits becomes their most important motive (Katona, 1951, p. 197).

A more comprehensive view of profit motives is put forward by those who regard profits as one of many factors affecting managerial decisions, and who distinguish between short- and long-range maximization of profits. In the latter case the building up of an industrial empire or the establishment of monopoly in a. given market may over time prove more beneficial in terms of profits than shorter-term policies. Many authors point out that managers of big companies are prepared to sacrifice profits when it comes to increasing the power of the company, building up its prestige and stabilizing the market. In the fight for survival, short- and long-run interests are evaluated: what is sought in the first place is control over the environment, which in the long run secures both stability and profitability, but it is also pursued for the sake of power itself. Marris (1964) argues that various features that have a positive value for managers — like salary, power, status, profits, turnover, capital, share of market and public image — are all strongly correlated with the size of the firm. Given the general preference of managers to advance within their firms rather than change them, they are therefore motivated primarily toward the growth of their enterprises, especially growth by diversification of activities. The pursuit of 'growth', however, is limited in Marris' model by the managers' desire for a reasonable degree of security — particularly security against collective dismissal from their jobs through a stockholders' 'raid'. To forestall the possibilities of such a 'raid', managers need to keep the rate of return on productive assets high and to avoid excessive retention of profits and high liquidity. In Marris' model, once a satisfactory degree of security vis-à-vis shareholders has been achieved, managers are likely to aim towards maximizing growth. Growth is therefore a function of the level of diversification and average profit margins.

In summary, one can say that the maximization of profits cannot be dismissed out of hand, although some qualification is needed where the interests of the owners (stockholders) and the managers are not identical. The stockholders expect a steady income through dividends and gradual appreciation of the market price of the stock, while managers' self-interest consists of maximizing the monetary and non-monetary benefits of their jobs. A *realistic* theory of managerial behaviour needs to consider this aspect of managerial motivation (Monsen and Downs, 1965). Monsen and Downs' approach is probably the most convincing, being based on the dualism of interests involved in running a company. They acknowledge the variety of interests among managers themselves (top, middle and lower management) and help us to understand that the divergence of goals does not necessarily eliminate the pursuit of profits by large firms.

An interesting contribution to this discussion was made by Nichols on the basis of data collected in a British city. Sixty-five directors and senior managers in fifteen companies were interviewed on various topics (redundancy, the role of the businessman in public life, giving information to employees) and views were elicited on the goals of companies:

Each of the three statements within each group was designed to fit on one of three broad conceptions about the role of business and the businessman. We termed these: 'Laisser-Faire' [i.e., attitudes corresponding to the traditional entrepreneurial philosophy]...'Long-term Company Interest' and...'Social Responsibility...'. [Nichols, 1969, p. 166]

The distribution of the attitudes of the respondents is shown in Table 6.1.

TABLE 6.1

THE DISTRIBUTION OF CHOICES BETWEEN THREE IDEOLOGICAL
FRAMES OF REFERENCE

| Ideological set | % of choices | Number of choices |
|---|---|---|
| Laisser-faire | 10.4 | 27 |
| Company interest | 57.3 | 149 |
| Social responsibility | 32.3 | 84 |
| Total | 100.0 | 260 |

*Source*: Nichols (1969) p. 169.

Nichols' further findings suggest that, in Britain, many directors have considerable holdings in the stock of large corporations. They are, according to Nichols, neither 'technocrats' nor 'professionals' in the sense used by the managerial theorists. He argues that on balance the interests of the shareholders are pretty well served, although he assumes that modern corporate leaders are more likely to be interested in steady growth than in policies of out-and-out profit maximization.

## THE STYLE OF MANAGEMENT

Among the many characteristics of bureaucracy identified by Weber, hierarchy and the wide use of formal rules and regulations seem to be the most relevant when considering industrial enterprises.

Those who study mass production techniques are unanimous in emphasizing the bureaucratization of management associated with this type of technology. The development of industries based on newer technologies like electronics, however, does cast doubt on the idea of a universality of bureaucratic patterns in industry. Similarly, present trends towards the decentralization of decision-making in many large-scale corporations lead some scholars to believe that a bureaucratic model of industry is obsolete.

A study of different styles of industrial management carried out by Burns and Stalker (1961) throws new light on the issue. They identify two styles of management; one, which they call mechanistic, can be regarded as a replica of the Weberian model of bureaucracy.

In mechanistic systems the problems and tasks facing the concern as a whole are broken down into specialisms. Each individual pursues his tasks as something distinct from the real tasks of the concern as a whole. 'Somebody at the top' is responsible for seeing to its relevance. The technical methods, duties and powers attached to each functional role are precisely defined. Interaction within management tends to be vertical, i.e., between superior and subordinate. Operations and working behaviour are governed by instructions and decisions issued by superiors. This command hierarchy is maintained by the implicit assumption that all knowledge about the situation of the firm and its tasks is, or should be, available only to the head of the firm. Management...operates a simple control system, with information flowing up through a succession of filters, and decisions and instructions flowing downwards through a succession of amplifiers. [Burns and Stalker, 1961, p. 5]

This mechanistic style of management is contrasted with the organic style, which is based on quite different principles:

The organic form is appropriate to changing conditions, which give rise constantly to fresh problems and unforeseen requirements for action which cannot be broken down or distributed automatically arising from the functional roles defined within a hierarchic structure. [Burns and Stalker, 1961, p. 121]

The organic style of management largely denies a hierarchical, highly structured and rigidly subdivided decision-making body. It implies communication that conveys primarily information and advice, rather than instructions and decisions. It requires identification on the part of individuals with the organization's goals and not just a purely contractual relationship. It does not allow for rigid definition of individual tasks but requires the sharing of responsibility and continuous readjustments as situations arise. Expertise is more important than formal authority; commitment to the task is more valued than loyalty and obedience. All these and many other characteristics have been recognized by Burns and Stalker as being associated with work that defies routine, repetitiveness and predictability of the environment.

Burns (1958) shows clearly that neither the mechanistic nor the organic model can be considered on its own, either is more or less effective depending on the nature of the goals to be met. When the technology does not change and market conditions are relatively stable, mechanistic procedures and hierarchy seem more appropriate. In unstable conditions, on the other hand, when standardized responses cannot be devised and applied, the organic style of management proves most successful. Little wonder, therefore, that this style is favoured in industries subject to frequent change and operating in very unpredictable environments.

Similar results from inter-industry comparisons were observed by Woodward (1958, 1965). Dividing the firms under investigation into the mechanistically and organically managed (while some were regarded as 'mixed'), Woodward found that organic management prevailed among unit production and process production enterprises, while mechanistic management was the dominant feature of mass production.

There was a tendency of organic management systems to predominate in the production categories at the extremes of the technical scale while mechanistic systems predominated in the middle ranges. Clearcut definition of duties and responsibilities was characteristic of firms in the middle ranges, while flexible organisation with a high degree of delegation both of authority and of responsibility for decision making and with permissive and participative management was characteristic of firms at the extremes. [Woodward, 1965, p. 64]

Supportive data have been provided by Zwerman's study (1970), which replicated Woodward's research under American conditions (see Table 6.2).

A conceptual refinement of this type of analysis may be found in an article by Stinchcombe (1959). He shows that while mass production industries are based on a bureaucratic style of management, construction-type industries are based primarily on a professional labour force operating without a large bureaucratic management. He explains that general trends in industry consist primarily of using workers with specialized competence, rewarding the participants financially, and using contractual obligations as the basis of duties and responsibilities. On the other hand, characteristics more akin to the Weberian concept of bureaucracy — like the hierarchical system of authority, the administration acting as the basis for the communication system, and continuity of performance — will only appear in some industries because of the very nature of their technology and goals.

TABLE 6.2
PRODUCTION TECHNOLOGY AND TYPE OF MANAGEMENT SYSTEM
IN MINNEAPOLIS FIRMS

| Management system | Type of technology | | |
| | Unit and small-batch | Large-batch and mass | Process |
| --- | --- | --- | --- |
| Organic | 14 | 11 | 3 |
| Mechanical | 2 | 15 | 1 |
| Total | 16 | 26 | 4 |

*Source*: Zwerman (1970) p. 53.

Drucker (1963) goes further and claims that modern management needs to be primarily management by objectives. In other words, it must liberate itself from the traditional bureaucratic approach. He argues that the traditional style is unsuited to the new industrial conditions and must be replaced by a highly decentralized and flexible system of management. In this system the gap between operations and centres of decision-making is reduced to a minimum, and, if possible, there are separate innovative divisions based on team work within the enterprise.

These findings have been generalized by Lawrence and Lorsch (1967), who demonstrate that the nature of an organization is contingent upon its situation (the contingency theory). The external environment affects the differentiation between functions and the way these functions are integrated into a working whole. The more dynamic is the environment, the greater is the differentiation of tasks and the more complicated are the means for their integration (Simon, 1961).

## LIMITATIONS TO MANAGERIAL RATIONALITY

The 'classical' approach to management assumes a high degree of rationality manifesting itself in a unity of command and impersonality in managerial decision-making. These assumptions, corresponding to or derived from the Weberian model of bureaucracy, were gradually challenged by social scientists. What is postulated is a 'realistic' theory of administrative behaviour (Simon, 1961). If 'organizations are tools designed to achieve various goals', social scientists have demonstrated that these goals are 'multiple, conflicting, pursued in sequence, open to group bargaining, and in general, problematical, rather than obvious and given' (Perrow, 1970, p. 180). Managers differ from the economic man of classical economics. They bring into firms their own motives, expectations and ambitions; they form groups with conflicting aims; they struggle for power within the organizations that employ them; and they make decisions that are a far cry from the perfect rationality implied by most theories of decision-making. The new approach to organizational decision-making, which found its best expression in Simon's study, uses a different perspective on managerial activity, so that the sociology of management has become an integral part of the study of organizational decision-making.

The new approach has also been used by Cyert and March (1963) in their behavioural theory of the firm. They assume that there are no goals in managerial decision-making except those pursued by individuals in groups in the administrative and managerial process. Instead of treating business firms as strategic units, they put forward a model in which many groups in the firm and outside it participate in the shaping of goals pursued by the firm. Two basic principles are taken for granted:

(1) Goals are set by bargaining among the units of the coalition.
(2) Goals are pursued in large measure independently of one another.

On the whole, Cyert and March assume five main targets that are pursued simultaneously and often independently of each other by different groups within the firm; these are goals related to production, inventory, market, sales and profit. Which of these goals dominates at any one time depends not so much on objective priorities as on the balance of power between managerial groups within the corporation.

A similar approach has been adopted by Gross (1964) in his criticism of the idea that an iron law of oligarchy operates in business organizations. He challenges the view that big firms are rigid hierarchies in which decisions at lower levels simply reflect those taken at the top. He points out that even at divisional level there is the possibility of highly concentrated power, although this is invariably counter-balanced by power centres in other parts of the organization.

Among the bureaucrats the dispersion of power reaches its highest point. Here it is created by the very process of formal organization and delegation and augmented by the proliferation of informal groups, leaders and lines of communication. [Gross, 1964, vol. 1, p. 404]

Much attention has also been paid to cleavages between staff and line management caused by the division of labour and the diverging perspectives of staff officers, who function in an advisory capacity, and line managers, who are responsible for meeting production targets. Dalton (1959) was one of the first to point out the conflicts that may arise in staff and line relationships. He explains these conflicts by:

functional differences between the two groups;

differences in age, formal education, potential occupational calling and status group affiliations (staff officers are younger and have a wider education but a lower occupational potential; they also form a prestige-oriented group with distinctive dress and recreational inclinations).

need on the part of the members of the staff group to justify their existence in the firm;

fear among the line officers that staff members undermine their authority by the expansion of their influence and through well-financed research activity;

the informal requirement that aspirants to higher staff positions may only gain promotion with the approval of influential line executives.

As far as other factors limiting the rationality of managerial decision-making are concerned, much research has been carried out on the individual's attitudes and preferences that affect the responses of managers to organizational requirements. For instance. Dill (1965, p. 1086) identifies among middle management:

*Men 'on the ladder'*: they are prospective candidates for promotion and ostensibly aspire to the executive group, whose values they share. Companies vary in the extent to which they publicly identify those who hold 'crown prince' status, but informally the occupancy of certain positions, various rough age—status ratios and patterns of movement make the active candidates visible to other members of the organization.

*Men 'in limbo'*: those who once aspired to executive positions but, for various reasons, have given up hope and have to adapt themselves to an occupation with little prospect of further advancement.

*Men who function primarily as 'mercenaries'*: these are rather indifferent to organizational goals and are primarily concerned with professional values. Employees in this category include some of the most important contributors to the organization; legal advisers, engineers, research scientists, branch managers and the like.

Gross (1964, p. 392—402) provides a long list of diverging attitudes revealed in organizational studies:

task-oriented, technique-oriented and people-oriented;
nay-sayers and yea-sayers;
rule enforcers, rule-evaders and rule-blinkers;
the involved and the detached;
regulars, deviants and isolates;
newcomers and oldtimers;
climbers and stickers;
cosmopolitans and locals;
gentlemen, middlemen and integrators;
builders and consolidators;
thinkers and doers;
grandstand players and behind-the-scene players;
authoritarians, laissez-faires and democrats;
impersonals, personals and charismatics.

Rational decision-making in large-scale organizations is also inhibited by structural constraints. Empire-building and unrestrained growth are well-known organizational phenomena (Parkinson, 1958). A whole range of organizational dysfunctions has been revealed by empirical studies. The trained incapacity of professional managers, whose activities are confined to one area only and who lose touch and lack experience of other parts of organizational activity, and the displacement of organizational goals and unavoidable red tape are but a couple of examples of negative organizational side-effects that can occur in large firms and which are bound to affect managerial decision-making.

## CROSS-CULTURAL AND INTERNATIONAL COMPARISONS

A new insight into managerial activities is afforded by a comparison of managers in different societies. The features of European, as distinct from US, management have been discussed by Granick (1962). He points out that, in Europe, management is not regarded in an exclusive professional manner: in Germany, the ethos is of a sort of mythical feeling of 'calling' and loyalty to private entrepreneurship; in France, business is open primarily to intellectuals who are academically trained; in England, business seeks people of 'breadth and character'. Granick also notes that there are barriers to managerial advancement because of type of education, the middle-class origins of managers (although not necessarily so in Britain) and a reversed hierarchy of values, in which business does not come first or, as is the case in Britain, is even scorned by the culture.

Several studies have highlighted the peculiarities of the British managerial culture. This finds expression in the fact that little attention is paid to purely professional specialized training, as compared with the desire for business graduates in the USA. In Nichols' survey of UK directors, we find the following statement:

The striking feature is the relatively small proportion with a university degree and the high number who think that experience alone qualifies them for a directorship...The professional, academic man as yet plays a minor part in industry. [Nichols, 1969, p. 80]

Table 6.3 shows the proportion of directors without formal qualifications by size of company in Great Britain.

TABLE 6.3
PERCENTAGE OF DIRECTORS WITHOUT QUALIFICATIONS,
BY SIZE OF COMPANY

| Size of company (capital) £ | Directors without qualifications % |
|---|---|
| less than 50,000 | 67.57 |
| 50,000–100,000 | 66.58 |
| 100,000–250,000 | 62.76 |
| 250,000–500,000 | 56.03 |
| 500,000–1 million | 46.31 |
| 1 million–5 million | 50.79 |
| 5 million and more | 43.14 |

*Source*: Quoted by Nichols (1969) p. 81.

Differences between managers and their strategies in various countries are explained by Kerr and his associates (1973) by the different historical trajectories leading towards industrialization. Similarly, an interesting argument concerning the differences between British and Japanese industries has been given by Dore (1973), who points out that Japanese industry developed at a much more advanced stage of industrialization, and that this entailed a greater sophistication of managerial methods. Japan faced the necessity of supplementing market forces with control by large corporations, had to accept unions as a fact of life, adapted its industrial structure to the idea of equality of opportunity, and sought ways of securing employee participation in decision-making. All these characteristics are part of what Dore calls the latecomer effect.

Comparisons of the social origin of European and American business leaders are shown in Table 6.4. It is obvious that European business offers fewer opportunities for professional advancement than the United States, where those from the lower classes have more chance of overcoming social obstacles. Even so, the proportion of managers of lower-class origin is still surprisingly limited, despite specialized business educational opportunities. A convergence in the development of management has been noted by Kerr and his associates. They point out that, as all industrial societies advance, management becomes more professional and less authoritarian in its attitude and policy towards workers (Kerr *et al.*, 1973, p. 165). However, some authors find that differences in managerial values and attitudes follow not so much the level of industrialization as the cultural traditions (Harbison and Myers, 1960) and ethnic patterns.

TABLE 6.4
SOCIAL ORIGIN OF EUROPEAN AND AMERICAN BUSINESS LEADERS

| *Social class* | *United States* | | | | *Europe* |
| | *1900* | *1925* | *1950* | *1964* | *1968–1970* |
| | % | % | % | % | % |
| --- | --- | --- | --- | --- | --- |
| Lower class | 12 | 16 | 12 | 23 | 7 |
| Middle class | 42 | 48 | 52 | 66 | 18 |
| Upper class | 46 | 36 | 36 | 11 | 75 |

*Source*: Bettignies and Evans (1977) p. 279.

The evidence for or against a convergence theory as far as managerial style and attitudes are concerned is far from conclusive. Differences between the command economy and the market economy, between the Scandinavian type of welfare capitalism and the US business culture, and between the Western economy and the Japanese model of economy and society, do not exclude possible similarities between managers in large corporations, who become surprisingly alike in their business behaviour and corporate decision-making.

The least known, but perhaps the most relevant, aspect of the new problems of management is, however, posed by multinationals, which, for many reasons, have successfully avoided close scrutiny. Studies show that they are characterized by an even greater lack of account-ability, growth orientation and divorce of ownership from control (Barnet and Müller, 1975). At the same time, Berle's (1960) prediction that community control would replace the profit motive and the pressures of the market economy seems more remote than ever: the multinationals are examples of industrial and financial empires that have no commitment to either governments or national interests, so that their management has acquired the status of sovereign power-holders.

However, some suggest that multinationals nevertheless retain the dominant features of the mother country and perpetuate these features at the managerial level, as for instance with Japanese firms operating in the UK and employing a British labour force or American multinationals pursuing their activities in Southern Europe. It may be that the multinationals constitute the highest stage of the bureaucratic business civilization, and incorporate a managerial ethos uniformly throughout the world. The evidence is, however, on too inadequate a basis to generalize.

From what has been said, it follows that the modern corporate situation characterized as 'capitalism without capitalists' creates new problems of analysis as far as the functioning of industrial society is concerned. The classical theory of profit motive needs to be revised in view of the variety of targets to be met by large corporations in a new social environment. At the same time, the very scale of productive, administrative and commercial activity poses new problems for the mechanisms of decision-making. The model of bureaucratic rationality is thus challenged and revised. Simon and March's view seems most plausible: rationality is still present on an unprecedented scale but operates within several constraints. These are caused by motivational and cognitive factors that distort the process of rational decision-making and shape both the goals pursued by managers and their perspectives on the course of action to be adopted (March and Simon, 1958).

# CHAPTER 7

# The Changing Image
# of the Working Class

A preoccupation with the position of the working class was a distinctive feature of nineteenth-century England and many other West European countries. Social thinkers considering the emerging industrial order pointed almost unanimously to the plight of factory workers and the poverty of life in squalid urban conglomerations. Although this gloomy picture was widely accepted, there were differences with respect to causes, and remedies for, the evils of capitalist industrialization.

## THE CONCEPT OF THE WORKING CLASS

As Simmel has pointed out, the generalized concept of the worker or, using his term, 'the *generalized* worker', appears to be a product of a relatively long development in social thought and social vocabulary. People had been classified for centuries according to their trade, skills, social position, functions and sectors of employment. It was some time before, in the course of industrial development, wider aspects of the working man's life were identified and integrated into a comprehensive concept of the working class (Simmel, 1955, pp. 172–8).

It should be noted that in all discussions about workers in the nineteenth and early twentieth century, defining the working class was the least concern. The *visibility* of the workers in Western societies left little room for misgivings or doubts. Compared with peasants, bourgeoisie, white-collar workers or nobility, workers were easily identifiable. Their specific position with regard to other sections of the 'plebeians' or 'urban mob' was linked to the nature of their employment in factories, mills or mines. The attributes of their existence associated with their position within the occupational structure were also relatively simple: poverty; lack of property; dependence; exploitation; and conflict.

The concept of the *working poor* preceded that of the working class. St Thomas Aquinas informed us that 'wage earners were poor and earned their daily living from their labours'. From the fourteenth century, English statutes regarding labour referred to 'poor laboureres' and 'poor artisans'. Such terms as 'poor labourer', 'working

141

poor', 'industrious poor' and 'laborious poor' were widely used in eighteenth-century England. After 1770 the term 'the labouring poor' was most frequently used (Briefs, 1975, pp. 1–5). Even J. S. Mill who, in his *Principles of Political Economy*, spoke of the labouring people, labouring classes, the operative classes and the working classes, identified all these with the poor (Mill, 1970).

The concept of the proletariat, derived from the Latin *proletarius*, originally signified an individual belonging to the poorest class in Roman society. In contrast with the other Roman classes, proletarians had no *familia* (dependants, slaves and livestock); all they possessed were their children. Hence the concept of the proletarian in modern times as a man without property (Briefs, 1975, p. 55). Briefs also mentions Simon de Sismondi, who noted that, as distinct from the Roman proletarian who did not work but lived at the state's expense, the modern proletarian not only works but is deprived, without compensation, of a considerable part of the goods he produces. In the view of Bensen about

...workers who so far as concerns their livelihood, the amount of their earnings, and their continuance in gainful occupation, are dependent upon the arbitrary exercise of power by others...The fact that they vary greatly as to their income at any given time and also as to their social and cultural standing does not change their status as here conceived. [Bensen, 1847; quoted in Briefs, 1975, p. 65]

The factory worker's dependence, and the exploitation to which he was subject, inevitably gave rise to conflict. As Von Stein remarked: 'From a state in which capital and labour are in separate fields to a state on which they are in hostile camps, is but a step' (Von Stein in Briefs, 1975, p. 69).

Anticipating industrial unrest in Western Europe, many writers portrayed the modern proletarians as the Messiahs of contemporary society. The Hegelian Left emphasized the plight of labourers exposed to the oppressive force of industrialism and expected that their liberation would bring the salvation of mankind. Following this approach and developing it into a consistent revolutionary theory, Karl Marx elaborated the concept of the working class into a comprehensive theoretical category related to the nature of capitalist society. The exploration of laws of the capitalist economy became the focus of Marx's theory. Wages, the level of employment, fluctuation in demand for the labour force, working conditions — all these could be explained by reference to these laws, to which capitalists were just as subject as workers.

It was this last point that enabled Marx to elaborate his theory of the class struggle, a struggle based on the concept of a fundamental conflict of interest between the workers and the owners of capital. The profit-oriented endeavours of the capitalists (the owners of factories, mines, firms and corporations), who purchase labour power like any other commodity and who appropriate the surplus-value produced by it, are opposed by the 'proletarian economy', so that workers press their claims and fight for their implementation.

In the long term however, there appeared to be no way of removing the hardships associated with the capitalist economy other than by abolishing the private market economy. The proletariat's role is therefore changed from being involved in a purely economic struggle, with demands for partial reforms, to full-scale revolution. For Marx, the proletariat was at the very centre of world history. At the same time, as part of the structure of the capitalist society, the workers depended on its dynamics. Poverty and deprivation were attributes of the propertyless labour force, which was dominated by the inexorable logic of the capitalist economy. The same logic impelled the labour force towards increasing resistance to the encroachments of capital (Laski, 1954).

To summarize, having followed the development of the image of the working class, we can conclude that poverty, propertylessness, dependence, exploitation and conflict became the ingredients of the concept of the working class in nineteenth-century social thought. On the level of colloquial language, the word 'workers' was subsequently associated with the visible status characteristic of industrial manual labourers, i.e. reflected the most conspicuous features of the existence of the working class as contrasted with other classes and strata in modern societies.

## THE WORKERS AS THE PARIAHS OF MODERN SOCIETY: STUDIES IN POVERTY

Marx's study of capitalism was based mainly on the experiences of industrial development in Great Britain. Indeed, England was a classic example of Marx's thesis that the deprivation and exploitation of the working class resulted in growing class consciousness and class conflict. Nevertheless, the impact of Marx's doctrine in England was less than elsewhere and English workers proved a far cry from the role of Messiah he attributed to them. With the expanding economy in the years 1851–1873 — the period of Victorian prosperity — the policy of conciliation, which defied pessimistic views about the calamity of the capitalist economy, seemed credible. However, the last decades of the nineteenth century were again marked by depression, unemployment and poverty.

The best evidence of the workers' plight at the turn of the century is provided by the studies in poverty that are to this day an unsurpassed collation of facts. Works by Sidney Webb, Beatrice Potter-Webb and H. M. Hyndman followed those of Mayhew and preceded a series of impressive investigations by Charles Booth and Seebohm Rowntree.

Booth, a wealthy Liverpool shipowner, undertook his studies as a challenge to the revealing survey carried out by Hyndman who had demonstrated that at least one-quarter of the population were so underpaid that their wages were insufficient to keep them in reasonable health (Thompson and Yeo, 1971, p. 91). Regarding these findings as sensational and politically biased, Booth decided to check Hyndman's data by making a detailed investigation of the living conditions of London workers. His findings were presented in an impressive study of seventeen volumes published in London between 1889 and 1904. The study, carried out house by house, covered more than a million families in the East End and Central London; the rest of London was surveyed street by street. In addition to fieldwork, written sources were used — documents kept by school attendance officers in the East End of London, Poor Law statistics, police reports, etc.

Booth was the first to define poverty. 'My "poor"', he wrote, 'may be described as living under a struggle to obtain the necessaries of life and make both ends meet; while the "very poor" live in a state of chronic want' (Booth, 1902–3, Vol. I, p. 33). He established a qualitative standard of measurement — a 'poverty line' of 18–21 shillings a week for a medium-sized family (p. 33). According to his findings, 30.7 per cent (that is, almost one-third of the total population in London) were on or below the poverty line (Vol. II, p. 21), with a much larger proportion of paupers among the old and unemployed. Booth's major innovation was to reject the idea of poverty as caused by personal negligence and maladjustment, and to show that the workers were exposed to squalor and poverty by their very position in the labour market.

At about the same time, a study was published by Rowntree in which similar findings were reported. Rowntree, who carried out his investigations in the northern city of York in 1899, provided a more precise definition of poverty by distinguishing between what he called 'primary' and 'secondary' poverty (Rowntree, 1901, pp. 86–7). A family was regarded as living in 'primary' poverty when its total income was insufficient to provide it with the minimum necessary for maintaining physical efficiency. Families whose total earnings were sufficient to maintain their merely physical efficiency but were spending part of this necessary minimum on other things — either useful or wasteful — were considered to be living in a state of 'secondary' poverty. In his door-to-door survey, Rowntree found that 9.9 per cent of the total population of York lived in 'primary' poverty. This meant that, irrespective of how they spent their money, even the most disciplined workers in this group were unable to cover their basic expenses. Another 17.9 per cent were living in a state of 'secondary' poverty. Thus over 27 per cent of the population of York could be regarded as having insufficient incomes to cover their basic necessities (Rowntree, 1901, p. 298).

Both of these surveys contributed to changing current ideas about working-class poverty by showing that insufficient wages, unemployment and old age were the main causes of the destitution of working people, irrespective of personality or individual attitudes. As Bowley and Burnett-Hurst, the authors of another survey covering Northampton, Stanley, Reading and Warrington, stated:

Of all the causes of primary poverty which have been brought to our notice, low wages are by far the most important...to raise the wages of the worst-paid workers is the most pressing social task with which the country is confronted today. [Bowley and Burnett-Hurst, 1915, p. 42]

## THE WORKING CLASS AS A NEW SOCIAL AND POLITICAL FORCE IN WESTERN SOCIETIES

At the end of the nineteenth century the role of the worker was determined by the growing political strength of organized labour. The power of the trade unions in Western Europe and the emergence of political parties backed by the votes of working men have been acknowledged as a major feature of what later came to be called mass democracy, based on political equality and electoral reform. In England, the percentage of the population aged over 20 years eligible to vote changed as shown in Table 7.1. In 1914 English workers not only had their own political organization but also had their own representation in parliament. In countries like Germany and France the progress of the working-class movement was even more pronounced, with socialist ideology becoming a distinctive feature of the continental parties. The Russian Revolution opened a new period in the history of the industrial labour force. The workers were henceforth viewed with fear and apprehension by those with economic and political power.

TABLE 7.1
PERCENTAGE OF POPULATION OVER 20 ELIGIBLE TO VOTE,
ENGLAND, 1831–1928

|  | | |
|---|---|---|
| | 1831 | 5.0% |
| after | 1832 | 7.1% |
| " | 1867 | 16.4% |
| " | 1884 | 28.5% |
| " | 1918 | 74.0% |
| " | 1928 | 96.9% |

*Source*: Ryder and Silver (1977) p. 82.

The economic malaise of the inter-war period was accompanied by the growth of radical demands voiced by both Left and Right. In many continental countries the communists succeeded in building up mass support; at the same time, the fascists proclaimed holy war against left-wing labour movements. In England, the collapse of the General Strike in 1926 left the workers demoralized, while the Labour Party could record only moderate success in 1929, and was defeated decisively in the general election of 1931. Simultaneously, despite prolonged unemployment and sluggish economic growth, there was a marked improvement in the standard of living of the working class in comparison with the pre-war period.

The real income of the average working-class family was 37% higher in 1938 than it had been in 1913, and might have been expected to go on rising. But it was still not feasible for a working-class family to aspire to anything approaching the standards of the family of the middle-class salary-earner. The average salary-earner was not only spending more on what could be regarded as luxuries; he was also better clothed, better housed and better fed. Above all, he was economically more secure. Even the prosperous wage-earner was still insecure for both of the two most familiar reasons: first, he was much more likely, even in a prosperous trade, to risk being unemployed, and second, he had no full and guaranteed insurance against the causes which, apart from unemployment itself, might at various stages of his life force him close to or below the poverty line. [Runciman, 1967, pp. 76–7]

To illustrate the points raised by Runciman, one need only mention that unemployment figures varied enormously according to occupational group (see Table 7.2).

TABLE 7.2
UNEMPLOYMENT AMONG DIFFERENT OCCUPATIONAL GROUPS,
ENGLAND, 1931

| | |
|---|---|
| Unskilled manual workers | 30.5% |
| Skilled and semi-skilled workers | 14.4% |
| Personal service workers | 9.9% |
| Salesmen and shop assistants | 7.9% |
| Clerks and typists | 5.5% |
| Higher office workers | 5.1% |
| Proprietors and managers | 1.3% |

*Source*: Pollard (1969) p. 245.

TABLE 7.3
CHANGES IN THE CAUSES OF POVERTY, YORK, 1899, 1936 AND 1950

| Causes of poverty | % of those in poverty | | |
| --- | --- | --- | --- |
| | 1899 | 1936 | 1950 |
| Unemployment of wage-earner or irregularity of work | 5.1 | 28.6 | NIL |
| Inadequate wages | 52.0 | 42.3 | 1.0 |
| Old age | 5.1 | 14.7 | 68.1 |
| Sickness | | 4.1 | 21.3 |
| Death of wage-earner | 15.6 | 7.8 | 6.4 |
| Largeness of family | 22.2 | 2.5 | 3.2 |

*Source*: Compiled from Rowntree (1941) pp. 110, 481; Rowntree and Lavers (1951) pp 34–5.

Rowntree repeated his survey of York in 1936 and 1950 and found considerable changes in the causes of poverty (see Table 7.3). As regards 'primary' poverty, Rowntree stated in 1941:

While the reduction in the amount of primary poverty due to inadequate wages is a matter for congratulation, the tenfold increase in the poverty due to unemployment is a matter for grave concern.... unemployment accounts for nearly half the primary poverty in York, and what is true of York may well be true of the country generally. The reason why these families are in primary poverty is that the unemployment benefit is insufficient to raise families with more than two children above the primary poverty line. [Rowntree, 1941, p. 111–2]

Referring to the gap that divided the working class from the world of middle-class citizens, Hobsbawm wrote:

A good deal of the pattern of life, the 'traditional working-class culture' which...developed towards the end of the nineteenth century, reflected their social isolation. They had been the pariahs of both economic and politics...The contacts between working-class and upper-class life (apart from servants) were hardly closer than those between white and Negro life in the inter-war USA..., for all the average middle-class citizen knew of the working class world, or it of him the two nations might have been living in different continents...Nothing much changed between the wars.... Over a large part of Britain depression welded all those who lived in its immediate shadow together into a grim block. A new class consciousness and sense of exploitation on one side, fear on the other, widened the gap between the two nations. A rigid educational system, a shaking economy, confined workers and their children to their own world. [Hobsbawm, 1968, p. 240–1]

It should, however, be noted that the pattern of development of the labour movement in the West in the nineteenth and first half of the twentieth centuries was by no means uniform, even if we disregard events in Nazi Germany and Italy, which may be interpreted as counter-revolutionary in terms of the rising strength of the proletariat. In America, for example, the workers' interests did not find expression in an independent working-class political movement. Characteristically, more often than elsewhere, sociologists in America seemed reluctant to apply the concept of the working class to what they regarded as an open society, which provided huge opportunities for individual advancement and had innumerable ethnic and other status divisions that cut across concepts of class society.

To conclude: the working class in some countries has been considerably more distinctive and more militant than in England, and vice versa, the variations being the result of many historical and social factors. As Briefs points out:

Capitalism is not the same phenomenon everywhere. Neither is labor. The leveling and − culturally at least − devastating sweep of a century of capitalism could not eradicate the historical forces that built up a nation through the centuries. Nor could it exterminate the influence of the political and social institutions of old. The economic and social fabric of every nation still has its particular brand. The type of man a nation molds is the material of all its institutions and the agent of all its accomplishments. [Briefs, 1975, p. 190]

## THE WORKING CLASS IN THE
## MASS CONSUMPTION SOCIETY

The end of the Second World War led to a new era that was described by many social scientists only a few years ago as 'the age of affluence'. The rapid amelioration of the living standards of workers in the Western world, the reallocation of political power based on the newly acquired strength of social democratic parties and unions, social reforms culminating in the rise of the 'welfare state' − all these changes transformed the very fabric of many Western societies. Rapid economic growth was, from this point of view, of major importance. It resulted in a radical change in the entire occupational structure − a shift from wage- to salary-earning jobs − as well as upward change in living standards.

Mannheim was one of the first to emphasize the ideological change brought out by post-war development:

Modern revolutionary theory was conceived at an early stage of capitalism, in a world of scarcity and ruthless exploitation, when one could think only of a life-and-death struggle between rich and poor in which the poor had nothing to lose but his chains. Since then a situation has developed in advanced industrialist countries where there are too many people who could lose only by revolution. [Mannheim, 1968, p. 27]

The changes in the position of the working class that took place after the Second World War were interpreted in different ways. The major theoretical viewpoints were as follows:

(a) The concept of an affluent society and the evaluation of its impact on the position of the worker.
(b) The thesis of the decomposition of the working class and the growing assimilation of some parts of it into the middle classes (embourgeoisement hypothesis).
(c) Theories of the institutionalization of industrial conflict and the dissociation of industrial conflict from political struggles.
(d) The concept of new forms of enslavement of the working class in a mass consumption society.

*(a) The new affluence*
The maintenance of high living standards became a key factor in an economy based on mass production and increasing mass consumption. The post-Keynesian belief has been that any slackening of workers' consumption owing to economic depression or falling wages would lead to economic disaster. Post-war governments seemed far more prepared to tolerate inflation with all its attendant difficulties than to permit a substantial drop in workers' real incomes, which it was thought would inevitably result in growing militancy and social unrest. (The accelerating increase in real wages in the course of the twentieth century is shown in Table 7.4.)

TABLE 7.4
INDEX OF REAL WAGES IN BRITAIN, 1890–1979 (1956=100)

| | |
|---|---|
| 1890 | 61.3 |
| 1910 | 62.7 |
| 1930 | 71.0 |
| 1950 | 94.8 |
| 1960 | 108.3 |
| 1965 | 111.1 |
| 1970 | 118.4 |
| 1974 | 140.8 |
| 1979 | 144.2 |

*Source*: Cronin (1979) p. 226; National Institute for Economic and Social Research.

New economic policies and social provisions were possible after the Second World War not only because of an increase in productive potential, but also because of state intervention and the increased scope of central planning combined with deliberate efforts to extend state-sponsored social services. Western European governments have become accustomed to intervening in the economy in order to strengthen the political stability of the system, to counteract its most salient inequalities and to extend safeguards against poverty, insecurity of employment and the deprivations of old age and disablement, which were frequently the lot of the underprivileged in preceding decades. Mass consumption has become a correlate of mass production among the working class (see Table 7.5). As Katona comments, 'the solution to mass poverty is not cutting the pie into different-size slices, but rather exerting every effort to increasing the size of the pie' (Katona, 1964, p. 53). This statement reflects the essence of post-war Western economic development: economic growth enabling the population's living standard as a whole to be improved.

TABLE 7.5
RELATION OF OCCUPATION AND INCOME
TO OWNERSHIP OF DURABLES
(PERCENTAGE OF FAMILIES)

| Country and occupation | Own a car | | Own a TV set | |
|---|---|---|---|---|
| | Low income | High income | Low income | High income |
| *Germany* | | | | |
| Blue-collar | 27 | 45 | 82 | 84 |
| White-collar | 33 | 56 | 65 | 85 |
| All respondents | 25 | 50 | 77 | 84 |
| *England* | | | | |
| Blue-collar | 24 | 59 | 89 | 98 |
| White-collar | 44 | 71 | 95 | 96 |
| All respondents | 34 | 73 | 92 | 95 |
| *Holland* | | | | |
| Blue-collar | 31 | 51 | 87 | 86 |
| White-collar | 31 | 59 | 87 | 85 |
| All respondents | 26 | 56 | 84 | 85 |

*Source*: Katona *et al.* (1971) p. 36.

Affluence, consumer power and importance of consumer psychology are for Katona the main features of the mass consumption society. This is not necessarily so for Galbraith, who in his famous book *The Affluent Society* opposed the concept of 'private opulence and public poverty'

(Galbraith, 1971). In this work of polemic, which became a sort of *Capital* for neo-liberals, Galbraith accepted that the traditional social problems of poverty, insecurity of employment and inequality persist even in the most prosperous countries, but rejected the idea that they are *major issues*, even if they are still regarded by many as part of the conventional wisdom. For Galbraith, if we try to cure the evils of modern life by resorting to the devices and procedures of the past, we are caught in a vicious circle. In their efforts to combat poverty, inequality and insecurity and to stimulate economic growth by increased private consumption, the Western governments aggravate the system's difficulties instead of solving them. This leads to further calls for inappropriate treatment, and so on.

The greatest difficulties arise because of an unbalanced relationship between private consumption and social consumption, as well as the inadequacy of the mechanisms of industrial growth. The gap between private and public expenditure (private affluence – public squalor) grows at the expense of all those who have to rely upon public spending for their access to good housing, leisure, education, unpolluted surroundings, etc. Economic and social development requires ever-increasing public subsidies, while expanded private consumption is the main cause of the acceleration and maintenance of industrial growth. The neglect of collective needs and the resulting disruptions in social life have gradually become the major problems of the modern world. Preoccupation with production, which is regarded as a necessary safeguard against poverty and economic insecurity, presupposes a steady increase in consumption: it is the stream of privately consumed goods that keeps the economy going. In Galbraith's words, 'more die in the United States of too much food than of too little' (Galbraith, 1971, p. 126). In order to maintain a high level of production, new needs must be created and maintained; also, the principle of mass wastage is encouraged, since the disposable economy helps to extend markets and enables newly designed replacements to be sold.

Galbraith was not particularly concerned with the working class; he regarded workers simply as part of the consumer society who have to pay the price of the new economic development while profiting from some aspects of it. The worker benefits as a private consumer from increased wages and an increased supply of cheap durables. At the same time, the less privileged sections of society are bound to suffer because of the insufficient financing of collective consumption. Galbraith illustrates this point in reference to the housing industry:

The housing industry functions well only in combination with a large, complex, and costly array of public service. These include land purchase and clearance for redevelopment: good neighbourhood and city planning, and effective and well-enforced zoning; a variety of financing and other aids to the housebuilder and owner; publicly supported research and architectural services for an industry which, by its nature, is equipped to do little on its own; and a considerable amount of direct or assisted public construction for families in the lowest income brackets. [Galbraith, 1971, p. 213]

The average blue- and white-collar workers are thus bound to suffer from poor housing, deteriorating schools, limited recreational facilities, air pollution and deficient public transport.

The contrast was and remains evident....the family which takes its mauve and cerise, air-conditioned, power-steered, and power-braked car out for a tour passes through cities that are badly paved, made hideous by litter, blighted buildings, billboards, and posts for wires that should long since have been put underground. [Galbraith, 1971, p. 208]

## (b) The decline and decomposition of the working class

It is not so much with affluence itself that we are concerned but with the question of how, if at all, the affluent society has changed the workers' position in society. An increasingly popular conviction in the West has been that in modern affluent societies we are witnessing the decline and decomposition of the working class. This decline relates not just to numerical change, but also to qualitative change. According to the embourgeoisement hypothesis, differences between the working and middle classes (or, rather, the new middle classes) are disappearing or being reduced to negligible proportions. One of the first studies that explicitly supported this line of thought was by Mayer (1956). He pointed out that, under the impact of recent socio-economic changes, the traditional distinctions between blue-collar manual workers and white-collar workers had become increasingly less valid: there was a spectacular rise — over 50 per cent — of working-class families entering the middle-income category; the educational level of working-class children was rising and differences between employees in white-collar and blue-collar jobs thus tended to be reduced; in automated industries there no longer existed the dirty jobs that had distinguished the manual trades from clerical occupations; changes in the consumption pattern of manual workers were increasingly pronounced so that their life style resembled more and more that of middle-class consumers.

If these trends continue — and there is no reason to assume otherwise at the present time, the class structure of American society will once again become predominantly middle class in the near future. [Mayer, 1956]

The standardization of American society becomes even more pronounced if we take into account the gradual disappearance of the 'old middle classes', that is, those in the self-employed categories (see Table 7.6).

TABLE 7.6
DISTRIBUTION OF THE US WORKING POPULATION, 1870–1954

| Occupation | Percentage of the working population | | | |
| --- | --- | --- | --- | --- |
| | *1870* | *1910* | *1950* | *1954* |
| Self-employed (farmers, business entrepreneurs, professionals) | 40.4 | 27.1 | 14.4 | 13.3 |
| Salaried employees | 6.6 | 16.1 | 29.1 | 30.8 |
| Wage workers | 52.8 | 56.8 | 56.5 | 55.8 |

*Source*: Mayer (1956) p. 78.

The thesis of the decomposition and decline of the working class has been elaborated most convincingly by Dahrendorf, who partly accepts Marxian views on nineteenth-century capitalism, but who argues that further development has contradicted Marx's notion of mature capitalism:

...neither capital nor labour have developed along these lines.... The proletarian, the impoverished slave of industry who is indistinguishable from his peers in terms of his work, his skill, his wage and his prestige, has left the scene... In modern industry 'the worker' has become precisely the kind of abstraction which Marx quite justly resented so much. In his place, we find a plurality of status and skill groups whose interests often diverge. Demands of the skilled for security may injure the semi-skilled; wage claims of the semi-skilled may raise objections by the skilled; and any interest on the part of the unskilled is bound to set their more highly skilled fellow workmen worrying about differentials.... As with the capitalist class, it has become doubtful whether speaking of the working class still makes much sense. [Dahrendorf, 1972, p. 51]

According to Dahrendorf, the changes that have transformed the very fabric of modern society are as follows: the decomposition of capital owing to the separation of ownership and control; the decomposition of labour and the growth of a new stratum of highly skilled workers; the emergence of the 'new middle class', which in its 'white-collar' component is increasingly convergent with the upper stratum of the workers; new patterns of social mobility, the rise of equality both in theory and in practice; and a new form of institutionalised class conflict.

Dahrendorf did not intend an outright refutation of Marxism, but substantially to replace it by a theory more appropriate to the society of the late twentieth century. He describes Marx's views as a reflection of a limited experience of nineteenth-century industrial society in which industrial conflict was superimposed on political cleavages and led to growing working-class militancy. In more advanced societies, industrial disputes can become separate from political struggles and are subject to well-established rules and procedures that render the whole concept of class war obsolete. The working class's role is transformed from being the 'gravediggers' of capitalist society, into an active force operating within the boundaries of the pluralistic post-capitalist order.

### (c) Institutionalization of conflict in post-industrial society

A new approach to the nature of conflict constitutes the substance of arguments about the transformation of the working class. Touraine (1971) argues that we have entered a new stage of social development, that of the technocratic societies in which new social divisions come to the fore. Features of the new order are, according to Touraine, that:

Ways of life peculiar to social classes have been replaced by quantitative differences in the level of consumption.

Industrial conflict has been institutionalized as a result of trade union activities and state interventionism.

Programming, and not accumulation, has become the dominant feature of modern societies.

The separation of organizational conflict and class conflict is accompanied by a distinction between a pragmatic defence of economic growth and revolutionary — or at least radical — activities aimed at transforming society.

The changing nature of industrial conflict is also the basis of Dahrendorf's views on the evolution of industrial societies. His theory of conflict was advanced as an explanation of the changes that have taken place in the West since the nineteenth century. He acknowledges the intellectual trend towards the replacement of the concept of class by the concept of elites and the masses, and seeks to formulate his own interpretation by retaining the historical perspective and the language of the conflict theory, while at the same time emphasizing systems of authority as the source of decisive divisions in modern society. Whereas Marx discussed conflict in terms of classes and class interests, Dahrendorf defines classes by referring to conflict. For Dahrendorf, classes are synonymous with 'conflict groups that are generated by the differential distribution of authority in imperatively coordinated associations' (Dahrendorf, 1972, p. 204). The substance of these conflicts is not explained by Dahrendorf: it acquires in his interpretation an almost metaphysical sense related primarily to the distribution of power within the enterprise. Laws of economics — market pressures, ups and downs in economic growth — seem irrelevant for an understanding of the nature of the conflict between the holders of power and their subordinates.

In Dahrendorf's opinion, the major causes of changes in the nature of the class conflict are:

the emergence of new patterns of regulation of conflict both in industry and in politics;

the development of democratic processes of decision-making, which has given both parties in the conflict — workers and employers — the chance to attain their goals peacefully;

the institutionalization of social mobility resulting from the needs of modern societies and expressed in more egalitarian educational policies;

the replacement of the absolute deprivation of some sections of society by relative deprivation;

the dissociation of political and industrial conflict.

As we can see, the workers in what Dahrendorf calls 'post-capitalist society' are quite different from workers under earlier capitalism: their position has changed because of the transformation of the social structure as well as the conflicts inherent in it. Dahrendorf's 'conflict theory' thus becomes a revised theory of class society with a different concept of the modern working class. Based on a sociological critique of Marx, it seems to explain the more recent developments in Western 'post-capitalist' societies.

### (d) New forms of oppression in the 'mass society'

The theme of the decomposition and decline of the working class has also been put forward by writers regarded as supporters of the radical Left. Fromm and Marcuse, although for different reasons, concluded that the traditional class antagonisms have disappeared and been replaced by a new type of conflict in which workers are not necessarily the most oppressed party. For Fromm (1973), it is primarily man's total alienation that causes the disruption of social life; this alienation afflicts not only the workers but their masters — the capitalists — too. In his view, the principal features of twentieth-century capitalism are:

the total disappearance of feudal characteristics of social organization;
the rapid increase in industrial production.
the concentration of capital and the growing size of business and government organizations;

the increasing number of people who manipulate figures and individuals, as compared with those who manipulate objects;
the separation of ownership from management;
the improved economic and social status of the working class;
the introduction of new working methods in factory and office.

This development goes hand in hand with the rise of the economic and social status of the working class. Especially in the United States, but also all over Europe, the working class has participated in the increased production of the whole economic system. The salary of the worker, and his social benefits, permit him a level of consumption which would have seemed fantastic one hundred years ago. His social and economic power has increased to the same degree and this not only with regard to salary and social benefits, but also to his human and social role in the factory. [Fromm, 1973, p. 108]

However, man's alienation has not disappeared — its character has changed. Human beings are subject to domination by uncontrollable alien forces.

In the twentieth century, such capitalistic exploitation as was customary in the nineteenth century has largely disappeared. This must not, however, becloud the insight into the fact that twentieth century capitalism is based on the principle that is to be found in all class societies: the use of man by man....
    The basic concept of *use* has nothing to do with cruel, or not cruel, ways of human treatment, but with the fundamental fact that one man serves another for purposes which are not his own but those of the employer. The concept of use of man by man has nothing to do even with the question whether one man uses another, or uses himself. The fact remains the same, that a man, a living human being, ceases to be an end in himself, and becomes the means for the economic interests of another man, or himself, or of an impersonal giant, the economic machine. [Fromm, 1973, p. 93]

Fromm assesses the conflict between capital and labour from the point of view of modern forms of alienation. The class basis of this conflict seems to him to some extent secondary in relation to the fact that capitalism incorporates principles in total opposition to the interests of a sane society, which is defined in terms of its adjustment to the needs of man. Capitalism operates as a system in which human beings are themselves turned into things through their labour, yet labour should incorporate cooperation based on mutuality, vitality, creativeness and independence, which, for human individuals, ought to be the ends.
    The tendency to treat modern societies in terms of conflicting

values rather than from the point of view of class interests is even more pronounced in Marcuse's writings. In *One Dimensional Man* (1964), Marcuse put forward an elaborate refutation of the traditional image of the working class, incorporating the following main points:

(1) Manual work has undergone basic changes as a result of the reduction in the quantity and intensity of *physical* energy in work processes, as compared with the *mental* and nervous effort.

(2) The manual labour force is bound to decline in relation to the white-collar elements, who increasingly dominate all sectors of production.

(3) The importance of existing labour tends to disappear, since mechanization shifts the emphasis onto past labour incorporated in automation and technical devices.

(4) The worker is thus deprived of his traditional power to withdraw his labour, since the withdrawal of manual labour means less and less in an age of full automation.

(5) Workers become more and more integrated culturally, that is, in their standard of living, in their leisure activities and in work itself, they identify themselves with the dominating values and standardized patterns. They lose their spiritual identity and become part of an organizational society in which they lose their individuality.

(6) Not only the process of cultural integration, but also the disappearance of reasons for rejecting the existing order, tend to disrupt the working-class ethos and rob the workers of their identity.

(7) Since 'domination is transfigured into administration', even the object of frustration and hatred seems to disappear: 'Mutual dependence is no longer the dialectic relationship between Master and Servant...but rather a vicious circle which encloses both the Master and the Servant' (Marcuse, 1964, p. 23).

According to Marcuse, the value of freedom becomes less important for the workers because increased production counteracts any *need* for freedom itself. Consumption needs, created and reinforced by the system, perpetuate the servitude of the exploited in that the workers are deprived of any good reason to revolt against this 'oppressive' system. This is the nature of modern totalitarianism, which, for Marcuse, does not consist necessarily of anti-democratic procedures but means 'a non-terroristic economic—technical coordination which operates through the manipulation of needs by vested interests' (Marcuse, 1964, p. 3).

One could conclude from Marcuse's writings that, apart from the suppression of 'pure freedom', no troubles afflict modern workers. Their tragedy is that the more affluent they become the more oppressed they are, since their will to resist and their desire for liberation are diminished. Small wonder that those who suffer most in modern affluent societies are the intellectuals and students: they are much more sensitive to a lack of freedom, resent spiritual oppression much more, and enjoy much less the affluence that they tend to regard as a superficial and degrading feature of modern life. The more developed the minds, the more they suffer under conditions of labour deprived of its attractions, and the more they feel enslaved by the anonymous forces in their organizational societies in which 'the irrationality itself had become rational' (Marcuse, 1964, p. 52).

## ANTI-EMBOURGEOISEMENT AND RADICAL SOCIOLOGY

The discussion about the working class today is totally different from the 1950s and early 1960s; the embourgeoisement theory is unacceptable to sociologists of many schools and persuasions. It is by no means easy to take a stand in these discussions since we are entangled in a muddle of theories and concepts. There is no single definition of the working class that would now be universally accepted. For some, workers are distinguished by the nature of their manual jobs, for others by their position in relation to the means of production, irrespective of whether they are in manual or non-manual occupations; yet others refer primarily to 'class awareness' or 'class consciousness' or use complex formulae of status characteristics. Differences in definition not only account for endless discussions about many non-existent problems, but also explain the difficulties in reaching useful conclusions about real problems.

The issues at stake also vary. For sociologists who refer to workers in terms of property relationships, the central question is usually why the modern proletariat develops (or does not develop) the class consciousness implied in Marx's theory of capitalist exploitation. On the other hand, the investigator who employs the criterion of manual/non-manual work will be particularly interested in the blurring of class boundaries because of the existence of marginal groups that are difficult to classify in terms of the white-collar/working-class dichotomy. Finally, sociologists who concentrate on consciousness as the distinctive feature of manual workers will be more interested in differences of opinions and political perspectives that are to be found right across the class spectrum of modern industrial societies.

All these approaches undoubtedly widen our knowledge of social life, but they do not necessarily clarify questions about the changing position of workers in the contemporary world. A comparison of the nineteenth century with the existing social structures in the West demonstrates why so many elaborate theoretical distinctions that are nowadays laboriously applied were non-existent and unnecessary at the earlier stage. Industrial workers constituted at that time a relatively easily distinguishable social category. They were propertyless and so easily contrasted with the world of small and large property ownership. They were uneducated and immersed in the culture or subculture of the 'lower classes', which differed completely from that of the educated strata in society. They were concentrated in industrial centres, where they led a separate bleak existence in high-density urban areas. Their living standard was not necessarily different from that of the indigenous peasantry (where one existed), but it was certainly much lower than that of the old and new middle classes. The *visibility* of the working class was, in other words, a most conspicuous feature of developing industrial society. Where grey areas existed (there were after all many marginal groups sharing one or more aspects of working-class life), the growing concentration of the industrial proletariat in expanding urban centres made it easy to resort to a simple model of working-class characteristics and structure.

Advanced technological development and the mixed economy as it now exists in the West have meant class boundaries have become even more ambiguous. Workers are employed in both private and nationalized industries, so that their 'propertyless' status cannot by itself be related to the 'oppositional class' of private capitslists. Their living standard is not only far above the breadline but often compares favourably with that of people in lower clerical jobs and in service industries. Their qualifications vary and do not permit a straight comparison between the education of people in manual and in simplified non-manual jobs. Their dependence on the market economy has been reduced. Their way of life has also changed considerably in many aspects: massive rehousing programmes, increased mobility, the standardization of mass production and the rising standards of education — all these factors have resulted in the transformation of many traditional patterns of working-class life.

It should, however, be noted that each of these factors implies different phenomena that have to be discussed on their own merits and that cannot be reduced, as often happens, to the all-embracing embourgeoisement hypothesis. The three issues that underlie the current controversy are:

(1) The question of possible differences between the working and the new middle classes.
(2) The question of the prevailing attitudes of the workers towards the establishment.
(3) The question of the possible diversification of the manual labour force, in terms of a decline in its former homogeneity.

Combining all these issues, we arrive at the scheme shown in Figure 7.1.

| Similarity with the middle classes | high | low |
|---|---|---|
| Attitudes towards the establishment | high | low |
| Homogeneity | low | high |
| | Embourgeoisement | Marxist orthodoxy |

FIGURE 7.1 *Differing views of working-class characteristics*

One could argue that workers becoming middle class include all the characteristics indicated in Figure 7.1. However, this would be based on the assumption that the middle classes are, by definition, firm supporters of the establishment. This view is challenged by the New Left, and more recently by Zweig (1976) who claims a process of embourgeoisement of the working class and de-bourgeoisement of the middle classes.

A challenge to the embourgeoisement thesis that does not rely upon anti-establishment working-class attitudes can be found in the *Affluent Worker* studies from Cambridge University. Goldthorpe and his associates (1969) assumed that the best way to test for embourgeoisement was to concentrate on the affluent manual worker: once it could be demonstrated that even this type of worker differed from white-collar workers in his attitudes, interests and life style, the whole 'embourgeoisement hypothesis' would be invalid. Through extensive empirical research, the authors were able to collect enough evidence to confirm their point. An earlier study by Lockwood (1966), a member of the research team, contains the main theoretical and conceptual assumptions of the investigation. He distinguishes between the traditional conception of the proletarian worker and two sub-types — the deferential worker and the affluent worker — thus revealing some features of the new working class as presented in studies like these of Klein (1965).

The focus of the study was the degree of distinctiveness of the affluent worker from his lower-middle-class counterparts. Having selected a sample of 229 manual workers and compared it with 54 lower level white-collar workers, the investigators were able to generalize about both the changing position of British workers as compared with the traditional working-class image, and the existing and by no means disappearing divisions between the world of manual and white-collar labour. Goldthorpe *et al.* did not find evidence of the progressive integration of the working class within the institutional structure of modern capitalism. Their sample, who could be regarded as affluent and hence much more prone to the adoption of middle-class consciousness and life style, proved to be separated from their middle-class counterparts by the nature of the work they performed, the collectivist orientation so characteristic of the traditional working class, their outlook on life, and the invisible barriers erected between them and the non-manual sectors of society. In fact, it is less a process of integration than a process of normative convergence of the affluent manual workers and the social world of the middle classes, argue the authors of *The Affluent Worker*. The transformation of working-class ends and aspirations is occurring less rapidly than the conversion of the middle classes to increased unionism and collectivism — characteristically working-class attitudes.

Similar arguments in respect of the American scene may be found in a study by Hamilton, who claims:

The hypothesis that the major line of class cleavage has shifted from the manual—nonmanual position to the skilled—semiskilled division does not appear to be supported. In the overwhelming majority of the comparisons made here, the skilled proved to be closer to the semi-skilled in their attitudes and behaviour [than to white-collar workers]. [Hamilton, 1965, p. 53]

Shostak (1969), discussing the social characteristics of US workers, points out that American manual workers are usually people of rural or blue-collar origin, with a very high proportion of persons of foreign stock, frequently Catholic and often poorly educated. Commenting on the argument that the better-educated and better-off workers were disappearing into the lower echelons of the white-collar middle class, he remarks:

Indeed, little support can be found for the 'class-centric' notion that all or even most of such mobile people want to become middle-class or are eager to assume the signs of membership in that group. The life of many blue-collar suburbanites suggests just the opposite. Their families, and the families of many others still in the cities, retain their working class mode of life...these adult blue-collarites remain a distinct and highly predictable working class type. [Shostak, 1969, p. 277]

An interesting viewpoint worth mentioning here was put forward by Banks (1970). In a critical revision of Marx's ideas about the working class, Banks found important features of the working-class movement that did not disappear with growing affluence. Working-class solidarity, militancy and commitment to the collectivist form of social organization are significant social phenomena in industrialized societies and, despite declining wage differentials between clerical and manual occupations, manual workers retain their distinctive characteristics. As such, they are in opposition to post-capitalist forms of exploitation and oppressive bureaucratic rule. The replacement of private enterprise capitalism by what Banks calls 'private enterprise collectivism involving

Welfare state politics' has not abolished class divisions and class conflicts. Ordinary workers often oppose their masters and seek protection against managerial bureaucracy through trade unionism, the institutions of industrial democracy, and various other means of collective action (Banks, 1970, p. 198).

The authors of an impressive study on Britain's class structure also discovered that manual workers' attitudes were a world apart from other sections of society (Roberts *et al.*, 1977). The workers' 'class awareness' persists, they argue, even if their views about specific issues do not differ much from those of the middle classes.

There are, finally, critics of the embourgeoisement hypothesis who claim that the growing similarities between manual workers and white-collar workers are associated with the increasing radicalization of these two groups, since both are exposed in the same way to the ill-effects of a capitalist economy. A complete refutation of the thesis of the embourgeoisement of the workers can be found in the writings of the so-called 'radical sociologists', many of whom are of orthodox Marxist persuasion. Their arguments, put briefly, are as follows:

The traditional working class is as strong and important as ever in social, economic and political life.

The laws of the capitalist economy put manual workers at a disadvantage as compared with white-collar workers.

The alienation of manual workers is thus inexorably increasing under the impact of both the market economy and technological change.

Growing working-class militancy is an inevitable result of this development.

The abundance of so many conflicting views is interesting in itself. Some of these views may be explained by the changing historical perspective: the contrast between the optimistic image of the establishment in the 1950s and early 1960s and the wave of radical criticism of that establishment in the late 1960s and 1970s is most illuminating in this respect. A broader interpretation of the current differences can, however, be achieved by applying two important concepts to an analysis of the position of the working class in the modern world: the concept of *transitional societies*, and that of the *fragmentary class structure*.

## THE WORKING CLASS IN THE TRANSITIONAL SOCIETY

Transitional societies are, in simple terms, societies in a state of structural change. In such societies all attempts to define existing groups and classes in distinctive terms invariably fail since elements of the past coexist with the new forms, which, emerging only gradually, do not help us to identify their specific traits and delineate new group boundaries.

Rigid either—or distinctions are hardly applicable and invariably lead to misleading generalizations in which either everything has changed or nothing has changed at all. The controversy about the working class is a typical example — some observers being inclined to believe that the substance of class relationships remains the same and others arguing that it has been completely transformed. The fact that present-day life is a mixture of the old and the new allows us to support each of these standpoints with solid empirical data simultaneously while ignoring or dismissing other data indicating the contrary.

Harrington (1963) was one of the first to signal this dilemma. He pointed out that there are at present in America two *different* working classes: the traditional working class, in which many traits of nineteenth-century labour are preserved, and the new working class, which increasingly resembles the lower strata of the middle classes. The dualism inherent in this distinction is not, however, confined to social status characteristics, but cuts right across the economy and society as a whole. There is no doubt that in most advanced countries some aspects typical of nineteenth-century capitalism remain; at the same time, new forces and mechanisms are at work that have nothing to do with nineteenth-century free competition and an unregulated market economy.

Aspects of the nineteenth-century past are for many people still a living reality and to be seen in backward industries, underdeveloped areas, sweated labour, ruthless exploitation, low wages and generally appalling working conditions. Technological progress does not eradicate small-scale production, nor does it eliminate the economic relationships typical of this mode of production. Many manual workers are therefore subject to a harsher kind of exploitation typical of the nineteenth century and early twentieth century, when private owners made their profits at the expense of the standard of living and working conditions of their employees. A similar situation may often be found in many 'modern' service industries — catering is perhaps the best example — but because of the low unionization of the employees in these industries their plight is often ignored.

The pressure of the market economy also takes its toll since technological development and the impact of economic stagnation aggravate the situation of many manual workers, who are left without jobs or are exposed to the insecurities of changing demands by employers, a phenomenon practically non-existent in the 'full employment' communist economies. Technological change, being the dominant feature of industrial production, results in rapid reductions in the number of people working in different industries, in a geographical relocation of the labour force — thus depriving entire areas of employment — and in pushing out of work the ageing worker who (because of the characteristic working man's life-cycle) is far more vulnerable to the threat of unemployment and downward mobility than the younger one.

Industrial production is particularly exposed to the fluctuations of the market economy when periods of expansion are followed by economic recessions. Closed factories, mass redundancies, entire areas deprived of places of work, are normal occurrences in industrial centres. In other words, the traditional phenomenon of insecurity of employment still exists for many working people, as does the inevitable lowering of living standards. The burden of sudden unemployment generates a feeling of helplessness toward indomitable market forces coupled with the drudgery of psychologically unrewarding low-paid jobs.

There is no doubt, however, that capitalism coexists today with many new social improvements. It is true that the life chances of manual workers are in many respects much worse than those of the so-called middle classes. This is true for life expectancy, education, mental health, the incidence of certain illnesses, earnings, provisions for old age, etc. However, it should be noted that these are differences that centre on the opposition between *occupational* groups. In other words, they have nothing in common with the classical relationship between proletariat and capital. This point is hardly, if ever, acknowledged by the radical sociologists, who are eager to demonstrate the validity of the revolutionary theories of the nineteenth-century heritage. In the communist countries, in which virtually no private property as a means of production is allowed, similar differences occur, with the more educated and more skilled groups being the main beneficiaries of the advanced industrial economy.

On the other hand, in terms of *interests* involved, the situation of many groups of workers is no different from the rank-and-file professionals who are also employed by private or public industries. Both are largely dependent upon union power and are subject to the ups and downs of the labour market. In other words, in relations with the employers, the statement 'we are all workers now' is increasingly applicable to both manual and non-manual employees. This makes generalizations about the working class as a whole, in the context of the power of capital, virtually obsolete.

The tendency towards class convergence has been analysed by Zweig (1976). The main points of the study are, firstly, that the major aspects of social change in highly developed societies are the *embourgeoisement* of the worker and the *de-bourgeoisement* of the middle classes. The worker leaves his ghetto, enjoys political influence and recovers his identity as an individual. At the same time, the middle classes suffer progressive bureaucratization and erosion of middle-class values; as their social and economic status declines, only by adopting a working-class strategy (i.e. joining unions and taking militant action) are they able to defend their interests, but with alienating consequences. Secondly, both the working and middle classes converge primarily by adopting new attitudes towards society — attitudes described by Zweig as 'the new acquisitiveness':

(1) 'The old acquisitiveness was confined to a small layer of business-men...In contrast the new acquisitiveness is almost universal...'
(2) 'The tool of the old acquisitiveness was first of all market pro-ficiency...The tool of the new acquisitiveness is primarily the negative power to inflict damage on the economy, industry or company...'
(3) 'The old acquisitiveness made no demands on the State, while the new acquisitiveness is primarily directed against the Welfare State or the State as an employer as the easiest target.'
(4) 'The old acquisitiveness was not a cause of imbalance in the economy...while the new acquisitiveness generates inflationary tendencies...' (Zweig, 1976, pp. 68 and 69).

Many years ago, Briefs, arguing along the same lines, pointed out that a process of deproletarianization was taking place in advanced industrial society. This meant that '"wage-earnerhood" loses much or all of its castlike character and that the hardships of the worker's life are removed or at least alleviated' (Briefs, 1975, p. 185). As a result of these processes, the proletariat in the traditional sense as described by Marx and Engels has almost disappeared in the old industrialized countries, although it has been preserved or even developed in many of the later industrializing societies. Briefs also noted the opposite process: proletarianization in different forms and on a massive scale:

The wage system has been extended to cover a number of occupations and types of service which it has never touched before....From this point of view proletarianisation is simply a name for the fact that an ever increasing number of propertyless individuals put their services on the market for sale. [Briefs, 1975, p. 186]

## INTEREST GROUPS AND THE
## FRAGMENTED CLASS STRUCTURE

In his book *The New Classes*, Millar predicted that the class structure in Great Britain would change into a system comprising four layers (Millar, 1966, pp. 28–30 and 171–87). At the top would be those belonging to organizational elites; they run political, industrial and social institutions. Next would be the administrators, who implement policies adopted by those at the top. Further down would be the technicists, i.e. the skilled workers, including professional people, small tradesmen, minor businessmen, rank-and-file trained white-collar workers. At the very bottom would be the artisans, i.e. the poorer paid workers in manual and non-manual jobs. A similar prediction is contained in the study by Touraine, who stresses the changing class position of the highly trained workers and compares them with middle-class technicians (Touraine, 1971, pp. 27–86).

The trend towards the decomposition of the manual labour force means that – in Leggett's words – 'it is foolish to generalise about the working class, treating it as a homogeneous lot' (Leggett, 1968, p. 3). As I said before, the argument that workers, or at least many of them, *are* rather homogenous and preserve their working-class culture, cannot seriously be used to refute the above opinion, since we are dealing with a transitional society and diversification will probably be charac-teristic of future society. So far, skills have been identified as the most diversifying factor, but the available evidence indicates that there are many other variables that cut across the traditional distinctions be-tween skilled, semi-skilled and unskilled workers. Among the variables that nowadays seem to be of paramount importance in forming distinc-tive interest groups among manual workers are: (a) the new distribution of industrial power, (b) a dichotomization of the labour market, and (c) the emergence of a new proletariat.

*(a) The distribution of industrial power*
In the second half of the twentieth century the unions in many coun-tries have become so powerful that some observers are inclined to speak of a new corporate state. What is often ignored, or dismissed as irrelevant, is the uneven distribution of this union power. Some sections of the labour force are better protected by unions than others, while in other sectors of the economy the impact of unions is either negligible or non-existent. Power workers, miners, sewage workers, gas workers, haulage drivers, airline pilots and railwaymen have a strong bargaining position because of the key role played by the industries in which they are employed and the virtual monopoly these industries enjoy in regard to market forces. A comparison between the crippling effects of strikes in these industries and the employers' resistance to the demands of say postal workers, agricultural workers, firemen or car workers, illustrates new divisions between different sections of the working class. Inflation adds fuel to these differences since it is possible in some industries to keep pace with price increases or even anticipate future rises, while other industries inevitably fall behind.

It should be noted that these differences are not confined to manual workers, since many groups of employees in clerical jobs receive salaries far below the national average.

## (b) The dual labour market

Recent studies of the labour market have highlighted another aspect of divisions based on the differences between the institutions that employ labour. Attention has been drawn in a series of articles and books, published mainly in the USA, to the dichotomization of the labour market between the *primary* labour market, which consists of large-scale corporations and some governmental institutions, and the *secondary* labour market, which consists to a large extent of small and medium-size firms in secondary and tertiary industries and of the less-privileged sections of the public sector. The concept of the dual labour market is based on the assertion that there are two separate parts of the national economy and that conditions of employment are totally different in each part. In one, employees can expect good wages, good working conditions, security, well established opportunities for advancement and vocational training. In the other part, wages are much lower, labour discipline is ill-defined and arbitrarily enforced, security of employment is very low and the chances of promotion, as well as training, are almost non-existent (Bosanquet and Doeringer, 1973). It has been found that years of schooling and previous vocational training are irrelevant as far as the secondary labour market is concerned. In America, black ghetto youths are found to be more likely than any others to be trapped in this market because of the combined ethnic and social discrimination exercised through the personnel policies of large firms and the recruitment practices of trade unions.

Differences in the nature of employment are obviously structural and reflect the dualism of the economy. But this dualism creates a vicious circle because of the negative characteristics of unrewarding positions: employers in the secondary labour market rely on unskilled and semi-skilled workers whose demands are low and whose training costs are negligible. They accept high labour turnover, and use it for cutting the costs of dismissals and redundancies. The low degree of unionization in such industries is also beneficial for the employers since it allows them to infringe many of the regulations governing working conditions and minimum wage rates.

Those who, like Edwards, have studied this problem with all its ramifications hold the view that it reflects a reversal of the 'homogenization' of the working class that is characteristic of nineteenth-century labour history. A transition from freely competitive local markets to an economy controlled by nation-wide monopolistic international corporations and strong trade union control in some sectors of the labour market has created a situation in which employees in the oligopolistic sector of the economy are effectively discriminating against the rest (Edwards *et al.*, 1975, pp. xi–xvi).

Since the dichotomization of the labour market in capitalist countries is linked to other divisions based on race, age, sex and social background, new forms of stratification are emerging in which some groups among the working population have fewer opportunities in life than others, and transfer the advantages or disadvantages of their positions to successive generations.

It should be noted that some ideas contained in the theory of the 'primary labour market' may be found in Mallet's study, in which he predicts the emergence of the 'new working class' under the impact of growing automation (Mallet, 1975, pp. 58–68). Mallet notes that in automated factories workers are remunerated not according to their individual contributions, since these are not measurable, but according to the overall performance of the enterprise. The workers' skills are the product of long and complex in-job training and, because of the costs incurred during training and because their skills are not marketable outside the enterprise, their security of employment is very high.

In Great Britain, where the problems of oligopolies have been overshadowed by differences in the distribution of industrial power, the theory of the dual labour market was not widely acknowledged. It should be noted, however, that in recent years some researchers have made wider use of this concept in considering the problems faced by racial minorities and deprived areas.

## (c) The new proletariat

An important aspect of the working class in a transitional society is the new proletariat. This term is often used nowadays to refer to the poorest sections of the population, who are sometimes regarded as part of the working class even if they are outside the labour force, that is they are not classified as currently employed or seeking employment – which applies to 35 per cent of the heads of low-income families in the USA (Miller, 1965, p. 24). Various names are used to designate this group: Miller talks of 'the new working class' as being synonymous with another concept that is currently used in America, the 'lower class' (Miller, 1965, p. 39); Myrdal speaks of the 'underclass' (Myrdal, 1965, p. 121–7). In all cases, the reference is to people at the very bottom of the scale in terms of income per head and per family and who, in most cases, rely not on employment in their daily struggle for survival but on public support and marginal activities. As Myrdal notes: 'There is an underclass of people in the poverty pockets who live an ever more precarious life and are increasingly excluded from any jobs worth having, or who do not find any jobs at all' (Myrdal, 1965, p. 122). This 'underclass' reminds us of the Roman *proletarii*; some aspects of the life of the old and the new proletariat are strikingly similar, while the difference between the new proletariat and the proletariat in the Marxist sense is considerable. Deprived of employment, leading a purposeless existence and supported by the state and welfare agencies, the new proletarians are the pariahs of modern industrial society. The stigma of idleness and squalor is transmitted from one generation to the next, and the chances of obtaining permanent employment are almost non-existent for the unskilled inhabitants of the most deprived areas.

## MANIFEST AND LATENT FUNCTIONS
## OF THE WORKING-CLASS IDEOLOGY

One wonders why the differences and divisions I have discussed are not adequately reflected in social and political thought, in which the traditional ideology of the working class's composition and role seems as popular as ever. Its appeal cannot be explained other than by assuming that it performs new functions and serves new interests. The relationship between social class (in this case, working class) and ideology may be depicted by using, to some extent, Marxist terms:

| Distinctive class existence | + | no class consciousness | = | Class in itself |
| Distinctive class existence | + | class consciousness | = | Class for itself |
| No distinctive class existence | + | class consciousness | = | Class as a myth |

In their book on the class structure of modern Britain, Roberts and his associates make the interesting point that the 'vague' character of the working class can be associated with the 'fragmented class structure' (Roberts *et al.*, 1977, pp. 37–65). I would go further and argue that, however vague and blurred class consciousness might be, there is always the possibility of it being dissociated from class existence too. In this case, working-class ideology simply serves different interests and demands. In other words, we might be facing an ideological shell that can be used to protect and legitimize many different demands. What makes this interpretation more plausible is the concept of the *transitional society* discussed above. In such a society, working-class ideology plays a dual role. On the one hand, it reflects the genuine and distinctive interests of the traditional working class whenever this class has been preserved; on the other hand it is associated with new occupational interests that are part of the emerging post-capitalist (or post-industrial) society, in which the old concept of the working class is largely irrelevant and obsolete.

Expanding on the latter point, we can say that, firstly, the spirit of militancy as reflected in socialist working-class ideology is a direct reflection of the survival of many elements of capitalism pure and simple, and expresses the grievances of workers subject to exploitation in the most traditional sense. Secondly, rising expectations amid relative affluence can explain the eagerness of those not subject to this kind of exploitation to accept socialist ideology as a response to their hopes and requirements, especially at a time when aspirations are threatened by the reality of economic stagnation. Thirdly, the most privileged blue-collar workers can resort to a militant and radical working-class ideology as a means of legitimizing and reaffirming their demands, which are addressed to the rest of society, including the weaker sections. (Interestingly, the same tendency appears among middle-class workers, many of whom are inclined to vote for left-wing union and political leaders, including communists, since the radical Left is more determined to fight against voluntary restraints and to push for wage claims irrespective of their impact upon other social groups.) A point of equal importance is the 'proletarianization' of the middle classes, which accounts for their growing radicalization. Their rhetoric is not only supported by radical left ideology, but also allows them to forge alliances with the workers where there is a possibility of opposing the government or playing for public sympathy. Finally, in the most developed societies, there is a growing army of underdogs (long-term unemployed, chronically sick, one-parent families, etc.) whose genuine and unsatisfied needs give rise to radical ideologies. No wonder that for some this army seems to be *the* working class. Their deprivation, hopelessness, dependence on the state and rate-payer and their vulnerability to the blind market forces that condemn them to an undignified and demoralizing existence – all this explains the growth of radical militancy among individuals who identify with them and believe that any socialism will give them far better opportunities than the present social order.

Many of these tendencies have little in common with traditional working-class problems but, since they operate within the framework of the market economy, they merge with the pressures and demands that stem from the genuine deprivation felt by the victims of a 'market economy'. In other words, we face a development of those aspects of socialist ideology that do not necessarily constitute a struggle against poverty and deprivation as such, but express instead the interests of the most voracious and powerful groups who use and abuse the support and popularity of the slogans they promote in the pursuit of their own interests. The mixed economy therefore generates a mixed ideology in which the interests of different groups are blended to such a degree that meaningful distinctions are not apparent.

One of the first to recognize the importance of the new 'class consciousness' was Johns (1972). Johns comment on the attitudes of British workers as follows:

Today only a minority of workers see society as divided into two warring camps of bosses and labour, and allow this concept to shape their entire social outlook; those who do are invariably concentrated in the least prosperous and most alienated sectors of the working population. In part, this declining hostility stems from the decay of the tightly knit, homogenous communities where feelings of in-group solidarity and conservatism were readily formed. At the same time, as Goldthorpe and his associates have shown, the affluent worker retains his working-class values and attitudes: while pursuing the goals of a consumption society, he rejects the status-striving values of the middle class. The affluent worker automatically resents the status superiority which middle-class people still seek to preserve even when their economic superiority has vanished — and, in the eyes of the worker, this status superiority is itself illusory. [Johns, 1972, pp. 101–2]

Unfortunately, few studies analyse the problem of the collective consciousness of the new working class. In many Western countries the problem is, moreover, obscured by new immigrants who take the least attractive jobs, thus leaving the native section of the new working class in a position of relative privilege.

It will be clear to the reader that one can hardly conclude that the concept of the working class can be dismissed overnight as a relic of the past. On the contrary, it seems to embrace new elements: despite the 'dissociation' of status characteristics and the 'decomposition' of the labour force to which so many writers refer, the myth of the working class remains an ideological reality to be reckoned with.

CHAPTER 8

# Sociology of Trade Unionism

The development of trade unionism is an essential part of the history of the labour movement and it is also of interest to those who wish to understand the institutions of the modern world. In the West, unions have become part of pluralistic democracy. In the communist East, they have been taken over by the party-state as a powerful instrument of the bureaucratic power structure. Their role and character is undoubtedly determined by the nature of the societies in which they operate, but at the same time they have proved to be, at least in the West, powerful agents of social change.

In Great Britain, the unions are the second largest set of associations (the largest being the state itself) and play a vital role in British economic and political life. Some observers refer to the unions in terms of a *third estate* in the tripartite power structure of the state, industrial management and organized labour. The importance of the unions is best illustrated by the tremendous growth in trade union membership, which now amounts to some 13 million (over 50 per cent of the labour force) (see Table 8.1).

TABLE 8.1
UK TRADE UNIONS, MEMBERSHIP AND DENSITY

| Year | Number of trade unions | Members (000's) | Union membership as % of labour force |
|------|------|------|------|
| 1900 | 1,323 | 2,022 | 12.4 |
| 1920 | 1,384 | 8,348 | 34.3 |
| 1939 | 1,019 | 6,298 | 31.6 |
| 1950 | 732 | 9,289 | 44.0 |
| 1960 | 664 | 9,835 | 42.8 |
| 1970 | 543 | 11,187 | 48.3 |
| 1978 | 462 | 13,003 | 53.8 |

*Sources*: *Labour Statistics — Historical Abstract 1886–1968* London, HMSO, 1968; *Department of Employment Gazette* December 1979.

The main body of knowledge about the trade unions has been provided in the specialized area of study referred to as industrial relations, a discipline defined by Flanders as 'a study of the institutions of job regulations' (Flanders, 1975, p. 86), by Dunlop as a study 'of the rules of the system and their variation over time' (Dunlop, 1958, p. 383) and (indirectly) by Simpson and Wood as an area covering 'a complex of relationships between workers, employers and government, basically concerned with the determination of the terms and conditions of employment of the working population' (Simpson and Wood, 1973, p. 3).

Industrial sociologists were at first inclined to disregard the institutional, formalized aspects of the enterprise; in 'classic' studies of industrial sociology, unions appear only in the background (if at all) as part of the organizational structures within which social relationships at work were investigated. But in recent years the sharp division between industrial relations and industrial sociology has disappeared. New trends in the theory of organizations favour an approach in which interrrelationships between formal and informal structures are being explored. The attention of many industrial sociologists is focused upon decision-making, power structures and social participation, that is, problems in which unions' activities are studied as well. Studies of bureaucracy stimulate research in trade union government. The revival of interest in Marxist approaches gives a new impetus to studies of industrial conflict and the role unions play in it. And, finally, discussion about the working class and its transformation poses many questions related to the attitudes of workers towards their unions.

By comparing unions in the West and East we notice considerable differences between systems dominated by the party-state and Western democracies in which union activities are based on the principles of group representation and free collective bargaining. In contrast to the traditional craft unions, which concentrated primarily on unilateral regulation of the terms of employment, present-day unions negotiate terms of employment with the employers and use their organized power to enforce their demands. Insofar as the formal framework of these negotiations is concerned, the unions do their best to secure legislation that enables them to negotiate in the most effective way. At the same time, unions are the leading force in the battle for the welfare of their members, which makes them interested in the major decisions concerning welfare state and economic policies pursued by the government.

Unions evolve in the performance of their functions, and it is this evolution that is most intriguing from the sociological point of view, and that is reflected in the many theories of trade unionism.

## EARLIER THEORIES OF TRADE UNIONISM

The rise and development of trade unions has become the subject of many studies and generalizations, which can be categorized into the following:

(a) Trade unions as instruments of workers' direct control of industry and society (syndicalism).
(b) Trade unions as an instrument of class war (Marx).
(c) Trade unions as an institutional element of social conflict (Simmel).
(d) Trade unions as a defensive mechanism of manual workers (Perlman).
(e) Trade unions as a response to social stress (Tannenbaum).
(f) Trade unions as an institutional component of democratic planning (Polanyi).

### (a) Syndicalism

Syndicalism was first promoted in France where working-class leaders were particularly suspicious of state power and believed that only through direct rule by the workers could the new socialist order emerge. They believed that local unions could take over enterprises and put an end to the exploitation of labour. Self-government by workers would thus replace capitalist management.

The syndicalists rejected the idea of a political party leading the workers' movement and instead expected that a general strike would abolish the dominance of private property so that a free and decentralized society would emerge (Edwards, 1970, pp. 180–3). Syndicalists asserted that once private industry had disappeared industries could be run by trade unions cooperating on a local basis through a so-called 'labour exchange'. This would be administered centrally to coordinate the production of different industrial sectors. Society was thus regarded in its socialist phase as a federation of producers' organizations replacing the coercive apparatus of the capitalist state.

### (b) Marxism

For Karl Marx, trade unions were an important yet subsidiary organization of workers whose struggle was supposed to start from the economic level and develop into a political and revolutionary movement (Lozowsky, 1935). He was opposed to both the anarchists, who regarded unions as the main instrument for the revolutionary liberation of labour, and the narrow trade unionist ideology, which saw the unions as a purely economic force, unconcerned with any wider political issues and not committed to any revolutionary programme.

Marx criticized those writers and politicians who at the very beginning of the trade union movement asserted that strikes and other forms of pressure exercised by the workers could not change the basic economic position of the proletariat because of the interconnection between rising wages and the consequent price increases that deprived the workers of any advantage gained through rising incomes ('the iron law of wages'). He argued that the labour movement could successfully oppose the pressure to reduce wages and compel the owners of capital to limit profits to the workers' advantage. By eliminating competition among workers and organizng them against capitalist exploitation, trade unions would then be able to enforce the 'proletarian economy' (Lozowsky, 1935).

In further elaboration of his ideas on unions, Marx pointed to the close relationship between the economic and political movements of the working class and the laws of capitalist economy and the nature of the capitalist state. He advocated that workers should widen the attack against capital by campaigning at first for economic and political reforms at the national level, and pressing gradually for the final emancipation of working men from the domination of the capitalist economy. Since the latter aim could not be achieved without political power, workers were directed towards revolutionary measures that could be implemented only under the direction of a revolutionary party. Trade unionism was thus only a *stage* and a *component* of the class struggle. 'Economism', the limited concern with wages, was a natural expression of the consciousness of the workers in the *initial* period of the working-class movement; but, even with the development of political organization and growing revolutionary pressures, the unions remained an important instrument for organizing workers and defending their economic interests.

### (c) George Simmel

Simmel, too, examined the issue of the relationship between class consciousness and workers' organizations (Simmel, 1955). He asserted that the very concept of 'working class' as covering manual workers of different skills and trades could be regarded as a product of historical development:

To achieve this result, industry had to develop to such an extent, that hundreds of thousands of workers were subject to identical working conditions and that the interdependence of the different trades would grow along with the increasing division of labor. A money economy had to become all-pervasive so that the value of the individual's performance would be reduced entirely to its monetary equivalent. Finally, demands for a high standard of living had to increase out of proportion to the level of wages. All these developments are the conditions which give a decisive significance to the role of labor in society. [Simmel, 1955, p. 173]

Once the abstract concept of 'the worker' had been formed, it became a new factor influencing and shaping working-class consciousness. From personal and local battles, workers' movements were transformed into objectified conflicts in the course of which individuals became gradually aware that they were defending not only their own personal interests but also more general class aims:

In Germany, this objectification was started more nearly by means of theory, in as much as the personal and individualistic nature of antagonism was overcome by the more abstract and general character of the historical and class movement. [Simmel, 1955, p. 40]

In England, the objectification of the conflict was determined by the trade unions' activities, and it was followed by the rigorous unity of their actions and of those of the corresponding federations of entrepreneurs. The development of trade unions proceeded by overcoming local exclusiveness and creating purpose-oriented organizations in which local bonds became less relevant while the promotion of common interests became the dominant trait of the movement.

Gradually, entrepreneurs realized that effective organization of the workers was favourable to themselves as well:

For, although the result of such organisation was that an incipient strike could rapidly spread and last a long time, this was still more advantageous and economical for both parties than were the many local quarrels, work stoppages, and petty conflicts which could not be arrested in the absence of a strict organisation of the employers and workers. [Simmel, 1955, p. 90]

For the same reasons, workers benefited from the existence of strong and well-organized employers associations: 'Only if there is such an organisation can the workers in a given industry be sure that the success achieved is not at once put in jeopardy by disagreeing employers' (Simmel, 1955, p. 90).

The model of the interrelationships between the objective factors in the workers' position, and the consequent development of the workers' movement, can be presented on the basis of Simmel's claims in diagrammatic form (Figure 8.1). According to this model, conflicts in which trade unions are involved are not static or relatively stabilized, they are dynamic processes in which every step ahead influences the essence of the conflict itself. The emergence of trade unions and the accompanying ideologies has therefore been an important factor in shaping the relationships between capital and labour. Once organized patterns of dealing with conflicting interests were established, that very fact *reinforced* the trend towards further development of workers' and employers' associations and towards the establishment of new institutionalized patterns in industrial relations.

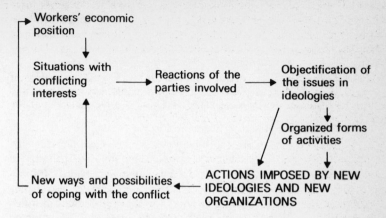

FIGURE 8.1 *Interrelationships between workers' economic position and development of workers' movement*

### (d) Selig Perlman – the theory of organic labour movement

One of the most prominent advocates of the separation of the trade union movement from political commitments was Perlman. He opposed both Kautsky and Lenin who believed that socialist consciousness has to be injected into working-class movements because by themselves these movements are unable to go beyond a pragmatic trade unionist ideology (Perlman, 1928).

Perlman believed that each section of society has interests of its own and develops both a consciousness and institutions that express these interests. Businessmen are competitively oriented. They are eternal optimists believing in a world of unlimited opportunities because it is only in such a world that they can develop their activities. They accept laissez-faire when it suits them, but abandon it and promote monopolistic practices when they can escape the risks of a free market. Workers, on the other hand, lack the adventurous entrepreneurial spirit and realise that competition gives them less security because of the fluctuations of the market economy. They learn by their own experiences that as far as better jobs are concerned opportunities are scarce and become even scarcer through competition among employees. They are henceforth interested in setting standards and rules that regulate their participation in job opportunities and act as safeguards against the insecurity of the market economy. While lacking competitive abilities, they are able to develop social instruments of self-defence by organizing themselves, eliminating competition among themselves and barring the ingress of outsiders.

While workers are bound to adhere to and develop the orientation towards trade unionism as an economic movement, all attempts at attributing political interests to them are based on abuse or misunderstanding. It is intellectuals who resent the existing social organization as it does not grant them the benefits they expect. In their pursuit of sectional interests, they attempt to divert the workers from acting on behalf of working-class goals, and try to use them as a militant force against the system that is so unresponsive to the needs of intellectuals.

*(e) Frank Tannenbaum: social anomie and the trade unions*

A psycho-sociological theory of trade unionism has been elaborated by another American writer, Tannenbaum. He starts his analysis with the concept of social anomie and regards the unions as a remedy for the disorganization of industrial societies (Tannenbaum, 1964). Tannenbaum points out that industrialization and the market economy tend to destroy the traditional social bonds without replacing them by any other adequate equivalent. The family has been disrupted because members of it work in different workshops and get their earnings independently from each other. The focus of social life has shifted towards the place of work, yet this is precisely where workers feel most isolated. A social and cultural gap widens until the workers take steps to restore their social integration and to protect themselves against the insecurities of modern life. Unionization can be regarded in the circumstances as the alternative to an authoritarian government, which might be adopted in order to maintain social cohesion and general welfare.

By joining unions, workers can recover their social identity, create some sort of occupational community and develop new patterns of social interaction with their colleagues. Trade unions are, then, a solution to both social and economic needs. They prevent the growth of social anomie due to the division of labour and to the progressive isolation of the individual, and at the same time they support the workers against the pressures of a competitive market economy. Trade unions thus counteract the dehumanization caused by rapid industrial change.

*(f) Karl Polanyi's liberal doctrine of trade unionism*

An attempt at combining the Marxist line with the democratic principles of liberalism can be found in Polanyi's writing (Polanyi, 1975). Polanyi saw trade unions as a response to the disappearance of community bonds under the influence of the market economy. Traditional society, as he points out, has been destroyed by capitalism, which by its price mechanisms undermined family structure and social institutions that previously protected the individual. In this new order both capitalists and workers seek protection and security by organizing themselves. Trade unions are used by the workers to restrain all-out competition, to promote factory legislation and to help employees in their struggle for fair wages.

Because of the general trend towards organization and the institutionalization of group activities, new forms of disruption have appeared, caused by the over-institutionalization of the system, which hinders the interplay of social forces. People who believe the solution can be provided by social planning and collective decision-making do not realise that it is the very idea of collectivism that poses new dangers and creates new dilemmas.

Polanyi contends that social planning can be exercised in two alternative ways: one consists in adopting totalitarian or fascist methods by introducing a system in which all personal and political freedom is eliminated; the other is what he calls 'planning for freedom', that is, the creation of some sort of representative socialism in which trade unions continue to act as an organized force protecting the interests of labour and acting against the bureaucratization and ossification of economic and social life.

## NEW UNIONISM AND INTEGRATION THEORY

Almost all the theories so far discussed have one thing in common: they relate to unions as they were in the past. Marx's conception of trade unions generalized the experience of nineteenth-century capitalism. Perlman's views reflected American labour's deeply ingrained distrust of intellectuals. Tannenbaum referred to the dislocation and alienation of the American worker during turbulent industrialization. Polanyi expressed the hopes inherent in the social democratic vision of a pluralistic and planning society. But Western societies have changed in many respects, and these changes have to be taken into account as far as trade unionism is concerned.

Looking at the history of the labour movement in Great Britain, we can distinguish five distinct stages in its development:

(1) The struggle for recognition extending from the emergence of the first unions at the end of the eighteenth century, throughout the period of illegality when the employers tried to stop industrial unrest by passing the Combination Acts in 1799 and 1800, to the repeal of the Acts and the emergence of the first National Association for the Protection of Labour in 1830.

(2) The period of expansion of the unions over different sections of the work force and consolidation of the unity of the movement at national level. In 1841 the Miners Association was created, in 1845

the National Association of United Trades; in 1868 the Trade Union Congress was set up. At the same time, union membership spread among the unskilled labour force, despite the bitter resistance of skilled workers.

(3) The period of struggle for the establishment of the legal status of trade unions and for direct political representation. The Taff Vale decision of 1901, the Osborne judgment of 1909, the Trade Unions Act of 1913 and the establishment of Labour representation mark this period.

(4) The period of consolidation of trade unions in the adverse conditions of the inter-war period, including the defeat of the General Strike in 1926, the passing of the Trade Disputes and Trade Union Act in 1927, and growing cooperation of the unions with the Labour Party.

(5) The period of integration of unions with the establishment, initiated by the cooperation of the unions and state during the war and followed by the establishment of direct and indirect relationships between unions and the central government in the 1950s and 1960s.

The new functions and policies carried out by the British unions account for the popularity of what one could call the integrative theory of trade unionism. A good presentation of that theory has been elaborated by Van de Vall (1970). He argues that because of the completely changed environment in which trade unions presently operate, and especially because of affluence, welfare activities, economic concentration, technological change and rapid urbanization, it is misleading to look at trade unions as if they are the same as in the nineteenth century when they were primarily organizations of working men against the world of private property. At the macro level, processes of integration are taking place: 'From an opposition movement, trade unions became a recognised institution, deeply rooted in our English economic and political system' (Van de Vall, 1970, p. 1). At the same time, as he points out, workers who once regarded trade unions as an important instrument of class warfare are nowadays much more concerned with the direct benefits they obtain from the unions' intervention in wage settlements. In effect there is much less working-*class* feeling among workers, and much more public spirit among trade union leaders who are increasingly involved in responsible cooperation with government and industry.

As for the workers...their macrosocial values of solidarity and idealism are replaced by a deeper concern with personal needs. This trend, partly conditioned by the welfare state, was described as 'the individualisation'

of the workers. The trade unions are undergoing changes in the opposite direction. While their micro-functions, on behalf of the individual
member, are being transferred to other institutions, their macro-
functions, on behalf of industry and nation, are expanding. [Van de
Vall, 1970, pp. 84–5]

The same line of argument was presented by Barbash, who introduced the term 'economic policy unionism' to denote the trade unions'
involvement 'in national economic policy dealing with planning, manpower, incomes and wages and industrial relations' (Barbash, 1972,
p. 161). He argues that the new trend in unionism is caused by the
impact of the development of the post-war European economy, in
which demobilization, recovery, full employment, structural change
and growth plus 'overfull' employment and inflation contributed to
the responsiveness of trade unions to national policy goals. He asserts
that ideological changes in trade unions also contribute to this development:

This ideological conversion is the result of several lessons learned during
the interwar and postwar years: 1) the enormous hazards to which ideological dogmatism subjects democracy and trade unionism, 2) reformist
capitalism's ability to produce full employment and the welfare state,
and 3) trade unionism's great stake in maintaining a stable and democratic order, even under reformist capitalism. [Barbash, 1972, p. 162]

The integration theory is to some extent an elaboration of Polanyi's
views on trade unionism. Its core argument is the necessity and possibility of institutionalizing conflicts and elaborating peaceful settlement
as an alternative to the industrial warfare that inevitably leads to
anarchy and possibly totalitarianism.

An interesting and coherent analysis of trade unions has been presented by Flanders. He criticizes Marxists because of their contempt for
'pure and simple unionism', while rejecting the rightist call for responsible cooperation by trade union leaders acting more as civil servants
than as partisans of militant labour (Flanders, 1976, p. 39). Flanders
emphasizes that the main function of the trade unions is representation:
they should neither neglect the variety of interests among workers
when they try to mobilize them nor adopt a 'responsible attitude' at
the expense of sectional (i.e. class) interests of labour. The trade unions
need to be aware that they act in larger society, the economic and
political laws of which cannot be ignored. The forms and targets may
change but the principle of responsibility and commitment to the
workers' interests remains. It is best reflected in collective bargaining,
which not only imposes the workers' terms and conditions of work
upon the industry, but tries to establish the rights and obligations of

employers towards their employees.

The integration theory is often contrasted with the conflict theory, which analyses unions in terms of conflicting interests, be it interests based on class contradictions, on the sectional aspirations of particular occupational groups or on the differences between elites and the masses. The difference between the integration and conflict approaches is, however, relative, since integration theorists do not deny the existence of conflict but assume that it can be regulated and contained within a commonly approved institutional framework. Real differences begin when we ask whether the mutual adjustment of conflicting interests is possible or acceptable for the parties concerned; the integrationists will argue that this is indeed so, while Marxists will claim that the existing institutions perpetuate the enslavement of working men and that escalation of the class war is a tendency inherent in capitalist society.

## UNIONS IN A CHANGING WORLD

The interesting point about institutions is not only their 'adaptability' and 'changeability' in a new social environment, but also the reverse: once institutions establish themselves they acquire a sort of life of their own; therefore in a changing environment a certain degree of 'dysfunctionality' is to be expected. Unions developed gradually as instruments of the working man's struggle for decent terms of employment and they are adjusted to the issues that dominated industry and society in the past. Whether they are prepared to cope successfully with the challenge of the world to come remains to be seen.

In the past, unionism was based on what one could call the 'classical' model of collective bargaining. It was assumed that agreements between employers and unions would be determined by the free interplay of collective forces of capital and labour. The market economy provided the framework within which the powers of the employers, and of the employees organized in unions, were decisive in shaping terms of employment throughout collective bargaining.

The legitimation of collective bargaining was the outcome of a long struggle by the labour movement and there is little doubt that unions are therefore regarded as *the* institution serving the working class and defending its interests. The ethos of unionism is inseparable from working-class ideology. It is generally accepted nowadays that workers have *the right* to their own form of representation, the position of the unions being thus derived from the position of the working class in modern industrial societies.

To summarize, the ideological heritage has endowed unions with the function of defending primarily the interests of *manual* workers in their struggle against the oppressive forces of *private capital* by use of the institution of *free collective bargaining*, which is regarded as the *inalienable right of the working class*. In the meantime, however, the economic structure in the West is undergoing important changes and we are now faced with a situation in which institutions inherited from and developed in the past operate in the new environment. Among the transformations that seem most characteristic for modern Western societies, the following are relevant to trade unionism:

*Occupational change*. Western societies have become predominantly societies *of employees*: employers and managers in all kinds of business establishments represent only 9.5 per cent of occupied males in England, the remainder being in one way or another employed. From an instrument of the working-class, unions have been transformed into institutions servicing employees of all occupations and ranks including doctors, teachers, civil servants and tax officers.

*The statization of the labour force*. The employers in turn consist not only of private owners of firms and corporations, but also, to a growing degree, of public corporations and public institutions supplying vital services to the state and to the public. Since the public sector is directly or indirectly subsidized by the taxpayers or supported by prices of services based on state monopoly, unions are involved in disputes over the distribution of the national income, and when industrial action is taken they confront the public by withdrawing vital services.

*Economic collectivism*. The growing interdependence of the economy is a fact of life unions have to reckon with. In order to survive in a rapidly changing and competitive world, a coordinated strategy is unavoidable. The power of the unions to disrupt fails to bring the kind of advantages reaped in the past when they struggled with individual employers.

*The corporate state*. No political party nowadays pursues a programme for a self-regulating economy. Whether exercising control by fiscal and monetary policies, or by direct intervention and centralized planning, it is the state that regulates and coordinates the economic level of activity. In order to do this it is inevitable that the state shares its own decision-making with private interest groups; in other words it lays the foundations of what is often referred to as voluntary corporatism (Thomson, 1979). Consensus and cooperation with the unions are an essential feature of the system and unions frequently surrender some of their power in order to support governments in their pursuit of prices and wages policies, long-term investment plans and other measures of 'national management'. In these circumstances, the very principle of free collective bargaining is often questioned, and indeed successive governments do appeal for the support of the unions when it comes to dealing with the dangerous undercurrents that threaten the economic equilibrium of Western societies.

There is no doubt that, whatever the prospects of further development in the relationship between unions and society, the structural changes I have just described affect the unions in the performance of their functions. The impact depends, of course, on the circumstances — countries differ with regard to the level of nationalization, the density of union membership and the development of the service industries. Some common trends can nevertheless be identified in:

a new configuration of the bargaining *parties*;
the *new framework* of rules and regulations in which negotiation takes place;
the new sections of society *affected* by the *outcome* of the negotiations; and
the *limitations* and *constraints* to which the possible results of the negotiations are exposed.

Within the framework of collective bargaining, wages and salaries are the main part of negotiated agreements, but the unions are increasingly turning their attention to other issues as well. Managers of corporations no longer pretend that they can manage against or even without some support of the unions. Some observers conclude therefore that we are approaching a new system of industrial management in which union participation might become a new powerful factor in the industrial and political balance. The politicians, comments Wilsher (1976), like many individual companies, have largely given up the attempt to manage large areas of their traditional responsibility. Not only are manning arrangements, job allocation, pay scales and shopfloor discipline now frequently decided, in both state and private industry, jointly with workers' representatives; but questions such as when the trains run, who will be admitted to hospital, or whether the garbage will be collected, are to an increasing extent settled in the same way. This does not mean that responsibility for some decision-making has disappeared: merely that it has changed hands.

At the first sight, the new functions of unions seem to support the integration theory: after all, in the changed circumstances unions are supposed to consider not only the interests of their own members but the interests of the public as a whole. Unionists are themselves members of the public and in their position as ordinary citizens they and their families often experience the inconvenience caused by action taken by their own, or other, trade unions. As Wilsher rightly puts it, referring to the unions as the 'new managers' of economic life:

Train drivers like to get their letters delivered. Garbage collectors like to know there will be ambulances available for their pregnant wives. Consultants like the banks to open when it is convenient for them to deposit their money. But these things will not happen by some kind of sympathetic magic. They will happen only if the new managers, as a group, can find a way to sink their differences, take a long look at what they really want from the society they have so boldly claimed the right to run, and find an institutional framework within which they can co-operate to make it all work. [Wilsher, 1976]

So far, however, the institutional framework within which unions act has not adjusted to the principle of cooperation; on the contrary, it is based on *sectionalism* — it implies that the interests of union members come first.

There is little doubt that the commitment of the unions to sectional interests poses serious problems when the welfare of society as a whole is concerned. There is also a natural contradiction between pluralistic liberalism and the requirements of a centrally regulated and directed economy. The unions themselves often seem torn apart when one occupational group tries to achieve its aims at the expense of the other groups. Sectional interests operate not only in the distribution of profits but also in the producing and selling of goods and services. The unions are inclined to associate with the employers in their attempts to establish secure markets for their products, to eliminate competition and to impose monopolistic prices, thus permitting not only higher profits but high remuneration of the labour force at the expense of the consumers concerned. Sectional interests are particularly conspicuous when unions negotiate about wages and salaries based on the allocation of public funds, that is, look to the improvement of the terms of employment at the expense of the taxpayer. High claims by the strongest unions often result in cuts in public expenditure to the detriment of weaker sections or the public at large.

As long as economic growth allows for general improvements in the living standard of the working population, these aspects of the pursuit of sectional interests are of minor importance as compared with the advantages of free bargaining. The situation changes radically, however, when the economy is brought to a standstill, so that claims in one sector are met only at the expense of others. In such circumstances, appeals for 'responsible unionism' are particularly strong, but many of those who wholeheartedly support such appeals when other interests are at stake do not hesitate to express their own claims when expedient. Unions are torn between loyalty to their own members, commitments to social welfare and commitment to the interests of the members of other unions — contradictions that manifest themselves in the ups and downs in union support for wage and price policies, in

TABLE 8.2
PUBLIC ATTITUDES TO THE UNIONS

| *Percentage agreeing that:* | *All trade union- ists* | *TU acti- vists* | *TU rank and file* | *TU in- active* | *Non- TU* |
|---|---|---|---|---|---|
| everyone who works should belong to a trade union | 47 | 56 | 46 | 37 | 26 |
| trade unions are the main cause of Britain's economic problems today | 37 | 26 | 39 | 49 | 57 |
| trade unions have too much power in Britain today | 66 | 50 | 72 | 77 | 76 |
| trade unions are essential to protect workers' interests | 86 | 96 | 87 | 69 | 69 |
| most trade unions today are conducted by a few extremists and militants | 56 | 49 | 57 | 68 | 67 |

*Source*: *Economist*, 10 January 1976, p. 13.

the factional struggles between Left and Right, and in the changing mood of the public when powerful unions exercise industrial muscle.

The extent to which trade unionists themselves have doubts and misgivings about current economic issues is best illustrated by the large proportion of unionists who do not approve of the power of the unions even if they regard them as an essential force in defending workers' interests (see Table 8.2). In an opinion poll in early 1977 three-quarters of the respondents again expressed the view that the unions had too much power (two-thirds of the members of unions held this view as well). The same uneasiness is reflected by the mass media in reports of hospital workers who unilaterally bar the use of private beds or of lorry drivers involved in secondary picketing.

The question of how to maintain the balance of power between unions and other interests in society is often raised, but it is not easy to answer. International comparisons offer a wide range of successful methods of regulating industrial relations: legal constraints; close cooperation of unions with the central government; enforcement of contractual obligations; and, finally, a dual structure of labour organi- zations via the unions and workers' councils. None of these approaches has much chance of being applied in Britain where the power of the unions is too firmly established to permit trade unionism according to recommendations of the Donovan Report (1968). (In order to resolve the conflict between the formal and informal system, the Donovan Report proposed limiting industry-wide agreements to those matters that they could effectively regulate. Companies and firms were encouraged to develop a collective bargaining machinery able to settle the terms and conditions of employment at the company and/or factory level. The importance of joint procedures for settlement of grievances according to collective agreements was strongly emphasized. Factory and company collective agreements were also to deal with the rights and obligations of shop stewards.) The collapse of the Conservative Industrial Relations Act and of the Labour government's incomes policy (based on the notion of social contract and social compact) typifies the relationship between the unions and the state in Britain over the past fifteen years.

One could conclude that British unionism has developed along different lines from that of Scandinavia and the Continent, with more influence enjoyed by organized labour at the shopfloor level and with trade unions playing a major role in the political structure of society. Will it mean some sort of revival of the syndicalist idea, that is, a voluntary corporatism with the producers having a say in shaping central policy and the state operating on the basis of union consensus for major economic and social decision-making? (Crouch, 1979). It is too early to answer that question in full. One thing is definite — once powerful unions emerged and reaffirmed their position, they became a major component of Britain's political life. The cost of this structural change is obvious: it results in a duality and ambiguity of union activities, which represent both the interests of the sellers of labour power and the producers and citizens (Korsnes, 1979).

RANK-AND-FILE UNIONISTS — MEMBERS OR CLIENTS?

In assessing the attitudes of workers towards their unions, we are dealing with two separate questions: one is why they join the union — the answer to which will depend on whether we deal with institutional constraints (closed shop) or not — and the other is how they feel about the union once they join it.

Table 8.3 shows how unionization varies from one country to another. It also varies from industry to industry. In the USA, a drop in union membership has been observed in most private sector industries owing to the resistance of managers using sophisticated methods, but there is a rapid increase of unionization among public sector employees, including the teaching profession, emergency services and municipal workers. In Great Britain, unionization is complete in coal-mining and in railways, but only 13 per cent in distributive trades and 5 per cent in hotels and catering, with an overall average of about 50 per cent of employees in unions (Coates and Topham, 1980, pp. 14–16).

TABLE 8.3
UNION STRENGTH IN DIFFERENT COUNTRIES

| | |
|---|---|
| Belgium–Luxembourg | 70% |
| Italy | 53% |
| Britain | 50% |
| Holland | 43% |
| Germany | 42% |
| France | 23% |
| USA | 27% |

*Source*: *Social Trends*, 1977, p. 217.

In these industries where saturation point has been reached or almost reached, the attitudes of members towards their unions could be far from what we would regard as a commitment to the *cause*, or expressing militancy and working-class solidarity. Gone is the ethos of revolt and the feeling that there exists a brotherhood of working men, gone are the dangers and uncertainties linked to union activities, and gone is the challenge of the fight against the oppressive, greedy employers when a considerable proportion of the manual and non-manual labour force is employed in the public sector.

Tagliacozzo and Seidman (1956) distinguished seven types of rank-and-file members according to their motivation for joining a union. The attitudes of the workers form a kind of continuum between the highest commitment and complete indifference towards the unions:

The ideological unionist, who, in addition to being a devoted and enthusiastic member, sees union activities as having the broader goal of promoting a different social order.

The 'good' union member, who is also devoted, but has no desire to change the existing social system.

The loyal but critical member, who is still devoted but is more critical of the leadership.

The crisis activist, who takes part in union activities only when strikes or other crises arise.

The member who is more sympathetic to management and may hope to gain a supervisory position.

The card carrier or indifferent member, who joins only because his work-mates have joined.

The unwilling unionist, who joins because he has to in order to keep his job.

Similar attitudes to union membership by union members can be seen in the few studies carried out in this area. Van de Vall (1970) divided the motives for joining a union into three groups: egocentric motives based on personal interests and benefits; sociocentric motives related to a commitment to the social community of fellow workers, solidarity, idealism etc.; and social control factors, i.e. submission to social pressures. The frequency of the motives within the group he investigated is shown in Table 8.4. Van de Vall states that workers who join and stay in the union give priority to the support of the union for the individual and to reasons of security — protection against unemployment and other occupational risks. He quotes among other things the following remarks made by his respondents: 'I joined as a kind of insurance. In case there is any trouble'; 'It's stupid not to be in the union. There are people who don't have any health insurance or fire insurance. Someone just had his house burnt down and he was not insured' (Van de Vall, 1970, p. 132).

TABLE 8.4
FREQUENCY OF MOTIVES FOR JOINING A UNION

| *Types of motive* | *Blue-collar* | *White-collar* |
|---|---|---|
| Egocentric | 44% | 30% |
| Sociocentric | 24% | 32% |
| Social control | 32% | 38% |

*Source*: Van de Vall (1970) p. 126.

An important examination of the question of workers' attitudes towards their unions was carried out for the *Affluent Worker* studies (Goldthorpe *et al.*, 1968). Motives for joining a union were similar to those in the Van de Vall study (see Table 8.5). From these findings the conclusion has been drawn that 'instrumental' attitudes to unionism prevail over moral and political commitment. The following remarks are quoted by the authors:

'The shop steward affects me more than the branch elections. It don't make a lot of difference which branch you're in so long as you pay your money and support the union. But the steward's the man I deal with if anything goes wrong — I want to know who he is.'

'You've always got interested in the things that happen in the shop. You're not all that interested in the affairs of the A.E.U. – except where it concerns yourself.' (Goldthorpe *et al.*, 1968, pp. 103–4]

TABLE 8.5
REASONS FOR JOINING A UNION

| | |
|---|---|
| Belief in unionism in principle or in worker's duty to join | 20% |
| Advantages of union representation on wages, conditions of service, grievances, etc. | 15% |
| Advantages of friendly society benefits and legal assistance | 15% |
| All work-mates were members | 8% |
| Coercion through existence of 'union shop' or pressure from stewards or work-mates | 23% |
| Other, don't know | 20% |

*Source*: Goldthorpe *et al.* (1968) p. 97.

The researchers draw the conclusion that:

unionism remains an integral part of working life;
unionism is regarded as being located in the workshop or plant, and is dissociated from wider, official unionism;
the focus is upon 'bread and butter' issues, i.e. on instrumental attitudes to union activities.

Following the suggestion made in an earlier paper by Goldthorpe and Lockwood (1963), unionism for these workers can be usefully described as 'instrumental collectivism' – that is, collectivism directed to the achievement of individual, private goals outside the work-place. Unionism is not losing its hold upon workers, but it assumes a new character, consistent with the wants and expectations that workers bring to their jobs. Instrumental collectivism is contrasted with the commitment to unions of traditional workers of the kind discussed by the Webbs, Zweig and Lockwood. The authors find evidence of the new unionism in the sizeable number of affluent workers who 'contract out' from paying the political levy, in the great number of those who do pay it who are not aware that they are doing so, and in the substantial minority (41 per cent) who believe that the unions have too much power in he country (Goldthorpe *et al.*, 1968, p. 113).

Corroboration of an instrumental attitude to unions among white-collar workers has been provided by the study *Shop Stewards in Action* (Batstone *et al.*, 1977), in which the authors compare and contrast white- and blue-collar unionization. The differences revealed in this study between the shop stewards operating on the shop floor and the shop stewards representing staff suggest that the authors of the *Affluent Worker* may have over-generalized their findings by concentrating their attention on workers in the motor car industry where instrumental attitudes (similar to those described by Batstone with reference to white-collar members and stewards) are more common than in many other industries.

In the light of an interesting study by Cyriax and Oakeshott (1960), trade unionism appears to mean different things to workers in different industries and trades. In their book, the authors discussed the following groups:

*The miners*: they are geographically isolated and involved in community life. 'As a result the union, with its lodge, its drinking club, its meetings, its welfare halls and libraries, its ramifications and openings into local and national politics, still remains one of the centres of community life' (Cyriax and Oakeshott, 1960, p. 15).

*The dockers*: they are relatively isolated, live a life of their own and use their union for frequent militant action.

*The printers and railwaymen*: their unions are primarily concerned with the specific problems of the respective trades. As far as the printers are concerned, the union is used for the defence of their skills; in the case of the railwaymen, the major factor is the protection of its members' relatively poor wages.

*The busmen*: they have a long list of grievances and are primarily interested in the union's protection of their living standards. 'Busmen tend to use their union vigorously to express these grievances and they take their official seriously enough so as never to accept a change in working methods without his sanction' (Cyriax and Oakeshott, 1960, p. 17).

*The engineers*: the majority are semi-skilled workers who expect their union to act in wage disputes and to settle minor grievances that arise on the shop floor without interfering in their outside life.

There is some further evidence that attitudes towards unions vary from one industry to another: studies by Blauner (1973), Chinoy (1955), Gouldner (1955) and many others allow us to understand the impact of occupational communities, job content, inter-group relationships and homogeneity of the labour force on the attitudes of workers towards their unions.

Van de Vall, whose findings I have discussed above, gives another explanation of attitudes to unions by pointing to the changes in the *functions* of the unions themselves. Taking into account his arguments and others to be found in similar studies, we can distinguish the following factors affecting the relationship between workers and their unions:

The growing range of state-provided services previously under the control of, or at least partly sponsored by, the unions — for instance, unemployment and sick benefits and death insurance.

The growing number of associations that compete with the unions to provide people with different facilities irrespective of their class allegiance and more in accord with their individual interests — private sports clubs and evening classes sponsored by local councils being the best examples of this trend.

The growing importance of state legislation that settles many problems without the direct interference of the unions — for example, legislation on conditions and safety at work.

The very extent of unionization, which accounts for the indifference of many workers to union allegiance. They know that whether they join or not the union will not disappear and will perform its functions on their behalf as if they were members.

The impact of these factors on different trades and occupations is of course variable; hence the inter-industry disparities in attitudes towards the unions. Finally, structural changes in the trade unions are regarded by many as the cause of the growing apathy of the rank-and-file workers and the development of purely instrumental client-like attitudes towards their unions, an argument discussed in more detail in the next section.

## TRADE UNION DEMOCRACY

The growing interest in trade union democracy found in current discussion and in numerous studies is a direct response to the bureaucratization of the trade unions, which is the inevitable result of their expansion and steady growth. As Weber stated: 'The choice is only between bureaucracy and dilettantism in the field of administration' (Weber, 1947, p. 310).

One of the first writers to raise the problem of the incompatibility of bureaucratic development with internal democracy in unions was Michels. He contended that:

competition and centralising tendencies in large and ostensibly democratic labor organisations could hardly be expected to reverse the advanced development of oligarchy, which flows from the technical requirements of organisation itself...It is organisation which gives birth to the dominion of the elected over the electors, of the mandatories over the mandators, of the delegates over the delegators. *Who says organisation, says oligarchy*. [Michels, 1959, p. 401]

Large-scale organizations are bound to become oligarchic: they endow their officials with enormous power, enable leaders to use their pre-rogatives so as to perpetuate their power, reduce the likelihood of organized internal opposition, and minimize the interest of rank-and-file members in direct participation. This even occurs in those organizations that by their very definition are supposed to incorporate democratic principles — political parties and trade unions being good examples of the 'iron law of oligarchy'.

One of the most important studies in this field examined an American print workers union, where the potential of membership influence over union policy seemed particularly great because a quasi two-party system functioned by which elections for trade union posts could be contested (Lipset *et al.*, 1956). The study relied upon many techniques, including historical exploration, interviews, questionnaires and the collection of documentary evidence. Factors found to have been most significant as far as the development of trade union bureaucracy were:

the structure of large-scale organization;
the attributes of the members of the union;
the functional adaptation of the union to its environment.

The main thesis of the study was that 'unions, like all other large-scale organisations, tend to develop bureaucratic structure, that is, a system of rational (predictable) organisations which is hierarchically organised' (Lipset *et al.*, 1956, p. 9). Taking into account these findings and other similar studies, the following causes of bureaucratization of the unions can be distinguished:

*The growing size of the unions.* As has been said before, the history of trade unions shows constant organizational growth and progressive concentration. In Great Britain the trend is best illustrated by the figures: whereas in 1900 there were 1323 unions with about 2 million members, in 1978 there were 462 unions with about 13 million members (see Table 8.1). The growing size of unions inevitably implies the growth of their administrative apparatus, which increases its influence in running union affairs.

*The growing complexity of functions* carried out by the unions. Rapid technological change, the growth of large firms, more sophisti-cated methods of management, the rise of the multinationals and growing cooperation with government and state agencies at national level, pose enormous problems for the unions concerned. Highly trained specialists like lawyers, financial experts, accountants, economists and statisticians are very necessary, and the influence of their opinions increases accordingly.

*The weight of centralized decision-making.* Once decisions are being made at company, or even more so at the national level, the union headquarters faces the task of enforcing them. 'Responsible unionism' assumes that local branches accept agreements elaborated in the course of national negotiations. The more complicated these negotiations are, the more difficult it becomes for the rank and file to understand the technicalities involved and to oppose the union leadership when controversies arise over policies related to those technicalities.

*Institutional pressures.* State officials and industrialists prefer to deal with a well-organized and competent union apparatus rather than with naive amateurs and welcome the progressive centralization, which facilitates negotiations at national level. (Lipset mentions the steel workers' union in the USA, which had to adjust to bargaining with a handful of huge corporations and had therefore to develop a structure parallel to that of the industry itself – Lipset, 1963, p. 390.)

*Leaders' vested interests.* The trend towards the bureaucratization of unions is reinforced by the tendency of the leaders to strengthen their hold over unions and reduce the uncertainty of their tenure of office. For their own sake, leaders are inclined to limit the influence of local units, to eliminate opposition and to strengthen their grip over current affairs.

Once a bureaucratic structure is developed, *the leadership can exert control over the formal means of communication within the union.* In consequence, the administration's views are often the only ones that the union members are likely to hear; it is extremely difficult to organize any movement of dissent *within* the union. The leader and union officers also have the opportunity of developing political and administrative skills that they can use against any internal opposition. For the same reason, the promotion of rank-and-file activists into the ranks of a union hierarchy is difficult; once a person acquires the necessary skills he is likely to remain among the union officers and become a supporter of the established oligarchy.

*Union officials tend to become a distinctive group* in terms of their life style, career, opportunities, habits and interests. They are reluctant to revert to their proletarian status and give up their union posts once they have adopted an essentially middle-class way of life. They are concerned with security and respectability, with holding down their jobs, with obtaining a good education for their children and with living in good residential areas, all of which can be put in jeopardy by organizational instability. They are therefore anxious to stabilize the organisations' goals, to stick to routine patterns and to build up safeguards against rebellion and dissension that threaten to disrupt the status quo.

Bureaucratization invariably results, as many observers point out, in *rank-and-file apathy*, which in turn contributes to the growth of organizational elites; the process is therefore self-reinforcing. In present conditions most of the functions performed by the unions can be effectively handled by the administrative apparatus without any direct involvement of rank-and-file members. As one of the steel workers commented: 'We don't have a union any more, we have a contract. The economists and statisticians negotiate contracts — all we can do is vote yes or no to them' (Lipset, 1963, p. 393).

The apathy amongst unionists is reflected in low attendance at branch meetings. The findings of Goldthorpe *et al.* are most illuminating in this respect. Let us take a closer look at the reported frequency of attendance at various union meetings and of voting in union elections (Table 8.6). Even if there are other sources that would suggest a higher rate of attendance and of participation in elections, the general picture can be seen. It is not so much lack of interest in the union *per se*, as an indifference to what goes on beyond the problems of the place of work.

TABLE 8.6
APATHY AMONGST UNIONISTS

| | Reported frequency | | |
| --- | --- | --- | --- |
| | of attendance at union branch meetings % | of voting at union branch elections % | of voting at shop steward elections % |
| Regularly | 7 | 26 | 83 |
| Occasionally | 14 | 12 | 5 |
| Rarely | 19 | 9 | 3 |
| Never | 60 | 52 | 7 |
| Other | 1 | 1 | 3 |

*Source*: Compiled from Goldthorpe *et al.* (1968) pp. 99–103.

The apathy of the rank and file is reflected in discrepancies between the policies carried out by the union leadership and the attitudes of the members. Moran (1974) reports that, in the Union of Post Office Workers, members' views differed on almost every political issue from the union's policy: only 21 per cent thought UPW should be affiliated to the Labour Party, only 51 per cent were aware that they were paying a political levy, and 85 per cent thought the union should not support a closed shop (Moran, 1974, pp. 54, 57. 91).

Tendencies towards the bureaucratization of trade unions are universal, but the degree of bureaucratization in individual unions depends upon various factors. Lipset and his associates identified at least three safeguards against fully fledged bureaucratization: (1) the nature of the membership; (2) the historical circumstances or — as they called them — 'the time-line factors'; and (3) the values and traditions predominant in the given union (Lipset *et al.*, 1956, pp. 393—400).

(1) Rank-and-file participation seems to be particularly high in those unions that are part of the occupational community. Within such a community, frequent interaction takes place between members, there are many common interests focused in union activities and a feeling of solidarity develops. There are also some occupations that enjoy a very high status and create the same spirit of occupational community.

(2) The 'time-line factors' are the historical circumstances that affect the present situation within the union, particularly past crises over succession. The character of the leader and his background may also be important, and at election time may amount to a choice between different candidates, that is, between democratic or bureaucratic rule in the future.

(3) The value system can be very significant. As Lipset stated: 'the more a given group holds a democratic anti-elitist value system, the more difficult it should be to institutionalise oligarchy' (Lipset, 1963, p. 425).

An explanation of why the trade unions in Great Britain resist the bureaucratization that occurs in other similar industrial and administrative organizations has been given by Banks. As he noted: (a) union leaders and union offices are filled by elected persons; even if they hold their offices for a long period they are still subject to re-election, the results of which might turn against them; (b) there is a difference between the posts filled in the trade unions by union officers and those filled by their staff — any increase in the latter tends to be kept under control (Banks, 1970, pp. 278—80). Commenting on the counter-forces that prevent full bureaucratization of the unions, Banks states that we are dealing not only with the iron law of bureaucracy but also with an 'iron law of democracy', which manifests itself in renewed attempts to rebuild democratic procedures whenever they may have been eroded is present in varying degrees in different countries. Comparisons between Great Britain and the United States are most illuminating in this respect (Edelstein and Warner, 1979). For instance, it has been found that the chances of opposition in filling higher level vacancies in the unions were much higher in Great Britain. In America, top officials were more powerful, conventions were less democratic and the number of potential competitors for top office was more limited.

## SHOP STEWARDS AND THE UNIONS' POWER STRUCTURE

One of the explanations of the growth of bureaucracy in voluntary organizations is the fact that, once they increase in size, participative democracy becomes impossible. As far as British trade unions are concerned, the evidence is to the contrary. The role of shop stewards defies the 'iron law of oligarchy'. Shop stewards emerge as 'participants' at the intermediate level; they represent the rank and file vis-à-vis union officials, and at the same time take an active part in trade union activities in their dual function of union functionaries and independent agents of the shopfloor membership.

The shop steward system has a long history. Studying it, we can see how the activities of shop stewards gradually outgrew the institutional framework within which they developed. At first, the duties of shop stewards consisted of helping to enrol new members, inspecting membership cards, collecting contributions, enforcing the observance of the general union rules and liaising with the district officers. It has been noted by many historians that in those early days union officials looked at shop stewards with some suspicion as there was always the possibility that employers would use local men to make agreements behind the unions' backs. The first clash between union officers and shop stewards occurred as a result of the radical Shop Stewards' Movement during the First World War. The movement, which started in the engineering and allied industries and spread among the miners and railwaymen, died out in the early 1920s, but it established a tradition of British stewardship being militant and socialist. The revival of the shop stewards' movement occurred on an unofficial basis shortly before the Second World War, but its impact was marginal. It was only after the Second World War that the shop stewards re-emerged as a powerful new force within the unions. Contributing to this development was the shift of collective bargaining from the national to local level, which took place because employers competed for labour in a booming economy. British unions and their branch organizations proved unable to cope with the innumerable local problems and shop stewards filled the *'institutional gap'* (Goodman and Whittingham, 1973, p. 11).

The relative independence of shop stewards from the bureaucratic apparatus of the unions is due primarily to the fact that they remain workers while carrying out their functions (the number of full-time shop stewards is about 10,000, i.e. no more than 3.5 per cent of the total – Clegg, 1980, p. 52). And since the workers can vote them out of their posts if they are not satisfied with them, the commitment of the shop stewards to rank-and-file interests defies pressures from above. Union officials remain for most workers remote figures, while 'the Shop Steward is for most rank-and-file members their first and only contact with the Union…the Shop Steward rather than the Branch is the Union' (Goldstein, 1952, p. 241).

Shop stewards are also a very important group. This is reflected in their growing numbers: according to various estimates there are between 250,000 and 300,000 shop stewards in Great Britain, compared with 200,000 in 1959 (Clegg, 1980, p. 51). At the same time the number of full-time union officers in British unions is rather low: the Donovan Report estimated that there were about 3,000 full-time officers, that is, one for every 3,800 members, although the average varies from one union to another (Donovan, 1968, p. 188). Among the factors that contribute to the shop stewards' importance, the following should be mentioned: (1) the structure of British trade unionism; (2) the impact of local agreements; (3) the informality of shopfloor bargaining.

(1) As far as the first issue is concerned, British trade unions represent a very peculiar mixture of craft, industrial and general unionism, which tends to reduce the opportunity of comprehensive plant-based bargaining. The standardization of central policy is almost impossible and the impact of 'rule books' limited because in most unions membership is spread over many unrelated industries. For the same reason close supervision is difficult; shop stewards are the only people who have inside knowledge of the problems of a given factory.

Multi-unionism increases the role of the shop stewards' committees at which joint decisions concerning enterprises are made (in 1973, 50 per cent of manual and 30 per cent of non-manual workers' establishments had more than one union – Coates and Topham, 1980, p. 145). These committees are not answerable to any single union and their decisions are presented to the unions as a *fait accompli*.

(2) The prevalence of work-place bargaining over national agreements is apparent throughout the UK; data presented in the Donovan Report (1968) were most illuminating in that respect. The structure of collective bargaining *implies* national level agreements at a time when terms and conditions of employment vary from one enterprise to another, so that local issues become the most important aspect of union activity. National agreements are regarded in the circumstances as the very minimum requirements, which are supplemented and expanded by work-place negotiations.

One of the many effects of this development is the *fragmentation* of work-place bargaining to the extent that decisions reached at that level reflect only the particular problems of the given enterprise and often of a given group of employees (Clegg, 1980, pp. 16–17). Thus the weight of union activity is shifted onto those who are conducting the negotiations – the shop stewards.

(3) The importance of the shop stewards has increased as a result

of 'the inevitable growth of informality' on the shop floor. The growing complexity of industry makes it almost impossible to regulate all aspects of labour relations by nationwide or even factory-based formal agreements. As Goldthorpe observed:

What is meant by saying that work place bargaining is informal is that it is to a large extent carried on within a context of 'custom and practice' rather than being guided by explicit procedural rules, and gives rise to understandings and arrangements which are mostly tacit, or at any rate rarely set down in a systematic, written form. [Goldthorpe, 1977, p. 187]

It is the shop stewards who act as the guardians and enforcers of these informal codes (Terry, 1977).

The growth of informality has been acknowledged by the Donovan Report (1968), where we read that Great Britain has two systems of industrial relations: the formal one sanctioned by rules and formal agreements, and the informal one of the shop floor. The degree of informality varies but is usually quite considerable. In a survey of workshop relationships in engineering, it was found that most aspects of the unions' activities at the work-place level were regulated by custom, current practices, the balance of power between management and workers and the goodwill of the management. In some companies, shop stewards build unofficial links with stewards in other plants; in 21.6 per cent of multi-plant companies, managers replied that they knew of such links (Warner, 1973, p. 92).

It has been found that the practice of informal negotiation over different aspects of wages is almost universal, but written procedure for these domestic agreements is virtually non-existent. The attitudes of managers towards compensating shop stewards for time spent in carrying out their official duties also vary. Similarly, agreements on wages, conditions of work and productivity are often made without any serious attempt at documentation, leaving open the possibility for reinterpreting the content of such agreements (Donovan, 1968, pp. 26–8).

Informality has the obvious advantage of flexibility in shopfloor agreements. There is ample evidence that shop stewards have a considerable freedom in defining their own role (Batstone *et al.*, 1977). Another study gives us an insight into the factors that affect the degree of independence of shop stewards from the union and helps us understand that what is often called 'informality' can also mean 'institutionalization in the making' (Boraston *et al.*, 1975). Thus there is an association between the size of an individual work force and the development of hierarchy, the regulation of procedures and the propensity of shop stewards' organizations to use sanctions (W. Brown *et al.*, 1978).

Although it is impossible to assess in full the impact of shop stewards on the consolidation of union democracy, it seems beyond doubt that their position must contribute to a changing balance of power between rank-and-file workers and the union headquarters. The unions have to rely on their shop stewards to no lesser extent than shop stewards rely on them. The officials seek a consensus with shop stewards, and adjust accordingly. In contrast to most employees, shop stewards have the chance to acquire considerable experience in dealing with the union matters. They participate in elections for union posts, they are able to censure motions and to assess the handling of union affairs by the elected leaders. The stewards play the major part in branch meetings; it is they who are the representatives at the annual conferences; and it is they who have first-hand knowledge of what is going on in the union offices when a conflict arises. If they are nowadays regarded as responsible for the militancy of the unions, it is nevertheless they who are given credit for the attention and concern that union leaders display in regard to the expectations and responses of the rank and file, who in turn expect their shop stewards to express grass-roots views in a decisive and uncompromising way.

As far as the relationship between the trade union structure and industrial democracy is concerned, it should be noted that trade unions in Great Britain operate as a three-tier structure: they have a bureaucratic apparatus consisting of professional or semi-professional officers, a rather apathetic and anonymous rank and file, and a mass of shop steward activists at the intermediate level, where the most important everyday negotiations take place. Insofar as shop stewards are recognized leaders of work groups, both in their expressive and instrumental functions, this structure combines the centralization of authority with delegated power vested in shop stewards as representatives of the rank and file.

CHAPTER 9

# Industrial Conflict

As long as industrial sociologists disregarded conflicts in industry and concentrated on problems of 'integrating the individual with the enterprise', strikes were not thought a proper subject of sociological inquiry. It is only recently that social scientists have become interested in industrial conflict. The first breakthrough occurred in the late 1950s when some scholars attempted to include the concept of conflict in the functional framework. Coser (1956) and Gouldner (1955) were pioneers in this respect. Research into the institutionalization of industrial conflict followed. Many sociologists declared optimistically that in advanced industrial societies industrial strife had been successfully regulated and would eventually be eliminated. It was only in the late 1960s and the 1970s that criticism of the conventional ideas regarding industrial conflict came to the fore, while renewed interest in Marxist theory contributed to the increase in studies of working-class militancy.

Strikes and industrial conflict are not, of course, synonymous terms. The term 'industrial conflict' is used in at least three different ways: (1) as related to long-term contradictions of interests between the workers and capitalists or employers and employees; (2) as a clash of demands connected with specific issues and generating some sort of hostility including warfare; and (3) as a direct confrontation of the parties involved.

As far as strikes are concerned, they are one of the many outward manifestations of industrial conflict. A general definition of strikes is that they are temporary stoppages of work by a group of employees in order to express a grievance or enforce a demand (Hyman, 1977, p. 17). There are, of course, many different ways of exercising this influence, for example: the go-slow; the overtime ban; informal refusal of cooperation and withdrawal of goodwill; the work-to-rule; obstruction of new policies; refusal to participate in joint committees; pursuit of exaggerated complaints that are not normally pursued. Strikes can be seen from this perspective as the culminating point of industrial action, short only of destructive riots or a direct takeover.

As a form of collective action strikes are a historical, social and

201

cultural phenomenon. They do not occur in societies in which individuals are unable to withdraw their labour, or in situations where withdrawal has little or no effect upon the interests of others. In many societies, such a withdrawal was, or is, regarded as open rebellion. Such was the case in societies based on slavery and serfdom. The right to strike is usually the first thing political dictators abolish. Strikes are banned in most communist states. In the West, they were legitimized only after a long and bitter struggle that lasted throughout the nineteenth century.

Some writers are inclined to approach strikes as part of the 'rules of the game', which are accepted by both employees and employers in the Western democracies to keep the industrial system going: 'My definition of harmony embraces conflict within the arms of common code and common purpose and there is nothing strange about this' (Homans, 1954, p. 49). In contrast to this view, many observers of the industrial scene believe there is a big difference between rules observed in a game and rules observed in situations of genuine conflict, the outcome of which is affected by the way people define their purposes.

...there need not be an implicit agreement that the rules should be equally fair to all the actors and, as a consequence, they may have different types of commitment to any existing set of rules....the participants may be involved in interaction for varying reasons and differ, therefore, in how they conceive 'winning' or 'losing'....their strategies may be designed to overturn the rules of the game rather than to obtain a larger slice of the cake (as presently defined) by means of legitimate actions. [Silverman, 1970, p. 212]

A team that scores a goal must agree to permit the other side to try to do the same from a position of equal strength....But in war, if one side wins a battle it pursues its enemy from a position of strength; in collective bargaining, if workers succeed in winning some concession from managers they use this to strengthen their future bargaining position. Games, tournaments and ritual contests may resemble other conflict situations in certain respects; but they cannot be treated as models in which most forms of social conflict are simulated. [Cohen, 1968, p. 148]

## CAUSES OF STRIKES

Strikes are explained in many different ways, which may be categorized as follows:

(1)  the common-sense approach;
(2)  the 'secret agents' or 'conspiracy' theory;
(3)  the psychological analysis;
(4)  the 'class war' frame of reference;
(5)  the 'social anomie' explanation.

→ Confusion on what one may want to accomplish

(1) The common-sense approach is applied by those who analyse strikes in terms of the demands put forward by the workers and who assume that the causes of strikes are precisely the reasons given by the strikers. Table 9.1 shows work stoppages in the United Kingdom in the years 1966–1979 in terms of their alleged causes. It illustrates the variety of demands that may underlie the strike and the necessity of taking into account aspects of industrial and social grievances that account for them.

(2) The 'secret agent' argument has become familiar through the expression 'reds under the bed', and reflects the attitude of those who explain strikes by the influence of insidious leaders causing industrial unrest. The 'conspiracy theory' places the blame on a handful of individuals or a secret cell of communists or Trotskyists, who, it is said, incite the workers to act against their employers and exploit their grievances for sinister, subversive purposes.

(3) In contrast to these simplified explanations, the psychological line of analysis concentrates on psychological processes and human interactions. The basic idea is that the reasons given by the workers who strike are not necessarily the real causes of their militancy. Workers are regarded as individuals angered or frustrated by factors of which they may be unaware; strikes are therefore assumed to express workers' frustration and discontent and are treated as *symptoms* of psychological stress rather than as an activity aimed at altering unfavourable circumstances. As Boulding observed:

The strike cannot be treated as the economist might like to treat it, as a rational phenomenon, in which each side nicely calculates the expected benefit of another day's strike and weighs this against an equally nicely calculated loss. It is, in part, a catharsis, a release of tensions, but it is also a drama, something that brings excitement and a sense of high purpose into otherwise humdrum lives. [Boulding, 1962, p. 217]

In psychological theories of conflict, both the instinctual and the environmental, the individual is at the center of attention. It is he who engages in conflicts, either because he is driven by primeval urges or because his psyche has been moulded by environment. Group conflicts are tacitly assumed to be summations of conflicts between individuals. [Rapoport, 1974, p. 135]

Psychological explanations do not have to be interpreted as exhaustive. Their value lies primarily in highlighting the causes of individual strikes in which underlying grievances and tensions may be more relevant than the overt reasons given for taking strike action.

(4) The 'class war' frame of reference is best illustrated by Marxist

## TABLE 9.1
## STRIKES BY CAUSE

| Causes of strikes | 1966 (a) | 1966 (b) | 1970 (a) | 1970 (b) | 1974 (a) | 1974 (b) | 1977 (a) | 1977 (b) | 1979 (a) | 1979 (b) |
|---|---|---|---|---|---|---|---|---|---|---|
| Wage rates and earnings levels | 43.0 | 65.7 | 62.0 | 82.0 | 61.5 | 85.0 | 52.4 | 73.5 | 57.2 | 92.7 |
| Extra wage and fringe benefits | 2.8 | 3.0 | 2.0 | 3.0 | 4.3 | 3.3 | 5.2 | 5.7 | 2.2 | 0.7 |
| All pay | 45.8 | 68.7 | 64.0 | 85.0 | 65.8 | 88.3 | 57.6 | 79.2 | 59.4 | 93.4 |
| Duration and pattern of hours worked | 2.1 | 2.7 | 1.4 | 0.3 | 1.8 | 1.4 | 1.7 | 0.3 | 1.5 | 0.3 |
| Redundancy questions | 3.6 | 5.6 | 3.1 | 2.0 | 2.9 | 0.7 | 2.8 | 1.6 | 2.9 | 0.6 |
| Trade union matters | 7.7 | 7.6 | 8.1 | 4.9 | 6.3 | 3.4 | 7.0 | 3.0 | 6.5 | 1.5 |
| Working conditions | 7.8 | 2.4 | 5.7 | 1.2 | 5.3 | 0.8 | 9.3 | 2.0 | 7.5 | 0.4 |
| Work allocation | 18.7 | 5.8 | 7.4 | 2.5 | 9.0 | 2.8 | 13.1 | 8.7 | 12.6 | 2.4 |
| Dismissals and other disciplinary measures | 13.1 | 7.2 | 7.4 | 4.0 | 8.9 | 2.8 | 8.5 | 5.1 | 9.6 | 1.4 |
| Miscellaneous | 0.4 | 0.2 | 0.6 | – | – | – | – | – | – | – |

(a) = % of total strikes
(b) = % of total days lost
(The different proportions show that strikers and/or employers feel more strongly about some issues than others, and that some issues are quite simply easier to resolve – either from a technical point of view or beacuse they do not involve a matter of principle)

Source: Compiled from various issues of the *Department of Employment Gazette*.

studies. According to Marxist theory, strikes are a direct outcome of the capitalist economy, in which workers are compelled to defend their interests against exploitation. Marx and Engels emphasized that the power of the unions was limited by market forces. In connection with the history of the trade union movement, Engels wrote:

All these efforts naturally cannot alter the economic law according to which wages are determined by relation between supply and demand in the labour market. Hence the Unions remain powerless against all *great* forces which influence this relation...But in dealing with minor, single influences they are powerful. [Engels, 1975, p. 505]

Lenin pointed out that strikes, apart from their economic functions, were 'A school of war', but not a war itself (Lenin, 1960, p. 317).

In present-day Marxist studies, strikes are seen as a major symptom of the exploitative capitalist market economy. The pressure of the owners of capital to reduce or limit wages is considered an inevitable aspect of a system based on private property. Only through the resistance of the workers can the 'proletarian' economy supplant the capitalist economy and a fairer share of existing surplus be allocated to workers.

(5) For some sociologists strikes appear as a consequence of the breakdown of the institutional order that regulates social behaviour. The 'social anomie' theory was elaborated primarily by Durkheim, who paid great attention to the disruptive forces that arise out of a state of normative disintegration. Durkheim distinguished three stages in the worker—master relationship: the early period, when worker and employer cooperated; a later period when employers and employees functioned separately and belonged to different associations with different rules and regulations (fifteenth century onwards); and the period of developing industrialism, when workers and managers lived and worked in two quite different worlds. It was from this time that conflict intensified. The growing division of labour led to the specialization and diversification of social functions. An elaborate system of cooperation had become a necessary condition of social life, yet the pace of change caused increasing difficulties in adjusting different interests and in shaping realistic expectations of the workers. Voluntary submission to the regulative system of norms and laws had become more important than ever; at the same time, it had become more difficult to achieve this because of rapid social transformation, when functional interdependence based on occupational differences was not associated with cultural values and social goals adapted to the new circumstances. Eldridge comments:

The social consequences of rapid industrial change posed for Durkheim both a threat and possibility. The threat was a total breakdown of industrial civilisation — a retreat to the Hobbesian war of all against all. The possibility was that men might by taking thought reconstruct the social order. For Durkheim this demanded not the imposition of a Leviathan but the encouragement of all the tendencies which promoted organic solidarity. Written into this perspective was a moral concern such that questions of social justice and individual freedom were paramount. [Eldridge, 1971, p. 91]

The concept of anomie was applied recently by Fox and Flanders (1969) in their analysis of the British industrial scene. They diagnosed a disruption of social regulation and normative disintegration of the system of industrial relations. This enabled them to analyse the differences between 'constitutional' and 'unconstitutional' strikes, and to attempt to explain the recent growth in the latter — an exercise also pursued in detail in the Donovan Report (1968). See also the criticism by Goldthorpe (1977).

These explanations and theories clearly demonstrate the ambiguity of the notion of 'cause' insofar as complex social phenomena are concerned. One could rightly conclude that, as far as strikes are concerned, several levels of analysis are to be identified. These take into account:

Overt reasons for strikes, i.e. the demands put forward as being the 'official' issue of the strike (reformulated if necessary in the further development of the conflict).

Underlying psychological causes and motives and the objective circumstances that give rise to the particular discontent and decision to strike at a given moment, as well as subsequent aggressiveness.

The institutional framework, which imposes certain requirements on the strategy of industrial conflict and shapes the responses of the parties.

General economic, political and social influences, which account for variation in both the propensity and intensity of striking.

Taking these distinctions into account, one must conclude that strikes cannot be explained by any 'one factor' theory. This conclusion is reached increasingly by the leading specialists in the field (for example, Hyman, 1977; Coates and Topham, 1980).

## EMPIRICAL STUDIES OF THE INCIDENCE OF STRIKES

The multi-causal approach to strikes does not mean that we are unable to investigate the impact of the various factors that may give rise to a strike. There is indeed a growing body of knowledge that enables us to understand the role of economic, institutional, social, organizational and psychological variables that determine the variations in the frequency of strikes. We can distinguish the following:

(1) Studies that cover many countries and concentrate on the historical trends in the incidence of strikes.
(2) Studies that compare strike statistics in various countries in order to explain strike-proneness by factors that occur in some countries but not in others.
(3) Studies focused on the incidence of strikes in one country.
(4) Studies concentrating on the inter-industry propensity to strike cutting across national boundaries.
(5) Studies of the inter-industry propensity to strike in one country.
(6) Studies of the incidence of strikes in one industry.

Each of these approaches offers a different perspective on the causes of industrial strikes. I shall examine some of these for illustrative purposes.

(1) In the first group of studies, Ross and Hartman's research is of major importance since it examines trends in strikes in the first half of the twentieth century. Table 9.2 contains the key statistics of their analysis. From these data Ross and Hartman conclude that strikes ceased to be tests of economic endurance and had become predominantly brief demonstrations of protest. They note a marked tendency for strikes to wither away. This, they explain, was the result of the following factors:

First, employers have developed more sophisticated policies and more effective organizations....Second, the state has become more prominent as an employer of labor, economic planner, provider of benefits, and supervisor of industrial relations. Third, in many countries (although not in the United States) the labor movement has been forsaking the use of strike in favor of broad political endeavors. [Ross and Hartman, 1960, p. 42]

Ross and Hartman point out that there are countervailing pressures like, for instance, 'shop steward revolts', unofficial strikes, etc., but these pressures are not strong enough to outweigh the tranquillizing factors (Ross and Hartman, 1960, p. 59)

An alternative explanation of the pattern of strikes was recently put forward by Snyder (1975). He concludes that different factors have influenced the incidence of strikes in different periods. In the pre-war period in particular, economic factors were much less relevant in generating strikes than now. When the unions were strong, workers

TABLE 9.2
TRENDS IN STRIKE ACTIVITY, 1900–1956

| Country | Stoppages per 100,000 employees | Average number of persons per stoppage | Average duration of stoppages (days) | Days lost annually per 1000 employees |
|---------|---------|---------|---------|---------|
| *Australia* | | | | |
| 1900–1929 | – | 308.8 | 14.1 | – |
| 1930–1947 | 25.2 | 348.0 | 5.5 | 449 |
| 1948–1956 | 51.4 | 305.1 | 3.1 | 485 |
| *France* | | | | |
| 1900–1929 | – | 301.2 | 15.1 | – |
| 1930–1947 | 34.1 | 303.3 | 6.5 | 591 |
| 1948–1956 | 22.9 | 1,134.1 | 2.6 | 682 |
| *West Germany* | | | | |
| 1900–1929 | – | 293.8 | 16.2 | – |
| 1930–1947 | – | 351.2 | 13.3 | – |
| 1948–1956 | – | – | 5.8 | 59 |
| *Sweden* | | | | |
| 1900–1929 | – | 209.7 | 40.9 | – |
| 1930–1947 | 7.2 | 205.3 | 58.5 | 851 |
| 1948–1956 | 1.3 | 259.8 | 24.1 | 81 |
| *United Kingdom* | | | | |
| 1900–1929 | – | 1,111.5 | 26.7 | – |
| 1930–1947 | 6.1 | 351.4 | 6.3 | 151 |
| 1948–1956 | 9.3 | 295.7 | 3.9 | 106 |
| *United States* | | | | |
| 1900–1929 | – | 500.9 | 13.3 | – |
| 1930–1947 | 8.5 | 523.0 | 14.2 | 624 |
| 1948–1956 | 9.0 | 562.2 | 14.7 | 751 |

*Source*: Ross and Hartman (1960) Appendix, pp. 183–211.

were much more prone to strike than in periods when the unions' strength declined. Snyder notes, however, that the pattern changed after the Second World War, when labour relations moved towards greater stability, collective bargaining became more institutionalized, and the political integration of labour took place. Once these elements were established, strike fluctuations seemed to be affected less by political than by economic processes.

In the post-war years, unemployment and the expectations—
achievements gap in real wage changes are both important predictors
of strike fluctuations...conversely, the organizational and political
variables...are unimportant in these recent years. [Snyder, 1975, p. 274]

(2) As far as comparative studies are concerned, the most important
contribution is undoubtedly the recent study by Clegg (1976b) of trade
union activities based on a comparison of the situation in six countries.
Discussion of strikes plays an important part in his analysis. Clegg
demonstrates the impact of institutional factors on the incidence of
strikes, their duration, the number of workers involved and the proportion of wildcat strikes. Another comparative study that highlights
the influence of institutional factors is Ingham's work (1974) based
on a comparison between Sweden and England. Both studies help us
to understand the close relationship between forms of protest and the
normative order within which employees exercise their influence and
resort to industrial action. The structure of trade unionism, the degree
of centralization, the level at which collective agreements are concluded,
the legal sanctions that follow a breach of contract, financial support
for strikers — all these and many other factors determine variations in
strike patterns in different countries, which are illustrated in a table in
Clegg's study (see Table 9.3).

TABLE 9.3
VARIATIONS IN STRIKE PATTERNS IN DIFFERENT COUNTRIES,
1970–1974

| Country | Stoppages per 100,000 employees | Average number of persons per stoppage | Average duration of stoppages (days) | Days lost annually per 1000 employees |
|---|---|---|---|---|
| Australia | 53.4 | 517 | 2.5 | 684 |
| France | 22.0 | 599 | 1.6 | 207 |
| West Germany | – | – | 5.3 | 56 |
| Sweden | 2.4 | 319 | 8.7 | 66 |
| UK | 12.4 | 545 | 9.0 | 606 |
| USA | 6.9 | 488 | 16.3 | 551 |

*Source*: Clegg (1976b) p. 69.

(3) Another aspect of the incidence of strikes has been investigated by
scholars who have studied the history of industrial conflict in one
country. One of the most illuminating books in this field is Shorter and
Tilly, *Strikes in France, 1850–1968* (1974). An important contribution to the analysis of the specific causes of industrial unrest is Crouch's

book (1979), dealing with industrial conflict in Great Britain after the Second World War. In both cases we are able to explore the incidence of strikes in depth as part of the economic and social situation that makes people more or less strike-prone.

(4) A fourth group of studies explores the inter-industry propensity to strike as a worldwide phenomenon. The major contribution in this field is by Kerr and Siegel (1954), whose study, although often criticized, has become a 'classic' in industrial sociology. They made a detailed analysis of the proneness to strike in various industries in leading industrial countries (see Table 9.4). Kerr and Siegel regard two factors as most relevant in explaining their findings: the location of the workers in society; and the character of the job and the corresponding features of the workers.

TABLE 9.4
INTER-INDUSTRY PROPENSITY TO STRIKE

| Industry | Propensity to strike |
|---|---|
| Mining<br>Maritime and longshire | High |
| Lumber<br>Textile | Medium high |
| Chemical<br>Printing<br>Leather<br>Manufacturing<br>Construction<br>Food and kindred products | Medium |
| Clothing<br>Gas, water and electricity works and services | Medium low |
| Railroad<br>Agriculture<br>Trade | Low |

*Source*: Kerr and Siegel (1954).

In discussing the location of the workers in society, Kerr and Siegel took into account the degree of geographical and social isolation and the extent of the integration of the workers or groups of workers within larger communities. As far as miners were concerned, their isolation helps to make them more cohesive and homogeneous than any other group of workers. Communities of miners or dockers usually develop their own standards, have rules of behaviour different from other groups and share a common mythology, legends and stereotypes. Low occupational mobility increases the homogeneous character of these groups. They are not only isolated from the broader society but even their own management is remote. For them, a strike is more than a struggle for economic aims, and operates on a different level as an expression of existing tensions, a rebellion against distant power centres, and a substitute for non-existent social and occupational change.

In contrast to employees living in isolated communities, workers who are better integrated in larger social groupings seem much less strike-prone. For various reasons, such workers are prevented from living in closely knit occupational groups: they may be geographically and occupationally dispersed; they may work in firms in which many trades are represented; they are often highly mobile; very often the small size of the firms contributes to their immersion in larger communities. They thus share the norms and standards of larger communities and are more responsive to public opinion. At the same time, they are less cohesive, their interests and grievances differ widely, and their expectations and life experiences are differentiated. Strikes by these groups do not affect occupational communities so greatly and at the same time tend to arouse a wider, and usually negative, public response.

Apart from the isolation—integration factors, Kerr and Siegel hypothesize that job characteristics lead to a concentration of workers with certain personality features: jobs requiring physical strength and endurance tend to attract workers who are harsher, tougher and more militant; on the other hand, jobs that are clean and provide a great deal of security are sought after by people unable to endure unpleasant and tough working conditions.

Kerr and Siegel emphasize that the second hypothesis is less satisfactory than the first, for it does not explain why textile workers are strike-prone, although their jobs do not require physical strength and endurance. They argue, on the other hand, that some findings seemed to corroborate the hypothesis that the relationship between job and personality features is related to strike-proneness: workers in some trades appear more exposed to middle-class patterns, and are less militant and conform more to the norms of the larger society.

(5) A good example of studies based on inter-industry comparisons of the propensity to strike in one country is Clegg's analysis (1976a) of the number of strikes in different periods of British history. He was able to demonstrate that the incidence of strikes in different industries varied from one period to another. He points out that in the years

1916–1926 the lion's share of working days lost was concentrated in a few industries: coal mining, cotton, engineering and shipbuilding (Clegg, 1976a, p. 314). On the other hand, in the years after 1927 there was a close relationship between the number of strikes and cycles of unemployment. Clegg emphasizes that the number of working days lost is likely to be high in depression years when employers may not be so concerned to get their men back to work until stocks are lowered.

An important point raised by Clegg is the concentration of strikes in certain industries within the period 1960–1964. He quotes the Ministry of Labour Report to the Royal Commission on Trade Unions.

The five or six industry groups losing most days per thousand employees have included motor vehicles, ship building and port transport every year from 1960....The four worst groups accounted for about 44% of the time lost in the last five years and over half the number of strikes. [Clegg, 1976a, p. 318]

Clegg notes that, since these industries included only 8 per cent of the total labour force, 'striking is an exceptional habit...Most workers strike rarely, if ever, and a few industries account for most of the strikes (Clegg, 1976a, p. 318). Clegg concludes that the propensity to strike could be explained only by taking into account *both* present conditions and historical factors. The latter include tradition, the atmosphere peculiar to the given industry, the memory of past depressions, etc. Among other factors common to all industries marked by a high propensity to strike are insecurity of employment, payment by results, fluctuation in earnings and inter-union differences.

Another study carried out along similar lines is that by Goodman (1967), who compares the rate of increase in strike activity in different industries. He discovered that electrical machinery, construction and the car industry are the most strike-prone in Britain. The number of strikes in the electrical machinery industry was seven times as high in the period 1963–1965 as in the years 1953–1955. In other industries like ship building, increases were smaller, while in some industries, like coalmining, strikes fell by 40 per cent. One might conclude in these circumstances that the private sector was becoming more strike-prone as compared with the state-owned coal industry – a generalization that proved utterly wrong in subsequent years when strikes in the public sector became the dominant feature of the industrial scene in Great Britain. Another conclusion Goodman drew was that industries were varyingly strike-prone within different categories of strikes.

(6) A separate group of studies on strike-proneness concentrates on the monographic study of one industry. This method allows for the

comparison of the given industry with others, as well as an examination of the specific features that seem conducive to strike activity.

A good example of this kind of inquiry can be found in the book by Turner *et al.* (1967). They investigated in great detail the causes of industrial unrest in the automobile industry. One of the factors that they found most relevant for high strike-proneness was: the preoccupation of the automobile workers with wages: 'Car workers...if they are not altogether "economic men", are probably more so than most other workers and nearly as much so as their employers' (Turner, *et al.*, 1967, p. 331). This attitude springs from the fact that most car factories do not recruit workers as juveniles, but deal with an adult labour force that derives from different occupations and who accept the strains and tensions of assembly-line work and mass production 'quite consciously as one price for the high wages that draw them into the industry' (Turner *et al.*, 1967, p. 331). Also, car workers are, because of their experiences, more familiar with the labour market; they realise that other jobs are available and are therefore not so committed to that particular industry.

Another point of equal importance is the combination of relatively high wages with anomalies in wage differentials and considerable instability of earnings.

There is a sense that since phases of high demand and output are fleeting, opportunities to extract concessions from managements should be exploited while they are available. And the frequency with which managements themselves lay men off, put them on 'fall-back' rates, or vary their overtime, makes it seem nothing abnormal for workers to withhold their labour. While high earnings make it easier for them to do so. [Turner *et al.*, 1967, p. 331]

The instability of earnings has complex causes, the most important of which are: fluctuations in demand experienced by the motor industry in recent years; minor disturbances, such as technical hold-ups or strikes in other departments or plants; and occasionally defective methods of calculating bonuses.

Summarizing their findings, Turner *et al.* reject the fashionable theories according to which strikes are the result more of general frustration that of specific economic grievances.

In sum then we are driven to the conclusion that strikes in the motor industry have been caused mainly by the kind of pressures that strikers themselves give as reasons for striking....The only background factor, which seems to us of unquestionable relevance to the high dispute proneness of the car industry is its pervasive irregularity of employment and earnings — and this in any case also emerges amongst the explicit causes of conflict. [Turner *et al.*, 1967, p. 333]

It is worth noting that the analysis by Turner *et al*. has thrown additional light on the difficulties of calculating strike-proneness on the basis of the number of days lost. It has been emphasized that many fluctuations could be explained by a greater or lesser willingness of managements to settle disputes without causing the workers to resort to strike action. In times of recession, workers seemed, on the one hand, more prone to strike, perhaps expecting strike action would postpone lay-offs; on the other hand, for large firms, 'high strike-incidence...has apparently represented the industry's substitute for formally agreed means of dealing with recurrent labour surplus' (Turner *et al*., 1967, p. 332).

Interesting contributions to the knowledge of strike-proneness are also to be found in monographical studies of declining industries. Wilson's study (1972) on dockers provides the best evidence of the reactions of workers to mass redundancies and the disappearance of traditional jobs.

## STRIKES AS A SOCIAL INSTITUTION

Strikes have become in recent decades an integral part of industrial life. In contrast to earlier periods of industrial struggle, when strikes were spontaneous, unpredictable and hardly subject to legal rules, nowadays they are well regulated and predictable events in which the parties observe certain rules of the game. The idea of the institutionalization of industrial conflict had become part of the ideology of the establishment in the 1950s and 1960s. Strikes were no longer regarded as a menace to the public order; on the contrary, many students of industry inclined to the view that they constituted a major component of social stability. What matters is the degree of regulation of industrial conflict. Once the rules of the game have been accepted by workers and employers alike, disputes can be kept within the bounds of the system while its requirements are respected and the procedures of industrial warfare followed.

Coser, author of the well-known book *Functions of Social Conflict* (1956), was one of the first to emphasize the 'functional' role of conflict in modern societies. He argued that:

Conflict, rather than being disruptive and dissociating, may indeed be a means of balancing and hence maintaining a society as a going concern....A flexible society benefits from conflict because such behaviour, by helping to create and modify norms, assures its continuance under changed conditions. [Coser, 1956, p. 154]

These rather general assertions lead to the more specific statement that conflict is a component of social change; without such change there is no development and necessary adjustments that are regarded as pre-conditions for the maintenance of the fabric of modern industrial societies.

Kerr *et al.* (1973) relate changes in the nature of industrial con-flict to the gradual progress of industrialization. During the early stages of industrialization, the commitment of workers to the industrial work-place and to the urban industrial community is low or non-existent. The authors therefore distinguish attitudes of non-commitment, semi-commitment, general commitment and specific commitment as reflecting stages of economic development and the loosening of ties with the pre-industrial order. As a consequence, forms of worker protest evolve and become more disciplined (see Table 9.5).

TABLE 9.5
COMMITMENT TO THE WORK-PLACE AND FORMS OF PROTEST

| *Stage of commitment* | *Characteristic forms of protest* |
| --- | --- |
| Uncommitted workers | Turnover<br>Absenteeism<br>Fighting<br>Theft and sabotage |
| Semi-committed workers | Spontaneous stoppages<br>Demonstrations and guerrilla strikes |
| Committed workers | Plant and industry strikes<br>Political protests and activity |
| Specifically committed workers | Grievance machinery, labour courts and disputes settlement machinery largely without stoppages<br>Political party and organizational alliances |

*Source*: Kerr *et al.* (1973) p. 212.

Kerr *et al.* acknowledge the positive role of workers' protest in implementing evolutionary change at earlier stages of industrialization. They argue that at the present stage of economic development organiza-tions of workers have become part of the establishment. Although the conditions of class warfare still exist, they are the exception rather than the rule. Only in the nineteenth century were they a prominent feature of the social scene and only then was the concept of class conflict advanced:

Earlier views on the role of worker protest reflected the facts of earlier times; periods when protest was more frequently against an authoritarian dynastic elite, a hard-pushing middle-class, harsh colonial masters; periods when protest was against the new technology itself. It then seemed reasonable to suggest the universal nature of class warfare, with the possibility of a few exceptions (the Netherlands and the United States). [Kerr *et al.*, 1973, p. 225]

The idea of the institutionalization of industrial conflict was also elaborated by Dahrendorf in his book, *Class and Class Conflict in Industrial Society*. Although references to strikes hardly appear in this study, the message is clear:

Conciliation, mediation, and arbitration, and their normative and structural prerequisites, are the outstanding mechanisms for reducing the violence of class conflict. Where these routines of relationship are established, group conflict loses its sting and becomes an institutionalised pattern of social life. [Dahrendorf, 1972, p. 230]

The institutionalization of class conflict is accompanied by the dissociation of political and industrial conflict. According to Dahrendorf, industrial conflict was particularly intense in early or developing capitalist society because the lines of political and industrial conflict were superimposed. In the later capitalist society, industry and industrial conflict have become institutionally isolated. One consequence of this is that:

...industrial strikes no longer affect the so-called public of post-capitalist societies immediately; indeed...strikes in one branch of industry leave workers in another branch relatively unaffected. If industry and society are two discrete social contexts, conflicts in one do not lead to conflicts in the other, i.e., the public does not identify itself with the striking parties on the basis of the respective class situation, but for completely different motives (e.g., harm to the economy, to one's own position, temporary discomforts, etc.). [Dahrendorf, 1972, pp. 274–5]

Once industrial conflict becomes institutionalized, strikes appear as legitimate trials of strength (and, in many cases, a mere demonstration of force) that help the contesting parties to reach agreements that cannot be settled otherwise. In other words, strikes become socially acknowledged, or even indispensable, devices for resolving and regulating conflict. Indeed, it is sometimes not the strike itself but its anticipation that permits a viable solution.

Sociological, economic and political studies seem to confirm the view that strikes have a role to play in modern institutionalized industrial relations. In particular, it has been said that strikes:

are by no means as disruptive as they are supposed to be;
help to maintain a sound balance in negotiations between capital and labour;
make it easier to carry out reforms and enforce popular demands;
are one of the vital safeguards of modern democracy.

As far as the disruption caused by strikes is concerned, it is frequently argued that the costs of such disruption are negligible as compared with other factors that affect production and the utilization of the labour force. If we take the total number of days lost through industrial accidents in Great Britain, we find that they amount to about 20 million working days per year. Unemployment of 1 million results in an annual 200 million working days lost, and certificated sickness costs 300 million working days. If we compare these figures with the total of working days lost by strikes in 1978 − 10 million − the amount seems negligible (Coates and Topham, 1980, p. 201). Another point to be noted in this respect is that, in most cases, lost working days are compensated for by overtime work and increased productivity when the strike is ended.

In some cases, strikes occur when the volume of production is shrinking because of falling demand. As Turner observes:

In these circumstances the strike becomes almost a form of 'work spreading'. To have a strike is not perhaps the most rational way to fill in a slump, but it is more interesting and sociable than some other forms of idleness, and helps to keep workers from drifting away to other jobs. [Turner *et al.*, 1967, p. 118]

Turner points out that the number of lost working days in the motor car industry is particularly high in periods of recession, when management tends to lay off workers in order to reduce production. This last point raises a further argument about the willingness of management to accept strikes as an alternative to laying off men in periods of recession: they can then blame the trade unions for lost production, while saving considerably on unproductive expenditure.

As for the relationship between employers and employees, industrial action is the principal trump card of the employees in the delicate structure of industrial power. The suspension or elimination of the right to strike puts an end to free collective bargaining and makes it far easier for the employer to impose his terms. Once strikes are legalized they become a powerful weapon in the fight for economic and industrial reforms. It can rightly be argued that a socio-economic system can operate only as long as it has enough inner resources to carry out the necessary reforms and adjustments in the face of internal conflicts and environmental pressures.

One of the big issues in communist countries in this respect is their inability to adjust and correct their economic policies. Strikes do not function in those countries as signals of popular discontent, the result being that the decision-makers usually learn too late, and often with disastrous consequences, of the necessity to 'change course'. On the other hand, in the West, industrial action makes the employers and the government aware of the problems of employees and allows them the opportunity to seek alternative courses of action in situations where popular discontent is increasing. Many observers therefore argue that strikes, or at least the threat of strikes, prevent the petrification of large organizational structures and compel managers to reform their policies and undertake structural rearrangements that they would otherwise have avoided or delayed.

In conclusion, it is commonly accepted that industrial conflict is not necessarily disruptive. Strikes are regarded as an integral part of the system of free collective bargaining and as an ultimate protective measure to which the workers may resort in defence of their living standard. A survey conducted between 25 and 30 November 1975 by NOP Market Research Limited, with a systematic probability sample of 1,827 electors, provided information about the attitudes of the British public to industrial action (see Table 9.6). From this it seems obvious that there is wide approval for strikes that are called for economic reasons only.

Another example of the attitudes of the public towards strikes is revealed in the results of a survey conducted by Marplan in July 1977 among a sample of 1013 respondents (Table 9.7).

Discussion of the positive functions of strikes is not confined to economic issues, however. For those who defend the right to strike and who wish to see strikes as a permanent institution of modern life, the strike is but one aspect of the fundamental right of citizens at large to defend themselves against private interests, managers, state bureaucracies and the majorities enforcing their views irrespective of minority interests. The social balance of power has thus become the focal point in legitimizing the right to strike: withdrawal of labour is regarded as the last resort of many groups that are deprived of any alternative means of influencing the decision-makers.

From this point of view, the right to strike plays a dual role. On the one hand, it is regarded as part of the mechanism of collective bargaining; on the other hand, it is treated as an institutional guarantee of the rights of employees and minorities in general as far as unfair decisions made by power elites and majority interests are concerned. What was previously regarded as being an economic weapon has gradually developed into a political device that is to some extent one of the major safeguards of democracy in the West. It is small wonder that restrictions

TABLE 9.6
PUBLIC OPINION ON INDUSTRIAL ACTION

*Do you agree or disagree with unions calling strikes?*

| Reason | Agree strongly & Agree % | Don't know % | Disagree & Disagree strongly % |
|---|---|---|---|
| To obtain better working conditions | 55 | 12 | 33 |
| To achieve security of employment | 45 | 14 | 41 |
| To obtain higher wages | 35 | 15 | 50 |
| To achieve shorter working hours | 20 | 14 | 66 |
| To get Parliament to change law | 18 | 17 | 65 |
| To get the government to change its policies | 17 | 14 | 69 |
| Against the laws they don't agree with | 13 | 14 | 73 |
| To get the government to call general elections | 12 | 12 | 76 |

*Source*: NOP (1976)

TABLE 9.7
REASONS FOR OFFICIAL AND UNOFFICIAL STRIKES

*Are official strikes usually called for good or bad reasons? And how about unofficial strikes?*

| | All adults | | Trade unionists | |
|---|---|---|---|---|
| | Official strikes % | Unofficial strikes % | Official strikes % | Unofficial strikes % |
| Very/quite good reasons | 76 | 23 | 83 | 34 |
| Very/quite bad reasons | 24 | 77 | 17 | 66 |

*Source*: Marplan, London, 1977.

on the right to strike are an integral part of authoritarian regimes. Both in Nazi Germany and in Soviet Russia the independence of the trade unions, and the right to strike in particular, have been regarded as a major danger to the regime. In the West, the strike is seen as a legitimate weapon that maintains the independence of the working population but does not damage the fabric of social life to the same extent as wars or guerilla action. It is thus a legalized procedure based on the real social balance of forces, yet is contained within limits acceptable to society as a whole.

## STRIKES AND STAGNATION ECONOMY
## – A REAPPRAISAL

As I have said, strikes are regarded nowadays as an integral part of free collective bargaining – as an ultimate sanction available to employees when all mechanisms of voluntary agreement have proved unsuccessful. It should be noted, however, that the very institution of free collective bargaining is often questioned. Inflation makes it more and more difficult to compensate workers with substantial wage increases at a time when economic stagnation does not encourage industrial firms to invest capital to increase productivity; and even if they do so, higher productivity invariably results in higher unemployment as long as markets do not expand to take up the increased output. At the same time, governments are determined to fight inflation by policies that restrict economic growth, thus intensifying these processes. In these circumstances, the aspirations of public and private sector employees cannot be met as easily as in periods of rapid economic growth. Yet the industrial power of many trades and occupations to an extent defies economic constraints. No wonder that in many countries governments have recourse to a prices and incomes policy, that is, suspend free collective bargaining and expect unions to toe the line. Strikes then become political even if they pursue limited economic aims: the employees who enforce wage increases directly challenge government guidelines and place into disrepute the parliamentary acts or voluntary agreements on which incomes policies are based.

Within the framework of free collective bargaining, the function of strikes changes too. Permanent inflation makes frequent wage/salary adjustments inevitable. Because these claims add further fuel to the inflationary spiral, especially in the public sector, there is a permanent wrangle over wage rises and the motivation to strike increases. Gradually, all sections of the labour force learn by experience that only by pressing their demands hard can they defend their living standards against inflation; those left behind find it very difficult to catch up later. Thus, in some sectors negotiations take place under the ever-present threat of strike action, while in other sections, where the threat of a strike is less effective, confrontations have become an annual ritual.

Strikes are more disruptive in economic and social terms than ever before. The growing 'systemness' of Western economies makes them much more vulnerable to prolonged strikes in key industries: for example, a strike by miners, power workers, lorry drivers or railmen, may paralyse the entire economy. As far as the services are concerned, their breakdown causes widespread inconvenience and suffering that increasingly affects ordinary people, usually those in the lowest income brackets. Thus, a strike by lift workers keeps old people virtually imprisoned in their council flats; a strike of railmen deprives those without cars of the ability to get to work; a strike by welfare workers affects those totally dependent on their services, etc. Thus the right to strike can be called into question. As Roberts comments:

When the costs of striking exceed the benefits to society, the case for an unlimited freedom to strike calls for re-examination. The right of any group to inflict great economic losses on society must be judged in the light of the situation of those who would stand to gain. When wages were very low, conditions of employment extremely bad, and power so distributed in society that redress was extremely difficult to secure, strikes were clearly justified. When, however, most strikes are not called to remedy a fundamental injustice, but to advance already high standards of living — often at the expense of those in a weak bargaining position — striking has little ethical justification in a society which gives its citizens a high standard of living, full freedom to change jobs, protection against adverse social circumstances and the opportunity to participate actively in the process of income determination at all levels. Social attitudes towards the right to strike are also likely to be greatly influenced in the future by the fact that under modern technological and economic conditions they are becoming increasingly costly. [Roberts, 1968, p. 22]

## WILDCAT STRIKES

The problem of wildcat strikes is a relatively new phenomenon caused by the historically changing nature, scope and institutions of collective bargaining. As long as the unions did not operate on a national scale and agreements were confined to single factories and companies, the distinction between local and industry-wide strikes was more relevant than that between official and unofficial strikes. The distinction is also more important when unions are supposed to support the strikers financially than when strikers are dependent on their own resources. Similarly, the concept of illegal strikes varies according to the institutional framework. The variations between different countries are set forth in considerable detail in Clegg's comparative study (1976b). These are summarized in Table 9.8, from which it can be seen that in some

*Industrial Conflict*

countries (for example, France) strikes cannot be illegal or unconstitutional. In other countries they might be illegal but not unconstitutional or both unconstitutional and illegal. Finally, in Great Britain, strikes cannot be illegal yet they are very often unconstitutional (although some strikes cannot be recognized as official simply because of their short duration). Thus what makes a strike unofficial or unconstitutional is, primarily, the institutional framework within which strike activities take place.

TABLE 9.8
INSTITUTIONAL FRAMEWORK OF STRIKE ACTIVITY

| | Legality | | |
|---|---|---|---|
| *Constitutionality (the requirement of union approval to make a strike official)* | *Some strikes outlawed* | *Agreements legally binding* | *Strikes not subject to legal restrictions* |
| All strikes need formal recognition | | USA Sweden | Great Britain |
| Some strikes need formal recognition | | Germany | |
| Strikes do not need formal recognition | Australia | | France |

*Source*: Compiled from Clegg (1976b).

Wildcat strikes are first and foremost *local* strikes that are neither initiated nor approved by the relevant union(s) and therefore take place without proper guidance by the unions. Such local strikes do not follow established procedures or conventions agreed on a national and local basis, but reveal a high degree of spontaneity. In other words, they contradict the principle of the institutionalization of industrial conflict to which I referred above.

For those who analyse industrial relations from the point of law and order, unofficial strikes are but one aspect of 'informal' industrial action at the shopfloor level. Dubois (1979), commenting on the situation in Britain, observes that many striking shop stewards today have no hesitation in condoning other kinds of disruption. They may refuse to cooperate if such cooperation assists management, they may insist on certain formal rights and customs, they may resort to a 'go-slow' or refuse overtime work. All these forms of pressure are generally approved of by the unions, but they are also largely spontaneous.

A different situation arises when a disruption, in particular a strike, is called in opposition to a union's instructions. Such cases have to be analysed in terms of a conflict between the union and local interests arising on the shop floor. From this viewpoint, wildcat strikes are seen as more anti-union than anti-employer. Eldridge and Cameron (1964) point out that unofficial strikes should be seen as:

an expression of dissatisfaction with complex rules;
an anarchic protest against the very existence of rules;
an expression of opposition to existing anomalies in the rules and a
    demand for reforms.

This line of argument leads to the 'anatomy' of unofficial strikes. It is obvious that, apart from legal considerations and ideological preferences, it is difficult to make a full analysis of the causes of unofficial strikes and of their dynamics because of the very limited numbers of studies carried out in this area.

Two detailed studies cast light on wildcat strikes. The first is by Gouldner, who describes an unofficial strike at a gypsum plant in the USA; the second is by Lane and Roberts, who provide a fascinating analysis of the well-known English strike at the Pilkington glass works in 1970.

Gouldner distinguishes between pseudo-wildcat strikes (those whose formal leaders claim they have little control over the situation but nevertheless exert influence) and genuine wildcat strikes, in which the formal union leaders have lost control and the strike is led by individuals whose position in the formal structure does not prescribe such a role for them (Gouldner, 1955, pp. 92–3). In the latter case, Gouldner emphasizes several features:

they may be regarded as 'an expression of aggression against the dila-
    tory manner in which workers' grievances are being dealt with';
they involve 'issues ordinarily of 'little interest' to labour and business
    leaders';
they mark a loss of power of official leaders (Gouldner, 1955, p. 95).

Gouldner notes that, prior to the strike he was investigating, relations between workers and management were fairly good, owing to what Gouldner calls 'indulgency patterns' and what workers themselves regarded as 'leniency'. Workers were permitted to organize their work the way they liked, provided they carried out their tasks properly; they were given a second chance if fired; they were allowed to swap their jobs; and those who were injured or fell sick could expect to do light work until they had fully recovered. They were also allowed access to firm's tools and materials for their private use. Only when management was changed and a new policy of rationalization was initiated did conflict arise. Gouldner discovered that technological changes, managerial succession and strategic replacement connected with technology resulted in closer supervision, which rejected the traditional 'indulgency patterns' and enforced rules that the workers regarded as irrelevant or petty. Faced by growing resistance to newly introduced bureaucratic rules, management responded by tightening up supervision — that is, by aggravating the original tensions. To counteract this effect, bureaucratic rules were used to allow the supervisor 'to show that he is not using close supervision on his own behalf, but is merely transmitting demands that apply equally to all' (Gouldner, 1964, p. 177). Nevertheless, a vicious circle had been created.

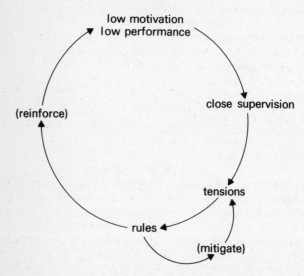

The important point in this case is the legitimacy of the workers' demands. As far as the 'indulgency patterns' were concerned, the workers themselves did not regard their grievances as legitimate, since they saw previous policy as owing more to managerial goodwill than to any formal obligations. This was one of the reasons why they reciprocated the indulgency by a willingness to obey and to work.

The issue of 'indulgency patterns' is particularly important for an understanding of the nature of many wildcat strikes because, as Gouldner points out, these were problems outside the scope of official union action. Even when workers translated their dissatisfaction into officially recognized claims, they were still concerned with the break in leniency patterns, something that could be neither defended nor officially promoted by the union. In consequence, the disparity between what the workers really wanted (or resented) and what the union could offer became the major factor of discontent. For the same reasons, the management could not easily come to terms with the workers even if they were prepared to satisfy their legitimate claims. The wildcat strike then developed into an outburst of frustration that was difficult to resolve. The managers, who were willing to deal with legitimate demands, could not attempt to remedy grievances that, in their opinion, were unjustified, especially within the context of market forces that limited their own course of action.

A similar point was raised by Lane and Roberts in their discussion of the Pilkington strike. This strike began as a minor dispute over a clerical error and only later was the purpose of the dispute transformed into a wage claim. As they put it:

Clearly there is a big difference between an organised strike and a wildcat. In the first there is a declaration of war in the form of a strike notice. In the second there is a revolt in which all the normal constitutional channels are thrown to one side. In these circumstances it is by no means unusual for the demands to be formulated *after* the strike has started. It often appears as though the only way that strikers can make themselves understood is by putting a price on their return to work even though the original reason for coming out may have possessed only the most tenuous relationship to money. [Lane and Roberts, 1971, p. 17]

The most interesting part of the study of Roberts and Lane concerns the anti-union character of the strike. In this respect, they seem to support Allen's view:

The existence in Britain of a high proportion of unofficial strikes indicates an important defect in formal union activity. It is an indictment of unions not of employees. The way to reduce unofficial strikes is to adapt union organisations so that they are involved in strike moves, thus making them official.... Unofficial action is informal trade unionism, occurring because formal unions are incapable of fulfilling their functions satisfactorily and have, for this reason, lost some control over their members. [Allen, 1966, p. 115]

The Pilkington strike arose ostensibly over wage miscalculations, but quickly developed into a struggle for higher wages. The union (the General and Municipal Workers' Union) aggravated the situation by insisting on the usual bargaining procedure and instructed workers to return to work before negotiations could start. As the workers had been dissatisfied with the union for a long time, they came to see the conflict as a reflection of the union's shortcomings. In this respect, the Pilkington strike was a rebellion not only against the management but against the union too.

The principal reason why such strikes are unofficial is that a union simply feels that a particular claim is not within its province, as was the case at the plant studied by Gouldner.

The analysis of the Pilkington strike reveals that the GMWU tended to regard its members as *clients* rather than as *participants*: 'The "members" pay their dues and in return are provided with certain services — provided they do as they are told' (Lane and Roberts, 1971, p. 55). Communications between the union hierarchy and the rank and file was poor. The union was undemocratic, officials held their posts indefinitely, many of them were graduates without shopfloor experience, union mechanisms eliminated the more militant contestants for union posts and in any case opposition was not tolerated. For union officials a wildcat strike immediately spelled trouble, since to concede their members' demands would mean to encourage them to take matters into their own hands again. The emergence of the Rank and File Strike Committee was, in the circumstances, an expression of anti-union feeling, even if the union's appeal for an early return to work was formally fully justified. Since differences with the management were settled within a fortnight, the prolonged strike was due mainly to wranglings between workers and union, the rebels fighting for their autonomy and their rights against the union headquarters. The GMWU obstinately refused to declare the strike official, thus contributing to the escalation of the strike. This took headquarters by surprise and challenged its authority. On the other hand, the crisis was aggravated by the full support given to the union by Pilkington's management. After three weeks, comment Lane and Roberts,

[the strike] became a very straightforward power struggle. It was not so much that each party misunderstood the aims of the others, indeed the contrary, for the opposing generals understood each other very well. The point was that the interests of one cut right across the interests of the others. [Lane and Roberts, 1971, p. 240]

Seen in this light, a wildcat strike may be regarded as an essential instrument of trade union democracy in a situation where rank-and-file workers are deserted by their union.

Yet an upward trend in the incidence of wildcat strikes leaves us with the unsolved problem of the extent to which they undermine the main principles of contractual agreements. The right of the minority to oppose and the duty of the minority to conform are very delicately balanced. When a revolt takes place this may be regarded as a symptom of a more serious conflict that is not confined to the formal opposition of minority—majority rights but arises out of contradictions and signals the shortcomings of the existing institutions.

The Donovan Report (1968) stated that wildcat strikes were the major problem of industrial relations in Great Britain (see Table 9.9).

National agreements were not officially binding on the parties concerned, legal constraints did not exist, informality prevailed in the negotiations at the shopfloor level and in consequence rank-and-file workers remained in a state of permanent confrontation with the employers. McCarthy (1970) emphasizes similarly that the major difficulty confronting industrial relations in Britain is an upward trend in unconstitutional strikes, which sometimes means strike-prone groups in particular firms or plants, and odd strikes that tend to paralyse large sections of plants or firms because substantial numbers of workers are involved in lay-offs.

TABLE 9.9
OFFICIAL, UNOFFICIAL AND OTHER STOPPAGES OF WORK
DUE TO INDUSTRIAL DISPUTES,
AVERAGE ANNUAL FIGURES, 1964–66

| *Type of stoppage* | *Number of stoppages* | *Number of workers involved* | *Number of working days lost* |
|---|---|---|---|
| Official strikes | 74 | 101,100 | 733,000 |
| Partly official strikes | 2 | 600 | 7,000 |
| Unofficial strikes | 2,171 | 653,400 | 1,697.000 |
| Others, e.g. lock-outs or strikes by unorganized workers, unclassified | 25 | 2,700 | 15,000 |
| All | 2,272 | 757,800 | 2,452,000 |

*Source*: Donovan (1968) p. 97.

The increased incidence of wildcat strikes identified by the Donovan Report (1968) indicates a tendency towards industrial anarchy, which manifests itself in unilateral action by sections of the labour force in several factories or in unilateral action by the workers of one factory. Donovan explains the reasons for this development as being the result of several factors, among which the following are most important:

the growing importance of local bargaining;
the relative independence of shop stewards and workers in regard to
    unions;
the lack of respect for voluntary agreements at the local level;
the lack of institutionalized procedures for dealing with grievances at
    the local level.

In other words, we face a growth of *i n f o r m a l i t y*. This is apparent not only in wildcat strikes but also in many other aspects of industrial relations, a tendency that has been described as the 'de-institutionalization' of industrial conflict. It may indicate that present-day institutions and organizational structures are often inadequate to cope with the many everyday problems that arise on the shop floor.

## STRIKE DYNAMICS: CONCLUDING REMARKS

Studies of both official and unofficial strikes reveal important aspects relating to their causes. In addition to the official demands that are presented as the reason for industrial action, there are many other motives that have to be taken into consideration. These may exist prior to the outbreak of the strike or they may develop after the strike has begun. We can distinguish:

*Replacement* of genuine goals, which may be regarded as illegitimate or less relevant legitimate demands, as happened in the strike described by Gouldner or in the stoppage at the Halewood factory of the Ford Motor Company in 1971 (analysed by Hyman, 1977, ch. 1).

*Escalation of the conflict* when original demands are expanded and new grievances arise during confrontation, as happens whenever there is victimization of the strikers or other events add fuel to the parties' militancy.

*Translocation of the issues* when original demands become less relevant or irrelevant in view of the new grievances and demands that arise during confrontation.

In these processes, new factors have to be taken into consideration to explain a particular strike. Some of these factors are rational, especially when underlying strategic considerations are more important for the strikers than their overt demands. Other factors are purely emotional: bitterness, resentment, frustration and hatred can motivate people as much as the prospect of financial gain and retaliation.

A series of studies in strike dynamics gives us an insight into these processes and mechanisms. The history of the miners' strike in Britain in 1926 (Morris, 1976), the monographic studies of wildcat strikes by Gouldner (1955), Lane and Roberts (1971), Beynon (1973) and many others have led to a growing understanding of why strikes occur. In other words, irrespective of the general causes that affect the incidence of strikes, each conflict has its own history, background and logic, and these must be carefully evaluated by all who wish fully to understand it.

# CHAPTER 10

# Industrial Democracy

## INTRODUCTION

No concept seems to be more fashionable among progressives of any orientation than 'industrial democracy': it is promoted by Labourites and Conservatives; it has become the battlecry of both the militant Left and of ordinary citizens; it is supported and praised on both sides of the 'iron curtain', by 'hawks' and 'doves' alike. The idea is by no means new. Many of the issues discussed nowadays go as far back as the doctrines of William Godwin (1756–1836), Robert Owen (1771–1858), Pierre Joseph Proudhon (1809–1865), Mikhail Bakunin (1814–1876), P. A. Kropotkin (1842–1921) and George Sorel (1847–1922), who all opposed the centralist orientation of state socialism. The most influential of the movements that followed this line of thought were syndicalism, industrial unionism and guild socialism.

The syndicalists denounced the state as the organ of centralized power and objected to those who were in favour of disciplined political parties acting on behalf of the workers. They pointed out that those parties were the bearers of a new elitism aimed at the creation of a new oppressive power at the expense of an independent and spontaneous working-class movement. They therefore wanted factories to be run entirely by trade unions. Syndicalism developed in France (from the late 1880s) in opposition to the Fédération Nationale des Syndicats and struck roots in other European countries despite attacks by orthodox unionism and socialist democratic parties. Industrial unionism developed in the United States: in 1905 'The Industrial Workers of the World' (Wobblies) was created to promote the doctrine of revolutionary unionism and to encourage direct worker action. Guild socialism developed in Great Britain as a movement on behalf of workers' control in industry, participative democracy, the extension of self-government in all spheres of social life, and a generally pluralist society based on organizations of producers, consumers, civil servants and citizens at large.

A generalized view of the links between mass action and industrial democracy was elaborated by Sorel in his theory of social myths. Sorel argued that social behaviour is governed primarily by feelings and ideals that lead people to try and transcend social reality and to act according to what they believe to be right and just. 'The myth must be judged as a means of action in the present; any attempt to discuss how far it can be taken literally as future history is devoid of sense', wrote Sorel (1961, p. 126). He referred to industrial democracy as an ideal directing human action; by resorting to a general strike the masses could liberate themselves from the yoke of private property.

The idea of the general strike (constantly rejuvenated by the feelings roused by proletarian violence) produces an entirely epic state of mind, and at the same time bends all the energies of the mind to that condition necessary to the realisation of a workshop carried on by free men, eagerly seeking the betterment of industry. [Sorel, 1961, p. 248]

The dispute within the labour movement between the advocates of direct industrial democracy and the 'centralizers' continued throughout the nineteenth and the first half of the twentieth centuries, but the tide obviously turned in favour of state socialism. The state socialists were able to support their case by pointing to the increasing power of the workers' political movement. In the West, social-democratic parties fought for political reforms and opted for state interventionism; in the East, the Soviet Communist Party from the onset doggedly opposed any idea of spontaneous mass action and devolution of political power. After the Second World War the ideology of state socialism was firmly established, but some progress toward industrial democracy was also taking place.

After the collapse of the short-lived Nazi 'empire' there was a general tendency throughout Western Europe towards the creation of workers' councils. In France, *comités d'entreprise* were established by the law of February 1945. In Germany, where the principle of codetermination had been incorporated into the Constitution of the Weimar Republic but where works councils were subsequently abolished by the Nazi regime, there was a post-war re-emergence under the provisions of the Codetermination Act of 1951. In Italy after the defeat of fascism, the demand for workers' councils increased and new status and functions were awarded to the internal commissions of workers. In Belgium, factory councils were created in September 1948. In 1951 the International Labour Organisation recorded more than thirty countries where permanent organs of workers' participation existed, of which the major ones were workers' councils, worker directors and joint committees (Horvat *et al.*, 1975, vol. I, p. 45).

However, in the 1950s and early 1960s the impact of these tendencies seemed to fade. The growing affluence of the Western world coincided with a marked decrease in working-class radicalism. The triumph of state interventionism and the rapid expansion of large corporations did not leave much room for codetermination; collective bargaining covered the most important aspects of industrial relations and unions did not press for the development of alternative forms of power-sharing and control. In these years the idea of industrial democracy was primarily the concern of social scientists who saw it as a pragmatic device of social engineering that could be used to increase worker satisfaction by supplying the work force with more information and permitting participation in group decision-making. Experiments in different forms of social participation were supported by big business and some social-democratic governments in an attempt to deal with apathy and the lack of commitment of workers. In Scandinavian countries like Norway or Sweden, trials in industrial democracy became official policy.

At the end of the 1960s the situation changed radically. New impetus to the development of industrial democracy was provided by the social and political movements of the late 1960s and early 1970s. Students' movements in the late sixties promoted the idea of direct participation and mass activism, which was also encouraged by the experiences of China and Cuba where revolution seemed to be progressing. Various minority groups in Western Europe enthusiastically supported the idea of direct representation to counter the shortcomings of parliamentary democracy in dealing with the claims and interests of minorities. The same trend was occurring with local interest groups: many resorted to direct action, set up community centres and voiced the need for further development of participation at all levels. There was also a strong undercurrent of opposition to the centralized administration in East European communist countries, where the experience of Yugoslavia had encouraged the idea of self-management. The Prague spring in Dubček's Czechoslovakia and the uprising of the workers in Poland in 1970 brought to light the growing dissatisfaction of the population in Eastern Europe with a command economy and authoritarian power structures. These new social and political trends were reflected in the ideology of the New Left, which dissociated itself from bureaucratic and authoritarian state socialism and promoted instead the idea of direct participation.

European governments did not remain indifferent to the new political climate. It should be noted that in EEC countries the principles of industrial democracy were integrated within the mainstream of industrial policy. The Statute for the European Community of June 1970 provided for a separation of managerial functions from those of supervision and control, and declared that workers' representatives should constitute one-third of the members of supervisory boards, which would have the power to appoint and oversee the managerial board. The draft Fifth Directive of the EEC Commission of September 1972 proposed the introduction of codetermination in all member countries. In April 1973 this proposal was reaffirmed by the Committee on Social Affairs. The European Commission has suggested that there should be a ten-year transitional period in which workers would be gradually given greater managerial power within Common Market countries. Even in Britain, where the idea of industrial democracy seems least advanced, the new approach gained favour with the main political parties. The TUC also modified its approach to workers' representation, contrary to its previous opposition to the EEC proposals, which it regarded as being inappropriate for Britain.

As we see, the idea of industrial democracy is rooted in different social and political conditions, including the experiences of industrial corporations in the West, mass movements of the late 1960s in the USA and Europe, revolutionary governments of the communist type, socialist democratic parties in capitalist countries, and ideological and political confrontation within the communist world. In view of the differing circumstances that have generated the pressure for industrial democracy, the concept must cover many inconsistent and even contradictory expectations and demands. There seems to be little point in defining industrial democracy in a manner equally acceptable to the many different parties committed to it. What can be done, however, is to take a generalized approach based on identifying those elements that reject the conventional wisdom of centralism and/or state socialism. Among the features that seem most relevant are the following:

A desire to restructure work situations faced by individual workers in terms of the values of self-expression, self-respect and control over the social environment: the *individual* worker, or employees in general, have become the focus of attention, in contrast to the anonymous masses identified by the various doctrines of industrialism.

An emphasis on relationships between workers and managers in industrial units, especially in factories: attention to *local* problems is based on the idea that participative democracy is relevant in the direct work environment as a counterforce to the growing bureaucracy of the corporation.

A new goal — employee *commitment* to the targets and aims of industry, as opposed to the class war dogma that has dominated the political and industrial scene for the past decades.

Further *encroachment* on managerial prerogatives, so far jealously guarded by management even if they do acknowledge the right of employees to use their bargaining power to influence managerial decision-making: the sacred principle that managers must manage and workers must obey has been directly challenged, along with the traditional reverence for technocracy and the authority structure in industry.

Growing acceptance of the *legitimacy* of claims for participation in a world of private property (or alternatively under systems of near-scared one partly rule communist countries) — based both on pragmatic arguments (effectiveness and efficiency) and on the ideological values of egalitarianism, which reflects the rising social status of the working man.

All these tendencies belong to a new political culture, which is increasingly dissociated from the traditional ethos that has dominated the world of industry and political and social movement in the twentieth century.

The appeal of the idea of industrial democracy is indeed widespread. Managers hope that the participation of workers in industrial decision-making will make them more satisfied with their work, more inclined to identify with managerial goals, and more willing to contribute voluntarily to the efficient running of enterprises. Social reformers of all persuasions believe that industrial democracy provides the world with an obvious answer to the problems created by the alienation of labour. Radicals advocate industrial democracy as the fulfilment of revolutionary ideals and hope it will serve as an instrument of resistance against the deviations of power-seeking dictators. Revisionist communists believe industrial democracy is the correct way to follow the Marxist road to socialism against the attempts of the 'red bourgeoisie' to maintain state capitalism in the guise of the proletarian state. Social scientists carry out innumerable investigations demonstrating all over again the psychological and social benefits of democratic participation (see Blumberg, 1968). Marxist scholars collect every scrap of information to prove that worker pressure for self-management is becoming the dominant focus of the class struggle (Coates and Topham, 1968). The democratic opposition in Eastern Europe uses the Yugoslav experience to corroborate its view of the economic superiority of workers' councils over all other forms of industrial management.

In all discussions and studies, one question reappears time and again — will industrial democracy really work and fulfil expectations? The findings in that respect seem pretty confusing. Paradoxically, in most experiments on group participation, the impact of the democratic style of leadership on individual satisfaction and group performance has been repeatedly demonstrated, and yet in many scholarly reports we typically find statements about workers' apathy and lack of interest in such participatory schemes. Managers who appear enthusiastic about participation in theory and who favour further study and experimentation are nevertheless reluctant to approve the implementation of more

radical schemes of worker control in their own enterprises. The British
labour movement, declaring sympathy for greater social control of
industry, gives only lukewarm support to the development of shop
steward committees and invariably promotes orthodox unionism with
its emphasis on centralized collective bargaining and national agreements. The concept of worker control appears also to be part of the
ideology of nationalization, yet in the nationalized sector worker participation seems often confined to trivialities.

The communist countries, which started their revolutions with
appeals for workers' (and soldiers' and peasants') councils, were and
are determined to prevent any attempt by workers to introduce self-
management in industry in opposition to the centralized power of the
state. Yugoslavia is the exception; it is where the implementation of
industrial democracy is most advanced, although regular complaints
are voiced about the limited influence of workers in the workers'
councils compared with the growing role of the managers and professionals. At the same time, more radical scholars emphasize that
the system of self-management does not counterbalance the dictatorial
power of the political elite in Yugoslavia.

Those who comment on these disparities adopt various arguments.
One argument is that the deficiencies of participatory schemes are the
result of the inadequacies of both capitalist and communist societies,
since participation at lower levels contradicts the status of dependence
of workers on higher levels of the power structure. As Gurvitch puts it:

The failure of the experiences realized up to the present in the non-
collectivist countries represents only the defeat of *reformism*, which,
relying on works councils, hoped to transform capitalism peacefully
into socialism. The first attempts of industrial democracy under a
capitalist regimen achieved no palpable result...Industrial democracy
will be either revolutionary or postrevolutionary, or else it will not be.
[Gurvitch, 1975, p. 20]

A second approach is gradualist, in its view that although it is difficult
for new ideas to take root in an unfavourable setting, at the same time
they generate new forces that will transform the existing social order.
A third perspective dismisses the whole idea of industrial democracy
at the macro level as purely utopian, although acknowledging some
positive aspects of participatory schemes within well-defined and
localized situations.

Arguments against industrial democracy often refer to the technological requirements of mass production, to organizational constraints
in large-scale enterprises, to the competitive nature of the market
economy, to the unavoidable clashes of interest of different occupational groups, to the detrimental effects of sectional pressures, and to

the shortcomings of workers not prepared for participation in managerial activities.

It seems that there are no black and white answers to all these objections and arguments. What we can do is to analyse the problems step by step, to evaluate methods and ways of solving the issues involved, and to try and delineate the areas of possible conflict and likely agreement among the various groups committed to industrial democracy.

## ANATOMY OF THE CONCEPT

The variety of interests and expectations surrounding the practice of industrial democracy accounts for the confusion about the concept itself. Industrial democracy can be defined as 'the term applied to a wide range of ideas of which the common element is the extension of the decision-making process within an enterprise, away from a single body and towards the whole work force' (Chiplin *et al.*, 1977, p. 15). However, there are at least two distinct meanings of the term: one is *social participation*, a concept derived primarily from psychological studies and social techniques applied in group dynamics; the second is *workers' control* (and *self-management*), based on socialist ideology and leading to the modification of the power structure in the enterprise. The two meanings partly overlap since participation and power-sharing can be presented on a single participation/influence scale that reflects the *degree* of workers' control:

(1)  sharing the information about the enterprise;
(2)  consultation and advice (before or after certain decisions are taken by management);
(3)  participation in decision-making;
(4)  decision-making.

It is clear that every step ahead in workers' participation means an encroachment upon the power structure of the enterprise. There are, however, other aspects to be considered before we are able to evaluate the specific ways in which social participation may be exercised.

An important distinction in the realm of participation and control is that between *negative* and *positive* power. Scanlon (1968) argues, for instance, that although 'there exists...a considerable degree of workers' control in individual factories...even the extension of the current type of "workers' control" can be seen as holding only a watching and limiting function on the "rights" of management'. Both positive and negative  power can be applied with varying effects, depending on whether they are exercised in regard to minor decisions, some important decisions, or all important decisions.

Participation or even full control is often granted only in those sections of work life where no important decisions are made from the point of view of managerial interests. Democracy within small work units in the enterprise does not necessarily erode managerial power at the middle and top levels. The sectors of little concern for the higher executives are areas such as sports clubs, welfare activities or nursery and health facilities, where both goals and means can be left to the discretion of employees. In communist countries, where control over workers in the enterprise is very tight, social activities and problems are left to the trade unions, which have a final say in the allocation of flats, granting loans, distributing tickets for sports events and supervising leisure grounds.

We need also to consider the degree of legitimization and *institutionalization* of workers' rights in contributing to decision-making. There is a basic difference between schemes of participation that have been granted by the management as a temporary or experimental device without any obligations on its part to preserve those schemes in the future, and institutions that are regarded as a basic workers' right, the preservation of which might be, if necessary, enforced upon management. Whether such institutions are based on custom, written agreements or legal acts is of secondary importance, provided a distinction is drawn between what belongs to the discretion of management and what constitutes part of the workers' prerogatives.

*Institutional forms* must also be taken into account when we discuss industrial democracy, each institution having a certain social potential and political dynamic of its own. It makes a lot of difference how elections to workers' councils are organized — whether regular conventions of workers' representatives take place, or alternatively, whether such councils operate within a framework of other institutions (unions, directors, etc.). There is also a wider social context that has to be considered, that is, the relationship between the constitution of an enterprise or of a firm and the power structure in society at large.

Figure 10.1 summarizes these elements of social participation (and workers' control). This typology can constitute a ranking order as well, so that different systems of participation can be seen roughly as 'different degrees of advancement on the road of effective application of the idea of workers' participation in management' (Tabb and Goldfarb, 1975, p. 63).

The belief that more democracy is always better than less democracy, and the view therefore that the ideal solution would consist of implementing the full range of self-management devices does, however, meet with serious objections and needs qualification.

1. Degree of participation: information — consultation — decision-making

2. Type of power: negative — positive

3. Scope: minor decisions — some major decisions — all major decisions

4. Basis: favour — custom — local agreements — national agreements — legal acts

5. Structure/institutions: informal meetings — joint consultation boards — advisory councils — referenda — worker directors — general councils

FIGURE 10.1 *Typology of various aspects of participation*

*Source*: See Tabb and Goldfarb (1975) p. 63.

## THE NEGATIVE ASPECTS
## OF SHOPFLOOR PARTICIPATION

Studies on industrial democracy pay much attention to 'shopfloor' participation, especially to decision-making within the work units that are the basis of the everyday tasks and operations. It is at this level that social psychologists and sociologists find worker participation to be most beneficial to the enterprise. Studies by White and Lippitt (1960), Coch and French (1948), French *et al.* (1960) and many others have demonstrated the impact of increased participation on group output, group morale and overall satisfaction.

A series of studies of the fragmentation of labour in mass production reveals the disruptive effects of an organization of labour that imposes meaningless tasks upon workers and transforms them into more or less 'happy' robots. The new work ethic is well summarized in the title of a *Newsweek* article: 'Too many US workers no longer give a damn'. As Westley and Westley state in their study:

The modern blue collar worker, in spite of his competence, his high aspirations and expectations, is unable to find a place in his society and feels alienated from his work and from his union. This frustration can only produce dissatisfaction and restlessness...He has a highly modern orientation, a different sense of self, and a much more equalitarian and liberal attitude toward his relationships and responsibilities to others...He finds the fragmentation and routinisation of tasks devised by men like Taylor to make him efficient, repulsive and demeaning. He is dissatisfied with his work, and increasingly challenges the competence of foremen and the rights of managers. [Westley and Westley, 1971, pp. 117–19]

There is also evidence of growing worker dissatisfaction with mass production methods in the communist countries. Russian and Polish sociologists report that the better educated the workers, the more they resent boring and repetitive jobs. Workers with ten or more years of education wish to apply their minds to the work they perform; they want to have a say and to exercise their independent judgement in work processes. As soon as they encounter unimaginative and dull jobs in big factories they become frustrated, embittered and resentful, in spite of the relatively good wages many of them enjoy.

Participation at shopfloor level is actively supported by the advocates of socialist transformation. Crosland, who seemed to be particularly concerned with the form of 'alienation which cannot be ascribed, as it was by Marx, to the system of property relations, nor yet to the absence of workers' management', emphasized this point:

But the predominant view among social psychologists appears to be that the problem is basically one of 'democratic participation' — not, however, the mass participation of *all* workers in the higher management of the enterprise, but the participation of the *primary* work-group in deciding how its *own* work should be divided, organized and remunerated. On this view, we must study the enterprise as a social organism, unravel the natural group relationships, and endeavour to align these with the technological necessities of the work process. The emphasis is on creating structured work-groups, rationally endowed with increased group responsibility and internal group leadership. [Crosland, 1959]

Bearing these arguments in mind one has to remember that collective decision-making is often ruled out by the nature of the circumstances. Technological requirements, organizational designs, economic pressures and social constraints are important factors to be reckoned with whenever we consider the scope of social participation and self-management at the shopfloor level. Work groups can sometimes be allowed and encouraged to decide on their own methods of production, pace of work and quality of output, but in most cases technology imposes serious constraints upon the structure of tasks within work units and does not allow for deviations from established patterns. There is also the economic pressure of the market: firms that are subject to the demands of the labour force may find it cheaper to solve their difficulties by further automation, which brings about a decrease in the number of the workers, increases unemployment and therefore reduces employee militancy. Social constraints are also important: in most communist countries there is still a large residue of rural population to take the most unattractive and unpopular jobs; in some developing countries a rapid improvement in wages and working conditions helps to maintain a submissive labour force; in some other countries the same effect can occur with high unemployment.

In view of all these limitations, advocates of industrial democracy at shopfloor level point out that reforms need to be incorporated into the technological and organizational framework through a policy of pragmatic gradualism rather than an 'all or nothing' approach to participation, and by combining participation on the shop floor with reform of the enterprise's organizational structure so as to give employees the right to exercise influence at higher levels of decision-making. Practical solutions consist of: introducing schemes based on a realistic assessment of the degree of decentralization achievable in a given sector; modifying the power structure where some independent decision-making can be left to workers; adopting techniques that maximize participation in some aspects of industrial processes even when full control is not feasible; and developing institutions that reaffirm the *right* of employees to use the channels of influence that are available.

## PARTICIPATION AT THE MANAGERIAL LEVEL

It is argued that although social participation may be limited on the shop floor and within work units, it could be implemented at the higher levels of decision-making either by the replacement of managers by workers' councils, or at least by reducing management and substituting joint decision-making. It is at the managerial level, however, that organizational requirements seem to be at odds with any substantial development of workers' participation in decision making.

Most studies of large-scale organizations show that collective decision-making has limited application when the organization has to react speedily and effectively to a changing and unpredictable environment. An army at war is the best example of an organization in which democratic government is made impossible by the pressure of circumstances. Industrial enterprises are similar in many respects.

The growing professionalism of industrial management is similarly inhibiting to joint decision-making, because the running of the enterprise cannot be given to people who are unable to work full time and do not have the necessary training and experience to perform managerial functions. For the same reasons, control of managerial activities by outsiders is usually ineffective. An outsider can hardly assess what is going on within an administrative unit unless (a) he is supplied with adequate information about what happens behind the scenes; (b) he has the training and experience to look for relevant data and to analyse the information supplied; and (c) he has time to absorb and interpret the information. No wonder, therefore, that auditors, accountants and other highly trained professional experts often have to be used in order to secure permanent and effective control of directors and managers.

The self-generating processes of oligarchy within organizations can create obstacles to attempts at democratizing managerial decision-making. The major reasons for such tendencies are: unequal access to information, giving those involved in top decision-making an advantage over others; unequal ability to solve problems and hence to influence the major processes that affect the positions of other participants; and unequal access to the means of power, that is, to the use of positive and negative sanctions.

When arguing for industrial democracy one can forget that, although authority structures generate some constraints and inconveniences for workers, democratic processes create many problems at managerial level. Adizes (1975, p. 183) has pointed out that, in group decision-making by workers, risk-taking is not necessarily related to expertise; long-range planning may be constrained because of the rotation of decision-makers; executives are placed in a passive role, yet are responsible for the outcome of decisions formally made by others; management status and prestige are undermined as formally they are left to deal with routine matters; generally there is little scope for individual responsibility; the results of hard work by management are not necessarily attributed to it, especially when much effort is expended in convincing the group to accept a decision — once the group is convinced, the decision may be considered theirs rather than management's; role ambiguity and group decision-making reinforce the difficulties of predicting behaviour, since they postpone feedback and make this feedback somewhat ambiguous.

Rank-and-file employees often lack the motivation and interest to participate in management discussion and to carry out control functions not connected with their direct interests. The everyday pressure of work, lack of adequate training, difficulties in following arguments incomprehensible to outsiders — all these factors deter rank-and-file employees from active participation and leave room in participatory bodies for careerists and operators who often use their position to promote their own interests.

The difficulties of participation at managerial level are particularly great in those plants that form part of multi-plant enterprises, and even more so in multinational corporations. The complexity of the organization greatly reduces the possibility of joint decision-making at the places from which orders emanate, and managers at lower levels are supposed to follow orders from above.

In view of all these factors, some determined advocates of self-management emphasize the necessity of designing new schemes and forms of industrial democracy that can offset the difficulties of exercising control at the managerial level. Horvat, who strongly argues for 'self-management' or 'associative' socialism, lists the following disadvantages of including workers in business decision-making:

1) A reduction of efficiency because it delays operational decisions and because correct operational decisions require that full working time be devoted to them, and not only sporadic meetings of an hour or two.
2) The illusion and deception that control is exercised, when it is in fact lacking because of inadequate expertise or insufficient information (full information requires full working time); and
3) The irresponsibility of people in the operational apparatus, who obtain without difficulty the cover for each of their dubious actions of self-management bodies entangled in operations. [Horvat, 1975, p. 142]

Referring to his investigations of seven industrial and sixteen handicraft work organizations in which the workers were much better informed than normal, Rus comments:

...we could almost agree with the thesis that, in handicraft enterprises, because of the non-specialized function of management and the homogeneous skill structure, collective decision-making is possible, while, in work organizations in industry and in *similar* organizations, *self-management* in the sense of collective *decision-making* is impossible. The consequence would thus be the following: we must urgently develop a type of self-management that will correspond functionally to those organizations that have already achieved a high level of division of labor. [Rus, 1975, pp. 103−4]

Worker directors are regarded as an answer to some of the problems indicated above, but even here there are many difficulties. Jones, in his discussion of employee directors in the British Steel Corporation, states:

Because the employee directors had to resign their trade union positions, it meant that they gradually ceased to have a detailed knowledge, arising out of their own activities, of the views of the trade unions and this resulted in their opinions becoming progressively more personal as opposed to representative. [Jones, 1973, p. 99]

A two-year experiment with worker directors in the British Post Office (Tylor, 1979) is a good example of the difficulties experienced by management, who felt the union representatives' attitudes were unhelpful. Both managers and independent observers believed that the union directors were mainly concerned with industrial relations, which impaired current business issues and long-term policy making, while the worker directors were concerned mainly with employee interests, and paid insufficient attention to the needs of the public and to organizational efficiency. The general lack of confidence in the benefits of worker directors can be seen in the failure of the report of the Committee of Inquiry on Industrial Democracy to recommend this strategy (Bullock, 1977).

The main criticisms of worker directors can be summarized as follows. Firstly, the introduction of worker directors is not a solution to the industrial unrest and wildcat strikes that are said to be crippling British industry. Secondly, the idea has been taken out of context by imitating German experience. In Germany, worker directors operate within a framework of workers' councils, while the unions concentrate their activities on local and national wage bargaining and other employment matters. In the British context, worker directors would simply extend the power of the unions or, if based on alternative principles of representation, would undermine the position of the unions and of the shop stewards' committees.

It is noticeable that in most countries the shift towards industrial participation has occurred through workers' councils rather than by formal representation on company boards. The reports by Emery and Thorsrud (1969), which cover the experiences of Norway, West Germany, Great Britain and Yugoslavia, point out that representation on company boards does not seem to make much difference to the rank-and-file member. The prerogatives of workers' councils usually go beyond the functions of direct management, which leads some writers to conclude that workers' control should not be exercised at the managerial level at all, so that the managers can manage without unnecessary interference.

Other authors distinguish between decision-making related to the social and technological issues and to commercial issues, and assert that only the former should be reserved for worker representation while the latter ought to be left to management. However, technical problems and personnel policy overlap to such an extent that any clear-cut division is difficult.

There is little possibility of giving managers the instruments of organizational power without running the risk of them abusing their position to the detriment of those who are subject to their control. Those at the top are always endowed with effective weapons for use against rebels, deviants and reformers, and it is no wonder that in all institutional systems there is discontent with authority and pressure from rank-and-file members to oppose it. But to challenge this inequality means, ultimately, to challenge organized hierarchies in general, that is, the very organizational principles upon which enterprises are run. It seems that there is no way out of the dilemma. Instead, we have to *acknowledge the contradictory nature* of effective leadership and of participative democracy at the managerial level, in the same way that it has been acknowledged in political life, where the administration and the democratic framework have to coexist somehow, and have to limit each other by constant conflict and readjustment.

## PARTICIPATION IN POLICY-MAKING AND THE LIMITS OF SELF-MANAGEMENT

Many observers of the industrial scene argue that if the principle of participation cannot apply to managerial activities, then the employees (similar to shareholders) should have a final say in top level policy-making decisions at which general targets are set and recommendations issued as guides to everyday managerial activities. Workers' councils are similar to parliaments in that they are sovereign with respect to all other sections and levels of administration in the enterprise. The hiring and firing of directors is one of the prerogatives of such bodies.

It goes without saying that such a system implies a complete shift of power from the owners of the enterprise towards the employees. Even under full socialism the success of such a system is by no means sure, since it implies full, or at least fairly advanced, decentralization. But decentralization, or in effect syndicalism, has its critics. Apart from the arguments put forward by the state socialists, the most pertinent criticism of the syndicalist approach is that of the guild socialists, who offer their own modified version of self-management in industry.

One of the most prominent advocates of guild socialism, G. D. H. Cole, emphasized that the ownership of the means of production should be vested in society, with none of its parts being allowed to impose its own interests upon the others. He distinguished three types of economic control:

(1) control over the products to be manufactured or supplied, i.e. decisions on 'what should be produced', 'in what quantities', 'where', and 'when';
(2) control over *methods* of production;
(3) control of the conditions under which work is performed, including pay, discipline, hours of work, etc. (Cole, 1920).

Cole believed that the proper form of external control over industry is through the expression of common needs and desires on the part of those who consume products. He argued that society as a whole should be the collective owner, but pointed out that it is at the same time subdivided into different sections in which people act as producers, consumers, civil servants or citizens. Since industry is a matter of both production and consumption, Cole rejected the proposals of the syndicalists who claim that *producers* should control all spheres of social life, and argued instead that it should be up to the consumers to decide what, when and in what quantities should be manufactured and supplied. Under private enterprise, that type of control is exercised by market forces. He foresaw, however, a system in which complete socialization of the economy could and should operate under essentially consumer control. The workers ought to control the normal conduct of industry, but they should not be permitted to regulate the prices of goods, to decide for the consumer what he shall consume or, in short, to exploit the community as the individual capitalist exploits it.

As far as control over methods of production is concerned, again Cole expressed doubts about whether workers should act as the sole decision-makers, and emphasized that their attitude towards technology was often biased against raising productivity through new processes because of the fear of unemployment. Occupational interests, insofar as they oppose technological change, could, he believed, be restrained in this post-capitalist order in such a way that producers would still enjoy a considerable say in the control of their methods of production. After all, consumers need not decide *how* things should be produced; experts could list the efficient alternative methods and technologies, while producers could decide which of the options to use.

The area under producers' control would be all the conditions of work — except for wages and hours, which could be regulated centrally. 'Just as the government does not interfere with the internal discipline of army or navy, it must leave the industrial armies to manage their own affairs, while keeping a share in supreme direction and telling them what it wants made, but not how to make it' (Cole, 1972, pp. 69–70).

Cole's important distinctions throw new light on much of the controversy arising from discussion of self-management at national level. The state socialists (that is, the centralizers) claim that there would be unavoidable conflict between sectional interests, decision-making and the interests of the general public. They criticize the syndicalists for their misgivings over the nature of a socialist economy and what they see as an over-emphasis upon central planning as the major feature of the socialist society. For Cole, that dilemma does not arise; his plan implies a combination of central decision-making with political and economic pluralism, thus allowing for the articulation and implementation of different social objectives and interests.

## WORKERS' SELF-MANAGEMENT AND STATE SOCIALISM

The dreams of the advocates of industrial democracy have tended to concentrate on the victory of socialism, which is seen as the way to the perfect society. Yet the greatest challenge to all democratic institutions has been the emergence of communist systems, which not only eradicate workers' autonomy, but turn the clock back by imposing on wage-earners harsh administrative rule reinforced by ideological manipulation and authoritarian supervision.

The idea of workers' control was first generated with the Paris Commune of 1871, which was regarded as a model of industrial democracy. In 1917 the slogan 'power to the soviets' became the battle cry of the Russian revolution. Factory committees were legalized by the provisional government in May 1917; in the same month the first congress of delegates of workers' and peasants' soviets took place in Petrograd and the first Petrograd conference of factory committees was organized. At the second congress of the soviets, the power of the soviets of workers, soldiers and peasants was proclaimed and soon afterwards factory committees were ordered to supervise industrial enterprises. In the years 1917–1919, workers' councils (often short-lived) emerged in the many revolutionary upheavals in Europe, including England (Leeds), Switzerland, Hungary, Germany, Poland and Italy (Horvat, 1975, vol. 1).

In no time at all, however, the idea of workers' self-management became anathema to the Bolshevik Party. The fate of the Workers' Opposition led by Kollontai and Shliapnikow in 1920 and 1921, the enforced incorporation of the left-wing socialists into the Communist Party, and the 'nationalization' of the trade unions, which have since been regarded as part of the centralized apparatus, marked the development of the communist order. Communist parties dissociated themselves from self-managed socialism and from the principle of devolution of revolutionary power. It was only after the Second World War that the traditional notion of worker self-management re-emerged in Yugoslavia, but this too was violently denounced by the Cominform as an anti-people imperialist plot.

If we view the Soviet Union as the embodiment of state control, Yugoslavia can be regarded as the only communist country where the model of self-management socialism has been at least partly implemented. Before 1950, political and economic centralism prevailed in Yugoslavia, and it was only when Tito broke his ties with the communist bloc in 1948 and was faced by an economic blockade and by internal economic difficulties because of the overcentralization of the national economy, that new ways of social and political recovery were sought. After initial attempts at encouraging greater worker participation, in June 1950 the federal Parliament passed the Basic Law on the Management of State Economic Enterprises and Higher Economic Associations by Work Collectives, which started the present self-management in Yugoslavia. Reform involved large-scale decentralization that shifted much of the responsibility and decision-making onto individual enterprises. At the same time, the councils have undermined the authoritarian structure of one party rule by depriving it of the power to intervene directly in many areas of the national economy and administration.

The three major steps in implementing the reforms were:

(1) The introduction of the decentralization of the economy whilst retaining the influence of the state in major decisions concerning wage policy and investment (1950–56).

(2) Gradual widening of the powers of self-management bodies in relation to the distribution of incomes within the enterprises, while leaving decisions about investment in the hands of the state (1956–65).

(3) A shift in decision-making since 1965 – as far as investment is concerned – to the enterprises. Central government is now concerned with decisions relating mainly to general purpose funding (including help for developing areas).

The whole development amounted to a gradual transformation of the nature and functions of the state. Apart from the decentralization of the national economy, which by itself restricted the central authority, the whole balance of power changed in favour both of the self-managed enterprises and also of the lower levels of administration.

What is characteristic of Yugoslavia is that self-managed institutions of all kinds and at all levels have become part of the very fabric of the society, and that they have become integrated with the political structure to an extent unacceptable in any other country within the communist bloc.

However these reforms have not eliminated authoritarianism. In fact, authoritarian management and participative institutions can coexist even within the formal democratic structure of the enterprise, and even more so at higher levels. As Zukin asserts:

All research...shows that the distribution of influence is hierarchical, with executives at the top and workers at the bottom...workers want only as much power as they already have...[N]ot only the actual decision-making power, but also the potential for sharing in this power ...is restricted to the ranks of a political-cum-technical elite...self-management as an ideological goal has little relevance to people's everyday lives. [Zukin, 1975, pp. 98, 189–91]

In spite of all these reservations and qualifications, workers' self-management has become the battle cry of the democratic opposition in all communist countries where any form of economic or political autonomy has been consistently denied by the ruling communist party.

All movements in these countries aimed at challenging the power of the ruling elites are accompanied by demands for the restoration of independent workers' organization. Where these movements can develop beyond the stage of political grievances, the claim is then for workers' councils and direct action to fight against the party and state bureaucracy. The Polish 'October' in 1956 developed along these lines with workers' councils mushrooming all over the country. Similarly the Hungarian revolution released the frustration of the workers in 1956, and the riots of Polish workers in 1970 culminated in workers' meetings presenting their demands to the leaders of the party-state.

From this perspective, industrial democracy in the Soviet bloc seems to be much more *a political device* than a formula for economic organization, although the idea of workers' self-management of the syndicalist type is periodically revived in discussions about the economy. But so long as the communist Leviathan consists of concentrating all power in the hands of the few at the top of the organizational hierarchy, incorporating all institutions and associations into the party-state system and monopolizing all instruments of coercive control, the very idea of workers' organization and workers' control is tantamount to heresy since it contradicts that system. The organizational elites do their best to prevent free associations and to destroy any attempt at creating self-governing bodies that are not subject to institutional supervision.

A careful analysis of the 'revolutionary demands' put by the democratic opposition in the peoples' republics reveals the same overall pattern. These demands are for the rotation of administrators and functionaries; for elections; for popular decision-making in all sorts of participative bodies — trade unions, youth organizations, cooperatives; for the wider use of referenda; and, above all, for self-management in places of work, which implies workers' power not only in the economic but also in the political field. Invariably there are additional demands for unrestricted information and for social supervision of the institutions that represent the system of organized force — the secret police, in particular. In this context, participative democracy can be seen as a means of institutionalizing safeguards against centralized power, a way of exercising influence and maintaining rank-and-file control over structures that by their very nature tend to subject individuals to unchallengeable dictatorship. Such ideas necessarily remain vague as long as there is no chance of transforming them into mass action. Yet it is clear that there is a general trend towards participative democracy, and that this is opposed to the traditional form of democracy, which involves periodic elections of full-time representatives who 'by general consent' exercise control over society as a whole.

## PROSPECTS FOR INSTITUTIONAL CHANGE

Progress towards industrial democracy implies not only developing a spirit of cooperation but building up new institutions complementary to or as alternatives to the existing ones. However, institutional change cannot be arbitrarily planned and implemented by law without taking into consideration other institutions that operate in the same area and the general patterns of social life, which make some forms of participation more acceptable than others.

The institutions regulating industrial relations in Great Britain are based on the principle of free collective bargaining, with the acknowledgement of the right of managers to manage. The idea behind this is that it is up to the managers to meet the workers' demands through improving industrial performance and by maximizing profits. The outcome of this system was acceptable in most developed countries during the 1950s and 1960s. It is only relatively recently that a new trend towards prices and wages policy has emerged, together with attempts to commit the unions and workers in general to national interests. At the same time, the growing concern of firms with labour unrest makes managers more responsive to the idea of industrial democracy.

The extent to which strikes have become a serious problem in large-scale industries can be seen from Table 10.1. The recommendations of the Ryder Report on British Leyland are pertinent for any large-scale enterprise:

Means must be found to take advantage of the ideas, enthusiasm and energy of British Leyland's workers in planning the future of the business on which their livelihood depends...The contribution which we are seeking to the reduction of industrial disputes and the improvement of productivity can only be made in an atmosphere of joint problem-solving by management and unions. There should be a framework, removed from the normal arrangements for collective bargaining, in which agreement can be reached on the action required. We have therefore proposed a new structure of joint management union councils, committees and conferences, in which BL's shop stewards particularly senior shop stewards will have a major rule. Trade union members will have to recognise the new responsibilities which the shop stewards are exercising on their behalf and ensure that the right people are chosen to exercise these responsibilities. [Ryder, 1975, pp. 37 and 42]

Industrial democracy is thus conceived of as *a new means* of ensuring the cooperation and commitment of workers and as *a new system* of protecting their interests, not at the bargaining table but from inside, by participation in decision-making and having common responsibilities. However, institutional change is difficult when it amounts to a set of alternative values and principles.

TABLE 10.1
STOPPAGES BY SIZE OF PLANT,
ANNUAL AVERAGE 1971—1973,
MANUFACTURING INDUSTRIES IN GREAT BRITAIN

| Plant size | Number of working days lost per 1000 employees |
|---|---|
| 11—24 | 14.8 |
| 25—99 | 72.4 |
| 100—199 | 155.0 |
| 200—499 | 329.1 |
| 500—999 | 719.4 |
| 1000 and more | 2046.1 |

*Source*: *Department of Employment Gazette* 26 November 1976.

There is little doubt that the obstacles to the development of industrial democracy in Britain lie not only in property relationships and
the authority structures of large-scale enterprises, but also in the
unions, which are well adjusted to their collective bargaining function
but for this very reason find it difficult to accept the responsibility of
collective decision-making. The traditions and structure of the union
movement, the sectional interests represented by different unions in
the same enterprise, and the delicate balance of the unions' relationship
with their members, are all factors to be reckoned with when we discuss
the prospects for industrial democracy. For these reasons, other countries' experiences are not necessarily valid; differences between the
position of the unions in Germany, Scandinavia, France and Great
Britain are enormous and so, correspondingly, are their reactions to
the progress of industrial democracy (Clegg, 1976b, pp. 83—98).

The dilemma faced by British unions is best seen in Clegg's argument that the basis of industrial democracy is the ability of the unions
to challenge and oppose management. Hence independent unions are
the condition for maintaining democracy in industry.

One of the main tasks of trade unions is to limit and control those
persons and institutions who wield direct authority over industry.
If trade unions were too closely connected with industrial management
they would not be able to do that job. [Clegg, 1963, p. 28]

According to Clegg, then, workers' participation is contrary to their
interests. By becoming part of management, unions would lose their
capacity to represent the workers and to oppose the management in
negotiating collective agreements.

...the syndicalists, the industrial unionists, the guild Socialists and even supporters of joint control all thought they had a means of creating a far better order in industry than capitalism could ever offer. Now we think we know better. Their proposals would not have led to an industrial democracy. On the contrary, they would have undermined the existing institutions of industrial democracy, already developed under capitalism. [Clegg, 1963, p. 76]

But in spite of reservations, interest in new institutions based on participation and power-sharing has increased. The appeal of participation and co-management is not confined to private enterprise but is on the increase in the public sector as well, where, because of state control, interventionism and macro-economic planning, industrial democracy is potentially more important. Long term-planning, high-cost capital investment, the cumulative effects of technological, economic and organizational change — all these factors mean it is virtually impossible to renegotiate *substantial* issues once they have been implemented. Far-reaching, large-scale and long-term decision-making seems incompatible with selective control, *ex-post* bargaining, and periodic revisions of current policies. Clearly it is at the very beginning that interested parties need to take part in the governmental process, be it deciding about wages, motorways, research and development, new industrial investment, housing projects or international agreements.

The whole economic framework has become more 'decisional', in that the situation of all groups is determined more and more by government decisions on economic and social policy. Efforts by workers to influence these decisions therefore increase — the focus of the power game is shifted from local to the governmental level, and the parties involved become more concerned with administrative expertise. This in turn has far-reaching effects on the strategic position of workers, as their cooperation has become potentially more useful to the state. It is at this level that a new controversy about self-management is bound to loom large. The governmental bureaucrat who used to be regarded as a mere tool of the privileged minorities has been transformed into an arbitrary master located in well-organized power structures that supply him with the means for controlling many aspects of social and industrial life. The debate over industrial democracy cuts right across the basic division between those who are for a socialist planned economy and those who are opposed to it. Post-capitalist societies seem to generate new problems that are not easily solved within the framework of traditional institutions.

# Guide to the Literature
*by Peter Cook*

The intention in this section is to provide a brief account of some of the issues raised in this book, together with a list of relevant reading for both students and teachers. With this in mind, the emphasis is upon the accessibility of sources. There are occasions when an article in a journal of decades past is difficult to obtain, but is nevertheless generally regarded as being a 'milestone' in the literature. In such cases, the use of an up-to-date summary of the original is necessary. Similarly with sources in general: if an easily obtainable summary of the main arguments is available, then it is used. Also, because the underlying purpose is to guide the newcomer to the subject through alternative analyses and interpretations, there is often an absence of what may be regarded as academically important, but nevertheless fairly inconclusive, work that does not amount as yet to a coherent or comprehensive school of thought in its own right.

The guide follows the structure of the book except that closely related chapters are dealt with as one section.

## INDUSTRIALISM AND INDUSTRIAL SOCIETY

As many of the issues that could be raised in this section appear later, only the most general approaches to industrialism will be dealt with.

The concept of industrial society may be said to include the ideas of progress, purpose, sequence and inevitability (Nisbet, 1967; Rostow, 1971). Industrialization creates a growth in possibilities and problems, and at the same time may be thought to proceed in a technologically determined manner.

The concept is not easy to discuss, for to refer to *industrialism* is to imply a technological determinism that relegates the descriptions 'industrial capitalism' or 'industrial socialism' to being mere sub-types. Essentially this is the argument of Kerr *et al.* (1973) and Dahrendorf (1976), who claim there are certain characteristics that one can associate with the increasing industrialization of society; as society develops, so does its effect on the socio-economic structure. This general trend toward structural consistency between societies, known as the 'convergence thesis' (Bell, 1974), has been subjected to much criticism. Generally the

251

case against is that, whatever the technologically determined tendencies, they are overshadowed by the differences between industrial societies based upon their system of productive ownership and the state as an independent political determinant (Giddens, 1974). A criticism of the critics (Watson, 1980), however, is that they often argue against the notion of convergence on the basis of an analysis that *starts* with industrial capitalism.

A useful general source on industrial society is Aron (1967), whilst both Durkheim (1964) and Weber (1968) were concerned with what they saw as some inherently dehumanizing features of industrialism.

## SOCIOLOGY OF THE ENTERPRISE

Before presenting sources relating to specific topics, there are a number of books that are sufficiently general and useful that they may be consulted throughout this section. Eldridge (1971), Child (1973) and Fox (1971), for example are all relevant to many of the issues. Parker *et al*. (1977), Vroom (1964) and Argyle (1972) also cover much of the ground in this section, whilst Dubin's (1976) book is a substantial collection of readings that will complement the field covered.

A general historical account of the changing conceptions of work over the ages may be found in Anthony (1977), whilst Braverman (1975) is a Marxist account of the change or 'degradation' of work under capitalism, linking this process with class structure.

General approaches to the relationship between man and technology include Friedmann (1955), who gives a comprehensive analysis of the major issues. Schneider (1957) and Miller and Form (1964) both have useful introductory chapters covering the way in which work in industrial society is fundamentally different from work in simpler societies. Bell (1961) examines the cult of efficiency in modern industrial society, but see also Meissner (1969). For personal accounts of the experiences of industrial workers, see Fraser (1969) and Palm (1977). Bendix (1963) analyses the ideological processes by which the work force in various countries was socialized into the factory work ethic.

Social scientists have long been concerned with and interested in the effects of certain types of technology upon workers – assembly-line work in particular, which intuitively at least has been regarded as the extreme application of technology for the division of labour. But any discussion of repetitive work eventually reaches the concept of *alienation*, a concept that has tended to be ill defined and broadly applied. Some of what Marx said on alienation may be found in Burns (1969), but much of the discussion of this phenomenon often includes the Durkheimian concept of *anomie*: Faunce (1968) summarizes most of the approaches that have been taken, but see also Seeman (1959), which has been used as the basis for much empirical research on the concept, and Form (1975), who takes a Durkheimian approach. Marcson (1970) includes readings on alienation and technology from many authors, including Seeman and Faunce. Blauner's (1973) is perhaps the best-known attempt to operationalize this concept, concluding that the degree of alienation in (manual) work varies with the kind of technology employed and that, as systems of production move from the more alienating mass production techniques to the less alienating process technology, the general level of alienating industrial work should therefore fall; see also Gardell (1971). This approach has been challenged by Form (1973a), and Davis and Taylor (1972); and for a thorough critique of Blauner's conception of alienation as a subjectively preceived experience, see Eldridge (1971).

The alienation perspective on modern work is consistent with the human relations/self-actualization approaches of such writers as McGregor (1960), Likert (1961), Maslow (1954) and Herzberg (1968), who argue that men are basically motivated toward autonomy, achievment and responsibility — innate tendencies that are subverted by the constraints of industrialism. Policy decisions that can flow from this type of analysis include attempts at job enrichment and a participatory style of management. This line of thought in industrial sociology has been influential in the past and has led many researchers to the car assembly lines: Chinoy (1955), Walker and Guest (1952), Goldthorpe *et al.* (1968).

Exponents of the socio-technical approach (Sayles, 1958; Trist *et al.*, 1963; Woodward, 1965) argue that technology largely determines social behaviour in that the division and allocation of tasks in the workplace is circumscribed by the technology; see also Burns and Stalker (1961) and Trist and Bamforth (1969). Although much research was based upon this perspective, especially since it held out great possibilities for restructuring the work environment, it has been criticized for being too narrow. In addition, some empirical research showed that because firms using the same technology were quite different from one another in many other respects, technology was not therefore the major explanatory variable (Turner *et al.*, 1967). Goldthorpe *et al.*'s (1968) criticisms were that the worker had been treated as a passive responder to technology, and that attention had not been paid to the values brought by the worker into the work situation.

This 'social action' perspective indicates that prior orientation to work is crucial in determining responses to the work situation (Dubin, 1956). But the social action approach has in turn been criticized because, it is claimed, orientations can arise as a *response* to the work situation (Beynon and Blackburn, 1972; Biddle and Hutton, 1976), whilst Daniel (1969) argues that it is an oversimplification to claim that any worker has a single orientation to work, and that the Luton studies came dangerously close to being rooted firmly outside the factory gates – the reverse of criticisms made against the socio-technical approach, which largely ignores the world beyond the work-place. Whelan (1976) provides a useful summary of both the action frame of reference and its critics, whilst Kalleberg (1977) provides empirical research drawing heavily on the action perspective.

Vamplew (1973) draws on both Blauner's and the social action perspective in his study of chemical process plants, finding that there is considerable explanatory merit in both. Useful general accounts in this area include Schein (1965), who challenges managerial assumptions on orientations to work, and Lawler (1973), who discusses the general theories of job satisfaction and fulfilment and the relationship between extrinsic and intrinsic rewards. Sutermeister (1976) also discusses, along with a useful collection of contributions from other writers, the whole area of work satisfaction, organizational structure and the way this relates to productivity.

Concern for the quality of working life, when it is not expressed in terms of the complete overthrow of the capitalist system, takes the form of proposals for job enrichment or job restructuring. Wild (1975) argues that mass production technology can be adapted to improve working life without endangering efficiency. He cites examples of job enrichment in practice, as does Weir (1976), who also provides a wide selection of readings on job satisfaction; see also Warr and Wall (1978). But for a critical review of such attempts see Clegg and Dunkerley (1980), although it is worth reading an account of work in Eastern Europe by Haraszti (1977).

The overall position after the development of all these perspectives is, firstly, that satisfactions or dissatisfactions with work may be regarded as either intrinsic or extrinsic and, secondly, that orientations and responses are dynamic in that they vary among individuals, according to time, place, circumstances and social background; see Watson (1980) and Blood and Hulin (1967). If, as is argued by some, job satisfaction is determined by the level of integration with middle-class work norms (Turner and Lawrence, 1965), then attempts at job enrichment will prove disappointing in terms of improving employee satisfaction. Morse and Weiss (1955) and Hyman (1967), for example, show that concern with the intrinsic aspects of work increases with the individual's position in the occupational hierarchy. Berg (1973) and Sheppard and Herrick (1972) relate level of education to expectations of intrinsic work satisfaction; see also Crozier (1964). If correct, and other things remaining equal, this will mean that work generally will be felt to be more alienating in the future (Rothwell and Zegveld, 1979). But the variables are many, making firm conclusions and clear-cut policy-making decisions tenuous.

Discussion of work groups in industry has tended to be an extension of orthodox organizational theory: the organization is seen as being a system of largely independent parts that in various ways work as a whole toward management-directed organizational goals (Barnard, 1956). This approach tends to ignore both the motives of those who set the goals and the wider social environment in which the organization operates (Watson, 1980; Clegg and Dunkerley, 1980). With this in mind, the relationships between management and workers, among the work-force itself and between small informal groupings of workers are relevant areas of sociological enquiry.

The most influential early research in this area is the human relations school of thought. This arose partly as an empirical refutation of scientific management or Taylorism, which see man as an asocial, self-seeking animal. Mayo (1962) described it as a 'rabble hypothesis'. Essentially, it claims that the worker is interested in work only in terms of reward, so that without close management supervision and planning of tasks he will tend not to work. But, managerial expertise should enable the enterprise to strike a bargain with the worker on the basis of maximum payment for maximum reward − the point at which this occurs being determined by management. A revealing account of the effects of Taylorism may be found in Beynon (1973), who reviews its application to motor car manufacture. Braverman (1975) shows that scientific management is not only still the predominant managerial approach but is really the logic of capitalist production. We can also refer here to Fox's (1974) argument that work relationships are moving increasingly toward relationships of low trust between employers and workers, and that this trend is increasing the instability of Western societies, as evidenced by the inability to control inflation and industrial conflict.

The human relations response to Taylorism revolved around the famous Hawthorne research project, which by and large showed that variations in the physical environment or money rewards would affect the worker's behaviour and output only through his social relationships and interactions at work. Details of the research may be found in Roethlisberger and Dickson (1964), although there are numerous summaries of both Taylorism and the development of human relations; see Clegg and Dunkerley (1980), Parker *et al.* (1977). Landsberger (1958) discusses the research, arguing that it has often been misinterpreted, whilst Carey (1967) offers a thorough critique. Mouzelis (1967) argues that there is a certain continuity in thought between Taylorism and human relations in that the industrial sociologist or psychologist came to assist the engineers in attempting to raise production. Further criticisms are that assumptions are still made about the individual and that a basic conflict of interests between workers and managers is largely ignored.

Even so, the influence of this school has been considerable, as it appears to offer solutions to low morale and productivity (Homans, 1968; Kahn and Katz, (1960), both in terms of participation at work (Coch and French, 1948) and in terms of 'styles' of leadership (White and Lippitt, 1953). Not surprisingly, given the general management orientation of much of the research in this area, the question of deliberately restricting output has arisen. The Hawthorne research showed that group norms are established regarding the 'normal' level of output for each worker, social sanctions being applied to those who under-, as well as over-, produce. Such behaviour can be seen as being 'rational' from both a human relations or a scientific management point of view, in that it may reflect a discrete form of wage rate bargaining with management, a strategy for improving job security or simply a 'norm' increasing group cohesion; see Roy (1952) and Katz (1965), who argues that the worker is bringing an element of his culture into the work-place and thus partly neutralizing the enterprise's organizational structure. Later work, however, produced the criticism that the study of group dynamics could not be contained within the confines of the organizational unit, that external factors and forces need to be taken into account (Rose, 1975).

The influence of the technology applied in a work setting upon social relationships and group formation has been the subject of a number of studies. Again, Blauner's (1973) work on the application of technologies is useful here, as is Sayles (1958). The technological approach to organization argues that technological complexity to a large extent determines organization, both formal and informal. The earliest studies using this perspective were on the mining and textile industries, where, it was said, the group was neither a technical entity nor a social entity as such, but an interdependent socio-technical system (Trist, 1976; Trist and Bamforth, 1969; Rice, 1963; Scott *et al.*, 1963; Trist *et al.*, 1963). Woodward (1965) took the argument a stage further, arguing that technical complexity influenced the kind of supervisory control and managerial hierarchy in an enterprise. This approach has been used extensively (see Perrow, 1970, and Pugh and Hickson, 1973), although structural differences seem to relate more to size than to technology; see Clegg and Dunkerley (1980) and Curran and Stanworth (1979). Further studies that tended to use or assess the technological perspective include Blauner (1973), Walker and Guest (1952), Chinoy (1955), Goldthorpe *et al.* (1968) and Form (1972).

An alternative line of thought much concerned with organizational effectiveness and job satisfaction is the neo-human relations school. Again, there is a reliance upon some notion of 'human nature , where 'man' is placed in a technological work environment and investigated to see if there is a 'fit' between his natural self and his work; the best known writers in this area are: Likert (1961), Herzberg (1968), McGregor (1960), and Argyris (1964). Central to the neo-human relations approach is the idea from Maslow (1976) of self-actualization: once human beings satisfy their lower-order physiological and psychological needs, they then look to self-fulfilment. Clearly, such a perspective argues for the importance of intrinsic rewards in work and for adapting work in order to improve such rewards. Although the later approach is more sophisticated than its predecessors, it still suffers from the same basic criticisms: that the concept of the enterprise remains unitary, so that there is no explicit acknowledgement of inherent conflict.

A comprehensive review and criticism of these various schools of thought is offered by Rose (1975), who finds that their main faults have arisen because they have tended to develop as a response to the recognized deficiencies of their predecessors.

Research on leadership or supervision in industry has tended to follow the general orientations of industrial sociology and psychology — namely, an early Taylorian approach, followed by human relations and more recently by other approaches integrating some elements of the previous perspectives. It has been assumed in the past that group effectiveness or, in the work context, group morale and productivity, are crucially dependent upon adequate leadership and supervision. The earlier approaches to leadership attempted to look for and identify leadership characteristics and skills (Cartwright and Zander, 1968). White and Lippitt (1960) carried out research along these lines, finding that different leadership styles, whether autocratic or democratic, resulted in different patterns of behaviour among group members. Coch and French (1948) also found in their study of leadership in an industrial setting that change is more acceptable to group members when introduced in a more democratic, participatory manner; see also McGregor (1960).

Often the 'trait' approach to leadership produces inconclusive or ambiguous findings. This has led to an alternative view that examines the characteristics of the group and the situation in which it is located; see Likert (1961), Gibb (1970) and Stogdill (1970). This allows that groups differ in many ways and that, not surprisingly therefore, the nature of the leadership in such groups will also need to vary if goals are to be achieved. Even so, supervision is seen as being important in that the correct leadership style can both raise work-group morale and assist in production decisions. A major impetus was provided by the stress on leadership in the Hawthorne studies (Kahn and Katz, 1960); although Argyle *et al.* (1958) point out that the rises in productivity that were attributed to leadership can also be explained by other factors, and that much of the evidence cited in support of the importance of supervision is methodologically suspect. This leads Homans

(1965) to point out that, from management's point of view, they may be wiser to concern themselves with the introduction of labour-saving technology rather than attempting to find an optimum formula for supervision.

The argument is taken a stage further by Fiedler (1968, 1969) who has developed a 'contingency model' for leadership effectiveness. This sees a connection between the leader's personal qualities and leadership style, and relates this connection to the needs of the task in hand. This allows for varying levels of effectiveness for both authoritarian and democratic styles of leadership, depending upon the circumstances.

The idea that organizational or technological structure determines the effectiveness of particular leadership styles is substantiated by the socio-technical approach: Woodward (1965), Burns and Stalker (1961). See also Goldthorpe (1959), who relates technology to supervisory style in the mining industry, although Bowey's (1973) empirical research illustrates the failings of any unitary approach.

The conclusion seems to be therefore that there is no one best method of supervision but, rather, a range of supervisory styles that are more or less effective according to the prevailing conditions. Further discussion of the complexity of supervision and the difficulty of reaching firm conclusions may be found in Mouzelis (1967) and Salaman and Thompson (1980).

A description of the basic tasks that supervisors perform may be found in Thurley and Hamblin (1963). Discussion of how the foreman's role and status have been changing over the years, and how the level of rewards and satisfactions has been on the decline, may be found in Dalton (1954) and Wray (1949). A comprehensive review of the literature may be found in Dunkerley (1975). Goldthorpe *et al.* (1968) provide useful additional information on workers' attitudes to their foremen. Etzioni (1961), in his general analysis of organizations and the integration of the individual, discusses the foreman as occupying a middle position in a work structure that may well be highly integrated or highly alienating. See also Gouldner (1964), who describes changes in supervisory styles and attitudes as a result of policy changes by higher management.

For an excellent summary of previous research in leadership style, see Rosen (1970), who also describes the transfer of foremen within a factory and the consequent decline in morale and productivity. Finally, an often neglected aspect of the supervisor is his position in the social structure. Child *et al.* (1980) show that foremen vary in their perception of their position in the class structure depending upon their identification with management.

A major issue in the study of management is whether or not non-owning company management pursue profitability with as much vigour as their nineteenth-century owner/manager counterparts are said to have done. The debate, although half a century old (Berle and Means, 1968), is by no means resolved. Part of the reason for this is that whether firms pursue profits or other objectives is not simply an academic point or the concern of the stock market fraternity, but is of great importance to the functioning and legitimizing of capitalism as a social system. Authors such as Dahrendorf (1972), Galbraith (1969), Bell (1961) and Parsons (1953) claim that the sociological effect of a divorce of ownership from control, with a consequent weakening of the profit orientation, amounts to a decomposition of the ruling class. Thus we have capitalism without capitalists, or capitalism with a human face, and therefore a far less class-like society.

The extent to which this separation has taken place is by no means clear because of data difficulties. Nevertheless, many researchers do find that the ownership/management split has occurred; for a useful review of the evidence see Zeitlin (1974). The split in itself is not important; it is the behavioural consequences that are relevant, and on profitability in particular the picture is unclear (Zeitlin, 1974; Larner, 1970). Most on the Left are quite prepared to accept there has been a change in terms of personnel, but claim that this is unimportant in that whatever management's subjective orientation, profit maximization in a capitalist market economy is an objective requirement upon which criteria of success are based and the pursuit of which is necessary for corporate survival (Nichols, 1969; Zeitlin, 1974; Miliband, 1969; Baran and Sweezy, 1966).

We can also refer here to what is seen as a cultural change in managerial style; the new 'technocracy', 'organization' or 'other-directed' manager is now the norm (Whyte, 1961; Riesman, 1953; Galbraith, 1969). The modern manager, it is said, is a communicator, a person who is responsive to the problems and desires of others. This view is undoubtedly correct but, again, it does not amount to a basic shift away from capitalistic principles so much as the adoption of a more humanistic approach toward the achievement of capitalistic goals.

The above focus on management is as a functioning economic entity; however, there are other approaches. Management may also be examined in terms of their being an elite status or professional group, or as a distinct political grouping (Burns and Stalker, 1961). Managers are becoming more professional in the sense that their general level of education and expertise is rising, along with the development of a body of professional knowledge or ideology (Child, 1969). On the other hand, we must allow that they are by no means an homogenous grouping, and that day-to-day management involves just as much in-fighting and power struggles as any other orgainzation or group (Burns and Stalker, 1961; Dalton, 1959).

Management as a group and their general effectiveness in running the enterprise may be analysed from many perspectives, some of which have been discussed earlier. Burns and Stalker's typology of organizational structures as either organic or mechanistic has been related for example to technology (Woodward, 1965), Cyert and March (1963) stress that corporate goals emerge from coalitions of different interest groups within the enterprise, each of which is attempting to pursue its own goals against various constraints and often at the expense of other groups' interests. Out of this multiplicity of interests, goals, coalitions, etc. arises the 'satisficing' behaviour of the enterprise as a whole. A useful collection of general readings in this field includes Gilbert (1972).

So, although the enterprise has its goals, its management face constraints like any other group. For an excellent general analysis of management and their relationship with other competing 'stakeholders' (consumers, labour force, investors, state), see Fox (1971). The usefulness of this approach is that it is applicable to management and enterprises under both private and state ownership.

Finally, some empirical research comparing and analysing managers' day-to-day activity may be found in Stewart (1970, 1976), and Stopford *et al.* (1975) provide a varied list of case studies that indicate the diversity of problems and issues faced by management.

## THE WORKING CLASS

For an historical account of a working or labouring class and its visibility see Briefs (1975). Marx, who holds a central place in any discussion of the working class in industrial society, is best read initially through the *Communist Manifesto* (1967), which although deliberately simplified does at least set down his own and Engels' view on the working class as an oppressed yet dynamic social force. For a general introduction to Marx, see McLellan (1975) and Aron (1965), and for further elaboration see Avineri (1979), Lukacs (1979) and Ossowski (1979).

Conditions since Marx have, of course, changed considerably and it is usually these changes and discernible trends that provide the basis for criticism and alternatives to Marx. One major alternative (Dahrendorf, 1972) argues that classes are now based upon authority rather than upon economic domination or subordination. Regardless of the merits of this argument, he does nevertheless offer a comprehensive critique of Marx based upon post-Marxian developments. Most of the alternatives to Marxist analysis of social structure attempt to account for change in terms either of affluence (Galbraith, 1971; Katona *et al.*, 1971), or of changes in the occupational structure and in particular the growth of the middle class (Millar, 1966; Mallet, 1975), or of technology and expanding bureaucracy as either a unifying or pacifying force (Touraine, 1971). Summaries and analyses of the various theoretical standpoints may be found in Giddens (1974) and Crompton and Gubbay (1977).

An excellent general analysis of class in Britain and the changes that have taken place this century is Halsey (1978), which gives empirical evidence on the distribution of both income and wealth over time. See also Johns (1972), Ryder and Silver (1977) and Westergaard and Resler (1975), who focus attention upon the many salient inequalities in what is still essentially a class-based society. A more descriptive historical account of changes in Western class structures is Marwick (1980), whilst a useful collection of essays containing criticism and re-analysis of many aspects of class is Benson (1978).

The role of education in particular as a transmitter of class advantage through the generations has been the subject of extensive study by sociologists (again Halsey, 1978; Douglas, 1972; Jackson and Marsden, 1973) and, for an overall summary of the education/class issue, see Banks (1976). Recent evidence on the differential role education plays in mobility may be found in Halsey *et al.* (1980), and a companion study of social mobility in general is Goldthorpe (1980).

Perceptions of society and the individual's place in the social structure are obviously relevant to issues of social conflict, cohesion, change, etc. Variations in working-class perceptions or images have been analysed by Popitz *et al.* (1969) and Lockwood (1966). One of the most significant theoretical developments arising out of the claim that members of the working class have been undergoing a fundamental change in attitudes and outlook is the embourgeoisement thesis. Some of the argument may be found in Zweig (1961) and Millar (1966), and an outline of the embourgeoisement thesis with a well-known attempt at investigating its credibility is Goldthorpe *et al.* (1969); but see also Mackenzie's (1974) critique. Claims that there are trends towards, rather than away from, traditional working-class solidarity (Brown *et al.*, 1972; Davis and Cousins, 1975) are often based upon research from older, now declining, industries. The incorporation of manual workers into the middle class may well be a very slow process in Britain, although some American sociologists claim that it is only a matter of time and affluence (Katona *et al.*, 1971; Westley and Westley, 1971). A further area of study from the point of view of working-class change and cohesiveness is that revolving around the idea that modern capitalism is creating a distinctive skilled manual grouping (Form, 1973b; Mackenzie, 1973). A related issue is that of the middle class; Mills (1953), Mackenzie, (1973) and Zweig (1976) argue that changes involving the proletarianization of the middle class are taking place and, coupled with changes in the working class, the net effect is still very much a class-based society. See also Kelly (1980). Discussion and examination of all these analyses and the relevant (and sometimes contradictory) evidence may be found in Roberts (1978), Roberts *et al*. (1977), Giddens (1974), Parkin (1971) and Mann (1973).

Clearly at one time most of the working class was affected by poverty (Engels, 1975; Booth, 1902–4; Rowntree, 1901), but little attention was paid to the problem from the end of the Second World War until the 'rediscovery' of poverty in the 1960s. In the United States, Galbraith (1971) directed attention to the existence of poverty in the world's wealthiest nation, whilst Harrington (1963) raised the question of whether there is a distinctive subculture of poverty that, although functioning as a defence mechanism, also exacerbates the position of the poor (Lewis, 1966; Coates and Silburn, 1973; Runciman, 1967). A summary of the issues may be found in Holman (1978), Wynne (1972) and Wedderburn (1974).

An area of study related both to the subculture of poverty and to changes in the working class as they are likely to affect social stability and social cohesion, is whether there are distinctive patterns of working-class cutlure. Accessible accounts of working-class culture and family life include Seabrook (1967), Klein (1965), Hoggart (1963), Newson and Newson (1976), Mogey (1956) and Jackson (1968). The extent to which this traditional culture has been eroded through, among other factors, social and geographical mobility is explored in Stacey (1960), Young and Willmott (1971) and Roberts (1973).

Regarding the issue of a new 'underclass', see Miller (1965), Leggett (1968) and the discussions in Mann (1973), Giddens (1974) and Zweig (1976). For the closely related issue of the dual labour market, see Bosanquet and Doeringer (1973). A good summary of dualist theory is to be found in D. M. Gordon (1972) and a review of the empirical evidence in Addison and Siebert (1979).

## ASPECTS OF INDUSTRIAL RELATIONS

For a general account of historical changes in the form and intensity of industrial conflict, see Kerr *et al*. (1973), particularly Chapters 5–7. The general argument of conflict becoming institutionalized under normal conditions may be found in Coser's (1956) work, which leans heavily on Simmel's (1955) classic treatment of conflict; also Cohen (1968). The institutionalization thesis as it applies specifically to industrial conflict is put forward by Ross and Hartman (1960) and Dahrendorf (1972); a comprehensive source of readings that includes institutional explanations is Kornhauser *et al*. (1954), particularly Chapters 2 (Ross), 3 (Dubin) and 40 (Kornhauser). A summary and critique may be found in Hyman (1977) and Ingham (1974), and a general review of the various theoretical approaches is in Eldridge (1968).

The various forms, including strike action, that industrial discontent and conflict can take are discussed in Kornhauser *et al.* (1954) Chapter 1. Fox (1971) presents a four-category classification of conflict, which in the industrial context has the merit of allowing for inter-union conflict. For summaries of the various alternatives to strike action, see Coates and Topham (1980) Chapter 7, and Jackson (1977) Chapter 7.

Studies covering industrial conflict in the early years of industrialization include a comprehensive review of individual British strikes between 1799 and 1926 by Frow *et al.* (1971). This book covers many mining strikes and lock-outs and the famous Match Girls' strike of 1888 and the Police Strike of 1918. For the 1871 engineering strike see also McCord (1980), which is a similar summary of significant strikes. Accounts of the 1926 General Strike may be found in Renshaw (1975), Mason (1970) and Kee (1976).

Studies of international differences in strike activity include Ross and Hartman (1960), Forchheimer (1948), Oxnam (1965); although more recently the argument is put that we are now experiencing a worldwide revival of industrial conflict (Knowles, 1960; Sweet and Jackson, 1977; Barkin, 1975). Also, there are indications that the strike itself is becoming de-institutionalized, with worker dissatisfaction expressing itself in a more overtly political manner through sit-ins, eviction of management, sabotage, mass picketing and generally greater civil disobedience (Crouch and Pizzorno, 1978; Dubois, 1979). Explanations based upon national differences in institutional structure include Garbarino (1969), Snyder (1975) and Stieber (1968), and Clegg (1976b) Chapter 6, presents a concise analysis of the differing levels of conflict within industrialized countries.

Studies of individual national trends include Shorter and Tilly (1974) on France, Cronin (1979) on the UK, and Ingham (1974) on Britain and Scandinavia. Industrial conflict, its basis and manifestations, in Eastern European societies is documented in Drulovic (1978), Brown (1963) and McAuley (1969).

Annual strike statistics on an international basis are published by the International Labour Organisation in their statistical Yearbook. Mitchell (1980) and Mitchell and Deane (1962) provide a comprehensive summary of British and European statistical trends to the 1970s, and *British Labour Statistics 1886–1968* (1971) contains valuable historical data on wages, strikes, employment and unemployment. Monthly strike statistics are published in the *Department of Employment Gazette* with comprehensive analyses of the previous year to be found in the May issues.

There are numerous studies of strike trends in the UK. The detailed and classic study by Knowles (1952) is now somewhat dated. Hyman's (1977) lucid introduction to the sociology of industrial conflict, with a general account of strikes and their dynamics, can be supplemented by the more empirical studies of Galambos and Evans (1966, 1973), Goodman (1967), Whittingham and Towers (1971), Clegg (1956), Silver (1973). For an excellent historical account of the British experience since the end of the nineteenth century, see Cronin (1979). Clegg, too, (1976a, 1980) provides a brief analysis of the British scene, and Smith *et al.* (1978), apart from being an invaluable source book for the recent British scene, does subject many theories and arguments to empirical statistical test.

Studies concerned with the reasons for striking include McCarthy (1959) and Batstone *et al.* (1978), who discuss the social processes leading to and defining strike action, whilst Jackson (1972) and Forward (1973) explain the method and rationale behind the offical classification of causes in the UK. In terms of analysing and explaining trends, see Pencavel (1970) who argues for the slow adaptability of British institutions in the face of rapid change; also Ashenfelter and Johnson (1969), Knowles (1954). Korpi and Shaler (1979) argue that institutional differences do not in themselves account for much of the variation in strike activity between countries, but instead argue that a process of 'political exchange' takes place where working-class political strength and mobilization forces a fundamental realignment of class relationships on a society.

The treatment of strikes in the UK as a 'problem' to be remedied was argued in the Donovan Report (1968) and, although the basis of the report has been criticized (Crossley, 1968), policy solutions were proposed by the Labour government (Department of Employment and Productivity, 1969) and the Conservative opposition. In the face of strong union opposition, nothing came of these legislative 'remedies'. The extent of the 'British problem' as argued by Donovan was challenged by Turner (1969), whose own interpretation was in turn criticized by McCarthy (1970). See Fox and Flanders (1969) for a perceptive Durkheimian analysis of the British scene; also Hanson (1968) and Phelps-Brown (1973).

Particularly relating to unofficial strikes and the British experience as compared to other countries, see Stieber (1968) and Eldridge (1968), whilst for the difficulties of clearly defining and categorizing strikes into official and unofficial, see Eldridge and Cameron (1964). Sayles' (1954) famous essay on wildcat strikes nevertheless argues the obvious – that such strikes are the only sure method for the rank and file to register their discontent, whether it be due to management, technology or the workers' own union.

Regarding media treatment of unofficial strikes in particular, see Blumler and Ewbank (1970), Turner (1969) and Glasgow University Media Group (1976), who after exhaustive monitoring of television news broadcasts, found certain topics, including strikes, are reported in a partisan manner. Hyman (1977) Chapter 6, attempts to explain why strikes are so socially visible and the process by which they are defined as 'problems'.

Public anxiety over the claim that taxpayers through state benefits have to a large extent been subsidizing strikers in Britain has little basis in fact (Gennard, 1977; Hunter, 1974; Durcan and McCarthy, 1974; Gennard and Lasko, 1975), although the argument is nevertheless seriously put (Conservative Political Centre, 1974).

On the relationship between the size of production units and conflict, see *Department of Employment Gazette* (1976), Eisele (1970, 1973), Cass (1957) and Britt and Galle's (1974) research, which shows that large plants are conducive to fewer and shorter strikes.

Attempts have been made to calculate the economic costs of industrial conflict; Coates and Topham (1980) Chapter 7, review the available evidence, as do Clegg (1976a) Chapter 8, and Knowles (1952) Chapter 5; the evidence does point to the relative insignificance of strikes as a cause of lost production as compared to sickness, unemployment, accidents, etc. (Silver, 1973; Hyman, 1977). For an examination of the costs of strikes that is much broader than the directly financial, see Fisher (1973).

Studies of specific strikes, or the pattern of conflict in certain industries, include Dennis *et al.* (1956), Rimlinger (1959), Scott *et al.* (1963) and Wellisz (1953) for coalmining. Mathews (1972), Turner and Bescoby (1961), Turner *et al.* (1967), Clack (1967), Beynon (1973) and Batstone *et al.* (1978) on the motor industry; Wilson (1972) and Sams (1967) on dockworkers; Cameron (1964) on shipbuilding; and Lipsky and Farber (1976) on the construction industry.

Works on individual disputes include Pope (1942), Gouldner's (1955) famous study of conflict at a gypsum plant, and Lane and Roberts' (1971) account of an essentially three-sided conflict in a British glass factory; see also Paterson and Willett (1951). An acrimonious and symbolic British dispute was that for trade union recognition at the Grunwick film processing factory; see Ward (1977) and Rogaly (1977).

The best-known work on strike incidence between industries and explanations is Kerr and Siegel (1954), whilst Kuhn's (1961) view is that differences in conflict reflect bargaining differences, which are in turn a function of technological imperatives. A good critique and more recent data are to be found in Edwards (1977) and Silver (1973), whilst Shorter and Tilly's (1974) work demonstrates that Kerr and Siegel's hypothesis does not apply to France. *The Department of Employment Gazette* (1976) gives strike propensities for various UK industries based on unpublished data.

Finally, Evans and Creigh (1977) contains reprints of many of the important articles on industrial conflict in Britain (McCarthy, Clegg, Pencavel, Goodman, Galambos and Evans, Silver) mentioned above.

A comprehensive recent review of the major theoretical perspectives on unionism (Marx, Lenin, Perlman, Lester, Kerr, the Webbs) is Schmidman (1979). There are a number of studies of Western trade unionism, most of which, in taking a comparative approach, explain the distinctive characteristics of individual movements by way of historical, economic and cultural factors. This is the approach of Kendall (1975). Kassalow (1969) compares North American and European trade union development, whilst Sturmthal (1972) surveys the ideological origins of the European labour movement. A more recent survey includes Barkin (1975), which covers developments during the 1970s. All these are not only useful in their own right, but are interesting in that they examine the British experience from a European and North American perspective. Clegg (1976b) argues that the variety found in the European trade union movement in terms of membership, structure, conflict, etc. can mainly be accounted for by differences in the structures of collective bargaining.

General works in the industrial relations field in Britain include Clegg's (1980) comprehensive account, Jackson (1977) and Goodman (1975). Coates and Topham (1980) is similarly wide ranging and includes a wealth of detail on trade union organization. For a history of the British movement, Pelling (1963) provides a well-known general account, setting the development of the movement in its economic and political context; Cooper and Bartlett (1976) also offer a brief account of the 'burden of the past', whilst Robertson and Sams (1972) and Hughes and Pollins (1973) are useful collections of trade union documents.

Moving to the more recent past, Allen (1966) examines the role of the trade unions, paying particular attention to their response to inflation, and Panitch (1976) traces the tensions that have arisen in Britain as a result of attempts at imposing incomes policies with trade union consent. Burkitt and Bowers (1979) examine the various economic arguments for trade unionism, whilst Robbins *et al.* (1978) offer an alternative viewpoint and raise such issues as the closed shop, trade union legal immunities, etc. Wilders and Parker (1975) examine the trend toward local bargaining and informality since Donovan (1968), as does Brown (1978).

Much of the discussion and criticism of the British trade union movement in recent years revolves around the unions' relationship with the state. Inevitably a closer relationship arises because of the growing role of the state as employer (Armstrong, 1975). Hyman (1975) argues that the role of the state in industrial relations depends upon the dominant economic and political philosophy during a movement's formative years. Nevertheless, trade unions do participate and expect to be consulted in national economic and social affairs. The dangers and criticism for them doing so is voiced in Taylor (1978), who argues that British unions cooperate with the state for short-term political and economic gain, rather than using such collaboration as a vehicle for longer-term working-class objectives; see Radice (1978) and Lane (1974).

A comprehensive analysis of state intervention in industrial relations with union collaboration is Van de Vall (1970), who argues that the unions' growing integration into public policy-making is the cause of member disaffection in the form of apathy, etc. Crouch (1979) warns of the corporatist dangers of such a trend; see also Thomson (1979) and Barnes and Reid (1980). Miliband (1969) discusses the ambivalent role that trade union leaders assume in capitalist societies; see also Wigham (1961). More critical approaches to unions in Britain include Jenkins' (1970) account of their determined and largely successful efforts to frustrate Labour government policy, whilst Milligan (1976) argues that union power threatens democracy.

Regarding membership participation in union affairs and tendencies toward oligarchy and bureaucracy, Bakke (1975) examines the reasons for joining, Tagliacozzo and Seidman (1956) offer a classic typology of union membership, and more recent literature examining the reasons for the sharp rise in white-collar unionization may be found in Lumley (1973), Bain (1970), Jenkins and Sherman (1979) and the study of unionized bank clerks by Blackburn (1967). Research on membership participation has consistently shown a high level of apathy on the part of rank-and-file members concerning union matters above the level of shop steward (Goldthorpe *et al.*, 1968; Roberts, 1956; Goldstein, 1952).

The classic work on oligarchic tendencies in trade unions is Michels (1959); also examined by Mills (1948). Discussion and a summary of this whole area may be found in Eldridge (1971). The question of effective opposition in unions as a means of maintaining democracy is is elaborated by Martin (1968), and an excellent case study of an American printing union is Lipset *et al.* (1977) Banks (1974) argues that the inevitability of oligarchy in unions is not substantiated, whilst Edelstein and Warner (1979) provide a good review of the arguments and case studies of individual American and British unions. Both Carew (1976) and Herding (1972) cover European unions, and Hemingway (1978) examines union government and membership opposition in three British unions.

The group in unions closest to the membership, the shop stewards, has been the subject of many studies: for example, Goodman and Whittingham (1973), and McCarthy (1966). Boraston *et al.* (1975)

examine the links between stewards and their full-time union officials, attributing differences to variations in managerial structure. Beynon (1973) is a study of steward activity in a particular car plant belonging to a multinational company; and *Batstone et al*. (1977) argue that manual and non-manual shop stewards see their roles quite differently, with different consequences in terms of industrial militancy.

The argument that the quest for more worker participation in the enterprise is merely an extension of Western values toward political democracy, and that the disputes that arise over participation are over form rather than principle, is summarized in Wall and Lischeron (1977). Vanek (1975), Section 1, gives an overall view of the arguments for and against participation, as does Horvat (1975), which contains a selection of readings on the history of industrial democratic thought (industrial unionism, guild socialism, syndicalism, etc.); also Cole (1917). Westley and Westley (1971) argue that increasing affluence and educational standards leads to a rejection and questioning of the legitimacy of the existing system in modern industry on the part of the labour force. Such dissatisfaction will increasingly be expressed in terms of demands for a greater control of production and the restriction of managerial power. For the Webbs (1897), industrial democracy was simply the presence of trade unionism in a formally democratic society. Similarly, Clegg (1960) has maintained that industrial democracy is synonymous with collective bargaining (Clarke, 1977), although his later work advocates some form of participation in the absence of adequate collective bargaining at plant level (Clegg, 1976b, Chapter 7). Also see the critique of Clegg's approach by Blumberg (1968).

There are many collections on experiences of worker participation in most European countries: Garson (1977) contains readings on participation in Britain, France, West Germany, Italy and Sweden. Garson also provides a useful introduction to the types of scheme available (employee share ownership, worker directors, etc.) and discusses the role of consumers as an interest group. See in particular Diamant (1977) on Germany and Jones (1977) on Britain for critical evaluation. Similarly, Pejovich (1978) provides a series of contributions to the theory and practice of codetermination, and argues that the lack of enthusiasm for such schemes from the work force has arisen because the case for it has not been presented in terms of the possibilities for raising workers' real incomes, but has been advocated by intellectuals who see it as a means for restructuring Western society. Sorge (1976) examines participation in Europe from a comparative institutional perspective, explaining how the different *types* of participation have evolved. Also on Europe generally, see Commission on Industrial Relations (1974), Sturmthal (1964), Carby-Hall (1977) for a more legalistic view, Furstenberg (1979), Rowley (1979) for Germany,

Oakshott (1973) and Johnson and Whyte (1977) for the Spanish Mondragon scheme, Markai (1972) and Hunnius *et al.* (1973) for the Kibbutz experience.

The Yugoslav system has received much attention. Most of the books of readings cited have at least one section on Yugoslavia, but in addition see Vanek (1972) and Broekmeyer (1970), which pay particular attention to economic performance and Pateman (1970) and Derrick and Phipps (1969) for a more political approach.

Studies of participation in Britain include the review of joint consultation schemes from the end of the nineteenth century (Renold, 1950). Pribicevic (1959) gives a history of the strong movement for workers' control in the railway, coalmining and engineering industries earlier this century and also discusses the movement's disintegration and argues for the inevitability of dictatorial and bureaucratic tendencies under direct workers' control. The same movement is covered in Coates and Topham (1968), which contains a wide selection of readings, although workers' control is presented as being synonymous with both trade union militant action and Left political leadership. Balfour (1973) stresses the difficulties trade unions as institutions pose for participation, and includes case studies of participation experiments in the British coal, steel and shipbuilding industries. Alexander and Jenkins (1970) found that trade union reluctance to take on the responsibilities of participation means they fail to take advantage of the possible benefits. In part, though, this can be seen as reflecting membership apathy toward participation (Ramsay, 1976; Hunnius *et al.*, 1973). Thomason (1971) is a collection of accounts of participation in 'progressive' British companies, whilst Banks (1963), Brown (1960), Daniel and McIntosh (1972) and Flanders *et al.* (1968) studied individual companies. Brannen *et al.* (1976) describe and evaluate a long-running scheme for worker directors in the nationalized steel industry.

Recent discussion in Britain on the extension of participation in order to overcome some of the basic industrial relations and motivational problems and as a means of conforming more with the European experience resulted in the Bullock Report (1977). Reviews and criticisms of the proposals (unlikely to be implemented for some time, if ever) include Jones (1977), Clarke (1977) and Elliott (1978). Jackson (1978) argues that industrial democracy is not possible under a capitalist system, a view shared to a large extent by Emery and Thorsrud (1969) who argue that board representation is not enough and that there needs to be a transfer of managerial power to employees. Ramsay (1977) argues that interest in worker participation arises only in times of economic difficulty when management feels it needs to secure worker compliance.

# Bibliography

ADDISON, J. T. and SIEBERT, W. S. (1979) *The Market For Labor: An Analytical Treatment* Santa Monica, California: Goodyear Publishing.

ADIZES, I. (1975) 'Balancing environmental requirements and personal needs through an organizational structure' in Horvat, *et al.*, Vol. 2; first published in 1971.

ALEXANDER, K. J. W. and JENKINS, C. L. (1970) *Fairfields: A Study of Industrial Change* London: Penguin.

ALLEN, F. R. *et al.* (1951) *Technology and Social Change* New York: Appleton Century Crofts.

ALLEN, V. L. (1966) *Militant Trade Unionism* London: Merlin Press.

ANTHONY, P. D. (1977) *The Ideology of Work* London: Tavistock.

ARGYLE, M., GARDNER, G., CIOFFI, F. (1958) 'Supervisory methods related to productivity, absenteeism, and labour turnover' *Human Relations* Vol. 11; reprinted in Vroom and Deci (1979).

ARGYLE, M. (1972) *The Social Psychology of Work* London: Penguin.

ARGYRIS, C. (1964) *Integrating the Individual in the Organization* New York: John Wiley.

ARMSTRONG, E. G. A. (1975) 'The role of the state' in Barrett *et al.* (eds).

ARON, R. (1965) *Main Currents in Sociological Thought* London: Penguin.

ARON, R. (1967) *18 Lectures on Industrial Society* London: Weidenfeld and Nicolson.

ASHENFELTER, O. and JOHNSON, G. E. (1969) 'Bargaining theory, trade unions and industrial strike activity' *American Economic Review* Vol. 59, pp. 35–49.

AVINERI, S. (1979) 'The proletariat' in Bottomore (ed.).

BAIN, G. S. (1970) *The Growth of White-Collar Unionism* Oxford: Clarendon Press.

BAKKE, E. W. (1975) 'To join or not to join' in Barrett *et al.* (eds).

BALFOUR, C. (ed.) (1973) *Participation in Industry* London: Croom-Helm.

BANKS, J. A. (1963) *Industrial Participation: Theory and Practice* Liverpool: Liverpool University Press.

BANKS, J. A. (1970) *Marxist Sociology in Action* London: Faber and Faber.

BANKS, J. A. (1974) *Trade Unionism* London: Collier-Macmillan.

BANKS, O. (1976) *The Sociology of Education* London: Batsford.

BARAN, P. A. and SWEEZY, P. M. (1966) *Monopoly Capital* New York: Monthly Review Press.

BARBASH, J. (1972) *Trade Unions and National Economic Policy* London: Johns Hopkins Press.

BARKAI, H. (1972) 'The Kibbutz, an experiment in micro-socialism'; reprinted in Vanek (ed.) (1975).

BARKIN, S. (1975) 'Redesigning collective bargaining and capitalism' in Barkin (ed.).

BARKIN, S. (ed.) (1975) *Worker Militancy and its Consequences, 1965–75* London: Praeger.

270

BARNARD, C. I. (1956) *The Functions of the Executive* Cambridge, Mass.: Harvard University Press.

BARNES, Sir D. and REID, E. (1980) *Governments and Trade Unions* London: Heinemann.

BARNET, R. J. and MÜLLER, R. E. (1975) *Global Reach: The Power of the Multinational Corporations* London: Jonathan Cape.

BARRETT, B., RHODES, E., BEISHON, J. (eds) (1975) *Industrial Relations in the Wider Society* London: Collier-Macmillan.

BATSTONE, E., BORASTON, I., FRENKEL, S. (1977) *Shop Stewards in Action* Oxford: Blackwell.

BATSTONE, E., BORASTON, I., FRENKEL, S. (1978) *The Social Organization of Strikes* Oxford: Blackwell.

BELL, D. (1961) *The End of Ideology* New York: Collier.

BELL, D. (1970) 'The post-industrial society: technology and politics' in *Transactions of the Third World Congress of Sociology* Vol. 6.

BELL, D. (1974) *The Coming of Post-Industrial Society* London: Heinemann.

BENDIX, R. (1963) *Work and Authority in Industry* New York: Harper and Row.

BENDIX, R. and LIPSET, S. M. (eds) (1967) *Class, Status, and Power* London: Routledge and Kegan Paul.

BENSEN, H. W. (1847) 'Die Proletarier, eine historische Denkschrift'; in Briefs (1975).

BENSMAN, J. and GERVER, I. (1963) 'Crime and punishment in the factory' *American Sociological Review* Vol. 28, pp. 35–49.

BENSON, L. (1978) *Proletarians and Parties* London: Tavistock.

BERG, I. (1973) *Education and Jobs* London: Penguin.

BERG, I. (1979) *Industrial Sociology* Englewood Cliffs, New Jersey: Prentice-Hall.

BERLE, A. A. (1954) *The Twentieth Century Capitalist Revolution* New York: Harcourt, Brace.

BERLE, A. A. (1960) *Power Without Property* New York: Harcourt Brace.

BERLE, A. A. and MEANS, G. C. (1968) *The Modern Corporation and Private Property* New York: Macmillan.

BETTIGNIES, H. C. De and EVANS, P. LEE (1977) 'The cultural dimension of top executives' careers: a comparative analysis' in Weinshall (ed.).

BEYNON, H. (1973) *Working For Ford* London: Penguin.

BEYNON, H. and BLACKBURN, R. (1972) *Perceptions of Work: Variations Within a Factory* Cambridge: Cambridge University Press.

BIDDLE, D. and HUTTON, G. (1976) 'Towards a tolerance theory of worker adaptation' *Human Relations* Vol. 29, pp. 833–60.

BLACKBURN, R. M. (1967) *Union Character and Social Class* London: Batsford.

BLACKBURN, R. (ed.) (1972) *Ideology in Social Science* Glasgow: Fontana/Collins.

BLAU, P. M. (1955) *The Dynamics of Bureaucracy* Chicago: University of Chicago Press.

BLAU, P. M. and SCOTT, W. R. (1963) *Formal Organizations* London: Routledge and Kegan Paul.

BLAUNER, R. (1973) *Alienation and Freedom* London: University of Chicago Press.

BLOOD, M. R. and HULIN, C. L. (1967) 'Alienation, environmental characteristics, and worker responses' *Journal of Applied Psychology* Vol. 51, pp. 284–90.

BLUMBERG, P. M. (1968) *Industrial Democracy: The Sociology of Participation* London: Constable.

BLUMLER, J. G. and EWBANK, A. J. (1970) 'Trade unionists, the mass media and unofficial strikes' *British Journal of Industrial Relations* Vol. 8, pp. 32–54.

BONJEAN, C. M. and VANCE, G. G. (1968) 'A short-form measure of self-actualisation' *Journal of Applied Behavioural Science* Vol. 4, pp. 299–312.

BONNER, H. (1959) *Group Dynamics* New York: The Ronald Press.

BOOTH, C. (1902–4) *Life and Labour of the People in London* London: Macmillan.

BORASTON, I., CLEGG, H., RIMMER, M. (1975) *Workplace and Union: A Study of Local Relationships in Fourteen Unions* London: Heinemann.

BOSANQUET, N. and DOERINGER, P. B. (1973) 'Is there a dual labour market in Great Britain?' *Econmic Journal* Vol. 83, pp. 421–35.

BOTTOMORE, T. (ed.) (1979) *Karl Marx* Oxford: Blackwell.

BOULDING, K. E. (1962) *Conflict and Defence* New York: Harper Torch Books.

BOWEY, A. M. (1973) 'The changing status of the supervisor' *British Journal of Industrial Relations* Vol. 11, pp. 393–414.

BOWLEY, A. L. and BURNETT-HURST, A. B. (1915) *Livelihood and Poverty* London: G. Bell & Sons.

BRANNEN, P., BATSTONE, E., FATCHETT, D., WHITE, P. (1976) *The Worker Directors: A Sociology of Participation* London: Hutchinson.

BRAVERMAN, H. (1975) *Labor and Monopoly Capital: The Degradation of Work in the Twentieth Century* New York: Monthly Review Press.

BRIEFS, G. (1975) *The Proletariat: A Challenge to Western Civilization* New York: Arno Press.

*British Labour Statistics: Historical Abstract 1886–1968* (1971) London, HMSO.

BRITT, D. W. and GALLE, O. (1974) 'Structural antecedents of the shape of strikes: a comparative analysis' *American Sociological Review* Vol. 39, pp. 642–51.

BROEKMEYER, M. (1970) *Yugoslav Workers' Self Management* Dordrecht, Holland: Reidel.

BROWN, E. C. (1963) 'Interests and rights of Soviet industrial workers and the resolution of conflicts' *Industrial and Labor Relations Review* Vol. 16, pp. 254–78.

BROWN, R. K. (1977a) 'Human relations and the work group' in Parker *et al.*

BROWN, R. K. (1977b) 'Technology, technical change and automation' in Parker *et al.*

BROWN, R. K. (1978) 'From Donovan to where? Interpretations of industrial relations in Britain since 1968' *British Journal of Sociology* Vol. 29, pp. 439–61.

BROWN, R. K. and BRANNEN, P. (1970) 'Social relations and social perspectives amongst shipbuilding workers – a preliminary statement' *Sociology* Vol. 4, pp. 71–84.

BROWN, R. K., BRANNEN, P., COUSINS, J. M. SAMPHIER, M. L. (1972) 'The contours of solidarity: social stratification and industrial relations in shipbuilding' *British Journal of Industrial Relations* Vol. 10, pp. 12 –41.

BROWN, W. (1960) *Exploration in Management* London: Heinemann.

BROWN, W., EBSWORTH, R., TERRY, M. (1978) 'Factors shaping shop steward organisation in Britain' *British Journal of Industrial Relations* Vol. 16, pp. 139–59.

BULLOCK REPORT (1970) *Report of the Committee of Inquiry on Industrial Democracy* London: HMSO, Cmnd. 6706.

BULMER, M. (ed.) (1975) *Working Class Images of Society* London: Routledge and Kegan Paul.

BURKITT, B. and BOWERS, D. (1979) *Trade Unions and the Economy* London: Macmillan.

BURNHAM, J. (1962) *The Managerial Revolution* London: Penguin.

BURNS, T. (1958) *Management in the Electronics Industry* Edinburgh: Social Science Research Centre, University of Edinburgh.

BURNS, T. (ed.) (1969) *Industrial Man* London: Penguin.
BURNS, T. and STALKER, G. H. (1961) *The Management of Innovation* London: Tavistock.

CAMERON, G. C. (1964) 'Post-war strikes in the North-East shipbuilding and ship-repairing industry 1946–1961' *British Journal of Industrial Relations* Vol. 2, pp. 1–22.
CAMERON, N. (1974) *The Psychology of Behavior Disorders* Riverside, Calif.: Riverside Press.
CAMPBELL, D. T. (1968) 'Social attitudes and other acquired behavioral dispositions' in Koch (ed.), Vol. 6.
CARBY-HALL, J. R. (1977) *Worker Participation in Europe* London: Croom-Helm.
CAREW, A. (1976) *Democracy and Government in European Trade Unions* London: Allen and Unwin.
CAREY, A. (1967) 'The Hawthorne studies: a radical criticism' *American Sociological Review* Vol. 32, pp. 403–16.
CARRE, R. (1964) *American Industry: Structure, Conduct, Performance* Englewood Cliffs, New Jersey: Prentice Hall.
CARTWRIGHT, D. and ZANDER, A. (eds) (1953, 1960, 1968) *Group Dynamics* (1st, 2nd & 3rd editions) New York: Harper and Row.
CASS, M. (1957) 'The relationship of size of firm and strike activity' *Monthly Labor Review* Vol. 80, pp. 1330–4.
CENTERS, R. J. and BUGENTAL, D. E. (1966) 'Intrinisic job motivations among different segments of the working population' *Journal of Applied Pshchology* Vol. 50, pp. 193–7.
CHILD, J. (1969) *British Management Thought* London: Allen and Unwin.
CHILD, J. (ed.) (1973) *Man and Organization* London: Allen and Unwin.
CHILD, J., PEARCE, S., KING, L. (1980) 'Class perceptions and social identification of industrial supervisors' *Sociology* Vol. 14, pp. 363–99.
CHINOY, E. (1955) *Automobile Workers and the American Dream* New York: Doubleday.
CHIPLIN, B., COYNE, J., SIRC, L. (1977) *Can Workers Manage?* London: Institute of Economic Affairs, Hobart Paper No. 77.
CHODAK, S. (1973) *Societal Development* New York: Oxford University Press.
CLACK, G. (1967) *Industrial Relations in a British Car Factory* London: Cambridge University Press.
CLARK, L. G. (1966) *Work, Age and Leisure* London: Michael Joseph.
CLARKE, T. (1977) 'Industrial democracy: the institutionalised suppression of industrial conflict' in Clarke and Clements (eds).
CLARKE, T. and CLEMENTS, L. (eds) (1977) *Trade Unions Under Capitalism* London: Fontana.
CLEGG, H. A. (1956) 'Strikes' *Political Quarterly* Vol. 27, pp. 31–43.
CLEGG, H. A. (1963) *A New Approach to Industrial Democracy* Oxford: Blackwell.
CLEGG, H. A. (1976a) *The System of Industrial Relations in Great Britain* (3rd edition) Oxford: Blackwell.
CLEGG, H. A. (1976b) *Trade Unionism Under Collective Bargaining* Oxford: Blackwell.
CLEGG, H. A. (1980) *The Changing System of Industrial Relations in Great Britain* Oxford: Blackwell.
CLEGG, S. and DUNKERLEY, D. (1980) *Organization, Class and Control* London: Routledge and Kegan Paul.
COATES, K. and SILBURN, R. (1973) *Poverty: The Forgotten Englishmen* London: Penguin.

COATES, K. and TOPHAM, A. (eds) (1968) *Industrial Democracy in Great Britain* London: MacGibbon and Kee.

COATES, K. and TOPHAM, T. (1980) *Trade Unions in Great Britain* Nottingham: Spokesman.

COCH, L. and FRENCH, J. R. P. (1948) 'Overcoming resistance to change' *Human Relations* Vol. 1, pp. 512–32; reprinted in Cartwright and Zander (eds) (1968).

COHEN, A. R. (1964) *Aptitude Change and Social Influence* New York: Basic Books.

COHEN, P. S. (1968) *Modern Social Theory* London: Heinemann.

COLE, G. D. H. (1917) *Self-Government in Industry* London: Bell and Sons.

COLE, G. D. H. (1920) *Guild Socialism Re-stated* London: Leonard Parsons.

COLE, G. D. H. (1972) 'Trade unions as co-managers of industry' in W.E.J.McCarthy (ed.) *Trade Unions* London: Penguin; first published in 1913.

COMMISSION ON INDUSTRIAL RELATIONS (1974) Study 4 *Worker Participation and Collective Bargaining in Europe* London: HMSO.

CONANT, E. H. and KILBRIDGE, M. D. (1965) 'An interdisciplinary analysis of job enlargement – technology, costs, and behavioral implications' *Industrial and Labor Relations Review* Vol. 18, pp. 377–95.

CONSERVATIVE PARTY (1968) *Fair Deal At Work* London: Conservative Central Office.

CONSERVATIVE POLITICAL CENTRE, (1974) *Financing Strikes* London.

COOPER, B. M. and BARTLETT, A. F. (1976) *Industrial Relations* London: Heinemann.

COSER, L. A. (1956) *The Functions of Social Conflict* London: Routledge and Kegan Paul.

CROMPTON, R. and GUBBAY, J. (1977) *Economy and Class Structure* London: Macmillan.

CRONIN, J. E. (1979) *Industrial Conflict in Modern Britain* London: Croom-Helm.

CROSLAND, C. A. R. (1959) 'What the worker wants' *Encounter* February; reprinted in Coates and Topham (eds) (1968).

CROSSLEY, J. R. (1968) 'The Donovan Report: a case study in the poverty of historicism' *British Journal of Industrial Relations* Vol. 6, pp. 296–302.

CROUCH, C. (1979) *The Politics of Industrial Relations* Glasgow: Fontana/Collins.

CROUCH, C. and PIZZORNO, A. (1978) *The Resurgency of Class Conflict in Europe Since 1968* 2 vols, New York: Holmes and Meier.

CROZIER, M. (1964) *The Bureaucratic Phenomenon* London: Tavistock.

CURRAN, J. and STANWORTH, J. (1979) 'Worker involvement and social relations in the small firm' *Sociological Review* Vol. 27, pp. 317–42.

CYERT, R. M. and MARCH, J. G. (1963) *A Behavioral Theory of the Firm* New Jersey: Prentice-Hall.

CYRIAX, G. and OAKESHOTT, R. (1960) *The Bargainers: A Survey of Modern Trade Unionism* London: Faber and Faber.


DAHRENDORF, R. (1972) *Class and Class Conflict in Industrial Society* London: Routledge and Kegan Paul.

DALTON, M. (1950) 'Conflicts between staff and line officers' *American Sociological Review* Vol. 15, pp. 342–51; reprinted in Burns (ed.) (1969).

DALTON, M. (1951) 'Informal factors in career achievement' *American Journal of Sociology* Vol. 56, pp. 407–15.

DALTON, M. (1954) 'The role of supervision' in Kornhauser *et al.* (eds).

DALTON, M. (1955) 'The industrial rate-buster' in W. F. Whyte (ed.). *Money and Motivation* New York: Harper Row.

DALTON, M. (1959) *Men Who Manage* New York: John Wiley.

DANIEL, W. W. (1969) 'Industrial behaviour and orientation to work – a critique' *Journal of Management Studies* Vol. 6, pp. 366–75.

DANIEL, W. W. and McINTOSH, N. (1972) *The Right To Manage?* London: Macdonald.

DAVIS, A. (1969) 'The motivation of the underprivileged worker' in Stuermeister (ed.).

DAVIS, L. E. and TAYLOR, J. C. (eds) (1972) *Design of Jobs* London: Penguin.

DAVIS, R. L. and COUSINS, J. M. (1975) 'The new working class and the old' in Bulmer (ed.).

DENNIS, N., HENRIQUES, F., SLAUGHTER, C. (1956) *Coal Is Our Life* London: Eyre & Spottiswoode.

DEPARTMENT OF EMPLOYMENT AND PRODUCTIVITY (1969) *In Place of Strife* London: HMSO, Cmnd. 3888.

*Department of Employment Gazette* (1976) 'The incidence of industrial stoppages in the United Kingdom' London: HMSO, February, pp. 115–26.

DERRICK, P and PHIPPS, F. J. (eds) (1969) *Co-Ownership, Cooperation and Control* London: Longman.

DEUTSCH, M. and KRAUSS, R. M. (1965) *Theories in Social Psychology* New York: Basic Books.

DIAMANT, A. (1977) 'Democratizing the workplace: the myth and reality of Mitbestimmung in the Federal Republic of Germany' in Garson (ed.).

DILL, W. (1965) 'Business organizations' in March (ed.).

DONOVAN, Lord (1968) *Royal Commission on Trade Unions and Employers' Associations, Report* London: HMSO, Cmnd. 3623.

DORE, R. (1973) *British Factory – Japanese Factory* London: Allen and Unwin.

DOUGLAS, J. W. B. (1972) *The Home and the School* London: Panther.

DRUCKER, P. F. (1950) *The New Society* New York: Harper.

DRUCKER, P. F. (1953) 'The employee society' *American Journal of Sociology* Vol. 58, pp. 358–63.

DRUCKER, P. F. (1963) *The Practice of Management* London: Heinemann.

DRULOVIC, M. (1978) *Self-Management On Trial* Nottingham: Spokesman Books.

DUBIN, R. (1954) 'Constructive aspects of industrial conflict' in Kornhauser *et al*. (eds).

DUBIN, R. (1956) 'Industrial workers' worlds: a study of the central life interests of industrial workers' *Social Problems* Vol. 3, pp. 131–42.

DUBIN, R. (ed.) (1976) *Handbook of Work, Organization and Society* Chicago: Rand-McNally.

DUBOIS, P. (1979) *Sabotage in Industry* London: Penguin.

DUNKERLEY, D. (1975) *The Foreman* London: Routledge and Kegan Paul.

DUNLOP, J. T. (1958) *Industrial Relations Systems* New York: Henry Holt and Co.

DURCAN, J. W. and McCARTHY, W. E. J. (1974) 'The state subsidy theory of strikes: an examination of the statistical data for the period 1956–70' *British Journal of Industrial Relations* Vol. 12, pp. 26–47.

DURKHEIM, E. (1964) *The Division of Labour in Society* London: Collier-Macmillan.

DUVERGER, M. (1964) *Introduction à la politique* Paris: Gallimard.

EDELSTEIN, J. D. and WARNER, M. (1979) *Comparative Union Democracy* New Brunswick, NJ: Transaction Books.

EDWARDS, P. K. (1977) 'A critique of the Kerr–Siegel hypothesis of strikes and the isolated mass: a study of the falsification of sociological knowledge' *Sociological Review* Vol. 25, pp. 551–73.

EDWARDS. R. C., REICH, M., GORDON, D. M. (eds) (1975) *Labor Market Segmentation* Lexington, Mass.: D. C. Heath.

EDWARDS, S. (ed.) (1970) *Selected Writings of P. J. Proudhon* London: Macmillan.

EISELE, C. F. (1970) 'Plant size and frequency of strikes' *Labor Law Journal* Vol. 21, pp. 779–86.

EISELE, C. F. (1973) 'Organization size, technology, and frequency of strikes' *Industrial and Labor Relations Review* Vol. 27, pp. 560–71.

ELDRIDGE, J. E. T. (1968) *Industrial Disputes* London: Routledge and Kegan Paul.

ELDRIDGE, J. E. T. (1971) *Sociology and Industrial Life* London: Michael Joseph.

ELDRIDGE, J. E. T. and CAMERON, G. C. (1964) 'Unofficial strikes: some objections considered' *British Journal of Sociology* Vol. 15, pp. 19–37.

ELLIOTT, J. (1978) *Conflict or Cooperation?* London: Kogan Page.

ELLUL, J. (1965) *The Technological Society* London: Jonathan Cape.

EMERY, F. E. and THORSRUD, E. (1969) *Form and Content in Industrial Democracy* London: Tavistock.

ENGELS, F. (1975) 'The Condition of the Working Class in England' in K. Marx and F. Engels *Collected Works* London: Lawrence and Wishart, Vol. 4.

ETZIONI, A. (1961) *Complex Organizations* New York: The Free Press.

ETZIONI, A. (1964) *Modern Organizations* New Jersey: Prentice-Hall.

EVANS, E. W. and CREIGH, S. W. (eds) (1977) *Industrial Conflict in Britain* London: Frank Cass.

FAINSOD, M. (1953) *How Russia is Ruled* Cambridge, Mass.: Harvard University Press.

FAUNCE, W. A. (1968) *Problems of an Industrial Society* New York: McGraw-Hill.

FELDMAN, A. S. and MOORE, W. E. (1962) 'Industrialisation and industrialism: Convergence and differentiation' *Transactions of the Fifth World Congress of Sociology* Vol. 2.

FESTINGER, L., SCHACHTER, S., BACK, K. (1963) *Social Pressures in Informal Groups* London: Tavistock.

FIEDLER, F. E. (1960) 'The leader's psychological distance and group effectiveness' in Cartwright and Zander (eds).

FIEDLER, F. E. (1968) 'Personality and situational determinants of leadership effectiveness' in Cartwright and Zander (eds).

FIEDLER, F. E. (1969) 'The contingency model: a theory of leadership effectiveness' in H. Proshansky and B. Seidenberg (eds) *Basic Studies in Social Psychology* London: Holt, Rinehart and Winston.

FISHER, M. (1973) *Measurement of Labour Disputes and their Economic Effects* Paris: OECD.

FLANDERS, A. (1975) *Management and Unions* London: Faber and Faber.

FLANDERS, A., POMERANZ, R., WOODWARD, J. (1968) *Experiment in Industrial Democracy* London: Faber and Faber.

FLEISHMAN, E. A. (1956) 'Leadership climate, human relations training and supervisory behaviour' *Personnel Psychology* Vol. 6, pp. 208–22.

FLETCHER, C. (1969) 'Men in the middle: a reformulation of the thesis' *Sociological Review* Vol. 17, pp. 341–54.

FLORENCE, S. (1953) *The Logic of British and American Industry* London: Routledge and Kegan Paul.

FOLLET, M. P. (1971) 'The giving of orders' in Pugh (ed.).

FORCHHEIMER, K. (1948) 'Some international aspects of the strike movement' *Bulletin of the Oxford Institute of Economics and Statistics* Vol. 10, pp. 9–31.

FORM, W. H. (1972) 'Technology and social behavior of workers in four countries: a socio-technical perspective' *American Sociological Review* Vol. 37, pp. 727–38.

FORM, W. H. (1973a) 'Auto workers and their machines: a study of work, factory, and job satisfaction in four countries' *Social Forces* Vol. 52, pp. 1–15.

FORM, W. H. (1973b) 'The internal stratification of the working class' *American Sociological Review* Vol. 38, pp. 697–711.

FORM, W. H. (1975) 'The social construction of anomie: a four nation study of industrial workers' *American Journal of Sociology* Vol. 80, pp. 1165–92.

FORM, W. H. and GESCHWENDER, J. A. (1962) 'Social reference basis of job satisfaction: the case of manual workers' *American Sociological Review* Vol. 27, pp. 228–37.

FORRESTER, J. W. (1971) *World Dynamics* Cambridge, Mass.: Wright-Allen Press.

FORWARD, N. S. (1973) 'Revision of the Department of Employment's classification for the causes of stoppages' *British Journal of Industrial Relations* Vol. 11, pp. 143–5.

FOX, A. (1971) *A Sociology of Work in Industry* London: Collier-Macmillan.

FOX, A. (1974) *Beyond Contract: Work, Power and Trust Relations* London: Faber and Faber.

FOX, A. and FLANDERS, A. (1969) 'The reform of collective bargaining: from Donovan to Durkheim' *British Journal of Industrial Relations* Vol. 7, pp. 151–80.

FRASER, R. (ed.) (1969) *Work: Twenty Personal Accounts* 2 vols, London: Penguin.

FRENCH, J. R. P., ISRAEL, J., and AAS, D. (1960) 'An experiment on participation in a Norwegian factory' *Human Relations* Vol. 13, pp. 3–19.

FRIEDMAN, E. A. and HAVIGHURST, R. J. (1954) *The Meaning of Work and Retirement* Chicago: University of Chicago Press.

FRIEDMANN, G. (1955) *Industrial Sociology* Glencoe: The Free Press.

FRIEDMANN, G. (1961) *The Anatomy of Work* London: Heinemann.

FRIEDRICH, C. J. and BRZEZINSKI, B. (1956) Totalitarian Dictatorship and Autocracy Cambridge, Mass.: Harvard University Press.

FROMKIN, H. L. and SHERWOOD, J. J. (1974) *Integrating the Organization* New York: Free Press/Collier-Macmillan.

FROMM, E. (1973) *The Sane Society* London: Routledge and Kegan Paul.

FROW, R., FROW, E., and KATANKA, M. (1971) *Strikes: A Documentary History* London: Charles Knight.

FURSTENBERG, F. (1979) 'Workers' participation: the European experience' in Sanderson and Stapenhurst (eds).

GALAMBOS, P. and EVANS, E. W. (1966) 'Work stoppages in the United Kingdom 1951–1964: a quantitative study' *Bulletin of the Oxford Institute of Economics and Statistics* Vol. 28, pp. 33–57.

GALAMBOS, P. and EVANS, E. W. (1973) 'Work stoppages in the United Kingdom 1965–70: a quantitative study' *Bulletin of Economic Research* Vol. 25, pp. 22–42.

GALBRAITH, J. K. (1969) *The New Industrial State* London: Penguin.

GALBRAITH, J. K. (1971) *The Affluent Society* London: Penguin.

GARBARINO, J. W. (1969) 'Managing conflict in industrial relations: U.S. experience and current issues in Britain' *British Journal of Industrial Relations* Vol. 7, pp. 317–35.

GARDELL, B. (1971) 'Alienation and mental health in the modern industrial environment' in L. Levi (ed.) *Society, Stress and Disease* London: Oxford University Press.

GARSON, G. D. (ed.) (1977) *Worker Self-Management in Industry: The West European Experience* New York: Praeger.

GELLERMAN, S. W. (1976) 'Supervision: substance and style' *Harvard Business Review* Vol. 54, pp. 89–99.

GENNARD, J. (1977) *Financing Strikers* London: Macmillan.

GENNARD, J. and LASKO, R. (1975) 'The individual and the strike' *British Journal of Industrial Relations* Vol. 8, pp. 346–69.

GIBB, C. A. (1954) 'Leadership' in Lindzey and Aronson (1954).

GIBB, C. A. (1970) 'The principles and traits of leadership' in Gibb (ed.); first published in 1947.

GIBB, C. A. (ed.) (1970) *Leadership* London: Penguin.

GIDDENS, A. (1974) *The Class Structure of the Advanced Societies* London: Hutchinson.

GILBERT, M. (ed.) (1972) *The Modern Business Enterprise* London: Penguin.

GINER, S. (1976) *Mass Society* London: Martin Robertson.

GLASGOW UNIVERSITY MEDIA GROUP (1976) *Bad News* London: Routledge and Kegan Paul.

GOLDSTEIN, J. (1952) *The Government of British Trade Unions* London: Allen and Unwin.

GOLDTHORPE, J. H. (1959) 'Technical organisation as a factor in supervisor/worker conflict' *British Journal of Sociology* Vol. 10, pp. 213–30.

GOLDTHORPE, J. H. (1964) 'Social stratification in industrial society' *Sociological Review Monograph* No. 8.

GOLDTHORPE, J. H. (1966) 'Attitudes and behaviour of car assembly workers: a deviant case and a theoretical critique' *British Journal of Sociology* Vol. 17, pp. 277–44.

GOLDTHORPE, J. H. (1977) 'Industrial relations in Great Britain: a critique of reformism' in Clarke and Clements (eds); first published in 1974 in *Politics and Society*.

GOLDTHORPE, J. H. (1980) *Social Mobility and Class Structure in Modern Britain* Oxford: Clarendon Press.

GOLDTHORPE, J. H. and LOCKWOOD, D. (1963) 'Affluence and the British class structure' *Sociological Review* Vol. 11, pp. 133–63.

GOLDTHORPE, J. H., LOCKWOOD, D., BECHHOFER, F., PLATT, J. (1968) *The Affluent Worker: Industrial Attitudes and Behaviour* London: Cambridge University Press.

GOLDTHORPE, J. H., LOCKWOOD, D., BECHHOFER, F., PLATT, J. (1969) *The Affluent Worker in the Class Structure* London: Cambridge University Press.

GOLEMBIEWSKI, R. T. (1961) 'Three styles of leadership and their uses' *Personnel* Vol. 38, July–August.

GOODMAN, J. F. B. (1967) 'Strikes in the U.K.: recent statistics and trends' *International Labour Review* Vol. 95, pp. 465–81.

GOODMAN, J. F. B. (1975) 'Great Britain: toward the social contract' in Barkin (ed.).

GOODMAN, J. F. B., ARMSTRONG, E. G. A., DAVIS, J. E., WARNER, A. (1977) *Rule-Making and Industrial Peace* London: Croom-Helm.

GOODMAN, J. F. B. and WHITTINGHAM, T. G. (1973) *Shop Stewards in British Industry* London: Pan Books.

GORDON, D. M. (1972) *Theories of Poverty and Unemployment* Lexington, Mass.: Heath Books.

GORDON, R. A. (1961) *Business Leadership in the Large Corporation* Berkeley, California: University of California Press.

GOULDNER, A. W. (1955) *Wildcat Strike* London: Routledge and Kegan Paul.

GOULDNER, A. W. (1960) 'The norm of reciprocity: a preliminary statement' *American Sociological Review* Vol. 25, pp. 161–78.

GOULDNER, A. W. (1964) *Patterns of Industrial Bureaucracy* London: Collier-Macmillan.

GRANICK, D. (1962) *The European Executive* London: Weidenfeld and Nicolson.

GROSS, B. M. (1964) *The Managing of Organizations* 2 vols, London: Collier-Macmillan.

GRUSKY, O. and MILLER, G. A. (eds) (1970) *The Sociology of Organizations* New York: The Free Press.

GUEST, R. H. (1957) 'Job enlargement: a revolution in job design' *Personnel Administration* Vol. 20, pp. 9–16.

GUEST, R. H. (1964) 'Of time and the foreman' in D. E. Porter and P. B. Applewhite (eds) *Studies in Organizational Behavior and Management* Scranton, Penn.: International Textbook Company.

GURVITCH, G. (1975) 'Three paths to self-management' in Horvat *et al.*, Vol. 2.


HALSEY, A. H. (1978) *Change in British Society* Oxford: Oxford University Press.

HALSEY, A. H., HEATH, A. F., RIDGE, J. M. (1980) *Origins and Destinations* Oxford: Clarendon Press.

HAMBLIN, R. L. (1958) 'Leadership and crises' *Sociometry* Vol. 21; reprinted in Cartwright and Zander (1960).

HAMILTON, R. F. (1965) 'The behavior and values of skilled workers' in Shostak and Gomberg (1965b).

HANDYSIDE, J. D. and SPEAK, M. (1964) 'Job satisfaction: myths and realities: *British Journal of Industrial Relations* Vol. 2, pp. 57–65.

HANSON, C. G. (1968) 'Trade union law reform and unofficial strikes' *National Westminster Bank Review* August, pp. 47–61.

HARASZTI, M. (1977) *A Worker in a Workers' State* London: Penguin.

HARBISON, F. and MYERS, C. (1960) *Management in the Industrial World* London: McGraw-Hill.

HARRINGTON, M. (1963) *The Other America: Poverty in the United States* London: Penguin.

HEILBRONER, R. L. (1977) *Business Civilization in Decline* London: Penguin.

HELLER, F. A. and PORTER, L. W. (1977) 'Perceptions of managerial needs and skills in two national samples' in Weinshall (ed.).

HEMINGWAY, J. (1978) *Conflict and Democracy: Studies in Trade Union Government* Oxford: Oxford University Press.

HERDING, R. (1972) *Job Control and Union Structure* Rotterdam: Rotterdam University Press.

HERZBERG, F. (1968) *Work and the Nature of Man* London: Staples Press.

HICKSON, D. J. (1965) 'Motives of people who restrict their output' *Occupational Psychology* Vol. 35, pp. 111–21.

HIRSCH, F. (1977) *Social Limits To Growth* London: Routledge and Kegan Paul.

HOBSBAWM, E. J. (1968) *Industry and Empire* London: Weidenfeld and Nicolson.

HOGGART, R. (1963) *The Uses of Literacy* London: Penguin.

HOLLANDER, E. P. and JULIAN, J. W. (1971) 'Contemporary trends in the analysis of leadership processes' in E. P. Hollander and R. G. Hunt *Current Perspectives in Social Psychology* London: Oxford University Press; first published in 1960 in *Psychological Bulletin*.

HOLLOWELL, P. G. (1968) *The Lorry Driver* London: Routledge and Kegan Paul.

HOLMAN, R. (1978) *Poverty: Explanations of Social Deprivation* Oxford: Martin Robertson.

HOMANS, G. (1954) 'Industrial harmony as a goal' in Kornhauser *et al*. (eds).

HOMANS, G. (1958) 'Social behavior as exchange' *American Journal of Sociology* Vol. 62.

HOMANS, G. (1965) 'Effort, supervision, and productivity' in R. Dubin (ed.) *Leadership and Productivity* San Francisco: Chandler Publishing.

HOMANS, G. (1968) *The Human Group* London: Routledge and Kegan Paul.

HORVAT, B. (1975) 'An institutional model of a self-managed socialist economy' in Vanek (ed.).

HORVAT, B., MARKOVIC, M. and SUPEK, R. (eds) (1975) *Self Governing Socialism: A Reader* 2 vols, New York: International Arts and Sciences Press.

HUGHES, J. and POLLINS, H. (1973) *Trade Unions in Great Britain* London: David and Charles.

HUNNIUS, G., GARSON, G. D. and CASE, J. (eds) (1973) *Workers Control* New York: Random House.

HUNTER, L. C. (1974) 'The state subsidy theory of strikes: a reconsideration' *British Journal of Industrial Relations* Vol. 12, pp. 438–44.

HYMAN, H. H. (1967) 'The value systems of different classes' in Bendix and Lipset (eds).

HYMAN, R. (1975) *Industrial Relations: a Marxist Introduction* London: Macmillan.

HYMAN, R. (1977) *Strikes* Glasgow: Fontana/Collins.

HYMAN, R. and FRYER, R. H. (1977) 'Trade unions: sociology and political economy' in Clarke and Clements (eds).

INDUSTRIAL FATIGUE RESEARCH BOARD (1924–34) *Reports* nos. 25, 26, 30, 32, 52, 56, 69, London: HMSO.

INGHAM, G. K. (1974) *Strikes and Industrial Conflict* London: Macmillan.

INKELES, A. and BAUER, R. A. (1959) *The Soviet Citizen* London: Harvard University Press.

INKELES, A. (1960) 'Industrial man: the relation of status to experience, perception, and value' *American Journal of Sociology* July.

INKELES, A. (1966) 'Models in the analysis of Soviet society' *Survey* Vol. 60, pp. 3–17.

JACKSON, B. (1968) *Working Class Community* London: Routledge and Kegan Paul.

JACKSON, B. and MARSDEN, D. (1973) *Education and the Working Class* London: Penguin.

JACKSON, M. P. (1972) 'The Department of Employment's method of classifying the causes of stoppages' *British Journal of Industrial Relations* Vol. 10, pp. 445–7.

JACKSON, M. P. (1977) *Industrial Relations* London: Croom-Helm.

JACKSON, M. (1978) 'Industrial Democracy: a Review of the Bullock Report' *Scottish Journal of Sociology* Vol. 2, No. 2.

JENKINS, C. and SHERMAN, B. (1979) *White Collar Unionism: The Rebellious Salariat* London: Routledge and Kegan Paul.

JENKINS, P. (1970) *The Battle of Downing Street* London: Charles Knight.

JOHNS, E. A. (1972) *The Social Structure of Modern Britain* Oxford: Pergamon Press.

JOHNSON, A. G. and WHYTE, W. F. (1977) 'The Mondragon system of worker co-operatives' *Industrial and Labor Relations Review* Vol. 31, pp. 18–30.

JONES, D. C. (1977) 'Worker Participation in Management in Britain: Evaluation, Current Developments and Prospects' in Garson (ed.).

JONES, P. A. (1965) *The Consumer Society* London: Penguin.
JONES, T. K. (1973) 'Employee directors in the British Steel Corporation' in Balfour (ed.) pp. 83–107.

KAHN, R. L. and KATZ, D. (1960) 'Leadership practices in relation to productivity' in Cartwright and Zander (eds).
KALLEBERG, A. L. (1977) 'Work values and job rewards: a theory of job satisfaction' *American Sociological Review* Vol. 42, pp. 124–43.
KASSALOW, E. M. (1969) *Trade Unions and Industrial Relations: An International Comparison* New York: Random House.
KATONA, G. (1951) *Psychological Analysis of Economic Behaviour* London: McGraw-Hill.
KATONA, G. (1964) *The Mass Consumption Society* New York: McGraw-Hill.
KATONA, G., STRUMPEL, B. and ZAHN, E. (1971) *Aspirations and Affluence* New York: McGraw-Hill.
KATZ, F. E. (1965) 'Explaining informal work groups in complex organizations: the case for autonomy in structure' *Administrative Science Quarterly* Vol. 10, pp. 204–23.
KEE, R. (1976) *General Strike Report* Leeds: Yorkshire Television.
KELLY, H. H. (1952) 'The functions of reference groups' in G. E. Swanson, T. M. Newcomb, E. L. Hartley (eds) *Readings in Social Psychology* New York: Holt.
KELLY, M. P. (1980) *White-Collar Proletariat* London: Routledge and Kegan Paul.
KENDALL, W. (1975) *The Labour Movement in Europe* London: Allen Lane.
KERR, C. and SIEGEL, A. (1954) 'The interindustry propensity to strike – an international comparison' in Kornhauser *et al.* (eds).
KERR, C., DUNLOP, J. T., HARBISON, F. H., MYERS, C. A (1973) *Industrialism and Industrial Man* London: Penguin.
KLEIN, J. (1965) *Samples From English Cultures* London: Routledge and Kegan Paul.
KNOWLES, K. G. J. C. (1952) *Strikes: A Study in Industrial Conflict* Oxford: Blackwell.
KNOWLES, K. G. J. C. (1954) 'Strike-proneness and its determinants' *American Journal of Sociology* Vol. 60, pp. 213–29.
KNOWLES, K. G. J.C. (1960) 'Strike-proneness and its determinants' in W. Galenson and S. M. Wiley (eds) *Labor and Trade Unionism* New York: John Wiley.
KOCH, S. (ed.) (1968) *Psychology: A Study of a Science* 6 vols, New York: McGraw-Hill.
KORNHAUSER, A. (1954) 'Human motivations underlying industrial conflict' in Kornhauser *et al* (eds).
KORNHAUSER, A., DUBIN, R., ROSS, A. (eds) (1954) *Industrial Conflict* New York: McGraw-Hill.
KORPI, W. and SHALER, M. (1979) 'Strikes, industrial relations and class conflict in capitalist societies' *British Journal of Sociology* Vol. 30, pp. 164–87.
KORSNES, O. (1979) 'Duality in the role of unions and unionists: the case of Norway' *British Journal of Industrial Relations* Vol. 17, pp. 362–75.
KUHN, J. W. (1961) *Bargaining in Grievance Settlement* New York: Columbia University Press.

LANDSBERGER, H. A. (1958) *Hawthorne Revisited* New York: Cornell University Press.
LANE, T. (1974) *The Union Makes Us Strong* London: Arrow Books.
LANE, T. and ROBERTS, K. (1971) *Strike At Pilkingtons* Glasgow: Collins-Fontana.

LARNER, R. J. (1970) *Management Control and the Large Corporation* Cambridge, Mass.: Dunellen University Press.

LASKI, H. (1954) *Communist Manifesto: Socialist Landmark* London: Allen and Unwin.

LAWLER, E. E. (1973) *Motivation in Work Organizations* Monterey, California: Brookes-Cole Publishing.

LAWLER, E. E. and PORTER, L. (1967) 'The effect of performance on job satisfaction' *Industrial Relations* Vol. 7, pp. 20–8.

LAWRENCE, P. R. and LORSCH, J. W. (1967) *Organization and Environment* Boston: Harvard University Press.

LEAVITT, H. J. (ed.) (1963) *The Social Science of Organizations* New Jersey: Prentice-Hall.

LEGGETT, J. C. (1968) *Class, Race, and Labor* New York: Oxford University Press.

LENIN, V. I. (1960) 'On strikes' in *Collected Works* London: Lawrence and Wishart, vol. 4; also reprinted in Clarke and Clements (1977).

LEWIS, O. (1959) *Five Families: Mexican Case Studies in the Culture of Poverty* New York: Basic Books.

LEWIS, O. (1966) *La Vida* New York: Vintage Books.

LIEBOW, E. (1967) *Tally's Corner* London: Routledge and Kegan Paul.

LIKERT, R. (1961) *New Patterns of Management* New York: McGraw-Hill.

LINDZEY, G. and ARONSON, E. (eds) (1954, 1969) *The Handbook of Social Psychology* (1st and 2nd editions) London: Addison-Wesley, vol. 4.

LIPSET, S. M. (1963) *Political Man* London: Heinemann.

LIPSET, S. M., TROW, M., COLEMAN, J. (1956) *Union Democracy* New York: Free Press.

LIPSKY, D. B. and FARBER, H. S. (1976) 'The composition of strike activity in the construction industry' *Industrial and Labour Relations Review* Vol. 29, pp. 388–404.

LOCKWOOD, D. (1966) 'Sources of variation in working-class images of society' *Sociological Review* Vol. 14, pp. 249–67; also in Bulmer (ed.) (1975).

LOZOWSKY, A. (1935) *Marx and the Trade Unions* London: Martin Lawrence.

LUKACS, G. (1979) 'Class consciousness' in Bottomore (ed.).

LUMLEY, R. (1973) *White Collar Unionism in Britain* London: Methuen.

LUPTON, T. (1972) *Payment Systems* Harmondsworth, Middx: Penguin.


MACKENZIE, G. (1973) *The Aristocracy of Labour* London: Cambridge University Press.

MACKENZIE, G. (1974) 'The affluent worker study: an evaluation and critique' in F. Parkin (ed.) *The Social Analysis of Class Structure* London: Tavistock.

MALLET, S. (1975) *The New Working Class* Nottingham: Spokesman Books.

MANN, F. C. and HOFFMAN, L. R. (1960) *Automation and the Worker* New York: Holt and Co.

MANN, M. (1973) *Consciousness and Action Among the Western Working Class* London: Macmillan.

MANNHEIM, K. (1968) *Freedom, Power and Democratic Planning* London: Routledge and Kegan Paul.

MARCH, J. G. (ed.) (1965) *Handbook of Organizations* Chicago: Rand-McNally.

MARCH, J. G. and SIMON, H. A. (1958) *Organizations* New York: Wiley and Sons.

MARCSON, S. (ed.) (1970) *Automation, Alienation, and Anomie* New York: Harper and Row.

MARCUSE, H. (1964) *One Dimensional Man* London: Routledge and Kegan Paul.

MAROT, H. (1918) *The Creative Impulse in Industry* New York: Dutton.

MARRIS, R. (1964) *The Economic Theory of Managerial Capitalism* New York: The Free Press.

MARTIN, R. (1968) 'Union democracy – an explanatory framework' *Sociology* Vol. 2, pp. 205–20.

MARWICK, A. (1980) *Class: Image and Reality* London: Collins.

MARX, K. (1962) *Capital* Vol. 3, Moscow: Foreign Languages Publishing House.

MARX, K. (1969) *Capital* Vol. 3, quoted in T. Bottomore and M. Rubel (eds) *Karl Marx: Selected Writings* London: Penguin.

MARX, K. (1971) 'Economic and Philosophical Manuscripts of 1944' in Z. A. Jordan (ed.) *Karl Marx* London: Michael Joseph.

MARX, K. (1979) *Capital* Vol. 1, London: Penguin.

MARX, K. and ENGELS, F. (1967) *The Communist Manifesto* London: Penguin.

MASLOW, A. H. (1954) *Motivation and Personality* New York: Harper.

MASLOW, A. H. (1976) 'A theory of human motivation' in Sutermeister (ed.) (1969, 1976); also in Vroom and Deci (eds) (1979); first published in 1943 in *Psychological Review* Vol. 50.

MASON, A. (1970) *The General Strike in the North-East* Hull: Hull University Press.

MATHEWS, J. (1972) *The Ford Strike* London: Panther.

MAYER, K. (1956) 'Recent changes in the class structure of the United States' London: *Transactions of the Third World Congress of Sociology* Vol. 3, pp. 66–80.

MAYO, E. (1933) *The Human Problems of an Industrial Civilization* New York: Macmillan.

MAYO, E. (1962) *The Social Problems of an Industrial Civilization* London: Routledge and Kegan Paul.

McAULEY, M. (1969) *Labour Disputes in Soviet Russia 1957–65* Oxford: Clarendon Press.

McCARTHY, W. E. J. (1959) 'The reasons given for striking' *Bulletin of the Oxford Institute of Economics and Statistics* Vol. 21, pp. 17–29.

McCARTHY, W. E. J. (1966) *The Role of Shop Stewards in British Industrial Relations* Royal Commission on Trade Unions and Employers' Associations (Donovan), Research Paper 1, London: HMSO.

McCARTHY, W. E. J. (1970) 'The nature of Britain's strike problem' *British Journal of Industrial Relations* Vol. 8, pp. 224–36.

McCORD, N. (1980) *Strikes* Oxford: Blackwell.

McGREGOR, D. (1960) *The Human Side of the Enterprise* London: McGraw-Hill.

McLELLAN, D. (1975) *Marx* Glasgow: Fontana-Collins.

MEADOWS, D. H., MEADOWS, D. L., RANDERS, J., BEHRENS, W. W. (1972) *The Limits to Growth* London: Earth Island Publishing.

MEISSNER, M. (1969) *Technology and the Worker* San Francisco: Chandler.

MERTON, R. K. (1970) 'The machine, the worker, and the engineer' in Marcson (ed.).

MICHELS, R. (1959) *Political Parties* New York: Dover Publishing.

MILIBAND, R. (1969) *The State in Capitalist Society* London: Weidenfeld and Nicolson.

MILL, J. S. (1970) *Principles of Political Economy* London: Penguin.

MILLAR, R. (1966) *The New Classes* London: Longman.

MILLER, D. C. and FORM, W. H. (1964) *Industrial Sociology* London: Harper.

MILLER, S. M. (1965) 'The American lower classes: a typological approach' in Shostak and Gomberg (eds) (1965a).

MILLIGAN, S. (1976) *The New Barons: Union Power in the 1970's* London: Temple Smith.

MILLS, C. W. (1948) *New Men of Power: America's Labor Leaders* New York: Harcourt.

MILLS, C. W. (1953) *White Collar* New York: Oxford University Press.

MILLS, C. W. (1974) *Power, Politics and People* New York: Oxford University Press.

MITCHELL, B. R. (1980) *European Historical Statistics 1750–1975* (2nd edition) London: Macmillan.

MITCHELL, B. R. and DEANE, P. (1962) *Abstract of British Historical Statistics* London: Cambridge University Press.

MOGEY, J. M. (1956) *Family and Neighbourhood* Oxford: Oxford University Press.

MONSEN, R. and DOWNS, A. (1965) 'A theory of large managerial firms' *Journal of Political Economy* Vol. 73, pp. 221–36; reprinted in Gilbert (ed.) (1972).

MONSEN, R. J., CHIN, J. W. and COOLEY, D. E. (1968) 'The effects of separation of ownership and control on the performance of the large firm' *Quarterly Journal of Economics* Vol. 82, no. 3, August.

MOORE, W. E. (1965) *The Impact of Industry* New Jersey: Prentice-Hall.

MORAN, M. (1974) *The Union of Post Office Workers* London: Macmillan.

MORRIS, M. (1976) *The General Strike* Harmondsworth, Middx: Penguin.

MORSE, N. C. and WEISS, R. S. (1955) 'The function and meaning of work and the job' *American Sociological Review* Vol. 20, pp. 191–8; reprinted in Vroom and Deci (eds) (1979).

MOUZELIS, N. (1967) *Organization and Bureaucracy* London: Routledge and Kegan Paul.

MUMFORD, E. (1970) 'Job satisfaction: a new approach derived from an old theory' *Sociological Review* Vol. 18, pp. 71–101.

MYRDAL, G. (1965) 'The war on poverty' in Shostak and Gomberg (eds) (1965a).


NESS, G. D. (ed.) (1970) *The Sociology of Economic Development* New York: Harper and Row.

NEVINS, A and HILL, F. E. (1957) *Ford: Expansion and Challenge* New York: Scribner and Sons.

NEWSON, E. and NEWSON, J. (1976) *Patterns of Infant Care* London: Penguin.

NICHOLS, T. (1969) *Ownership, Control and Ideology* London: Allen and Unwin.

NISBET, R. (1967) *The Sociological Tradition* London: Heinemann.

NOP (1976) *Political, Social and Economic Review* Vol. 5, London: National Opinion Poll.

NOVICK, D. (1976) *A World of Scarcities* London: Associated Business Programmes.


OAKSHOTT, R. (1973) 'Mondragon: Spain's oasis of democracy' *The Observer* 21 January; reprinted in Vanek (ed.) (1975).

OPSAHL, R. L. and DUNNETTE, M. D. (1966) 'The role of financial compensation in industrial motivation' *Psychological Bulletin* Vol. 66, pp. 94–118; reprinted in Vroom and Deci (eds) (1979).

ORZACK, L. H. (1959) 'Work as a central life interest of professionals' *Social Problems* Vol. 7, pp. 125–32.

OSSOWSKI, S. (1979) 'The Marxian synthesis' in Bottomore (ed.).

OXNAM, D. W. (1965) 'International comparisons of industrial conflict: an appraisal' *Journal of Industrial Relations* Vol. 7, pp. 149–63.


PALM, G. (1977) *The Flight From Work* London: Cambridge University Press.

PANITCH, L. (1976) *Social Democracy and Industrial Militancy: The Labour Party, The Trade Unions and Incomes Policy* New York: Cambridge University Press.

PARKER, S. R., BROWN, R. K., CHILD, J., SMITH, M. A. (1977) *The Sociology of Industry* (3rd edition) London: Allen and Unwin.

PARKIN, F. (1971) *Class Inequality and Political Order* London: MacGibbon and Kee.

PARKINSON, C. N. (1958) *Parkinson's Law* London: John Murray.

PARSONS, T. (1953) 'A revised analytical approach to the theory of social stratification'; in Bendix and Lipset (eds) (1967).

PATEL, S. J. (1970) 'Rates of industrial growth in the last century 1860–1958' in Ness (ed.).

PATEMAN, C. (1970) *Participation and Democratic Theory* London: Cambridge University Press.

PATERSON, T. T. and WILLETT, F. J. (1951) 'Unofficial Strike' *Sociological Review* Vol. 43, pp. 57–94.

PEJOVICH, S. (ed.) (1978) *The Codetermination Movement in the West* Massachusetts: Lexington Books.

PELLING, H. (1963) *A History of British Trade Unionism* London: Penguin.

PELZ, D. C. (1952) 'Influence: a key to effective leadership in the first-line supervisor' *Personnel* Vol. 29, pp. 209–17.

PENCAVEL, J. H. (1970) 'An investigation into industrial strike activity in Britain' *Economica* Vol. 37, pp. 239–56.

PENROSE, O. (1946) 'Elementary statistics of majority voting' *Statistical Journal* Part I.

PERLMAN, S. (1928) *A Theory of the Labor Movement* New York: Macmillan.

PERROW, C. (1970) *Organizational Analysis: A Sociological View* London: Tavistock.

PHELPS-BROWN, E. H. (1973) 'New wine in old bottles: reflections on the changed working of collective bargaining in Great Britain' *British Journal of Industrial Relations* Vol. 11, pp. 329–37.

POLANYI, K. (1975) *The Great Transformation* New York: Octagon Books.

POLLARD, S. (1969) *The Development of the British Economy 1914–1967* (2nd edition) London: Edward Arnold.

POPE, L. (1942) *Millhands and Preachers* New York: Yale University Press.

POPITZ, H., BAHRDT, H. P., JUERES, E. A., KESTING, A. (1969) 'The worker's image of society' in Burns (ed.).

PRESTHUS, R. (1979) *The Organisational Society* London/Basingstoke: Macmillan.

PRIBICEVIC, B. (1959) *The Shop Stewards' Movement and Workers' Control* Oxford: Blackwell.

PUGH, D. S. (ed.) (1971) *Organizational Theory* London: Penguin.

PUGH, D. S. and HICKSON, D. J. (1973) 'The comparative study of organizations' in G. Salaman and K. Thompson (eds) *People and Organizations* London: Longmans.

RADICE, G. (1978) *The Industrial Democrats: Trade Unions in an Uncertain World* London: Allen and Unwin.

RAMSAY, H. (1976) 'Participation: the shop floor view' *British Journal of Industrial Relations* Vol. 14, pp. 128–41.

RAMSAY, H. (1977) 'Cycles of control: worker participation in sociological and historical perspective' *Sociology* Vol. 11, pp. 481–506.

RAPOPORT, A. (1974) *Conflict in Manmade Environment* London: Penguin.

RENOLD, C. G. (1950) *Joint Consultation Over Thirty Years* London: Allen and Unwin.

RENSHAW, P. (1975) *The General Strike* London: Eyre Methuen.

RICE, A. K. (1958) *Productivity and Social Organization* London: Tavistock.

RICE, A. K. (1963) *The Enterprise and its Environment* London: Tavistock.

RIESMAN, D. (1953) *The Lonely Crowd* New York: Anchor Books.

RIMLINGER, G. V. (1959) 'International differences in the strike propensity of coalminers: experience in four countries' *Industrial and Labour Relations Review* Vol. 12, pp. 389–405.

ROBBINS, Lord, HANSON, C. G., BURTON, J., GRUNFELD, C., GRIFFITHS, B., PEACOCK, A. (1978) *Trade Unions: Public Goods or Public Bads?* London: Institute of Economic Affairs.

ROBERTS, B. C. (1956) *Trade Union Government and Administration in Great Britain* London: Bell.

ROBERTS, B. C. (ed.) (1968) *Industrial Relations* London: Methuen.

ROBERTS, K. (1978) *The Working Class* London: Longmans.

ROBERTS, K., COOK, F. G., CLARK, S. C., SEMEONOFF, E. (1977) *The Fragmentary Class Structure* London: Heinemann.

ROBERTS, R. (1973) *The Classic Slum* London: Penguin.

ROBERTSON, N. and SAMS, K. I. (eds) (1972) *British Trade Unionism: Selected Documents* 2 vols, Oxford: Blackwell.

ROETHLISBERGER, F. J. and DICKSON, W. J. (1964) *Management and the Worker* Cambridge, Mass.: Harvard University Press.

ROGALY, J. (1977) *Grunwick* London: Penguin.

ROHRER, J. H. and SHERIF, M. (1951) *Social Psychology at the Crossroads* New York: Harper Row.

ROSE, M. (1975) *Industrial Behaviour: Theoretical Development Since Taylor* London: Allen Lane.

ROSEN, N. A. (1970) *Leadership Change and Work-Group Dynamics* London: Staples Press.

ROSOW, J. M. (ed.) (1974) *The Worker and the Job* Englewood Cliffs, New Jersey: Prentice-Hall.

ROSS, A. M. (1954) 'The natural history of the strike' in Kornhauser *et al.* (eds).

ROSS, A. M. and HARTMAN, P. T. (1960) *Changing Patterns of Industrial Conflict* New York: John Wiley.

ROSTOW, W. W. (1971) *The Stages of Economic Growth* (2nd edition) London: Cambridge University Press.

ROTHWELL, S. and ZEGVELD, W. (1979) *Technical Change and Employment* London: Frances Pinter.

ROWLEY, R. K. (1979) 'A skeptical view of the West German model' in Sanderson and Stapenhurst (eds).

ROWNTREE, B. S. (1901) *Poverty: A Study of Town Life* London: Macmillan.

ROWNTREE, B. S. (1941) *Poverty and Progress* London: Longmans Green.

ROWNTREE, B. S. and LAVERS, G. R. (1951) *Poverty and the Welfare State* London: Longmans Green.

ROY, D. (1952) 'Quota restriction and goldbricking in a machine shop' *American Journal of Sociology* Vol. 57, pp. 427–42.

ROY, D. (1960) 'Banana time: job satisfaction and informal interaction' *Human Organization* Vol. 15, pp. 158–68.

RUNCIMAN, W. G. (1967) *Relative Deprivation and Social Justice* London: Routledge and Kegan Paul.

RUS, V. (1975) 'Problems of participatory democracy' in Horvat *et al.* (eds) Vol. 2, pp. 101–11.

RYDER, Sir D. (1975) *British Leyland: The Next Decade. Report* London: HMSO, 23 April.

RYDER, J. and SILVER, H. (1977) *Modern English Society* (2nd edition) London: Methuen.

SALAMAN, G. (1974) *Community and Occupation* London: Cambridge University Press.

SALAMAN, G. and THOMPSON, K. (1980) *Control and Ideology in Organizations* Milton Keynes: Open University Press.

SAMS, K. I. (1967) 'The Devlin Committee and unrest in British ports' *Journal of Industrial Relations* Vol. 9, pp. 65–71.

SANDERSON, G. and STAPENHURST, F. (eds) (1979) *Industrial Democracy Today* Toronto: McGraw-Hill.

SAYLES, L. R. (1954) 'Wildcat strikes' *Harvard Business Review* Vol. 32, pp. 42–54.

SAYLES, L. R. (1958) *Behavior of Industrial Work Groups* New York: Wiley and Sons.

SCANLON, H. (1968) *The Way Forward For Workers' Control* Nottingham: Institute for Workers' Control, Pamphlet No. 1.

SCHEIN, E. H. (1965) *Organizational Psychology* Englewood Cliffs, NJ: Prentice-Hall.

SCHMIDMAN, J. (1979) *Unions in Post-Industrial Society* University Park, Pennsylvania: University Press.

SCHNEIDER, E. V. (1957) *Industrial Sociology* New York: McGraw-Hill.

SCOTT, W. H., MUMFORD, E., McGIVERING, I. C., KIRKBY, J. M. (1963) *Coal and Conflict* Liverpool: Liverpool University Press.

SEABROOK, J. (1967) *The Unprivileged* London: Longman.

SEEMAN, M. (1959) 'On the meaning of alienation' *American Sociological Review* Vol. 24, pp. 783–91.

SHANKS, M. (1978) *What's Wrong With the Modern World. Agenda for a New Society* London: Bodley Head.

SHEPPARD, H. L. and HERRICK, N. Q. (1972) *Where Have All the Robots Gone?: Worker Dissatisfaction in the 70's* New York: The Free Press.

SHILS, E. B. (1963) *Automation and Industrial Relations* New York: Holt, Rinehart and Winston.

SHORTER, E. and TILLY, C. (1974) *Strikes in France 1830–1968* London: Cambridge University Press.

SHOSTAK, A. B. (1969) *Blue Collar Life* New York: Random House.

SHOSTAK, A. B. and GOMBERG, W. (eds) (1965a) *New Perspectives on Poverty* Englewood Cliffs, New Jersey: Prentice-Hall.

SHOSTAK, A. B. and GOMBERG, W. (eds) (1965b) *Blue Collar Worlds: Studies of the American Worker* Englewood Cliffs, New Jersey: Prentice-Hall.

SILVER, M. (1973) 'Recent British strike trends: a factual analysis' *British Journal of Industrial Relations* Vol. 11.

SILVERMAN, D. (1970) *The Theory of Organisations* London: Heinemann.

SIMMEL, G. (1955) *Conflict* Glencoe: The Free Press.

SIMON, H. A. (1961) *Administrative Behavior* New York: Macmillan.

SIMPSON, R. C. and WOOD, J. (1973) *Industrial Relations and the 1971 Act* London: Pitman.

SLICHTER, S. H. (1966) *Economic Growth in the United States* London: Collier-Macmillan.

SMELSER, N. J. (1968) *Essays in Sociological Explanation* Englweood Cliffs, New Jersey: Prentice-Hall.

SMITH, C. T. B., CLIFTON, R., MAKEHAM, P., CREIGH, S. W., BURN, R. V. (1978) *Strikes in Britain* London: Department of Employment Manpower Paper 15; HMSO.

SNYDER, D. (1975) 'Institutional setting and industrial conflict: comparative analyses of France, Italy and the United States' *American Sociological Review* Vol. 40, pp. 259–78.

*Social Trends* London: HMSO.

SOFER, C. (1972) *Organizations in Theory and Practice* London: Heinemann Educational Books.

SOREL, G. (1961) *Reflections on Violence* New York: Collier Books.

SORGE, A. (1976) 'The evolution of industrial democracy in the countries of the European Community' *British Journal of Industrial Relations* Vol. 14, pp. 274–94.

SPENCER, M. H. and SIEGELMAN, L. (1959) *Managerial Economics* Homewood, Ill.: Irwin Publishing.

STACEY, M. (1960) *Tradition and Change* Oxford: Oxford University Press.

STAGNER, R. (1969) 'The level of aspiration' in Sutermeister (ed.); first published in 1956.

STEDERY, A. C. and KAY, E. (1971) 'The effects of goal difficulty on performance' in Warr (ed.); first published in 1966 in *General Electric Company Technical Report*.

STEWART, R. (1970) *Managers and Their Jobs* London: Pan.

STEWART, R. (1976) *Contrasts in Management* London: McGraw-Hill.

STEWART, R. (1979) *The Reality of Management* London: Pan.

STIEBER, J. (1968) 'Unauthorized strikes under the American and British industrial relations systems' *British Journal of Industrial Relations* Vol. 6.

STINCHCOMBE, P. (1969) 'Bureaucratic and craft administration of production' *Administrative Science Quarterly* Vol. 4, pp. 168–87.

STOGDILL, R. M. (1959) *Individual Behaviour and Group Achievement* New York: Oxford University Press.

STOGDILL, R. M. (1970) 'Leadership, membership, organization' in Gibb (ed.); first published in 1950.

STRAUSS, G. (1974) 'Workers – attitudes and adaptation' in Rosow (ed.).

STOPFORD, J. M., CHANNON, D. K., NORBURN, D. (1975) *British Business Policy: A Casebook* London: Macmillan.

STURMTHAL, A. (1964) *Workers' Councils: A Study of Workplace Organization on Both Sides of the Iron Curtain* Cambridge, Mass.: Harvard University Press.

STURMTHAL, A. (1972) *Comparative Labor Movements* Belmont, California. Wadsworth.

SUTERMEISTER, R. A. (ed.) (1969, 1976) *People and Productivity* (2nd and 3rd editions) London: McGraw-Hill.

SWEET, T. G. and JACKSON, D. (1977) *The World Strike Wave 1969–7?* Aston, England: University of Aston Management Centre, Working Paper Series No. 63.

SYKES, A. J. M. (1969a) 'Navvies: their social relations' *Sociology* Vol. 3, pp. 157–72.

SYKES, A. J. M. (1969b) 'Navvies: their work attitudes' *Sociology* Vol. 3, pp. 21–35.


TABB, J. Y. and GOLDFARB, A. (1975) 'The typology of systems of participation' in Horvat *et al.* (eds), vol. 2; first published in 1970.

TAGLIACOZZO, D. L. and SEIDMAN, J. (1956) 'A typology of rank and file union members' *American Journal of Sociology* Vol. 61, pp. 546–53.

TANNENBAUM, A. and SEASHORE, S. (1964) 'Some changing conceptions and approaches to the study of persons in organizations' *XV International Congress of Applied Psychology* Ljubljana, Yugoslavia.

TANNENBAUM, F. (1964) *The True Society: A Philosophy of Labour* London: Jonathan Cape.

TAYLOR, F. W. (1911) *Introduction to the Principles of Scientific Management* New York: Harper.

TAYLOR, R. (1978) *The Fifth Estate: Britain's Unions in the Seventies* London: Routledge and Kegan Paul.

TERRY, M. (1977) 'The inevitable growth of informality' *British Journal of Industrial Relations* Vol. 15, pp. 76–90.

THOMASON, G. F. (1971) *Experiments in Participation* London: Institute of Personnel Management.

THOMPSON, E. P. and YEO, E. (1971) *The Unknown Mayhew* London: Merlin Press.

THOMSON, A. W. J. (1979) 'Trade unions and the corporate state in Britain' *Industrial and Labour Relations Review* Vol. 33, pp. 36–54.

THURLEY, K. E. and HAMBLIN, A. C. (1963) *The Supervisor and his Job* London: HMSO.

TOURAINE, A. (1955) *L'évolution du travail ouvrier aux usines Renault* Paris: CNRS.

TOURAINE, A. (1962) 'An historical theory in the evolution of industrial skills' in C. R. Walker (ed.) *Modern Technology and Organization* London: McGraw-Hill.

TOURAINE, A. (1966) *La conscience ouvrière* Paris: Editions du Seuil.

TOURAINE, A. (1971) *The Post-Industrial Society* London: Wildwood House.

TRIST, E. (1976) 'The work of the Tavistock Institute' in Pugh *et al.* (eds).

TRIST, E. L. and BAMFORTH, K. W. (1951) 'Some social and psychological consequences of the longwall method of coal-getting' *Human Relations* Vol. 4, pp. 3–38.; reprinted in Pugh (ed.) (1971).

TRIST, E. L. and BAMFORTH, K. W. (1969) 'Technicism: some effects of material technology on managerial methods and on work situation and relationships' in Burns (ed.); first published in 1951.

TRIST, E. L., HIGGIN, G. W., MURRAY, H., POLLOCK, A. B. (1963) *Organizational Choice* London: Tavistock.

TURNER, A. N. (1955) 'Interaction and sentiment in the foreman–worker relationship' *Human Organization* Vol. 14, pp. 10–16.

TURNER, A. N. and LAWRENCE, P. R. (1965) *Industrial Jobs and the Worker* Cambridge, Mass.: Harvard University Press.

TURNER, H. A. (1969) *Is Britain Really Strike Prone?* Cambridge: Cambridge University Press.

TURNER, H. A. and BESCOBY, J. (1961) 'Strikes, redundancy and the demand cycle in the motor car industry' *Bulletin of the Oxford Institute of Economics and Statistics* Vol. 23, pp. 179–85.

TURNER, H. A., CLACK, G., ROBERTS, G. (1967) *Labour Relations in the Motor Industry* London: Allen & Unwin.

TYLOR, C. (1979) 'Post Office Worker–Directors Fall From Favour', London: *The Financial Times* 11 December.

UDY, S. H. (1970) *Work in Traditional and Modern Societies* Englewood Cliffs, New Jersey: Prentice-Hall.

URWICK, L. (1947) *The Elements of Administration* London: Pitman.

VAMPLEW, C. (1973) 'Automated process operators: work attitudes and behaviour' *British Journal of Industrial Relations* Vol. 11, pp. 415–30.

VAN DE VALL, M. (1970) *Labor Organizations* Cambridge: Cambridge University Press.

VANEK, J. (1972) *The Economics of Workers' Management* London: Allen&Unwin.

VANEK, J. (ed.) (1975) *Self-Management* London: Penguin.

VITELES, M. S. (1955) *Industrial Psychology* London: Jonathan Cape.

VROOM, V. H. (1964) *Work and Motivation* New York: Wiley and Sons.

VROOM, V. H. (1969) 'Industrial social psychology' in Lindzey and Aronson (eds); reprinted in Vroom and Deci (eds) (1979).

VROOM, V. H. and DECI, E. L. (eds) (1979) *Management and Motivation* London: Penguin.

VROOM, V. H. and MANN, F. C. (1960) 'Leader authoritarianism and employee attitudes' *Personnel Psychology* Vol. 13, pp. 125–40.

WALKER, C. R. and GUEST, R. H. (1952) *The Man on the Assembly Line* Cambridge, Mass.: Harvard University Press.

WALL, T. D. and LISCHERON, J. A. (1977) *Worker Participation* London: McGraw-Hill.

WARD, G. (1977) *Fort Grunwick* London: Temple Smith.

WARNER, M. (1973) *The Sociology of the Workplace* London: Allen & Unwin.

WARR, P. B. (ed.) (1971) *Psychology At Work* London: Penguin.

WARR, P. B. and WALL T. (1978) *Work and Well Being* London: Penguin.

WATSON, T. J. (1980) *Sociology, Work and Industry* London: Routledge and Kegan Paul.

WEBB, B. and WEBB, S. (1897) *Industrial Democracy* London: Longmans Green.

WEBER, M. (1947) *The Theory of Social and Economic Organization* London: William Hodge.

WEBER, M. (1968) *Economy and Society* New York: Bedminster Press.

WEDDERBURN, D. (ed.) (1974) *Poverty, Inequality and Class Structure* Cambridge: Cambridge University Press.

WEINSHALL, T. D. (ed.) (1977) *Culture and Management* London: Penguin.

WEIR, M. (ed.) (1976) *Job Satisfaction* London: Fontana.

WELLISZ, S. (1953) 'Strikes in coal-mining' *British Journal of Sociology* Vol. 3, pp. 346–66.

WESTERGAARD, J. and RESLER, H. (1975) *Class in a Capitalist Society* London: Heinemann.

WESTLEY, W. A. and WESTLEY, M. W. (1971) *The Emerging Worker* Montreal: McGill University Press.

WHELAN, C. T. (1976) 'Orientations to work: some theoretical and methodological problems' *British Journal of Industrial Relations* Vol. 14, pp. 142–58.

WHITE, R. and LIPPITT, R. (1953) 'Leader behaviour and member reaction in three social climates' in Cartwright and Zander (eds).

WHITE, R. K. and LIPPITT, R. (1960) *Autocracy and Democracy* New York: Harper and Row.

WHITTINGHAM, T. G. and TOWERS, B. (1971) 'Strikes and the economy' *National Westminster Bank Quarterly Review* 2–8.

WHYTE, W. F. (1961) *The Organization Man* London: Penguin.

WIGHAM, E. (1961) *What's Wrong With the Unions?* London: Penguin.

WILD, R. (1975) *Work Organization: A Study of Manual Work and Mass Production* London: John Wiley.

WILDERS, M. G. and PARKER, S. R. (1975) 'Changes in workplace industrial relations 1966–72' *British Journal of Industrial Relations* Vol. 13, pp. 14–22.

WILENSKY, H. L. (1957) 'Human relations in the workplace' in C. M. Arensberg (ed.) *Research in Industrial Human Relations: A Critical Appraisal* New York: Harper and Row.

WILKIE, R. (1961) 'The ends of industrial sociology' *The Sociological Review* Vol. 9, pp. 215–24.

WILSHER, P. (1976) 'New bosses in the dock' *Sunday Times* 28 March.

WILSON, D. F. (1972) *Dockers: The Impact of Industrial Change* Glasgow: Fontana/Collins.

WOODWARD, J. (1958) *Management and Technology* London: HMSO.

WOODWARD, J. (1965) *Industrial Orgainzation: Theory and Practice* Oxford: Oxford University Press.

WOYTINSKY, W. S. and WOYTINSKY, E. S. (1953) *World Population and Production* New York: Twentieth Century Fund.

WRAY, D. (1949) 'Marginal men of industry – the foremen' *American Journal of Sociology* Vol. 54, pp. 298–301.

WYNNE, M. (1972) *Family Policy* London: Penguin.

YANKELOVICH, D. (1974) 'The meaning of work' in Rosow (ed.).

YOUNG, M. and WILLMOTT, P. (1971) *Family and Kinship in East London* London: Penguin.

ZEITLIN, M. (1974) 'Corporate ownership and control: the large corporation and the capitalist class' *American Journal of Sociology* Vol. 79, pp. 1073–119.

ZUKIN, S. (1975) *Beyond Marx and Tito* New York: Cambridge University Press.

ZWEIG, F. (1961) *The Worker in an Affluent Society* London: Heinemann.

ZWEIG, F. (1976) *The New Acquisitive Society* London: Barry Rose.

ZWERMAN, W. L. (1970) *New Perspectives on Organization Theory* Westport, Connecticut: Greenwood Publishing.

# Name Index

Aas, D. 106, 237
Addison, J. T. 262
Adizes, I. 240
Alexander, K. J. W. 269
Allen, F. R. 3
Allen, V. L. 225, 266
Anthony, P. D. 252
Aquinas, St Thomas 141
Argyle, M. 50–1, 63, 64, 69, 85, 252, 257
Argyris, C. 76, 257
Armstrong, E. G. A. 99, 116, 266
Aron, R. 1, 2, 18, 252, 260
Ashenfelter, O. 264
Avineri, S. 260

Back, K. 64
Bahrdt, H. P. 261
Bain, G. S. 267
Bakke, E. W. 267
Bakunin, M. 229
Balfour, C. 269
Bamforth, K. W. 58, 253, 256
Banks, J. A. 161–2, 196, 267, 269
Banks, O. 261
Baran, P. A. 259
Barbash, J. 181
Barkai, H. 269
Barkin, S. 263, 266
Barnard, C. I. 50, 78–9, 118, 255
Barnes, Sir D. 267
Barnet, R. J. 139
Bartlett, A. F. 266
Batstone, E. 190, 199, 264, 265, 268, 269
Bauer, R. A. 10

Bechhofer, F. 38, 67, 160–1, 171, 189–90, 195, 253, 256, 258, 261, 267
Behrens, W. W. 20–1
Bell, D. 16–17, 251, 252, 259
Bendix, R. 252
Bensen, H. W. 142
Bensman, J. 116
Benson, L. 261
Berg, I. 18, 47–8, 126, 254
Berle, A. A. 126, 128, 139, 259
Bescoby, J. 265
Bettignies, H. C. de 139
Beynon, H. 228, 253, 255, 265, 268
Biddle, D. 39, 253
Blackburn, R. vi, 253, 267
Blau, P. M. 110, 115–16, 121
Blauner, R. 41–2, 52, 57–8, 67, 89, 191, 253, 256
Blood, M. R. 254
Blumberg, P. M. 233, 268
Blumler, J. G. 264
Bonjean, C. M. 36
Bonner, H. 61
Booth, C. 144, 262
Boraston, I. 190, 199, 264, 265, 267, 268
Bosanquet, N. 167, 262
Boulding, K. E. 203
Bowers, D. 266
Bowey, A. M. 258
Bowley, A. L. 145
Brannen, P. 58, 261, 269
Braverman, H. 252, 255
Briefs, G. 142, 148, 165, 260
Britt, D. W. 265
Broekmeyer, M. 269

292

Brown, E. C. 263
Brown, R. K. 32, 55, 58, 252, 255, 261, 266
Brown, W. 200, 269
Brzezinski, B. 14
Bugental, D. E. 109–10
Bullock, Lord 242, 269
Burkitt, B. 266
Burn, R. V. 264
Burnett-Hurst, A. B. 145
Burnham, J. 126
Burns, T. 132–3, 252, 253, 258, 259, 260
Burton, J. 266

Cameron, G. C. 223, 264, 265
Campbell, D. T. 71
Carby-Hall, J. R. 268
Carew, A. 267
Carey, A. 255
Carre, R. 129
Cartwright, D. 109, 257
Case, J. 269
Cass, M. 265
Centers, R. J. 109–10
Channon, D. K. 260
Child, J. 252, 255, 258, 259
Chin, J. W. 129
Chinoy, E. 33, 47, 191, 253, 256
Chiplin, B. 235
Chodak, S. 10
Cioffi, F. 257
Clack, G. 213–14, 217, 253, 265
Clark, L. G. 74
Clark, S. C. 162, 169, 262
Clarke, T. 268, 269
Clegg, H. A. 197, 198, 199, 209, 211–12, 221–2, 249–50, 263, 264, 265, 266, 267, 268
Clegg, S. 254, 255, 256
Clifton, R. 264
Coates, K. 188, 198, 206, 217, 233, 262, 263, 265, 266, 269
Coch, L. 105–6, 237, 256, 257
Cohen, A. R. 65
Cohen, P. S. 202, 262
Cole, G. D. H. 243–4, 268
Coleman, J. 193, 195–6, 267

Conant, E. H. 37–8
Cook, F. G. 162, 169, 262
Cooley, D. E. 129
Cooper, B. M. 266
Coser, L. A. 201, 214, 262
Cousins, J. M. 58, 261
Coyne, J. 235
Creigh, S. W. 264, 265
Crompton, R. 261
Cronin, J. E. 149, 263, 264
Crosland, C. A. R. 238
Crossley, J. R. 264
Crouch, C. 187, 209–10, 263, 267
Crozier, M. 254
Curran, J. 256
Cyert, R. M. 135, 260
Cyriax, G. 191

Dahrendorf, R. 2, 126, 153–5, 216, 251, 259, 260, 262
Dalton, M. 88–9, 101, 136, 258, 259
Daniel, W. W. 93, 253, 269
Davis, A. 82–3
Davis, J. E. 99, 116
Davis, L. E. 253
Davis, R. L. 261
Deane, P. 263
Dennis, N. 58, 265
Derrick, P. 269
Deutsch, M. 72
Diamant, A. 268
Dickson, W. J. 53–4, 255
Dill, W. 136
Doeringer, P. B. 167, 262
Donovan, Lord 187, 198–9, 206, 226–7, 264, 266
Dore, R. 69, 138
Douglas, J. W. B. 261
Downs, A. 131
Drucker, P. F. 19, 60–1, 134
Drulovic, M. 263
Dubin, R. 66, 73, 252, 253, 262, 263
Dubois, P. 222, 263
Dunkerley, D. 101, 254, 255, 256, 258
Dunlop, J. T. 2, 8, 9, 11–13, 15, 23, 24, 138, 139, 173, 215–16, 251, 262
Dunnette, M. D. 80, 84

Durcan, J. W. 265
Durkheim, E. 26, 41, 52, 54, 71, 205, 252

Ebsworth, R. 200
Edelstein, J. D. 196, 267
Edwards, P. K. 265
Edwards, R. C. 167
Edwards, S. 174
Eisele, C. F. 265
Eldridge, J. E. T. 205–6, 223, 252, 253, 262, 264, 267
Elliott, J. 269
Ellul, J. 2, 14
Emery, F. E. 96–7, 242, 269
Engels, F. 165, 205, 260, 262
Etzioni, A. 58–9, 72, 118–19, 258
Evans, E. W. 264, 265, 266
Ewbank, A. J. 264

Fainsod, M. 14
Farber, H. S. 265
Fatchett, D. 269
Faunce, W. A. 3, 252, 253
Fayol, H. 103
Feldman, A. S. 8–9
Festinger, L. 64
Feuerbach, L. 39
Fiedler, F. E. 111–14, 258
Fisher, M. 265
Flanders, A. 173, 181–2, 206, 264, 269
Fleishman, E. A. 108
Follet, M. P. 103
Forchheimer, K. 263
Form, W. H. 42, 89, 252, 253, 256, 261
Forrester, J. W. 20, 21
Forward, N. S. 264
Fox, A. 206, 252, 255, 260, 263, 264
Fraser, J. A. 35–6
Fraser, R. 252
French, J. R. P. 105–6, 237, 256, 257
Frenkel, S. 190, 199, 264, 265, 268
Friedman, E. A. 74
Friedmann, G. 31–2, 33, 34–5, 45, 53, 252
Friedrich, C. J. 14
Fromkin, H. L. 83
Fromm, E. 155–6

Frow, E. 263
Frow, R. 263
Furstenberg, F. 268

Galambos, P. 264, 266
Galbraith, J. K. 72–3, 74, 128, 150–2, 259, 260, 262
Galle, O. 265
Garbarino, J. W. 263
Gardell, B. 253
Gardner, G. 257
Garson, G. D. 268, 269
Gellerman, S. W. 120
Gennard, J. 265
Gerver, I. 116
Geschwender, J. A. 89
Gibb, C. A. 100, 257
Giddens, A. 16, 252, 261, 262
Gilbert, M. 260
Giner, S. 19
Godwin, W. 229
Goldfarb, A. 236–7
Goldstein, J. 198, 267
Goldthorpe, J. H. 9, 38, 67, 120, 160–1, 171, 189–90, 195, 199, 206, 253, 256, 258, 261, 267
Golembiewski, R. T. 109
Goodman, J. F. B. 99, 116, 197, 212, 264, 266, 267
Gordon, D. M. 167, 262
Gordon, R. A. 129
Gouldner, A. W. 68, 114, 116, 191, 201, 223–5, 226, 228, 258, 265
Granick, D. 137
Griffiths, B. 266
Gross, B. M. 19, 103, 135–7
Grunfeld, C. 266
Gubbay, J. 261
Guest, R. H. 33, 45, 56, 121–2, 253, 256
Gulick, L. 103
Gurvitch, G. 234

Halsey, A. H. 261
Hamblin, A. C. 258
Hamblin, R. L. 110
Hamilton, R. F. 161
Handyside, J. D. 89

Hanson, C. G. 264, 266
Haraszti, M. 254
Harbison, F. H. 2, 8, 9, 11–13, 15, 23, 24, 138, 139, 215–6, 251, 262
Harrington, M. 163, 262
Hartman, P. T. 207–8, 262, 263
Havighurst, R. J. 74
Heath, A. F. 261
Heilbroner, R. L. 17, 23–4
Hemingway, J. 267
Henriques, F. 58, 265
Herding, R. 267
Herrick, N. Q. 43–4, 254
Herzberg, F. 91, 94, 253, 257
Hickson, D. J. 86, 256
Higgin, G. W. 253, 256
Hill, F. E. 32
Himes, J. S. 83
Hirsch, F. 22
Hobsbawm, E. J. 147
Hoggart, R. 262
Hollander, E. P. 118
Hollowell, P. G. 58
Holman, R. 81–2, 262
Homans, G. 51, 61–3, 108, 114, 202, 256, 257
Horvat, B. 230, 240–1, 245, 268
Hughes, J. 266
Hulin, C. L. 254
Hunnius, G. 269
Hunter, L. C. 265
Hutton, G. 39, 253
Hyman, R. 201, 206, 228, 254, 262, 263, 265, 266
Hyndman, H. M. 144

Ingham, G. K. 209, 262, 263
Inkeles, A. 7, 10
Israel, J. 106, 237

Jackson, B. 261, 262
Jackson, D. 263
Jackson, M. P. 263, 264, 266, 269
Jenkins, C. 267
Jenkins, C. L. 269
Jenkins, P. 267
Johns, E. A. 170–1, 261
Johnson, A. G. 269

Johnson, G. E. 264
Jones, D. C. 268, 269
Jones, P. A. 19
Jones, T. K. 241
Jueres, E. A. 261
Julian, J. W. 118

Kahn, R. L. 105, 256, 257
Kalleberg, A. L. 254
Kassalow, E. M. 266
Katanka, M. 263
Katona, G. 130, 150, 260, 261
Katz, D. 105, 256, 257
Katz, F. E. 256
Kautsky, K. 177
Kay, E. 81
Kee, R. 263
Kelly, H. H. 63
Kelly, M. P. 261
Kendall, W. 266
Kerr, C. 2, 8, 9, 11–13, 15, 23, 24, 138, 139, 210, 215–16, 251, 262, 265, 266
Kesting, A. 261
Kilbridge, M. D. 37–8
King, L. 258
Kirby, J. M. 58, 256, 265
Klein, J. 160, 262
Knowles, K. G. J. C. 263, 264, 265
Kornhauser, A. 73, 262, 263
Korpi, W. 264
Korsnes, O. 187
Krauss, R. M. 72
Kropotkin, P. A. 229
Kuhn, J. W. 265

Landsberger, H. A. 255
Lane, T. 223, 225–6, 228, 265, 267
Larner, R. J. 126, 130, 259
Laski, H. 143
Lasko, R. 265
Lavers, G. R. 147
Lawler, E. E. 36, 71, 80, 90–1, 94–5, 254
Lawrence, P. R. 36, 134, 254
Leavitt, H. J. 96
Leggett, J. C. 166, 262
Lenin, V. I. 177, 205, 266

Lester, R. A. 266
Lewin, K. 105
Lewis, O. 81–2, 262
Liebow, E. 83
Likert, R. 107, 253, 357
Lippitt, R. 103–4, 237, 256, 257
Lipset, S. M. 193, 194, 195–6, 267
Lipsky, D. B. 265
Lischeron, J. A. 268
Lockwood, D. 38, 67, 160–1, 171, 189–90, 195, 253, 256, 258, 261, 267
Lorsch, J. W. 134
Lozowsky, A. 174–5
Lukacs, G. 260
Lumley, R. 267
Lupton, T. 89

McAuley, M. 263
McCarthy, W. E. J. 227, 264, 265, 266, 267
McClellan, D. 260
McCord, N. 263
McGivering, I. C. 58, 256, 265
McGregor, D. 106–7, 253, 257
McIntosh, N. 269
Mackenzie, G. 261
Makeham, P. 264
Mallet, S. 168, 260
Mann, F. C. 109
Mann, M. 262
Mannheim, K. 148–9
March, J. G. 79, 91, 135, 140, 260
Marcson, S. 253
Marcuse, H. 155, 157–8
Markovic, M. 230, 245
Marot, H. 30
Marris, R. 130
Marsden, D. 261
Martin, R. 267
Marwick, A. 261
Marx, K. 23, 26, 28–30, 39–41, 52, 56, 125, 142–3, 153, 155, 158, 165, 174, 175, 179, 205, 252, 260, 266
Maslow, A. H. 76–7, 253, 257
Mason, A. 263
Mathews, P. 265

Mayer, K. 152–3
Mayhew, H. 144
Mayo, E. 34, 54–5, 75, 105, 255
Meadows, D. H. 20–1
Meadows, D. L. 20–1
Means, G. C. 126, 259
Meissner, M. 31, 252
Merton, R. K. 51
Michels, R. 192, 267
Miliband, R. 259, 267
Mill, J. S. 142
Millar, R. 165–6, 260, 261
Miller, D. C. 252
Miller, S. M. 168, 262
Milligan, S. 267
Mills, C. W. 14, 261, 267
Mitchell, B. R. 263
Mogey, J. M. 262
Monsen, R. J. 129, 131
Moore, W. E. 8–9, 73, 84
Moran, M. 195
Morris, M. 228
Morse, N. C. 74, 254
Mouzelis, N. 255, 258
Muller, R. E. 139
Mumford, E. 58, 89, 256, 265
Murray, H. 253, 256
Myers, C. A. 2, 8, 9, 11–13, 15, 23, 24, 138, 139, 215–16, 251, 262
Myrdal, G. 168

Nevins, A. 32
Newson, E. 262
Newson, J. 262
Nichols, T. 127, 131–2, 138, 259
Nisbet, R. 251
Norburn, D. 260
Novick, D. 21

Oakeshott, R. 191, 269
Opsahl, R. L. 80, 84
Orzack, L. H. 66
Ossowski, S. 260
Oxnam, D. W. 263
Owen, R. 229

Palm, G. 252
Panitch, L. 266

Parker, S. R. 252, 255, 266
Parkin, F. 262
Parkinson, C. N. 137
Parsons, T. 118, 259
Patel, S. J. 5–6
Pateman, C. 269
Paterson, T. T. 265
Peacock, A. 266
Pearce, S. 258
Pejovich, S. 268
Pelling, H. 266
Pelz, D. C. 114
Pencavel, J. H. 264, 266
Penrose, O. 127–8
Perlman, S. 174, 177–8, 179, 266
Perrow, C. 135, 256
Phelps-Brown, E. H. 264
Phipps, F. J. 269
Pizzorno, A. 263
Platt, J. 38, 67, 160–1, 171, 189–90, 195, 253, 256, 258, 261, 267
Polanyi, K. 174, 178–9, 181
Pollard, S. 146
Pollins, H. 266
Pollock, A. B. 253, 256
Pomeranz, R. 269
Pope, L. 265
Popitz, H. 261
Porter, L. 94–5
Presthus, R. 19
Pribicevic, B. 269
Proudhon, P. J. 229
Pugh, D. S. 256

Radice, G. 267
Ramsay, H. 269
Randers, J. 20
Rapoport, A. 203
Rathenau, W. 126
Reich, M. 167
Reid, E. 267
Renold, C. G. 269
Renshaw, P. 263
Resler, H. 261
Rice, A. K. 64, 256
Ridge, J. M. 261
Riesman, D. 259
Rimlinger, G. V. 265

Rimmer, M. 199, 267
Robbins, Lord 266
Roberts, B. C. 221, 267
Roberts, G. 213–14, 217, 253, 265
Roberts, K. 162, 169, 223, 225–6, 228, 262, 265
Roberts, R. 262
Robertson, N. 266
Roethlisberger, F. J. 53–4, 105, 255
Rogaly, J. 265
Rohrer, J. H. 65
Rose, M. vi, 105, 256, 257
Rosen, N. A. 258
Rosow, J. M. 96
Ross, A. 73, 207–8, 262, 263
Rostow, W. W. 10–11, 73, 251
Rothwell, S. 46–7, 49, 254
Rowley, R. K. 268
Rowntree, B. S. 144–5, 147, 262
Roy, D. 70, 86, 256
Runciman, W. G. 146, 262
Rus, V. 241
Ryder, Sir D. 248
Ryder, J. 145, 261

Salaman, G. 69, 258
Samphier, M. L. 58, 261
Sams, K. I. 265, 266
Sayles, L. R. 52, 253, 256, 264
Scanlon, H. 235
Schachter, S. 64
Schein, E. H. 75, 254
Schmidman, J. 266
Schneider, E. V. 28, 30–1, 252
Schumpeter, J. A. 23
Scott, W. H. 58, 256, 265
Scott, W. R. 110, 121
Seabrook, J. 262
Seashore, S. 108
Seeman, M. 252, 253
Seidman, J. 188–9, 267
Semeonoff, E. 162, 169, 262
Shaler, M. 264
Shanks, M. 22
Sheppard, H. L. 43–4, 254
Sherif, M. 65
Sherman, B. 267
Sherwood, J. J. 83

Shils, E. B. 48
Shorter, E. 209, 263, 265
Shostak, A. B. 161
Siebert, W. S. 262
Siegel, A. 210, 265
Silburn, R. 262
Silver, H. 145, 261
Silver, M. 264, 265, 266
Silverman, D. vi, 202
Simmel, G. 141, 174, 175–6, 262
Simon, H. A. 79, 91, 92, 134–5, 140
Simpson, R. C. 173
Sirc, L. 235
Sismondi, S. de 142
Slaughter, C. 58, 265
Slichter, S. H. 3
Smelser, N. J. 10
Smith, A. 125
Smith, C. T. B. 264
Smith, M. A. 252, 255
Snyder, D. 207–9, 263
Sofer, C. vi, 105
Sorel, G. 229–30
Sorge, A. 268
Speak, M. 89
Stacey, M. 262
Stagner, R. 91–2
Stalker, G. H. 132, 253, 258, 259, 260
Stanworth, J. 256
Stedery, A. C. 81
Stein, L. von 142
Stewart, R. 129, 260
Stieber, J. 263, 264
Stinchcombe, A. 133–4
Stock, F. G. L. 35–6
Stogdill, R. M. 64, 257
Stopford, J. M. 260
Strauss, G. 89, 91, 92–3
Strumpel, B. 260, 261
Sturmthal, A. 266, 268
Supek, R. 230, 245
Sutermeister, R. A. 254
Sweet, T. G. 263
Sweezy, P. M. 259
Sykes, A. J. M. 52, 58, 68

Tabb, J. Y. 236–7
Tagliacozzo, D. L. 188–9, 267

Tannenbaum, A. 108
Tannebnaum, F. 174, 178, 179
Taylor, F. W. 53, 85, 102
Taylor, J. C. 253
Taylor, R. 267
Terry, M. 199, 200
Thomason, G. F. 269
Thompson, E. P. 144
Thompson, K. 258
Thomson, A. W. J. 183, 267
Thorsrud, E. 96–7, 242, 269
Thurley, K. E. 258
Tilly, C. 209, 263, 265
Topham, A. 188, 198, 206, 217, 233, 263, 265, 266, 269
Touraine, A. 17, 33, 56–7, 154, 166, 261
Towers, B. 264
Trist, E. L. 58, 253, 256
Trow, M. 193, 195–6, 267
Turner, A. N. 36, 110, 254, 264, 265
Turner, H. A. 213–14, 217, 253
Tylor, C. 241–2

Udy, S. H. 78
Urwick, L. 102, 103

Vall, M. Van de 180–1, 189, 191–2, 267
Vamplew, C. 254
Vance, G. G. 36
Vanek, J. 268, 269
Viteles, M. S. 35
Vroom, V. H. 94, 109, 252

Walker, C. R. 33, 56, 121, 253, 256
Wall, T. D. 102, 254, 268
Ward, G. 265
Warner, A. 99, 116
Warner, M. 196, 199, 267
Warr, P. B. 102, 254
Watson, T. J. 252, 254, 255
Webb, B. 144, 190, 266, 268
Webb, S. 144, 190, 266, 268
Weber, M. 26, 71, 110, 125, 132, 192, 252
Wedderburn, D. 262
Weir, M. 254

Weiss, R. S. 74, 254
Wellisz, S. 265
Westergaard, J. 261
Westley, M. W. 237, 261, 268
Westley, W. A. 237, 261, 268
Whelan, C. T. 254
White, P. 269
White, R. K. 103–4, 237, 256, 257
Whittingham, T. G. 197, 264, 267
Whyte, W. F. 259, 269
Wild, R. 254
Wilders, M. G. 266
Wigham, E. 267
Wilkie, R. 4
Willett, F. J. 265
Willmott, P. 262
Wilsher, P. 184–5
Wilson, P. F. 58, 214, 265
Wood, J. 173
Woodward, J. 122–3, 133, 253, 256, 258, 260, 269

Woytinsky, E. S. 5
Woytinsky, W. S. 5
Wray, D. 258
Wyatt, S. 35–6
Wynne, M. 262

Yankelovich, D. 73, 90
Yeo, E. 144
Young, M. 262

Zahn, E. 260, 261
Zander, A. 109, 257
Zegveld, W. 46–7, 49, 254
Zeitlin, M. 259
Zukin, S. 246
Zweig, F. 19, 51–2, 160, 164–5, 190, 261, 262
Zwerman, W. L. 123, 133–4

# Subject Index

abseenteeism, 34, 36, 43, 45, 215
acquisitive society, 19, 165
adjustment to work, 39, 91–3
affluent worker, 160–1, 170–1, 260
alienation in industry, 39–40, 49, 52, 68, 118–19, 155–6, 162, 238, 252–3
anomie, 52, 54, 178, 205–6, 252–3
assembly line, 33, 37–8, 56, 252
automation, 31, 41–2, 48, 56

boredom, 34–8
bureaucracy, 99, 115–16, 125, 132–7, 140, 173, 192–6, 260, 269
Bullock Report, 242, 269

capitalism, 177, 178, 252, 254, 261; alienation and 40, 155–6; corporate management and 140; communism and 25; degradation of work in 252; future of 23–4; industrial democracy and 234; managerial 128–32; separation of ownership and control in 125–6; without capitalists 140, 259; class conflict and 142–3, 154–5
class conflict, 142–3, 154–5
Club of Rome, 20–1
contingency theory, 111–13, 258
contractual obligations, 78; and motivations 78–9
convergence theory, 8–16, 139, 251–2
corporate management, 125–8, 130–1, 259
corporate state, 183, 267
craftsmanship, 27–8

discrepancy theory, 91
division of labour, 27–32, 56, 252
Donovan Report, 187, 198, 199, 226–8, 264
dual labour market, 167–8

economic growth, 5, 19–23, 148–52, 185
embourgeoisement theory, 152–4, 158–62, 261
equity theory, 91
expectancy theory, 79–80

foreman, 98–124, 257–8; authority of 118–20; changing role of 98–9; contingency theory 111–13; day-to-day activity 258; exchange theory 114–17; as man in the middle 100–2; role conflict 101–2; substance of supervision 120–4; unionization of 101
fragmentation of labour, 32–34, 237
free collective bargaining, 173, 182, 183, 184, 198–200, 217–18, 220
fulfilment theory, 91

goldbricking, 85
groups in industry, 50–71, 255–6; cohesion 63–5, 256; concept of 50–2; conflict 65; dynamics 61–6, 256; formal and informal 51, 52, 54; formation of 63–4; importance of affiliation to 53–5, 66–70; passive and active contacts in 64; and segmentation of life 66
guild socialism, 229, 243–4

Hawthorne investigations, 52–4, 255, 256
human relations school, 54, 103, 255, 256–7

inducement-contribution theory, 78–9
industrial conflict, 201–28, 262–6; deinstitutionalization of 228, 263; functions of 214–15, 217–9; general studies in 262–5; institutionalization of 201, 214–20; objectification of 176; small groups and 60–1; social change and 215; strikes and 201–28, 262–6
industrial democracy, 229–50, 268–9; appeal of 229–35; comparative perspective, 244–7, 268–9; concept of 235–7, 268; development of 229–32; in GB 248–50; on managerial level 239–43; on shopfloor level 237–9; state socialism and 232–3, 244–7; in Yugoslavia 245–6
industrial feudalism, 94
industrial relations, 173, 266
industrial revolution, 29
industrial society, 1–26, 251–2; stages of development of 3, 10–11; and industrial conflict 215, 263
industrial unionism, 229
industrialization, 1–26, 251–2; concept of 1–2; and industrial conflict 215, 263; modes of 16; totalitarianism and 14; stages of 5, 16; variations in 14–16
industrialism 1–26, 251–2; concept of 1, 4; dehumanizing features of 252; ethos of work in 73; motivations and 72–4, 78, 83–4; social correlates of 4–8
inequality, 261
informal relations 53; functions of 58–61; see also groups in industry
integration theory, 180–2
iron law of democracy, 196
iron law of oligarchy, 192, 267

job enrichment, 45–6, 253–4; through enlargement 45–6; through improvement 43–6; through rotation 45–6
job satisfaction, 36–8, 49, 254, 256; and absenteeism 96; and labour turnover 96; and productivity 89–97; and shopfloor participation 237–8

leadership style, 104–7, 256–8; see also foreman and supervision
labour force in USA, 18
labour turnover, 34, 43, 46, 47, 96, 215

man, and technology 27–49, 252–5
man–machine system, 29–31, 32–4, 38
management, 125–40, 259–60; attitudes of managers 136–7; cross-cultural comparisons 137–40; day-to-day activity 260; limitations of rationality 134–7; mechanistic 132–4, 260; line and staff 136; organic 132–4, 260; and profit motives 128–32; styles of 132–4, 260; professionalization of 137–9, 259
managerialism, see management
manufacture, 28, 30
mass consumption, 11, 148–9
mass production, 32–8, 46–8, 56, 237–8
mass society, 19, 155–8
marxism, 142–3, 153–4, 158, 162, 173, 174–5, 181, 203–5, 252, 260–1
meaning of work, 66–70, 74
money as an incentive, 72–3, 75, 80, 84–9
motivations, 71–97, 253–7; concept of 71–2; contractual obligations and 78–9; culture and 81–4; hierarchy of needs and, 76–7; models of man, 75–6; outcome oriented behaviour and, 79–81, sub-culture

of poverty and, 81–4; types of production and, 72–3
motor car industry, 33, 41, 213–14
myth, 169–71, 230

occupational structure, 18, 153

payment by results, 84–9
personality traits, 7, 35
post-capitalist society, 155
post-industrial society, 3, 16–22, 154
poverty: causes of, 146–7; primary and secondary 144–5; studies in 143–5; subculture of 81–4
power, 59, 113, 117, 127–8, 166
productivity, 60, 256; shopfloor participation and 237–8; style of supervision and 104–8, 257–8
proletariat, 141–3, 168–9

quota restrictions, 86
quality of working life, 96–7, 237, 254

rate busters, 88
repetitiveness, 33–6, 252
restricters, 88
rewards at work, 95, 97, 254; *see also* motivation
Ryder Report, 248

scientific management approach, 75, 102–3, 255
self-actualization, 253, 257
separation of ownership and control 125–40, 153, 259
shop stewards, 197–200, 267–8
social action perspective, 253–4
society: adaptive 55; established 55; industrial, *see* industrial society; capitalist, *see* capitalism; post-capitalist 155; post-industrial, *see* post-industrial society; technocratic 3, 154; transitional 10, 162–5, 169
socio-technical approach, 253, 256, 258
strikes, 201–28, 262–6; in automo-

bile industry 213–14; case studies 223–6, 228, 265; causes of 202–6; costs of 217, 265; in declining industries 214; free collective bargaining and 217–18; inter-industry differences 265; international trends 208, 263; Marxist explanation of 205; propensity to 210–14; psychological explanation of 203; public opinion and 219; by size of plant 249; as a social institution 214–20; trends in GB 263–4; wildcat 221–8, 264–5
supervision in industry, *see* foreman
syndicalism, 174, 187, 229–30
systemness, 9–10

Taylorism, 53, 255, 257
technological development, 56–8; social relations and, 72–3; *see also* industrialization
tolerance theory, 39
totalitarianism, 14, 157, 179
trade unions, 172–200, 266–8; attitudes of members of 189, 191–2; bureaucracy in 267, 192–6; changing world and 182–7; democracy in 192–6, 197–200; history of 179–80, 266; integration theory of 184; iron law of oligarchy in 192–3; membership 172; motives for joining 189–90; public attitudes to 186; rank and file in 187–92; shop stewards and 197–200; the state and 182–7, 194, 266–7; strength in different countries 188; theories of 174–82, 266; wildcat strikes and 221–8
transitional society, 10, 162–5, 169
two-factor theory, 91

unemployment, 146, 147, 151, 163–4, 168–9, 217, 220
urbanization, 7

wildcat strikes, 221–8, 264–5
working class, 141–71, 260–2; the affluent worker 148–52, 160–1,

capitalism and 142–3, 148; class consciousness 169–71, 175–6; concept of 141–3; decline and decomposition 152–4, 165–9; dual labour market and 167; education and 46–7, 261; embourgeoisement theory of 152–4, 158–62; fragmented class structure and 165–9; generalized worker 141; mass consumption society and 148–9; middle classes and 146, 147, 152, 158–62; new proletariat 168–9; transitional society and 163–5; visibility of 141, 159; the 'working poor' 141–2

worker directors, 241–2

workers' control, *see* industrial democracy